INTRODUCTION TO LAW ENFORCEMENT

INTRODUCTION TO LAW ENFORCEMENT

GEORGE L. KIRKHAM

FLORIDA STATE UNIVERSITY

LAURIN A. WOLLAN, JR.

FLORIDA STATE UNIVERSITY

1817

HARPER & ROW, PUBLISHERS, New York
Cambridge, Hagerstown, Philadelphia, San Francisco,
London, Mexico City, São Paulo, Sydney

Photo Credits

Page 3, West, Photo Trends; 13, Granger; 43, Warshaw, Photo Trends; 81, Wolinsky, Stock, Boston; 125, Harper & Row Police Surveillance Training; 147, Franken, Stock, Boston; 177, Hamlin, Stock, Boston; 205, Abramson, Photo Trends; 237, Ross, Photo Trends; 271, Krathwohl, Stock, Boston; 305, Brody, Stock, Boston; 331, Wolinsky, Stock, Boston; 367, West, Photo Trends; 391, Franken, Stock, Boston.

Sponsoring Editor: Alan M. Spiegel
Project Editor: Karla Billups Philip
Designer: Robert Sugar
Production Manager: Marion A. Palen
Photo Researcher: Myra Schachne
Compositor: P & M Typesetting, Incorporated
Printer and Binder: Halliday Lithograph Corporation
Art Studio: Vantage Art Inc.

Introduction to Law Enforcement

Library of Congress Cataloging in Publication Data
Kirkham, George.
    Introduction to law enforcement.

    Includes bibliographies and index.
      1. Law enforcement. 2. Law enforcement—United States. I. Wollan, Laurin A., Date- joint author.
II. Title.
HV7921.K57   363.2'3'0973   79–28089
ISBN 0–06–043666–2

To our parents
William and Elizabeth Kirkham
and
Laurin and Louise Wollan,
whose generous support and encouragement made this book possible.

CONTENTS

Law enforcement is one of the most complex, dynamic, and little understood institutions of modern society. *Introduction to Law Enforcement* goes beyond the traditional scope of a basic text by exposing students to a number of critical issues and provocative problems that are not ordinarily considered in introductory books on law enforcement.

Perhaps paramount among these "new" subject areas is an in-depth treatment of the human dimension of modern policing—a perspective on police officers as human beings and the problems and pressures confronting them because of the nature of their work. In our society we too often think of the police as an impersonal class of robots—rigid and mechanical beings who are programmed to react to crimes and criminals with a set of neat, stereotyped responses. The complex range of human services, interpersonal skills, and sometimes agonizingly difficult decisions that police officers make each day is often lost sight of. This text seeks to remedy that long-standing deficiency by helping students develop a better understanding of policing as one of the most difficult and demanding (but rewarding) forms of "people work" in modern society.

The senior author decided to include major sections on subjects such as stress in policing and the human dimension of law enforcement, after a number of his police-officer students persuaded him some years ago, to leave the university environment, go through a police academy, and spend a number of months working as a uniformed officer in a major metropolitan department. The years since that first revolutionary exposure to the real world of law enforcement have seen the senior author in the role of a "professor–policeman," alternating time in the classroom and at the typewriter with time in the blue uniform of a patrolman and the plainclothes garb of an investigator.

The junior author, a former prosecutor, viewed law enforcement from a quite different perspective as a result of several years of policy-making work in the United States Department of Justice. We think the contribution of a policy-oriented lawyer adds considerable depth and scope to our overall treatment of the subect, by raising such important issues as the involvement of the police in the community, and vice versa, and in the sharing of police functions by public and private elements of the community.

Introduction to Law Enforcement covers the basics of law enforcement in a structure that can be thought of in terms of journalism's "who, what, where, when, and why," but without, however, much attention to the "how" of law enforcement. This is because the authors have not attempted to write a manual or handbook of law enforcement techniques. As discussed in the concluding chapter on professional policing, these important aspects of the subject are best relegated to the police training academy and ultimately to "the street," where experience is the best—indeed often the only—teacher.

Part One of the text opens with an introduction to the "what" of law enforcement: its origins in the nature of social life and the need for order; then moves to the evolution of the police function in social control from primitive times; and continues through the modern patrol functions, the specialized activities in the traffic, investigative, juvenile, and vice and narcotics fields, and such supporting services as communications and criminalistics.

Part Two surveys the "where" of law enforcement—in a sense broader than geography—that reveals many influences that shape law enforcement. It puts the police at the beginning of the flow of cases into the criminal justice system; places the police in relationships with systems closely associated with social control (e.g., the mental health system); and finally locates the police within the governmental, political, and social systems.

Part Three turns to the "when" and "why" of law enforcement: it defines the "why" in terms of purposes, particularly the police officer's concern for crime and for the criminal law he or she is responsible for enforcing. Attention is given to the limitations on the police that are aimed at the protection of individual liberties. The "when" of law enforcement identifies the occasions when police action is taken—what triggers police intervention and what does not. It deals with the difficulties of police discretion—the range of choices the police have as to whether they will act at all, with what means, to what extent, and under what limitations. The conclusion of Part Three presents the problem of discord between legality and legitimacy in police authority—the power to do what they should not do, and the lack of power to do what they should.

Part Four takes up the "who" of law enforcement: it presents the personal or "human" dimension of policing, especially its social and psychological stresses and their effects on the officer's work, health, and family. The text concludes with a discussion on the professionalization of the police, with special attention to the controversy over the relationship of higher education to law enforcement.

We hope our collaboration has enriched the text with insights and concerns that will make it valuable not only to the present or future law enforcement practitioner but also to workers in other parts of the criminal justice system and to citizens who seek a better understanding of the police role in modern society.

Because the authors believe firmly in the value of supplementing conventional lecture and reading material on the subject of law enforcement with periodic exposure to the issues and problems being dealt with, the text can fruitfully be used in conjunction with a series of films the senior author has developed. These serve to illustrate graphically such key subjects as stress in policing, the exercise of discretion, and a wide variety of other topics discussed in the text. Information on these audio-visual supplements may be obtained from the Media Division, Harper & Row, Publishers, Inc., 10 East 53rd Street, New York, New York, 10022.

We have many people to thank for contributions of various kinds to the development of this book, but especially Frank Niland and Dennis Hauptly for providing some important information, and Jim White and Gus Dalley for reading portions of the manuscript, Donna Whitaker for typing most of it, and the senior author's wife, Merry Ann Kirkham, who somehow always managed to find time for valuable editorial advice, despite her other responsibilities as a full-time criminal investigator, wife, and mother of four.

George L. Kirkham
Laurin A. Wollan, Jr.

ACKNOWLEDGMENTS

The authors gratefully acknowledge permission to reproduce passages from the following works:

American Bar Association Section of Criminal Justice, "Urban Police Function," *Standards Relating to the Administration of Criminal Justice,* Second Edition Tentative Draft approved February 12, 1979, chapter 1 (two-volume edition available). Reprinted by permission.

David H. Bayley, "Learning About Crime—The Japanese Experience." Reprinted with permission from *The Public Interest* 44 (Summer 1976), p. 55. Copyright © 1976 by National Affairs, Inc.

Nathan Goldman, *The Differential Selection of Juvenile Offenders for Court Appearance.* Copyright © 1963 by National Council on Crime and Delinquency. Reprinted by permission.

Herman Goldstein, *Policing a Free Society.* Copyright © 1977 by Ballinger Publishing Company. Reprinted by permission.

George L. Kirkham, *Signal Zero* (J. B. Lippincott).Copyright © 1976 by George L. Kirkham. Reprinted by permission of Harper & Row, Publishers, Inc.

William H. Kroes, *Society's Victim.* Copyright © 1976 by Charles C Thomas, Publisher, Springfield, Illinois. Reprinted by permission.

Robert Nisbet, "Knowledge Dethroned," *New York Times Magazine,* September 28, 1975. Copyright © 1975 by the New York Times Company. Reprinted by permission.

Herbert L. Packer, *The Limits of the Criminal Sanction.* Copyright © 1968 by Herbert L. Packer. Reprinted by permission of Stanford University Press.

Jerome H. Skolnick, "Coercion to Virtue: The Enforcement of Morals," *Southern California Law Review* 41:588 (1968). Copyright © 1968 by the *Southern California Law Review*. Reprinted by permission.

Jerome H. Skolnick, *Justice Without Trial,* 2nd ed. Copyright © 1975 by John Wiley & Sons, Inc. Reprinted by permission.

Arthur Train, *From the District Attorney's Office.* Copyright © 1939 by Arthur Train. Reprinted by permission of Charles Scribners' Sons.

One

THE ORIGINS AND FUNCTIONS OF THE POLICE

Part One of *Introduction to Law Enforcement* introduces the reader to the origins, evolution, and functions of the police. Chapter 1 puts the police into perspective against a background of social order. It sketches the social origins of law enforcement within the universal need for order—a need that had historically been filled with very little deliberate, formal action by established social institutions. The need for order is met by social control mechanisms in many forms, only one of which is the enforcement of the law by the police. But the police, despite the impression made by the media, are neither omnipotent nor omnipresent. They are a fragile, "thin blue line," few in number, a scarce resource, and limited in many ways, including limitations placed on them by society. The police are, in short, a backup for many other means of social control and are called up when others fail to bear their share of the burden.

The need for social order and control is so fundamental to a society that some form of law and police force are found, in one form or another, in all but the most primitive cultures. The study of one civilization after another reveals remarkable parallels to our modern law enforcement system, such as Augustus Caesar's *vigiles*.

Chapter 2 traces from antiquity the evolution of law enforcement systems, from the developments in the days of Moses and Hammurabi, through ancient Greek and Roman times, to early English history, from which so many later American institutions and procedures have emerged. This historical background sets the stage for a survey of modern law enforcement systems.

Chapters 3 and 4 accordingly review the activities of the modern police force. Chapter 3 describes the patrol functions—the most basic responsibility of the municipal police, the eyes and ears of the department as a whole. This chapter looks at the characteristics of the patrol officer, the tasks involved in a typical

1

workday on patrol, the organization of patrol operations, and the types of influences affecting what the officer does. In addition, Chapter 3 deals with such issues as the relative importance of law enforcement, order maintenance, and public service; the deterrent effects of patrol; and the findings of recent experiments with different patrol procedures. It concludes with the traffic function— a responsibility that has grown rapidly with the importance of the automobile to the American way of life, yet one that is easily viewed negatively and underestimated despite its importance (given the significance of 50,000 traffic deaths per year). The chapter also examines the social and psychological influences on the encounter of a motorist and police officer.

Chapter 4 brings Part One of the text to a close by reviewing additional police functions, beginning with the detective function. The chapter delves beneath the romantic stereotype of the fictional detective to deal realistically with the role, organization, and daily operations of the criminal investigator. Less visible components of the police are also discussed, such as the juvenile unit, the importance of which is seen in the 5 percent of America's children who have some contact with the police each year, and the detective specialties of vice and narcotics investigation. The chapter concludes with a review of police support services, such as communications systems and criminalistics, to provide a rounded picture of the police organization and its activities.

1
LAW AND SOCIAL CONTROL

Social Order

What exactly do we mean when we speak of *order*? The word, like so many others in our language, holds very different meanings for different people. If we turn to the dictionary, we find that order is defined as "A social condition of peace or harmony." For a great many people in our society today, however, the word holds a far more emotional and complex significance than that simple definition suggests. During the mid and late sixties in America, in the face of soaring crime rates and mounting civil protests, *order* became a highly volatile and often-used term. For some—those who saw our society's survival as gravely threatened by the forces of crime and anarchy—*order* became a political rallying point. For still others during the same era, the word became the hated symbol of a totalitarian future, a police state filled with mindless robots and characterized by the absence of individual liberty.

The idea of order carries with it an inescapable connotation of sameness, conformity, and uniformity. It therefore bristles the backs of many of us who feel strongly committed to the values of individuality and diversity in human thought and action. As members of a free society, we have come to cherish each person's right to be unique, to march to a different drummer if he or she so chooses. Despite this, the truth is that order has been an essential part of every human society, whether democratic or totalitarian, since the beginning of time.

The earliest people discovered the elementary reality that, if they wished to interact regularly with one another on a cooperative basis, they would first have to agree upon and enforce certain standards of conduct. Human social life was possible, they found, only in proportion as it was to some extent predictable, stable—in a word, orderly over time.

A certain degree of our innate capacity for being different, for deviating from agreed-upon social rules, had to be harnessed and controlled, in the interest of group survival. Even in a democracy individuality and personal liberty have been able to flourish only once a foundation of basic social order has been established: A promising artist can scarcely produce a great painting or a scientist a major invention, if social disorder is so rampant that people must devote every waking hour to devising ways to protect themselves from the depredations of other human beings.

The necessity for order is found not only in the societies that humans have built over the ages, but also in those fashioned by far simpler social creatures. Ant colonies, for instance, represent highly complex societies within which patterns of order have remained virtually unchanged for over 60 million years! As in human civilization, the survival of each ant colony depends upon the preservation of essential forms of order. Individual ants must cooperate with one another according to the "rules" of conduct established by nature and instinct, and they must be able to safely "predict" the actions and reactions of those with whom they have daily contact, if social life is to be an ongoing reality.

Individual deviance in any society contains the seeds of social disorganization, and therefore must be controlled and kept within safe limits. Individual ants must not be allowed to suddenly abdicate their roles as builders, drones, or warriors, or to run amuck and begin destroying egg chambers within the colony. Each of you reading these words must be prevented from seizing the property of others and from venting your anger toward them in the form of physical attack. The iron grip of biologic instinct operates to prevent such manifestations of disorder among our lowly brethren the ants, while the rules of life we humans have devised operate with considerably less success in our own societies.

The maintenance of order enables the members of every society—whether ants or *Homo sapiens*—to interact cooperatively with others of their kind, and makes the dictionary definition of *order* as "A social condition of peace or harmony" a reality. In our own lives, the existence of order around us becomes so routine and natural that we often come to take for granted what has been called the miracle of social order. Despite this fact, however, scarcely a day passes when we do not stake our very lives and those of our loved ones on the preservation of order. Consider the motorist, a position that many of us occupy for some part of each day. We breeze along the street, a relatively fragile object encased in a mass of metal and glass, secure in the expectation that drivers approaching our road will stop at the red lights facing them. But will they? Imagine the social chaos—the paralysis of modern urban life—that would quickly result if even a small minority of all drivers suddenly decided to disregard the traffic law which commands us to stop at red lights. And this is only one of the many thousands of rules of order that operate in our daily lives.

These rules or norms represent, in a very real sense, the cement that binds our social order together. The vast majority of social norms are unwritten and highly informal in nature. Most of us follow them automatically, unthinkingly, in blind obedience to customs and traditions we have been raised to recognize and respect since earliest childhood. We refrain from eating peas with a knife, wear shoes, and brush our teeth simply because we have been *socialized* to regard such things as right and appropriate conduct. We might just as easily have grown up in a social order where the norms decree that no foot coverings be worn, that food be eaten with the hands rather than with pieces of metal, and that healthy teeth be chipped and blackened for ornamental purposes. A given society's norms may either support or condemn premarital chastity, taking multiple wives, and eating one's enemies. The study of other cultures leads one to appreciate the extent to which norms vary from one society to another. Yet whatever their particular form may be, norms serve to lend order and stability to life. Each of us, whether Alorese or American, comes to accept the particular fabric of norms surrounding us as a natural part of the environment.

Law

In our society a very small number of social norms—generally those deemed to be most closely linked to group welfare and survival—have been elevated to the status of *laws*. Laws, unlike other social norms, do not depend primarily on informal group pressures for their support. Rather, they are always backed by the threat of official coercion on the part of society or its representatives. It is this essential element of *force* and *authority* which sets laws apart from other social norms.

Yet laws need not be enacted by a legislature or even written down to exist. Most primitive laws are not legislated and may consist of nothing more than a tribal council convening after some deviant act to determine the question of guilt or innocence according to well-established traditions. The same elements of legitimate authority and power to act officially in behalf of society are as much present in the West African Ashanti court as in our modern American courts. Primitive peoples, like ourselves, have recognized that certain forms of deviant behavior pose such a potential threat to social order that they dare not be left to such informal control devices as group pressure and ostracism. To leave such things as homicide and theft to individual notions of justice and revenge may be to risk deadly feuds and even outright warfare within a society.

It is impossible to separate the idea of *enforcement* from the idea of *law* itself, for some system of legitimate coercion or force must underpin any law, regardless of how primitive or civilized the society evolving it may be. Such force may be embodied in the person of a figure in blue with a badge pinned to his or her chest, or in the head-hunting Ifago *monkalun* of Luzon, whose official responsibility is to mediate disputes in the interest of group peace. But it must exist. It has been rightly said that "legal rule without coercion is a fire that does not burn, a light that does not shine."[1]

Law can best be thought of as a backup system that is intended to sharpen and strengthen the impact of certain social norms which are already supported by the society. Law can rarely be used to shoreup weak norms or to create new ones. Indeed, it is an imprudent legislature that seeks to "legislate morality" by passing laws that run against the grain of prevailing morality. Our own disastrous experiment with Prohibition is a classic case in point, in that it provided a breeding ground for serious forms of organized crime that are still very much with us today. The use of alcohol was simply too deeply imbedded in American folkways to be legislated out of existence, and its illegalization appears to have done little more than encourage disrespect for the institution of law.

However difficult their birth may be, laws die very hard and often linger long after the values which brought them into being have disappeared. Our own statutes books are replete with examples—some of them quite amusing—of such outmoded laws. For instance, even as late as 1950, the Commonwealth of Massachusetts still had a law on its books that made any Rhode Island citizen found within its boundaries liable to death by hanging. The absurdity of some laws still in existence makes it hard to even guess at the social events and circumstances that brought them into being. For example, we find that it is against the law in Natchez, Mississippi, for elephants to drink beer, while the town of Walden, New York, has a law that makes it illegal to give a drink of water to another person without first securing an official permit.[2]

Our system of written or formally enacted law has its roots in the English tradition known as *common law*. During the Middle Ages a system of law evolved in Britain that placed great emphasis on allowing judicial action in each case to be heavily guided by precedent and custom. Each king's court looked to the manner in which a particular crime had been dealt with by similar courts in the past, something which led within a few hundred years to a system of law whose authority rested on tradition rather than statutory enactment. This, in turn, became the basis for modern case law, which similarly looks for legal principles established by the weight of precedent.

A great deal of our English heritage is evident in other aspects of our legal system. In our modern criminal codes we have retained the distinction between felonies and misdemeanors—a means of differentiating the seriousness of crimes which was established in the year 1116 by Henry I. Under English common law, a felony was a crime that might lead to having to give up one's property, as well as imprisonment or death. Common-law *felonies* included the very acts that represent the focus of crime statistics and public concern today: murder, manslaughter, rape, larceny, robbery, arson, and burglary. *Misdemeanors,* unlike felonies, were lesser offenses which did not carry the penalty of forfeiture of one's real and personal property.

Our manner of grading offenses in terms of their seriousness reflects the ancient common-law distinction between conduct considered inherently wrong or evil in itself (*mala in se*) and conduct considered wrong merely because the law prohibits it (*mala prohibita*).Whereas common-law felonies have always and unequivocally been regarded as *mala in se* acts, our modern society has spawned increasingly large numbers of *mala prohibita* offenses. Marijuana use, homosexuality, gambling, and prostitution represent only a few instances of *mala prohibita* crimes which are presently the subject of widespread debate. There are many who contend that such "crimes without victims" ought to be legalized, enabling the attention of our police and courts to be diverted to dealing with more serious, *mala in se,* conduct.

We also inherited from the British a tradition of distinguishing between *crimes* as public wrongs and *torts* as injuries to private parties. "A crime," in the words of the common-law scholar William Blackstone, "is an act committed, or omitted, in violation of a public law either forbidding or commanding it."[3] Conversely, a tort or civil injury is considered an entirely private offense. Historically, a crime calls for legal action and penalties imposed by the state in its own name, whereas redress for a tort is left to legal action by private indivduals. The difficulty for modern law-enforcement officers comes from the fact that the same act may simultaneously be *both* a crime and a tort.

Crime

The extent to which the criminal law is violated is usually taken as an indication of the amount of disorder within a society. This has led many to suggest that the United States is fast approaching a crisis of lawlessness, one that threatens to undermine the foundation of order in our lives. Newspapers daily assail us with accounts of steadily increasing crime, much of it violent in nature. By any set of measurements one might wish to employ, crime has become a national problem of major proportions: Since 1961 the rate for all serious crimes has more than doubled. From 1973 to 1974 it increased 17 percent—the largest increase in the 44 years that national crime statistics have been collected. The rise of violent crime has been even more pronounced. During the 14-year period prior to 1975, the rate of robberies increased 255 percent, forcible rape 143 percent, aggravated assault 153 percent, and murder 106 percent. Besides the official statistics compiled by the FBI in its *Uniform Crime Reports,* victim surveys conducted in recent years suggest that the actual crime rate may be several times greater than that indicated by police. America today is generally recognized as having probably the highest crime rate among the world's industrial societies. The effectiveness of our criminal-justice system in dealing with the mounting problem of lawlessness is reflected in a special message to Congress delivered by President Ford in 1975:

> America has been far from successful in dealing with the sort of crime that obsesses Americans day and night—I mean street crime, crime that invades our neighborhoods and our homes—murders, robberies, rapes, muggings, holdups, break-ins—the kind of brutal violence that makes us fearful of strangers and afraid to go out at night.[4]

The kind of public alarm over crime reflected in the president's speech is far from unique to our time and country. Indeed, the following words, written in 1730 by Daniel Defoe in a pamphlet dedicated to the Lord Mayor of London, reveal a remarkably similar tone:

> The Whole City, My Lord, is alarm'd and uneasy; Wickedness has got such a Head, and the Robbers and Insolence of the Night are such, that the Citizens are no longer secure within their own Walls, or safe even in passing their Streets, but are robbed, insulted and abused, even at their own Doors . . . The Citizens . . . are oppressed by Rapin and Violence; Hell seems to have let loose Troops of human D----ls upon them; and such Mischiefs are done within the Bounds of your Government as never were practised here before (at least not to such a degree) and which, if suffered to go on, will call for Armies, not Magistrates, to suppress.[5]

While today's crime problem is certainly deserving of our concern, it is essential that we respond to it in a rational and objective—rather than an emotional or hysterical—manner. It is important to bear in mind that any form of crime, however sharply increasing and heinous it may seem, exists against a far greater backdrop of social order. For every criminal there exist hundreds and thousands of law-abiding citizens, and for every criminal act committed there exist an infinitely greater number of acts that support the social order around us. The point is an important one, especially in an era of mounting public fears over "crime in the streets." Although it is suggested by some that disrespect for the law has become a characteristic of our time, the simple truth is that society as we know it would be impossible unless most of our citizens voluntarily followed and respected most of the laws most of the time: 420,000 law-enforcement personnel in the United States may sound like a large number, but as a social-control device in a society of well over 200 million people, it represents a feeble resource indeed. No society on earth—neither ours nor any other—can possibly place a police officer at the elbow of each of its citizens in the hope of dissuading everyone from criminal activity. Rather, each society must, in a very real sense, gamble on the effectiveness of informal group pressures in producing support for the institution of law. Such pressures appear to work remarkably well for the vast majority of our citizens, even in an era marked by unprecedented social change and the destruction of many traditional values.

Law and the system of criminal justice that surrounds it can function effectively only when it does not have to be formally applied against more than a small minority of society's members. As we suggested earlier, the machinery of law enforcement is essentially a backup system, a scarce resource which is brought to the fore only when more informal means of social control have failed or been inadequate. As such, law enforcement is inherently limited in its potential for application.

An example may illustrate this point more clearly. Our laws against armed robbery rest on the implicit and unwritten assumption that they will never have to be enforced against anything more than a relatively few individuals. Even the previously mentioned 255 percent increase in robbery is still small when it is considered in terms of our society's *potential* for armed robbery. Our law-enforcement and criminal-justice systems can—indeed, have—absorbed such increases and continued to function. But suppose that 10 percent of the citizens in this country decided tomorrow that they would no longer follow laws prohibiting armed robbery, and that they would disregard informal peer pressures against engaging in this form of deviant conduct. What would be the result? Our criminal-justice system could scarcely contend with the resultant surge in armed robbers, even though only, still, a relatively small minority of our citizens would be involved. Overnight, our court dockets would be logjammed with the influx of new cases, police departments would strive in vain to keep pace with the steady stream of robbery complaints, most of us would barricade ourselves in our homes at night, understandably reluctant to venture out into a world where 1 in every 10 people might confront us with a gun or knife. Social life as we know it would quickly grind to a halt.

Such examples should not be construed as arguments for complacency in the face of what are obviously serious national crime problems. Rather, they should serve to illustrate the fact that order—perhaps miraculously—continues be to a fact of daily life for most of us, a backdrop of calm and predictability against which the turmoil of crime is sharply silhouetted in modern society.

SUMMARY

In this chapter we have seen that a certain degree of *order* is basic to any society, whether animal or human. In order to live and interact together on a regular basis, individuals must be able to predict the actions of others. The preservation of order—defined as a minimal level of uniformity and conformity—is essential to social life as we know it. Every society can and does tolerate a measure of deviance from prescribed social norms. Societies display considerable variation in just what kinds of actions are defined as *deviant* versus *conforming*. Yet every society from the beginning of time has had to find ways of controlling and preventing certain universally threatening acts. One society, for instance, may value scarring the face for religious purposes, whereas another society associates such conduct with severe mental illness. But both societies face the common concern of controlling such acts as murder, rape, and theft as behavior that intrinsically threatens the social order. Without the control of such forms of disorder—the holding of them to a minimal level—humanity is consigned to life in a social jungle.

In the attempt to control crime, most people in our society have a tendency to overestimate the role and power of law and the machinery that exists for its enforcement. The cold truth is that, given the vast potential for deviance which exists in every society at any given moment, law enforcement represents at best an extremely small and limited social-control resource. We have seen in this chapter how even small increases in the volume of crime can completely overload our entire justice system. Law enforcement will always be a backup system—albeit an important one—useful in dealing with that small segment of the total population which engages in those forms of disorder that we regard as most threatening to our social order. For most of us, most of the time, it is the socialization process and the informal reactions of friends, relatives, and acquaintances that represents the most powerful force of social control in our daily lives.

NOTES

1. R. von Jhering, "Law as Means to an End," in E. Adamson Hoebel, *Man in the Primitive World* (New York: McGraw-Hill, 1958), p. 470.
2. For an interesting and humorous account of outdated laws that still remain on the books in many states, see Barbara Seuling, *You Can't Eat Peanuts in Church and Other Little-Known Laws,* (Garden City, N.Y.: Dolphin Books, 1975), p. 76.

3. Bernard C. Gavit, ed., *Blackstone's Commentaries on the Law* (Washington, D.C.: Washington Law Book Company, 1941), p. 748.

4. *Time,* June 30, 1975, p.10.

5. Allan Silver, "The Demand for Order in Civil Society: A Review of Some Themes in the History of Urban Crime, Police and Riot," in *The Police: Six Sociological Essays,* David J. Bordua, ed, (New York: Wiley, 1967).

SELECTED   Robert Bierstedt, *The Social Order,* 3rd ed. (New York: McGraw-Hill, 1970).
READINGS   E. Adamson Hoebel, *Man in The Primitive World* (New York: McGraw-Hill, 1958).
Gerald R. Leslie, Richard F. Larson, and Benjamin L. Gorman, *Order and Change* (New York: Oxford, 1973).

2
THE EVOLUTION OF LAW-ENFORCEMENT SYSTEMS

Origins

In attempting to trace the thread of time which leads from antiquity to the twentieth century, it becomes impossible to identify the birth of law enforcement with anything approaching pinpoint accuracy. We have already said that preserving order and limiting potentially destructive acts of deviance on the part of individuals were necessarily major concerns in even the earliest of human societies. In a sense, therefore, law enforcement is as old as group life itself, and has always existed in one form or another.

Among the first known human societies, enforcement of group laws was primarily a matter of individual and kin responsibility. One who had suffered an injury against person or property personally retaliated against the offender, sometimes exacting only that which he had lost, but often escalating the original crime through even more serious acts of vengeance. In the event of a victim's disability or death at the hands of an offender, the task of securing "justice" fell to the family, tribe, or clan. As can be readily imagined, prolonged and bloody feuds between kin groups became a common occurrence, and the level of social existence was accordingly limited and precarious. Human life in general during this period of time was, to borrow the words of the British philosopher Thomas Hobbes, ". . . solitary, poor, nasty, brutish and short."

Under this early system of individual justice, each member of a society was, in a sense, invested with police authority, although in time formal responsibility for enforcing certain group laws began to be delegated to particular individuals by the community and its leaders.

Some historians feel that formal codes of law backed by enforcement systems made their appearance as early as 4000 B.C. in China and Egypt.

A Sumerian king named Ur-Nammu is known to have formulated a legal code somewhere around 2400 B.C. Our search for tangible evidence of the first known system of recorded law takes us to an eight-foot-high piece of black diorite located today in the Louvre Museum in Paris. On it is engraved the famous *Code of Hammurabi,* a Babylonian king who ruled around 2100 B.C. The column of stone containing the code was discovered in 1901 by a French government expedition exploring the Persian Gulf region.

The laws of Hammurabi represent the first known attempt to comprehensively define the responsibilities of individuals to one another, as well as to the society of which they are a part. As such, it was a system of both criminal and civil law. It is within Hammurabi's code that we find the origin of the ancient legal principle of *lex talionis*—literally, "an eye for an eye and a tooth for a tooth." This concept is often misunderstood as something which was intended to justify blood feud and sanction vengeance; however, *lex talionis* was brought into being for very opposite reasons: it was intended to bring an end to the kind of wanton violence that was so common among individuals and groups pursuing their own ideas of justice and vengeance in the wake of some wrongdoing. Under *lex talionis*, an aggrieved person or any survivors could exact *no more* than had been lost: an eye for an eye, a life for a life. The principle thus ushered in the notion of uniform and socially prescribed reactions to law violation, something which underpins our modern system of law. While *lex talionis* served to limit the possibility of irrational individual reactions to crime and civil injury, it was far from equitable and impartial in its manner of application. The penalties of Hammurabi's code—many of them unconscionably harsh to our modern eyes—reflect the sharp class differences which existed between freemen, serfs, and slaves in Babylonian society at the time it was developed. We find, for instance, that despite the underlying philosophy of *lex talionis*, a noble could put out the eye of a slave and "pay one mina of silver," whereas the same offense against a noble by a slave would result in the loss of eye.[1] Like our own society, Hammurabi's Babylonia was characterized by considerable wealth and personal property—something which is reflected in a complex set of legal regulations governing such things as the fixing of prices and the marketing of goods.

Mosaic law, which appeared over one thousand years after the Code of Hammurabi, was similarly intended to standardize offenses and the kinds of penalties accompanying them. Like Babylonian law, many aspects of early Jewish law were harsh and retributive in nature. Mosaic law, which was administered by kings, high priests, and tribal elders, included 36 capital crimes. Among the actions for which death was prescribed were cursing one's parents, worshiping false gods, and engaging in sexual relations with a betrothed female.[2] Historians find a great many similarities between the structure of Mosaic law and the Babylonian code which preceded it.

Both the Babylonian and Mosaic systems signaled the start of a trend that was to increasingly standardize law and formalize the procedures for its enforcement. The historical movement away from blood feud and private vengeance, initiated by Hammurabi, was intensified and strengthened by the early Greek city-states. It was under the Greeks that we find the very first origins of true formal systems of policing. The Athenian ruler Pisistratus (605–527 B.C.), for instance, established an ancient forerunner of our modern city police when he created a body of guards and charged them with responsibility for protecting the tower and highways. At the start of the sixth century B.C., the Athenian statesman Solon made a major contribution to our democratic legal tradition by extending to every citizen of Athens, as well as the state, the right to initiate prosecutions for certain crimes.[3] Under his rule juries were selected from the citizenry and an assembly of freemen passed the laws. In sharp contrast to the democratic legal system of Athens, the authoritarian Greek city-state of Sparta was characterized by an iron-fisted control of law by its rulers, who appointed and maintained a police force that is often referred to as the first "secret police" system.[4]

Law-enforcement history took a giant stride forward with the emergence of the Roman ruler Augustus Caesar (63 B.C.–A.D.14). Augustus, the grandnephew and heir of Julius Caesar, utilized military units known as *urban cohorts* to preserve the peace of the city. Three cohorts were deployed from his legions, each of them consisting of between five hundred to one thousand men, and assigned throughout Rome. With the growth of civil disorders in the city during the reign of Augustus, the urban cohorts increasingly took on the functions of riot police, controlling disturbances by slaves as well as citizen mobs. The use of urban cohorts replaced an earlier and highly ineffective reliance on groups of superivsed slaves to perform peacekeeping activities in Rome. Augustus also created a highly elite and carefully selected force known as the Praetorian Guard, which was similarly drawn from his military legions but assigned to the palace to protect the emperor's life and property.

In the wake of ongoing problems of "law and order," as well as a series of disastrous fires which swept the city of Rome, Augustus established a nonmilitary force of men known as *vigiles*. These men, numbering several thousand, were geographically assigned to specific districts or regions of the city and were charged with responsibility for fighting fires as well as preserving the public peace. For this reason the *vigiles* are often referred to by law-enforcement historians as the first known example of an *integrated police-fire service*. Armed with cudgels and swords, and with authority to arrest thieves and other law violators, the *vigiles* of Rome represent the very first civilian police force. To his enduring credit, Augustus was farsighted enough to recognize the modern law-enforcement principle that police, if they are to be at all effective, must be deployed on the basis of geography. His organization of the city into a series of *wards*, and his assignment of *vigiles* to each of them, anticipates our modern allocation of police personnel to *precincts*.

Anglo-Saxon Development

With the fall of Rome in A.D. 395, throughout Europe centuries of bitter warfare followed, with large-scale invasions and governmental instability all but obliterating whatever gains in social order had been made up to that point. During the fifth and sixth centuries, Germanic tribes known as Angles and Saxons poured into England as conquerors, bringing with them new ideas and forms of government which would radically transform the history of law enforcement.

One of the most important developments during this period was the establishment of a system of local law-enforcement responsibility by the Anglo-Saxon King Alfred the Great (872–901). In addition to formulating a new legal code or *dooms*, which specified the penalties to be levied for particular offenses, Alfred sought to place the burden of keeping the peace squarely on the backs of the citizenry. He did this through what has become known as the *mutual pledge system*.

England at this time was characterized by a highly rural population, most of it clustered in small villages known as *tuns* (the origin of our word *towns*). For purposes of peacekeeping, each tun was subdivided into a number of ten-family units called *tithings*. Every able-bodied male in the realm over the age of 12 was required by law to attach himself to a tithing, which was held strictly accountable for the conduct of all of its members. An entire tithing might, therefore, be required to make restitution for the acts of a single individual within its ranks.

In the event of a crime, it fell to the elected head of the tithing (the *tithingman*) to mobilize his group for pursuit and apprehension of the offender. This process, known as raising a *hue and cry,* was the beginning of what we today call a *citizen's arrest*. Once the miscreant was caught, it was the tithingman's responsibility to see that a just punishment was meted out. The task of protecting the entire tun was rotated among the tithings within it, and each tithingman was in a very real sense the tun's chief of police during his group's period of service.

Organizations, once they are established, seem to have an inherent tendency to expand and become more complex. From the tithing, there gradually emerged a larger unit known as a *hundred*. Each hundred consisted of ten tithings and was presided over by a person known as a *reeve,* while the task of equipping and maintaining its ranks fell to the *comes stabuli* or *constable* ("horse master"). In keeping with the growing tradition of local self-government, the hundred began to hold regular monthly meetings for the purpose of settling disagreements among the groups comprising it. In time, a *hundred's court* evolved from these town meetings and began to perform such judicial functions as affixing punishment for offenses and mediating territorial conflicts.

Still a larger enforcement unit to appear in Anglo-Saxon England was the *shire,* an area roughly corresponding to an entire county and placed under the authority of a new official known as the *shire-reeve* (the predecessor of our modern-day and historical "sheriff"). The shire-reeve assumed the duties of collecting taxes and generally acting in the crown's best interests, as well as enforcing the law. In his attempts to do the latter, the shire-reeve was possessed of the power of *posse comitatus,* which authorized him to summon any adult male within the county to his assistance. *Posse comitatus* is a traditional power of office which is still possessed by most American sheriffs. Although the English shire-reeve was nominally under an *earldom man* or *earl,* a noble appointed by the crown to preside over several shires, he became an increasingly powerful and autonomous figure—another tradition which persists in many parts of our own country today.

The administration of justice within hundreds and shires became ever more involved with the passage of time. *Trial by ordeal* was introduced as a means of determining the guilt or innocence of an accused person. Thus, for instance, a person might be compelled to walk across burning coals or be bound and thrown into a body of water. Injury or death—or the lack of it—would then be taken as God's sign of the accused's guilt or innocence. *Trial by combat* was also utilized, with the vanquished party bearing the stigma of guilt. Finally, a system of *compurgators* was devised, which involved the coming forward of one or more reputable persons to take an oath supporting an accused's protestations of innocence. The compurgator was an early character witness, who might or might not be familiar with the action a person was accused of. His social stature and prestige in the community was of principal importance in assessing the worth of his support.

As might be expected, a great many innocent people readily confessed to the crimes of which they were accused rather than endure such horrors as trial by ordeal and battle. In light of the use of such barbaric techniques as immersion in scalding water and burning with hot coals to determine guilt or innocence, it is interesting to note that capital punishment was rarely applied under Anglo-Saxon law once an offender was adjudged guilty even of a serious crime. Punishment by fines graded to fit both the offense and the social class of the perpetrator were far more common, as was placing a guilty person in the service of the victim, or the victim's family or tun for a stipulated period of time.

The local system of law enforcement established under Anglo-Saxon rule worked well only as long as communities remained relatively small, tightly knit, and closely bound to the land. Under such conditions of life informal group pressures are sufficiently effective in achieving social control and the formal machinery of justice seldom needs to be invoked.

Early England

The kind of community-based law enforcement nurtured throughout the Anglo-Saxon era came to an end in 1066, with the Battle of Hastings and the subsequent invasion of England by William, Duke of Normandy, who became known as William the Conqueror. Under his rule law enforcement was quickly centralized under national control through the establishment of a series of 55 individual military districts, each of them under the supervision of a Norman official responsible directly to the crown. Saxon earls and shire-reeves were replaced in short order by Norman officials and landowners as the country was brought under military control. While the office of shire-reeve was preserved, it was divested of much of its former power and transformed into a military rank. The shire-reeve was no longer enpowered to try cases as well as apprehend offenders. For trying cases, William established the *vice comites,* a traveling predecessor of the later circuit judge. During his reign the Norman king also introduced the notion of what we today call a *curfew,* requiring that all fires be put out at nightfall. William earned the enduring hatred of many throughout his realm by setting aside vast amounts of land for himself and his nobles to use for hunting. His *forest laws* were backed by severe penalties for any who trespassed or poached on royal lands.

The changing conception of law and its enforcement as something to be regulated by the state, rather than the local community, was given additional impetus by Henry I (1100–1135), the son of William the Conqueror. It is with Henry I that we find clearly articulated the idea of crime as a wrong committed against the *state* and the *public peace,* rather than just against particular individuals or groups within it. In the famous proclamation *Leges Henrici,* he sought to identify such acts as robbery, murder, arson, false coinage, and violent crime as acts against the king's peace, and established our modern distinction between *felonies* and *misdemeanors.* Henry I's seminal contributions in the field of law earned him the title "Law Giver."

No consideration of the history of law enforcement could possibly fail to take into account the contribution of Henry II (1154–1188), for it was he who first introduced our modern criminal–justice principle of *trial by jury* and the *grand jury system.* Henry II provided for the selection of 12 men from each township to serve as *jurors* in cases being heard by the king's circuit justices. It was the responsibility of jurors to hear the facts and examine evidence in a given case, and then render a *verdict.* Witnesses were heard, although at first only those for the prosecution. In marked contrast to our system of justice today, an accused person was apt to be regarded as guilty by the very fact of having been charged with an offense, and there was little concern with the accused's rights as an individual. In time, however, witnesses for the defense were allowed to come forward, and rules of evidence and methods of jury selection were established as the scales of justice began to slowly balance. The idea of trial by a jury of one's peers was born at the *Assize of Clarendon* in 1166, in the case of an individual accused of a violation of the king's peace, and was at first regarded as a *privilege* rather than what we think of today as an inalienable right. An accused person, therefore, might or might not be accorded a choice between a jury trial and the traditional methods of determining guilt or innocence: trial by combat and trial by ordeal.

The jury system established by Henry II also functioned as a prototype of our grand juries by impaneling citizens and requiring them to tell under oath all they knew about anyone suspected of having committed a major crime. In cases in which there was concensus concerning the commission of a serious offense, an *indictment,* or charge might be handed down. Juries thus took on an accusatorial function, in addition to the responsibility of weighing the guilt or innocence of someone already accused of a crime.

Finally, the period during which Henry II was in power witnessed the emergence of what is known as *common law,* the law as embodied in custom and traditional usage. In each case heard by one of the crown's circuit justices, an effort was made to carefully record the decision and the grounds on which it was reached. The purpose here was to establish legal *precedents,* which might serve to guide the hearing of similar kinds of cases throughout the realm. A measure of uniformity and constancy was thereby brought to the entire judicial system. It was also during the rule of Henry II that offenses against the state (*crimes*) were clearly differentiated from private injuries (*torts*).

The influence of the church during this time was so strong that it was able to obtain immunity for its clergy from conventional trial and punishment, a practice known as *benefit of clergy.* Separate church courts were established to try members of the clergy accused of wrongdoing, as well as to hear cases involving church lands, wills, inheritance, and marriage. Only ecclesiastical courts had the authority to deal with such matters, which were completely exempt from the normal process of justice. It was also during this period that the tradition of church *sanctuary* first appeared, something which provided fugitives with safety from arrest for so long as they were within the confines of a church.

One of the most important events in the history of law and its enforcement took place at Runnymede, England, in the year 1215 when King John was forced by bitterly oppressed nobles, clergymen, and citizens to sign the *Magna Carta* or *Great Charter*. This document, brought into being by widespread resentment of King John's tyrannical practices, established as law such critical democratic rights as *local governmental control, due process,* and the *right to trial by jury.*These basic protections form a cornerstone of modern American criminal justice, and were incorporated by the founders of our Consitution in both the Fifth and Sixth Amendments. Our Fifth Amendment stipulates that no person shall be ". . . deprived of life, liberty, or property, without due process of law," while our Sixth Amendment provides that "In all criminal prosecutions, the accused shall enjoy the right to a speedy and public trial, by an impartial jury of the State and district wherein the crime shall have been committed." These taken for granted but precious freedoms were born on the field at Runnymede.

It was suggested in the preceding chapter that the problem of effectively controlling widespread lawlessness is not unique to the time in which we live. Citizen apathy and unwillingness to accept responsibility for bringing criminals to justice was every bit as big a problem in thirteenth-century England as it is in twentieth-century America. Juries, then as now, often failed to convict, and individual citizens typically shunned even the reporting of crime out of fear of reprisal by criminals, particularly from the nobility.

This state of affairs led in 1285 to issuance of the *Statute of Winchester* by Edward I. The Statute of Winchester was intended to reaffirm and strengthen the old tradition of local responsibility for law enforcement. The statute not only made it unlawful to either conceal felonies or harbor felons, but also made everyone within the county where a crime occurred accountable for making certain that the offender was apprehended. The hue and cry was to be raised immediately in the event of a crime and the offender to be pursued and captured regardless of the time or distance involved. Citizens could no longer seek to exempt themselves from personal responsibility in enforcing the law, for the statute decreed that "cries shall be made in all counties, markets, hundreds, fairs, so that none shall excuse himself by ignorance."[5] The price of failure to apprehend criminals was shared liability by the entire community for the crime and whatever damages it might involve.

As might be imagined, the Statute of Winchester stimulated local communities to search for more effective and better organized systems of law enforcement than had existed in the past. It required them by law to post men at every town gate from dark to dawn. Walled towns were ordered to close their gates at nightfall, and every town and borough in the country was required to maintain a *watch* or guard, the size of which was to be in proportion to its population. The watch for a given *ward* or area was made up of the citizens within it, who rotated the duty among themselves. The modern concept of police *patrol* made its appearance with the advent of a *marching watch,* consisting of citizen watchmen who banded together and walked certain wards. The marching watch was doubtless brought about more by a desire for personal safety on the part of these early citizen-policemen than any real desire to deter crime and criminals.

Since the notion of environmental design looms large in contemporary planning for crime control, it is interesting to note that the seeds of this concept were present during the watch and ward era. Thus, for instance, because of the constant peril of highwaymen, the Statute of Winchester required that well-traveled roads connecting towns be kept clear of growth for a distance of two hundred feet on either side, the purpose being to deny robbers any place of concealment.[6] Landlords who failed to comply with this law were liable to fines, as well as being responsible for any crimes occurring as a direct result of their negligence.

Another effort at controlling crime through environmental measures at this time was the prohibition against adult men being in areas beyond the town after dark, unless they were lodging with a responsible citizen. Criminals were thereby denied a community perimeter within which they might comfortably nest and venture out to stage crimes at night. An attempt was made to keep track of strangers who might pose future trouble in a town through the appointment of *bailiffs,* who were to check on such individuals at regular fifteen-day intervals and take whatever action they deemed necessary. Bailiffs were assisted in this enforcement activity by officials known as *sergeants* (meaning "great scrutinizers"). We see here the beginning of our own tradition of *vagrancy* and *loitering* laws.

It is also during this same period that we see the first appearance of organized law-enforcement effort aimed at regulating what is often referred to as society's oldest profession, prostitution. The *police des mouers,* the earliest known predecessor of today's sex detail or morals squad, was formed for the specific purpose of keeping track of prostitutes and confining their activities to certain parts of the city.

In the year 1361 a new and quite powerful law-enforcement position was added to the roster of those we have already discussed. King Edward

III appointed certain members of the landed gentry as *justices of the peace,* conferring on them broad judicial as well as law-enforcement authority. William the Conqueror had greatly reduced the traditional powers of the shire-reeve or sheriff. Many of these very powers now came to be vested in the justice of the peace under Edward III. Justices of the peace were not only authorized to hear cases and pass sentence in a wide variety of offenses against the king's peace, ranging from major felonies to public drunkenness and idleness, but were also empowered to pursue, apprehend, and incarcerate offenders. Justices of the peace evolved the familiar practice of permitting an accused person to post *bail,* when the individual in question appeared sufficiently trustworthy and responsible, as an alternative to languishing in jail until the date the case was heard. By virtue of the broad judicial and enforcement functions of the office, the justice of the peace quickly came to eclipse the shire-reeve in political importance. Indeed, the justice could initiate investigations into suspected misconduct on the part of the shire-reeves and take action against any who had violated the law.

The development of civilization has witnessed the steady growth of new forms of law and procedures for their enforcement. During the reign of Edward III there appeared for the first time *Statutes of Treason,* which made it a crime punishable by death to give aid and comfort to England's enemies. These same statutes expanded the concept of treason far beyond our modern definition, to include the *counterfeiting* of English money, something which was regarded as a serious crime against the entire country.

History convincingly demonstrates that such problems as large-scale unemployment, poverty, and overcrowded living conditions tend to be associated with high crime rates regardless of the period during which they occur. Around the start of the sixteenth century, such conditions of life began to characterize England's larger cities as ever-increasing numbers of people poured out of farms and villages and into the country's urban centers. Much of this mass migration was a direct result of the so-called *enclosure movement,* which caused vast areas of farming land throughout England to be converted to grazing pastures for sheep as the country sought to keep pace with the rising national and international demand for wool.

As the urban exodus produced soaring crime rates, the pressure on the country's woefully inadequate law-enforcement machinery mounted and led to demands for new measures to combat the rising tide of lawlessness. The watch and ward system, never very effective and at most grudgingly accepted by citizens impressed into its service, now crumbled as householders insisted on hiring substitutes to take their increasingly risky watches. Even though this practice was allowed, crimes against business establishments in such large cities as London reached such staggering proportions that merchants were forced to begin employing their own *private police*. Known as the *Commercial and Parochial Police,* these early forerunners of today's "rent-a-cop" or private security officers performed many of the functions of their modern counterparts.

The sixteenth century marked the beginning of a dark period in English law-enforcement history, not only because of skyrocketing crime rates, but also because this era witnessed the erosion and temporary loss of most of the hard-won freedoms wrested from King John under the Magna Carta. Due process of law became a thing of the past with the appearance of the *Court of the Star Chamber* under Charles I. Operating under the guise of being a judicial body, the crown-appointed counselors making up this "court" not only accused persons out of favor with the king, but also sought to elicit confessions of guilt from them through the use of legalized torture methods known as the *third degree.* In this kangaroo court virtually all the constitutional safeguards enjoyed by an accused person in our society were nonexistent: defendants were not entitled to legal representation or trial by jury, and might not call witnesses in their behalf, although the prosecution was free to do so. There was no way to appeal the typically harsh sentence meted out by the court. Indeed, merely being accused by the Court of the Star Chamber carried with it the certainty of conviction once the mockery of a trial or hearing had been taken care of.

The tyranny of Charles I led in 1628 to the passage of a *Petition of Right* by an outraged and increasingly rebellious Parliament, determined to stem the king's growing abuse of power. The petition was intended to reestablish the right of due process of law and end the practices of the Court of the Star Chamber, as well as to prevent the king from coercing illegal gifts and taxes from his subjects. Although Charles signed the petition, he promptly disregarded its contents and returned to his former ways, which led to the outbreak of civil war and his execution in 1649.

With the death of Charles, the country fell under harsh military rule as Oliver Cromwell (1653–1658), a former general, became Lord protector of England. Cromwell divided the country into a total of 12 districts, placing a military official known as *provost marshal* in charge of each, and giving him absolute law enforcement and judicial authority over all civilians and military personnel within his area. With the advent of Cromwell's military dictatorship, whatever gains were achieved in curbing the spread of rampant social disorder were more than offset by the complete suppression of individual liberty.

Following the death of Cromwell, Parliament succeeded in gaining control of England's governmental system and greatly limiting the king's heretofore vast power, something that paved the way for the development of a more democratic and just system of law enforcement. In 1689 Parliament enlarged the basic human rights established by the Magna Carta, with the passage of a *Bill of Rights,* which provided that people might speak openly without fear of punishment for whatever views they expressed.

It also extended to individuals a legal protection against being forced to incriminate themselves. We see here the origin of two of our most cherished constitutional rights as American citizens: *freedom of speech* and *freedom from self-incrimination.* Other legal safeguards basic to the operation of our modern system of criminal justice were also established during this same general period of time. In 1679 a *Habeas Corpus Act* was introduced by Charles II, requiring that prisoners be arraigned before a judge following their arrest and that cause be established for their continued detention. The judge was either to set a date for the prisoner's trial or order the person's immediate release if there appeared to be no legal grounds for pursuing the case. In addition to passing the Habeas Corpus Act, Charles II is also remembered in the history of law enforcement for introducing a force of one thousand nightwatchmen in London. The timidity and ineffectiveness of these paid constables in the face of ever-increasing crime problems led to public ridicule of them as "Charlies" and the "shiver and shake watch," the latter appellation apparently coming from their practice of shaking the doors of shops and businesses between sunset and daybreak.

Later English Contributions

With the beginning of the Industrial Revolution during the mid-eighteenth century, already serious problems of mass poverty, unemployment, and crime reached major, epidemic proportions throughout England. The crowded slums spawned over two centuries before by the enclosure movement now festered with every form of social illness, and the introduction of machines such as the steam engine eliminated much of the need for even cheap human labor. The country's poor and dispossessed flocked to urban centers as never before in search of the promise of a better life. They typically found, instead, only squalor and even more intense desperation. Men, women, and children worked for up to 16 hours a day in congested, unsafe factories, returning each evening to slum dwellings and the nightmare of urban crime surrounding them. Historical accounts of this period make our contemporary problems of "crime in the streets" seem pale, indeed, by comparison.[7] Gangs of thugs roamed the streets at will, robbing, beating, and often killing their victims. Highwaymen preyed on travelers entering and leaving the city. In London alone hundreds of bank robberies occurred each year. Only the most foolhardy citizens failed to carry guns virtually everywhere they went. No social class was safe from the terror that affected rich and poor alike, no area of the city immune to the depredations of violent crime.

Thousands of pickpockets gravitated to large cities such as London and Liverpool, where the high population density afforded them constant opportunities to ply their trade and interact with *fences,* who bought and sold the fruits of their labor. Counterfeiting was so prevalent that it is estimated that far more illegal currency was in circulation than that issued by the English government. Large numbers of women were forced into prostitution by economic necessity. At one time there were over 25,000 prostitutes in London alone. Alcoholism, particularly gin drinking, became a major national problem for the first time, as did juvenile delinquency.

Such dire conditions led to constant experimentation with new law-enforcement methods as society sought to place a lid on the boiling kettle of urban lawlessness. As is true of our current, federally sponsored "Help Stop Crime" programs, one of the most perplexing problems facing the English was how to motivate citizens to become actively involved in the war on crime. We have already noted how the law-abiding population chafed under and resisted the requirement of watch and ward service, many of them hiring derelicts and vagabonds to take their place.

One solution to the problem of citizen apathy, it was hoped by the English, might be the provision of rewards for the apprehension of criminals. As early as 1693, Parliament enacted a law which provided a scale of reward payments for the capture of different classes of offenders. Thus, for instance, highwaymen, burglars, and housebreakers, yielded the highest bounties. In contrast, sheep thieves brought only ten pounds and army deserters only a single pound apiece. Unfortunately, the system had a boomerang effect, often producing more crime than it eliminated as criminals themselves discovered the ease with which they might frame innocent men and collect rewards for their capture. The English experiment with rewards brought into being the historical forerunners of our own Western *bounty hunters.*

By 1737 individual city councils were authorized to establish taxes to pay persons serving on the nightwatch, thereby introducing the principle of a tax-supported public police. To aid the fight against crime, citizen groups known as *vigilantes* came into being, and the penalties for every kind of crime were greatly increased. At one point the death penalty was prescribed for 160 different offenses. The mere pilfering of a loaf of bread was punishable by hanging, and each day dozens of minor offenders were executed alongside dangerous felons as society became progressively more desperate in its efforts to combat crime. Even in the face of such severe measures, however, the crime rate continued to climb dramatically.

The first real effort to examine the crime problem systematically and prescribe more effective law-enforcement methods for dealing with it came in 1749, when the novelist and lawyer Sir Henry Fielding published his work, "An Enquiry into the Causes of the Late Increase of Robberies."[8] Fielding, who was at the time chief magistrate for Middlesex and Westminster, concluded on the basis of his surveys that inferior police personnel were themselves a major cause of crime. In addition to setting forth other advanced law-enforcement principles, Fielding called for improved methods of police selection and better pay as essential first steps in dealing with crime. With the help of his blind brother John, he sought to put such concepts into practice by establishing a new kind of force at the Bow Street station. It involved the use of mounted officers to patrol the crime-infested highways leading into the city, and foot patrolmen in the densely populated residential and business areas, both of them based on the modern notion of a *mobile patrol force*. Fielding is usually best remembered, however, for his introduction of what is believed to be the first real detective force in history: the "Bow-Street Runners" or "Thief-Takers." These early police investigators moved quickly and in plain clothes to the scene of a crime, where they began examining the facts surrounding it, a major incentive for their efforts being the possibility of collecting a reward for apprehending the culprit.

In addition to these contributions, Fielding also introduced special daily hearings, which were the beginning of today's *police and traffic courts*. Few of those who read Fielding's popular work *Tom Jones* are aware of the author's contribution to the history of law enforcement.

Fielding's emphasis on competent, well-qualified police personnel paved the way for other major strides toward professionalism. One such event was the publication of a code of conduct intended to guide police officers in the performance of their duty. Written by *Saunders Welch*, onetime assistant chief of the "Runners," the document contains basic principles that are still taught to British police officers and are every bit as sound today as when they were first written. In it Welch cautions officers against "officious, wanton acts of power," noting that "imperiousness of conduct too frequently seen in constables . . . may be called the drunkenness of power."[9] Constables were at all times to display "temper and sobriety," courtesy and good humor. Above all, they were to avoid the use of physical force whenever possible:

> I advise never to strike, except it be absolutely in your own defense; but striking at all, if possible, should be avoided, for the sword of justice not the arm of constables, was intended for punishment.[10]

One of the major barriers to law-enforcement progress was a widespread fear of political oppression that rivaled even the fear of crime in eighteenth-century England. Certainly this fear was well grounded in reality, for the country had endured more than its share of tyrants who had twisted the law and its enforcement systems to their own advantage—from the ruthless King John to Charles I and his Star Chamber to Oliver Cromwell's military dictatorship. Such things as taxation for police service and the provision of equipment and better-organized personnel came slowly, with great difficulty, and always with the fear of many in Parliament that such developments were the first steps toward creation of a police state. They had seen far too many instances of widespread abuse of power that went along with strong police organizations in France and other continental countries.

If the title "father of modern policing" is deserved by any one individual, that man is without a doubt, Sir Robert Peel, Britain's Home Secretary in 1829. Peel had been greatly impressed by Fielding's argument that poor police personnel were themselves a major contributing cause of crime. He also believed very strongly that effective crime control depends on the existence of a body of law that the public can respect and clearly understand. For this reason he regarded the generally harsh and vague laws of his time as woefully inadequate, and set about introducing far-reaching legal reforms. Peel abolished the death penalty for most crimes, and greatly reduced or altogether eliminated what he regarded as unreasonably severe and unproductive penalties for a great many other offenses.

This being accomplished, he turned his attention to the country's law-enforcement system itself, which at the time was little more than a mishmash of countless uncoordinated agencies with divided authority and responsibility. Unifying the police under a single organizational roof was an essential first step in Peel's plan for law-enforcement reform. In 1829 he succeeded in pushing through Parliament "An Act for Improving the Police In and Near the Metropolis," not without considerable opposition from the Tories of his own party, who saw in the act the seeds of totalitarianism. Peel countered their arguments that his act posed a threat to individual liberty by stressing that England's crime problem had reached such proportions that it demanded bold action, and asking if liberty " . . . consist[s] in having your house robbed by organized gangs of thieves?"

The Metropolitan Police Act provided for the immediate creation of a force of 1000 men, operating in six divisions, and under the supervision of two commissioners who reported directly to Peel himself. This new enforcement body was to have responsibility for safeguarding life and property in London's crime-ridden metropolitan area, and to be guided in its organization and operation by the following 12 principles, each of them formulated by Peel:

1. The police must be stable, efficient, and organized along military lines.
2. The police must be under governmental control.
3. The absence of crime will best prove the efficiency of the police.
4. The distribution of crime news is essential.
5. The deployment of police strength by *time* and *area* is essential.
6. No quality is more indispensable to a policeman than a perfect command of temper; a quiet, determined manner has more effect than violent action.
7. Good appearance commands respect.
8. The securing and training of proper persons is at the root of efficiency.
9. Public security demands that every police officer be given a number.
10. Police headquarters should be centrally located and easily accessible to the people.
11. Policemen should be hired on a probationary basis.
12. Police records are necessary to the correct distribution of police strength.

We see in these guidelines the essence of what is often referred to as the *Peelian Reform,* the establishment of modern law-enforcement concepts destined to profoundly affect the history of policing in both England and America. The basic structure and operation of police departments in both countries still reflect the influence of Peel's principles.

Such was the level of Peels' personal commitment to making the Metropolitan Police experiment a success that he himself participated in the examination of over 12,000 applicants for the available 1,000 positions. His commitment to seeing the principles of policing he had established carried out was no less. During the first two years of its operation, roughly 50 percent of the Metropolitan Police force was either dismissed or forced to resign, thus firmly establishing the modern law-enforcement concept that every officer must be held accountable to high standards of conduct.

Despite such efforts to allay the fears of both Parliament and the public that the new force would operate with flagrant disregard for personal liberty, its first constables were met with incredible hostility—and even violence—on the part of London's law-abiding citizenry. Constables were derided as "crushers," "blue devils," and "raw lobsters."

Although the appearance of today's English "bobby" in public typically evokes a reaction of respect, the sight of his predecessor was more apt to lead to catcalls or an assault. Early constables were frequently attacked and beaten. Some were literally kicked to death by mobs and others seized and thrown into the Thames. Such public reactions, as well as strict internal discipline, doubtless contributed greatly to the high attrition rate during the first years of the force.

Realizing the widespread resentment of them, the first force of constables made extraordinary efforts to win the respect of the public. Such was the hatred of anything even remotely military at the time that the "uniform" worn by Peel's men, though it was intentionally designed to make the constable easily distinguishable from ordinary citizens, was not all that different from civilian garb in general appearance. It consisted basically of a blue cloth suit, frock coat, and "chimney-pot" hat.

Within the short space of 10 years, the Metropolitan police succeeded not only in demonstrating their ability to deal effectively with crime and criminals, but also won the enthusiastic support of the citizenry. Earlier, hostile labels for them were now replaced with the affectionate designation "bobbies" (after Sir Robert) and "peelers." With the demonstrable success of the new police organization, Peel was acclaimed as a national hero and plans were made to export his system to other municipalities throughout the country. Legislation allowing other communities to establish police forces modeled on the Metropolitan Police was passed in 1839, followed in 1856 by laws which made the creation of tax-supported police agencies mandatory throughout England.

London's Metropolitan Police force by this time had better than tripled its original size, now numbering 3314, and consisting of some 2906 constables, 17 superintendents, 68 inspectors, and 323 sergeants. For purposes of policing, the city's metropolitan region was divided into areas of 80,000 residents, with a superintendent being placed in charge of each. In each of these residential areas or *divisions,* there were eight *patrol sections,* with each of the latter being further subdivided into eight *beats.* A rotating shift system operated, with two-thirds of the force serving night duty for eight months, and one-third serving day duty for four months.

The organization and operation of the Metropolitan Police remains basically the same today as when Peel first established it almost 150 years ago at 4 Whitehall Place, behind a courtyard that had once been used by Scottish kings—which led over time to the designation of police headquarters as Scotland Yard. Today the force numbers over 20,000 and provides law-enforcement service for an area consisting of approximately 742 square miles. Yet it continues to operate on the same 12 principles that first brought it into being on September 29, 1829.

Early American Police

The first colonists who settled in the new world naturally brought with them the law-enforcement systems which had been used in their homeland. Since well over 90 percent of these early settlers came from England, this meant that the evolution of American law enforcement for the most part closely paralleled its British counterpart. The highly diverse geography of colonial America strongly influenced the manner in which various English methods of policing came to be adopted. Thus, for instance, the vast expanse of flat and fertile farmland in the South naturally attracted large numbers of people who had relied on agriculture as a means of livelihood in the Old World. Such individuals, already accustomed to the nature of rural life, brought with them a county form of government and the familiar county enforcement office of *sheriff*. The latter made his first appearance in America as early as 1634, when the first counties were established in Virginia. A tradition was thereby created in the southern United States which was to see the sheriff become the most powerful law enforcement figure in that part of the country, something that continues to be true even today.

The North was a different matter. There the colonial era witnessed the steady growth of towns and villages whose population depended heavily on commerce and industry, and who typically had emigrated from the cities and larger communities of England. Unlike the South's rural population, these people were most familiar not with the county tradition of the sheriff, but with the urban practice of *watch and ward*. They accordingly began to adopt this enforcement system to deal with the problems of crime and disorder which soon appeared in the New World. Boston formed a *night watch* in 1636 to combat theft by Indians and to be on the lookout for the omnipresent peril of fires in the city. A "*rattle watch*," so called because its members carried something closely akin to today's Halloween noisemakers, appeared in New York in 1658. Rattles were not only an early antecedent of today's two-way police radio, insofar as they allowed communication between those charged with enforcing the law, but they also represented an application of the idea that police patrol personnel should make their presence well known to potential offenders. In this sense New York's "rattle watch" was a historical forerunner of the marked patrol unit. Other northern cities soon established similar versions of the English watch and ward system.

The citizen enforcement effort of the watch and ward in America soon led to experiences remarkably similar to those which had been encountered in England, most notably to citizen resistance and general ineffectiveness in the face of growing crime problems. People of the time resented the common requirement that all males over the age of 16 serve without pay on the watch, and went to great lengths to evade service. Many refused outright to accept such duty, while others nominally agreed but used the long hours of the night watch to nap in some secure spot. So odious was the watch and ward in early America that minor offenders were often sentenced to serve on it as part of the punishment for their crimes. Cities found themselves forced to pass detailed regulations prohibiting watchmen from sleeping on duty and commanding these generally dull and apathetic guardians of the public peace to ". . . walk their rounds slowly and now and then stand and listen."[11] Even the eventual payment of nightwatchmen did little to sweeten the bitter pill of serving in such an unpopular capacity.

Even in such Northern cities as Boston, New York, and Philadelphia, American law enforcement was extremely slow to develop. As late as 1830, the policing of cities by day was totally unheard of. The city was guarded only during the vulnerable nighttime hours, while it slept. In attempting to understand the reasons behind such limited police service, it is important to bear in mind that even the nation's largest cities at the time were small villages by modern standards. Indeed, by 1790 there were only six cities in the country with populations in excess of 8,000.

The concept of *daytime policing* made its first appearance in Philadelphia in 1833. At that time a wealthy philanthropist provided sufficient funds to enable the city to pass an ordinance creating a 24-man day force to supplement the efforts of the city's nightwatch. Unfortunately, the ordinance was repealed within two years and Philadelphia returned to its nightwatch system. Following the lead of Philadelphia, Boston created a day watch of its own in 1838, and Cincinnati did likewise in 1842. Under these early day-night systems, separate supervisors were in charge of each force, and considerable rivalry and friction developed between the members of each. Steps to eliminate this problem were taken in 1844, when New York's legislature passed a law authorizing the creation of a *unified* day and night force.

New York became the first city in the country to establish a truly *modern police force,* one closely modeled on the 12 principles set forth by Sir Robert Peel in 1829. In 1845 New York's day and night forces were unified under a superintendent and paid out of state legislated funds. The new force was quickly increased to 1000 men and the selection and training of officers began to proceed along professional lines.

The New York City police became the first *fully uniformed* force in the country in 1856, but this development was not without great internal resistance on the part of the department's officers. As was true of most early American police departments, New York's officers regarded wearing any external identifying insignia as a stigma and an invitation to displays of hostility—from the law-abiding citizenry as well as criminals. Even wearing of distinctive caps or badges on outer garments was steadfastly resisted. It was not until 1855, a full 12 years after the New York department was founded, that officers were compelled to begin carrying an identifying badge on a chain beneath their jackets and to exhibit it when enforcing the law. A year later the entire force began wearing a full police uniform, although there was great variation in the appearance of these from one ward to another. Contrary to Sir Robert Peel's basic principle that a policeman's outward appearance is an essential element of his ability to command respect, police officers in other American cities displayed a resistance to police uniforms very similar to that encountered in New York.

Despite the attempt of many American cities to model their own law enforcement agencies on the British Metropolitan Police, basic cultural and historical differences between the two countries soon began to produce dramatic departures from the English system. The spread of violence in America's burgeoning urban centers saw early constables in our country up against problems even more severe that those experienced by their British counterparts. The following account of conditions in mid-nineteenth-century America gives us some appreciation of the hazards of being a police officer at the time:

> New York City was alleged to be the most crime-ridden city in the world, with Philadelphia, Baltimore and Cincinnati not far behind. . . . Gangs of youthful rowdies in the larger cities . . . threatened to destroy the American reputation for respect for law. . . . Before their boisterous demonstrations the crude police forces of the day were often helpless.[12]

In addition to the staggering growth of street crime, American police departments found themselves facing a succession of bitter urban riots centering upon such issues as poverty, immigration, race, religious freedom, and opposition to the draft. In July, 1863, New York police battled thousands of angry rioters who roamed the city, burning and looting in protest over the Draft Act. The conflict was so severe that units of the Union Army had to be rushed in just after the Battle of Gettysburg to restore order. Large numbers of both police and rioters were killed. Police departments in cities across the country were increasingly drawn into violent industrial disputes between labor and management as unions began to emerge as powerful organizations. In the wake of the large-scale urban disorders which took place in such cities as Los Angeles, Chicago, and Newark during the 1960s, we sometimes lose sight of the fact that such violent clashes are nothing new in the history of our country.

The cumulative effect of the emerging patterns of violence and lawlessness in nineteenth-century America was the production of what still represents one of the major differences between police in England and the United States: the carrying of *firearms*. Given the fact that all police officers in our country today are armed, we are inclined to forget that their ancestors were *not*. The first American patrolmen carried only sticks or truncheons, as did their British equivalents. As departments became better organized, quantities of sabers were kept on hand for emergency situations, but were promptly collected once the crisis had passed.[13] By the 1850s the task of patrolling American cities had become sufficiently dangerous that large numbers of officers began purchasing and carrying firearms on their own, without official permission. Much of this was in direct response to the fact that growing numbers of both criminals and citizens were arming themselves.

The all-too-common murder of unarmed patrolmen by gun-toting offenders led to recurrent public demands that the police be armed and further extended the growing practice of officers informally carrying weapons. The widespread gun ownership which appeared during and immediately after the Civil War, and the attendant increase in violent crime, led to the official arming of police in cities throughout the country in an effort to both assure the safety of patrolmen and regulate the kinds of weapons that were carried. Given the proliferation of guns of every kind and description in America today, and the astronomical rise of gun-related violent crime, it seems unthinkable that any American policeman will ever begin a tour of duty armed only with the stick carried by British "bobbies." In light of the statement just made, the senior author might parenthetically note that until 1973 he was an outspoken advocate of an unarmed American police modeled on the English system. In that year, largely on the basis of a "dare" from a number of police officers enrolled in one of my university law enforcement courses, I decided to become a uniformed patrolman for a period of several months in order to study social and psychological dynamics of the police role in modern society. After graduating from the academy and meeting other departmental requirements, I began working a high-crime beat in the slum section of a large American city. To make a very long story short, the ensuing exposure to the realities of violent crime in our society today was a sobering experience. Among other changes, the author went during this short period of time from being an opponent of armed police to personally carrying a gun off duty as well as on, supplementing its protective effects by wearing a ballistic vest while on patrol.[14]

Aside from their early adoption of firearms, American police officers were also different from England's bobbies by virtue of the problem of widespread political interference with their attempts to enforce the law. Where British constables were, from their very inception, under the tight control of a democratically elected Parliament and of police commissioners who refused to accept traditions of patronage in making appointments, police officers and administrators in this country soon became targets of political control. The 1830s witnessed the birth in the political arena of what became known as the *spoils system,* a corrupt philosophy of government which decrees that the party in power should enjoy such perquisites as immunity from arrest and prosecution, and the right to manipulate the law for their own political ends. Police positions during this era were typically awarded as political favors by mayors, city councilmen, and aldermen, many of whom exacted in return a license to violate the law with impunity. With the waxing and waning of different politicians, the administration and organization of entire departments changed overnight. The results were predictable: Corruption and extortion became traditions in many departments. Discipline and a sense of professional pride in the work of enforcing the law were virtually impossible to sustain.[15]

Numerous unsuccessful attempts were made over the years to minimize political control of the police. One of the most notable of these was the practice of creating *police administrative boards* comprised of prominent local citizens to deal with issues and problems affecting the police, the intent being to eliminate the meddling of mayors and councilmen. Unfortunately, such groups—despite their good intentions—lacked sufficient understanding of the police and the problems facing them at the time. For the most part, the experiment with police administrative boards was demonstrably ineffective. Because police corruption tended at the time to be primarily a problem in urban areas, some state legislatures sought to bring the appointment of department administrators under their control, something that aroused considerable resentment on local levels and did little if anything to alleviate the basic problem. Indeed, many state-appointed police administrators had so little awareness or appreciation of local law-enforcement problems that they inadvertently introduced policies which actually worsened conditions.

Wholesale political interference in the business of American law enforcement extended all the way from the early thirties until 1883. In that year the idea of insulating governmental machinery from political influence was ushered in by the *Pendleton Act,* which provided *civil service* for federal empoloyees. The years following the passage of this act saw the gradual extension of civil-service protection to employees at the local and state levels, as well. Today all but a tiny fraction of those employed at all three levels of government are covered by civil-service procedures.

From what has been said so far about the evolution of municipal law enforcement in the United States, we can see how our British heritage was uniquely shaped and molded to fit both the culture and geography of the new land in which it was applied. As America's population slowly drifted westward across the frontier, these same traditions were modified still further in the face of changing social and environmental demands. Northern settlers carried to rugged western and southwestern communities the office of the town constable, who was to become the much romanticized *marshal* of television and motion-picture folklore. However, because the towns that existed out West were few and far between, the sheriff—brought westward by the first rural migrants from the South— was destined to become the dominant law-enforcement figure in that part of the country.

Emergence of State and Federal Law Enforcement

In contrast to municipal police, state law-enforcement agencies were relatively slow to develop. The earliest form of state police force was the Texas Rangers, brought into being in 1835 as a supplement to Texas military forces and to combat cattle rustling by Mexicans along the border. Massachusetts created a statewide force of constables to deal with violations of vice laws in 1865, and Connecticut followed with a similar investigative agency in 1903. Around the same time, both Arizona and New Mexico created mounted border police modeled closely on the Texas Rangers. The first truly modern state police force appeared in Pennsylvania in 1905. The Pennsylvania State Police were a uniformed, mounted body of officers under direct control of the governor. This force was in response to a series of violent coal strikes throughout the state.

Generally speaking, state police agencies emerged as a direct result of two major problems: (1) The inefficiency and corruption of many local law-enforcement officials charged with responsibility for enforcing state statutes led to public demands for state involvement. (2) The increasing mobility of criminals, who could strike in one area of a state and then move quickly on to another, sorely taxed the resources of local enforcement personnel. Significantly, most state police forces were created shortly after World War I, a point in American history when the automobile was exerting its greatest influence in terms of producing large amounts of car theft and making the rapid flight of offenders easier than ever before. Today, every state in the Union has some form of state law-enforcement organization, with the sole exception of Hawaii. The actual structure and operation of these agencies show great variation from state to state, with some having general, state-wide law-enforcement powers, and others being restricted to traffic and highway safety functions. Many large states today have highly specialized state law-enforcement units, with some being entirely devoted to such areas as criminal identification, narcotics, and liquor control.

The very idea of federal involvement in the law-enforcement process has always been touchy and controversial in the United States. If anything, it has become even more so in the post-Watergate era in which we live. The specter of government use of law-enforcement powers to infringe on the rights of individual citizens served, during the Watergate scandal, to awaken ancient fears in the American psyche, fears that clearly guided the framers of our Constitution, fears that are as much a part of our heritage as the watch and ward.

It was these very fears that led to a Constitution that specifically reserved police authority to the individual states. Congress was, however, given the authority under Article I, Section 8 to take steps necessary to assure the common defense and promote the general welfare of the country's population. Under this authority it was clear from the beginning that Congress might pass and enforce laws deemed essential to protect the Constitution and its amendments.

However much the citizenry and founders of our country, in their zeal to prevent the dreaded reality of a police state, might have wished to limit the law-enforcement role of the federal government, forces beyond their control soon forced the reluctant creation of police at the federal level. Certain problems clamored for solutions that were far beyond the resources of both local and state governments. Thus, for instance, as the country began to grow and develop, there was the pressing question of who would make certain that lawful taxes were paid. Who would take responsibility for dealing with the growing number of smugglers who began operating along the nation's vast borders? Who would seek to prevent the counterfeiting of currency, deal with mail robberies and fraud, pursue offenders who had fled beyond the boundaries of individual states? The answers to these and a host of related questions brought the first federal law-enforcement agencies into being. It should be emphasized that the creation of federal law enforcement was a slow and piecemeal business from the beginning, with Congress enacting highly specific legislation to deal with a problem such as internal revenue or narcotics, and federal agencies with highly limited powers of enforcement later emerging to deal with it. The American aversion to federal control has always been far too strong to allow the creation of a single national police entity with broad powers of enforcement.

Federal law enforcement first became a reality in the United States in 1789, when Congress created the *Revenue Cutter Service* to help prevent smuggling. During the same year Congress passed legislation authorizing the appointment of *federal marshals* throughout the country. An incumbent in the office of U.S. marshal was appointed to serve for a four-year term and was held responsible for the enforcement of all laws of the United States. Early federal marshals enjoyed enforcement powers comparable in many respects to those held by sheriffs within their respective counties, including the ancient common-law tradition we described earlier as *posse comitatus*,[16] the right to summon all able-bodied men in the vicinity to their assistance. The office of *attorney general* was also created in 1789, along with our federal court system, although the attorney general was not given authority over U.S. marshals until as late as 1861.

After the position of U.S. marshal was introduced in 1789, there followed a gap of some 40 years before Congress undertook to create additional federal law-enforcement personnel. The problem of mail fraud led to the establishment of a *Post Office Inspection* system in 1829. Following this, the postmaster general was authorized to pay agents investigating postal matters in 1836.

Although Congress passed a counterfeiting law in 1842, the agency charged with responsibility for its enforcement was not established until 1865. In that year the *U.S. Secret Service* was formally organized under the Treasury Department as the first general investigative agency at the federal level. The new agency was extremely small at its inception, with some 30 investigators being scattered in 11 field offices across the country. Their sole concern at this time was the task of detecting counterfeiters and restoring public confidence in the nation's currency. Because of the magnitude of this task and their limited resources to accomplish it, the Secret Service requested and obtained the assistance and cooperation of the country's U.S. marshals. To their credit, the first secret-service agents were remarkably successful in dealing with counterfeiters, and their agency continued to operate and grow with annual appropriations from Congress. In 1903, in the wake of President McKinley's assassination, the heretofore single responsibility of the Secret Service was expanded to include protection of the president.[17]

Although Congress introduced a Department of Justice into the federal system in 1870, it was reluctant to allow this powerful new arm of government to operate with its own independent investigative personnel. Indeed, as late as 1906, Congress was still authorizing the temporary loan of Secret Service agents to the attorney general in lieu of allowing the Justice Department to maintain its own force of investigators. Finally, in 1909 funds were appropriated for the purpose of establishing a small group of detectives to operate under direction of the attorney general. These men comprised what was known at the time as the *Bureau of Investigation,* an agency destined for later fame as the *Federal Bureau of Investigation.* The FBI itself was formally established in 1924 by the late J. Edgar Hoover, then a 29-year-old attorney, who remained director of the agency until the time of his death in 1972. Despite whatever criticisms have been leveled at Hoover in recent years, it should be remembered that he successfully built one of the world's most respected and efficient law-enforcement agencies.

The past hundred years has witnessed the steady emergence of ever new federal enforcement agencies in response to mounting problems of lawlessness in our society, problems which are often far beyond the scope of local and even state law enforcement to deal with. Some of the most important federal developments since 1870 include:

1870	Department of Justice established
1882–1886	Border Patrol established under the Customs Service
1895	Federal investigation of lotteries sent through the mail
1906	Pure Food and Drug Act established
1909	narcotics control initiated; along with controls over interstate transportation of diseased fruits, vegetables, and plants
1910	White Slave Act, to prevent interstate transport of females for immoral purposes, and the Motor Vehicle Theft Act, covering interstate movement of vehicles, adopted
1913	federal controls over the manufacture of liquor adopted
1915	narcotic control becomes a section of the Internal Revenue Service
1918	national prohibition laws enacted
1924	Federal Bureau of Investigation organized in the Department of Justice by J. Edgar Hoover
1934	National Kidnapping Act, Banking Act, Racketeering Act and Interstate Compact Act passed by Congress[18]

SUMMARY   In a very real sense, law enforcement is as old as human society itself. We have seen in this chapter how in even the earliest societies certain common "rules of the game" had to be evolved and agreed upon. Moreover, certain individuals have always had to be charged with responsibility for enforcing basic societal rules—whether such laws are formally codified in a set of written statutes or informally agreed upon by tribal elders and passed from one generation to another by word of mouth.

The first "police officers" were individuals and their kinspeople on whom responsibility for avenging wrongs and obtaining justice fell in the absence of any more formal arrangements. To study the history of law enforcement is to appreciate more fully the truth of the old expression, The past is prologue. So much of what we associate with modern American law enforcement has its roots in earliest antiquity: thus, for instance, we saw how the Athenian ruler Pisistratus (605–527 B.C.) developed a forerunner of today's police when he created a force of guards and charged them with responsibiliity for protecting his city's tower and highways. In a like manner, the *vigiles* of Augustus Caesar were the first instance of what we think of today as an integrated police-fire service. Moving into more recent history, we saw how very much of our modern municipal police system was borrowed from the Metropolitan Police established by Sir Robert Peel in England: everything from uniforms and identifying numbers to beat assignment and standards of selection and training. We saw also in our discussion of the history of law enforcement how certain ancient ideas have come into recent prominence in our society's attempt to deal more effectively with crime and criminals. The idea of citizen involvement in the law-enforcement process, initiated by Alfred the Great in the ninth century, has, in a sense, reemerged in a myriad of programs such as Neighborhood Watch, Help Stop Crime, and Operation Identification—which have as a common goal getting the person in the street involved in the business of law enforcement. Certainly there is much in modern law-enforcement activity that is altogether unique and novel in human history. Yet there appears to be much more that involves the modification or use of ideas and behavior that has been part of law enforcement for a very long time.

NOTES

1. Seagle, William "Hammurabi: King of Babylon," in Seagle, *Men of Law: From Hammaurabi to Holmes* (New York: Macmillan, 1947), pp. 13–30.
2. Goldin, Hyman E., *Hebrew Criminal Law and Procedure,* (New York: Twayne, 1952), pp. 18–37.
3. Linforth, Ivan M., *Solon The Athenian* (Berkeley: University of California Press, 1919), chapter 3.
4. A. C. Germann; Frank D. Day; and R. R. H. Gallati, *Introduction to Law Enforcement and Criminal Justice* (Springfield, Ill.: Thomas, 1976), p. 46.
5. Ibid., p. 56.
6. Vern L. Folley, *American Law Enforcement* (Boston: Hollbrook, 1976), p. 47.
7. Royal Commission on the Police, *Royal Commission on the Police; Final Report* (London: Her Majesty's Stationery Office, 1962), p. 12.
8. Douglas G. Growne, *The Rise of Scotland Yard* (New York: Putnam, N.D.), p. 27.
9. Walter Arm, *The Policeman* (New York: Dutton 1969), p. 18.
10. Ibid.
11. James R. Waters and Sheree A. McGrath, *Introduction to Law Enforcement* (Columbus, Ohio: Merrill, 1974), p. 9.
12. Arthur Charles Coe, "The Irrepressible Conflict: 1859–65," *A History of American Life in 12 Volumes,* Vol. III, Arthur M. Schlessinger, Sr. and Dixon Ryan Fox, eds. (New York: Macmillan, 1934), pp. 154–55.
13. Johnathan Rubenstein, *City Police* (New York: Farrar, Straus, and Giroux, 1973), p. 285.

14. For a complete account of the author's experiences as a university professor turned slum patrolman, see George Kirkham, *Signal Zero* (New York: Lippincott, 1976).
15. See Bruce Smith, Sr., *Police Systems in the United States*, 2nd ed., rev. (New York: Harper and Row, 1960), pp. 105–6.
16. Rita W. Cooley, "The Office of U.S. Marshal," *Western Political Quarterly* 12, Part I (March, 1959), pp. 123–140.
17. Walter S. Bowen and Harry Edwards Neal, *The United States Secret Service* (Philadelphia: Chilton, 1960), pp. 14–16, 126, 190–92.
18. From Waters and McGrath, *Law Enforcement*, p. 11.

SELECTED READINGS

Douglas G. Browne, *The Rise of Scotland Yard* (New York: Greenwood, 1973).

James Cramer, *The World's Police* (London: Cassel, 1964).

Wilbur L. Cross, *The History of Henry Fielding*, vol. 1, (New York: Russell and Russell, 1963).

Raymond Fosdick, *American Police Systems* (New York: Century, 1920).

———, *European Police Systems* (New York: Century, 1915).

J. M. Hart, *The British Police* (London: Allen and Unwin, 1951).

Roger Lane, *Policing the City: Boston, 1822–1885* (New York: Atheneum, 1971).

Charles Reith, *A New Study of Police History* (Edinburgh: Oliver and Boyd, 1956).

Bruce Smith, *Police Systems in the United States* 2nd rev. ed. (New York: Harper & Row, 1960).

D. Whitehead, *The F.B.I. Story* (Garden City, N.Y.: Doubleday, 1963).

3
THE PATROL AND TRAFFIC FUNCTIONS

When most citizens mention the word *police,* they think of local or municipal police. The tendency to conceive of the police in our society largely in terms of local law enforcement is justified to some extent by the fact that ours is basically a country of municipal police agencies—large and small, scattered in cities, towns, counties, boroughs, and villages throughout the land. Today, there are over 40,000 separate law-enforcement agencies in the United States, only 200 of which are state-level agencies and a bare 50 federal.[1] The remaining 39,750 consist of municipal police and sheriffs' departments, which collectively comprise the essence of American law enforcement.

From the very beginning, our country's strong emphasis on the principle of local governmental control meant that there were potentially as many different forms of police organization as there were municipalities. However, the fact that local police agencies, regardless of their size or location, have always faced certain common problems and tasks, has made for basic similarities in both their organization and their manner of operation. If there is a single unifying thread which runs through the fabric of virtually every municipal law-enforcement agency—large or small, rural or urban—that thread is the *patrol* function. Indeed, to most Americans the words *patrol* and *police* have become almost synonymous. To the average person, the police are personified by the uniformed figure of the patrol officer seated behind the wheel of a marked cruiser.

Patrol

The patrol division is often referred to as the backbone of any police department. This is because the success of the police organization as a whole depends most directly on the effectiveness of its patrol operation. The concept of patrol refers to the movement of police personnel within a designated or assigned area, most commonly known in the United States and England as a beat. Such movement may involve the time-honored practice of foot patrol, or it may encompass the use of automobiles, aircraft, motorcycles, horses, boats, or bicycles. Regardless of how it is actually accomplished, the essence of every police patrol operation is a round-the-clock, seven-days-a-week, presence in the community to be protected. It is because of this required omnipresence, and the number and complexity of tasks to be accomplished, that the patrol division is always the largest single organizational unit within any police department.

The expression "To Protect and Serve," which is seen today on the doors of marked police cars in many American communities, captures the essence of the patrol mission. The responsibility of patrol officers includes detecting and preventing crime, preserving public peace, safeguarding human life and property, apprehending law violators, and providing a great many community services which have little or nothing to do with the business of law enforcement itself.

The actual work done by today's patrol officer is greatly misunderstood by the public, largely as a result of the false images and stereotypes about the police that are conveyed by television programs and sensational news stories. One of the most glaring of these misconceptions is the impression that the average patrol officer spends most of his or her time fighting crime. In contrast to the nightly high-speed chases, shoot-outs, and scuffles of television and motion picture Supercops, our real-life patrol officer typically devotes 75 percent or more of his or her work time to social-service activity. Getting a child's cat out of a tree, transporting a dazed and crusty alcoholic from the sidewalk to a detoxification center, and trying to calm a landlord-tenant or family dispute are, to be sure, less colorful activities than pursuing armed robbers. Yet they are far more typical of the things police officers do during a normal workday. Many of these service activities, while less glamorous than crime fighting, are highly complex and difficult to handle. The task of confronting people daily who have pressing emotional, social, legal, and physical problems often forces the patrol officer to play, during a single tour of duty, the roles of psychiatrist, social worker, curbside lawyer, and physician. The service role is often one that would test the mettle of an experienced practitioner from any of the professions just mentioned—something that the senior author discovered firsthand when he left his university post in 1973 and spent several months working as a uniformed patrolman in a large American city as part of a research project.[2]

PREVENTIVE PATROL

While it has been estimated that only about two-tenths of 1 percent of the time a police officer spends on patrol is occupied with criminal matters,[3] deterrence and prevention of crime have always been the main justification for the practice of *preventive patrol*. From the very first use of patrol officers in our country to the present day, it has been assumed that the conspicuous and unpredictable presence of law-enforcement officers in public places serves to deter an unknown—but presumably substantial—number of people from committing crimes. Crimes that involve rational planning and a profit motive, such as burglary, auto theft, and robbery, are generally thought to be more deterrable through preventive patrol than those that stem from emotion or passion (e.g., murder), and usually occur in private places where police presence is unlikely.

Randomness of movement and *high visibility* are basic elements in the operation of preventive patrol. The patrol officer carefully avoids following any predictable pattern of movement along the streets of his beat. He varies the times during his shift that he checks a given warehouse or cruises by a frequently robbed liquor store. Everything, even down to when and where he stops for a cup of coffee or dinner, are calculatedly intended to be random and unpredictable to those considering committing a crime. At the same time, his appearance at points along the beat is intended to be highly visible. His uniform and the markings on his vehicle are intended to signal his sudden presence to all.

The rationale for the patrol officer's traditionally high visibility is really twofold: Not only does it serve warning to criminals in the area, but it also provides an important sense of psychological security to law-abiding citizens as well. Many of us who have found ourselves traveling in strange cities have personally experienced the sense of security that comes from seeing a marked police car turn the corner in front of us. Some argue that, quite aside from its value as a deterrent to crime, preventive patrol provides an essential psychological service for the average citizen, who feels increasingly menaced by the threat of street crime in our society.

Preventive patrol is described as both being both *reactive* and *proactive*. Because the patrol force of every department represents a scarce resource in relation to the total area to be covered and the numbers of people to be protected, real life—as opposed to television—police officers seldom come upon crimes in progress during the course of routine patrol activity. Rather, in most cases they are directed to crimes which have occurred through the actions of victims or other citizens. Whether an officer is flagged down by a pedestrian or dispatched by communications in response to a complaint call, contact with most crime is basically reactive in the sense that the officer himself does not initiate it. Officer-initiated discovery of crime and the apprehension of offenders, which is best described as proactive policing, are very difficult because of the unpredictability of most crime. As Albert J. Reiss, Jr., has observed:

In the absence of massive police manpower, proactive policing is a feasible method for discovery only when crime is routine and organized, and therefore predictable. From a sociological point of view, the patterned activity of vice, traffic, and organized groups such as gangs, lend themselves to proactive forms of policing.[4]

THE USE OF PATROL RESOURCES

Every police department has a limited amount of officers, equipment, and other resources which can be committed to the task of patrol. Even the largest and best equipped of agencies can scarcely place a patrol officer on every street corner or in front of every residence and place of business on a round-the-clock basis. Since patrol resources are always scarce, it is essential that they be deployed in such a way as to afford the public maximum protection and service for its tax dollars. A number of considerations should guide the development of a meaningful patrol plan in every community.

In the creation of beats or designated areas to be patrolled, the distribution of people in the community is always important. Population density—the sheer number of people in a given area—bears a close relationship to the volume of crime within it. As a general rule, the more people any area contains, the more crime that will occur within it. This is particularly true where high population density is accompanied by such criminogenic conditions as poverty, large-scale unemployment, and deteriorated housing. Humans are territorial creatures who require a certain amount of physical and social space to call their own. When they are forced, under modern, urban living conditions, into suffocating proximity to their own kind, they often lash out against others in the symptoms represented by crime.

Population density, and the resultant need for patrol resources, often varies with the factor of time. Commuters, for instance, pour into downtown business and commercial districts during the daylight hours, swelling the numbers of people within these areas and creating conditions ripe for many forms of crime. During the evening hours these formerly bustling streets are changed into semideserted canyons of concrete and steel with different law-enforcement problems than those that obtained during the day. With the setting of the sun, shoplifters and con-artists in downtown business districts, for instance, give way to other species of criminal, such as street muggers and commercial burglars.

Time bears an important relationship to many forms of crime and, therefore, heavily influences the use of patrol resources. For instance, the fact that the majority of industrial and commercial burglaries occur at night makes business offices and warehouses especially vulnerable during the hours of darkness and demands more frequent and careful patrol of them during these times. Just the opposite is true of residential areas, for homes and apartments are most often invaded by burglars during the daylight hours, while residents are away at work, school, or shopping. So it is that the size and shape of patrol beats commonly expand and contract with the changes in human behavior signaled by changes in the clock.

Even once patterns of crime and service needs within a given patrol beat appear clear on a 24-hour basis, they must still be regarded as tentative and subject to change on the basis of new information. Volume and types of crime within a beat must be regularly and carefully reevaluated, with an aim to making any indicated adjustments in patrol operations. The availability of daily computer data on conditions within individual beats has recently begun aiding such ongoing evaluation. Because every community and the volume of crime within its boundaries is in a constant state of flux, there can never be such a thing as a truly permanent patrol beat.

Despite the general impermanence of beats, the history of the types of service most commonly called for within a particular area tends to establish patterns which determine the amount and kinds of patrol service needed by it. A street that has a sizeable number of cheap bars, pool halls, and sleazy hotels will usually disclose a record of many police responses to crimes of violence within it. In contrast, patrol officers will seldom be called to a semiaffluent residential suburb to handle assaults or family arguments, but their service in these areas may be requested fairly often for such incidents as burglary and vandalism. To experienced patrol officers the economic level of neighborhoods within their beats becomes an important guide to the kinds of criminal or service problems they are likely to encounter during a tour of duty.

In allocating patrol resources, the 24-hour day is commonly broken into three shifts, or watches, as follows:

day shift	8 A.M.–4 P.M.
evening ("swing") shift	4 P.M.–12 midnight
"graveyard shift"	12 midnight–8 A.M.

A group of officers known as a platoon is then assigned to cover each of these shifts. In the past many departments have followed the unfortunate tradition of assigning an equal number of officers to each of their three platoons. This places an excessive burden on certain patrol officers, since the work load often varies tremendously from shift to shift. Studies usually reveal, for instance, that a department's peak hours of activity run from about 8 P.M. to 3 A.M. Because a greater number of critical criminal problems occur during this span of hours, and the risk to each officer's safety is therefore presumed to be greater, many departments "double-up" or place two officers in each patrol unit on swing (evening) and graveyard shifts. As a result, these shifts may have fewer patrol cars cruising the streets than the less active day watch, which typically operates one officer or "solo" cars. Changes in work load usually indicate that the greatest number of officers should be assigned to the evening watch, followed by the midnight and day watches, respectively.

It is important that some strategy be employed to assure that patrol coverage is not lost or reduced below acceptable levels during the times when shift changes occur. For instance, it is quite easy for criminals to discover the shift pattern within a given department. Indeed, more and more sophisticated offenders are equipped with police "scanners" or radio monitors, which enable them to follow patrol-unit assignments as well. Under the traditional three-shift system, armed robbers might elect to hit a grocery or liquor store between 3:45 and 4:15 P.M., or perhaps later in the evening, between 11:45 and 12:15 A.M. Patrol units on either shift about to go off duty presumably leave their assigned beats 15 or 20 minutes early and head for the station in order to have sufficient time to turn in equipment, reports, and check off. Another 15 or 20 minutes of critical patrol time is lost by the oncoming shift as it gets keys to and fuels the vehicles being turned in, checks out other equipment and gets ready to go on duty. In all, the community may be left utterly vulnerable and without patrol coverage for a half-hour or more under this system.

To remedy this problem, departments commonly utilize overlapping shifts. Simply by splitting each platoon and having half its officers go on duty an hour before and half an hour after the usual starting time of each shift, patrol coverage is provided during periods of shift change. Thus, for example, on the 8 A.M. to 8 P.M. shift, our hypothetical armed robbers face the knowledge that although an "early car" will be leaving Beat X to check off just before 3 P.M. (since it came on duty at 7 A.M.), a "late" or overlapping car (which came on at 9 A.M. and will work until 5 P.M.) is already available to cover the beat in question.

A department may rotate its platoons from one shift to another on a monthly basis, or it may assign them to permanent shifts. Many people argue that permanent shifts enable an officer to learn more about the character of a particular beat and its problems than does the practice of shift rotation. Certainly it is true that permanent shifts work less hardship on such important aspects of an officer's life as eating and sleeping patterns. Changing one's hours of work each month (or more often, in the case of some departments) not only disrupts the human body's established rhythm of life, but may pose emotional and social hardships for the officer and his or her family as well. These will be discussed in some detail in a later chapter. On the other hand, in the case of permanent shifts, some hours will be much sought and others dreaded by officers. A new, young officer may eagerly welcome a permanent assignment to the graveyard watch, because it affords the chance to enroll in afternoon classes at a local university. A ten-year veteran with a spouse and three very young children, however, may deeply resent the same assignment because it disrupts normal family interaction. For instance, more than one such officer's youngsters have asked their now-police parent, upon being told to stop making noise in the house, "Why can't Daddy (or Mommy) sleep at night like everybody else?"

A new work plan being tried by a growing number of departments is called the "Ten-Four" or "Four-Forty" plan. Very simply, it is an extension of the current American trend toward a shorter work week. Instead of working the usual five-day, forty-hour week, under this system the patrol division moves to a four-day week and has its officers work ten hours each day.[5] While the plan has not yet been in use long enough to properly evaluate it, indications to date are that it increases officer morale because of the additional time off each week. It also permits an overlap of shifts not possible under the eight-hour system, and enables a department to beef up its street force during times of high activity. As shown below, a full six hours of additional patrol service is picked up during the busy hours between 8 P.M. and 3 A.M. because of the overlap between shifts two and three:

TEN-FOUR OR FOUR-FORTY PLAN

shift one   7 A.M.–5 P.M.
shift two   4 P.M.–2 A.M.
shift three 9 P.M.–7 A.M.

One factor that at least partially offsets the workforce gains of the Ten-Four Plan's shift overlap during peak activity times is the fact that additional patrol vehicles must be acquired to operate it. Cars cannot simply be gassed up and kept in 24-hour continuous service under the Ten-Four Plan. The expense of buying or leasing more patrol cars may, however, be worthwhile, since data from departments using this patrol system reveal a substantial rise in productive activity by officers as well as in their arrest rates.

Another procedure that may be used to increase the available patrol force during the hours that the work load is greatest is the creation of a fourth or additional platoon, and the permanent assignment of it to either the 7 P.M. – 3 A.M. or 8 P.M. – 4 A.M. shift, where it supplements the work of regularly rotating platoons.

TYPES OF PATROL

Foot Patrol. The once-common image of the hulking, red-faced cop walking the streets of his beat has largely faded from the public mind in recent years. The feeling of personal familiarity evoked in citizens by the foot patrolman of yesteryear has given way to a sense of anonymity and impersonality at the sight of the passing blur of light that is today's motorized patrol officer. Police officers on wheels are a relatively recent innovation in the history of American law enforcement, first ushered in in 1895 when Theodore Roosevelt organized a "bicycle squad" within the New York City Police Department.[6] Prior to that, the business of patrol was accomplished exclusively through the use of shoe leather.

Certainly one of the greatest advantages of foot patrol as it was traditionally practiced was the degree of familiarity it afforded officers with the people and problems of their individual beats. Typically, foot patrolmen came to know the merchants, families, and criminals who inhabited their assigned areas very well. Beats were necessarily small and compact enough to permit frequent, personal interaction between an officer and the inhabitants of a neighborhood. Because of his usually thorough familiarity with the places and people of his beat, the foot patrolman was undoutedly more apt to notice suspicious individuals and situations than his modern, motorized counterpart, who generally patrols a far larger area and must observe people and their behavior from the vantage point of a moving car. Lest we become too nostalgic over the passing of the foot patrolman in our society—the traditional "cop on the beat"—it should be noted that this form of patrol had a number of distinct disadvantages. Paramount among these was the fact that each officer's mobility and potential range of movement within a given time were extremely limited. Contact with headquarters was poor at best. Prior to the introduction of the one-way radio and the use of police cars, communication with the foot-patrol officer depended on the use of bells and lights installed at different points along the beat. These were a means of alerting an officer to contact headquarters. Beyond these measures, the communication of officers with one another was limited to the shouted calls for assistance and rapping curbs with nightsticks.

The conditions of modern walking patrol officers is, of course, vastly improved. Highly portable walkie-talkie radios carried on each officer's belt afford instant communication with headquarters in the event of an emergency, and keep the officer constantly aware of conditions on the beat. Yet, like their nineteenth-century counterparts, today's foot-patrol officers generally suffer from the same limitations of physical mobility. An officer can move only so fast and so far on foot. For this reason, where resources permit, walking patrol officers may be assigned vehicles which can be parked and utilized as necessary. Indeed, in some agencies vehicle and foot-patrol functions may be effectively merged by providing every officer on duty with a portable radio, which enables him or her to alter the method of patrol as time and circumstances dictate. Where this is done, it becomes possible to preserve at least a measure of the personal contact that is possible through the tradition of foot patrol.

The spread of our population and crime problems to geographically large suburban and even rural areas in recent decades, has made foot patrol impractical and prohibitively expensive, for the most part. Its use today is generally restricted to downtown business districts, where both population and crime are still contained within walkable distances. On such beats both the nature and volume of an officer's work will change with different shifts. On the midnight watch, he will be concerned basically with checking the security of businesses and stores because of their vulnerability to burglary during these hours. Because an officer on foot can move quietly down alleys and streets and can generally observe things more closely than a car-patrol officer, the foot officer's chances of detecting and apprehending commercial burglars are increased. For the downtown foot-patrol officer, the day watch may bring a large volume of traffic problems and citizen complaints over panhandlers and "winos" in the area. Where there are a number of bars and taverns operating, the evening watch may witness the appearance of liquor-fueled arguments and fights for the officer to mediate, as well as a general increase in the street movement of such undesirables as addicts, prostitutes, and muggers.

It is worth noting, in light of the general decline in the use of walking patrol officers, that at least some departments that had previously eliminated their use on grounds of economy and efficiency have returned at least partially to them in recent years. Some have done so because of their obvious community-relations value, while others have done so because performance studies failed to show that motorized officers were any more effective in their cities.

Car Patrol.   If the invention of the automobile had a revolutionary effect on our society as a whole, its impact on crime and law enforcement was no less dramatic. The increasing use of cars in police service necessarily followed the widespread use of cars by criminals of all kinds, making it necessary that patrol service be extended to areas too vast to be covered by either foot or bicycle. From its inception motorized patrol offered a number of clear advantages. One obvious one was the great reduction in *response time*—the sometimes long interval between the time an officer learned of a crime or a call for assistance and the time he actually arrived at the scene. The installation of one-way (and later two- and three-way) radios in police cars further improved the response time of patrol units, since valuable minutes were no longer lost putting out and clarifying assignment information for officers in the field. Rapid and coordinated movement by patrol officers pursuing law violators became a reality for the first time.

Throughout the history of the patrol car's use, an attempt has been made to make it as visible and conspicuous as possible. Such things as roof-mounted emergency lights, distinctively painted door panels, and official lettering to denote its presence have always been presumed to have a deterrent effect on those considering the commission of crime. High visibility is thus presumed to be another major advantage of the patrol car—an assumption which, as we will see later in this chapter, has been challenged in recent years.

While "marked" patrol cars are most commonly used in preventive or routine patrol, police departments also maintain a number of low-visibility or unmarked units for special-assignment purposes. Thus, for instance, when intelligence information reveals that a given area is having serious problems with nighttime robberies of quick-service or convenience stores, a department may deploy uniformed officers in "plain-clothes" cars to conduct a special and concentrated patrol of the area in question. Such effort may be supplemented by—or even rendered unnecessary by—the operation of highly specialized *tactical* or *selective-enforcement* units in some departments. Officers in such units characteristically operate in civilian clothes and drive unmarked cars. By the appearance of both their clothing and cars, the latter may create an impression of being anything from bums to average citizens.

Much controversy has taken place in recent years over the relative value of one-person versus two-person patrol cars. In general, police officers—who, like most people, understandably feel safer in numbers—have opted for two-officer patrol systems, at least at night, on the ground that this increases their safety. Police administrators, on the other hand, are concerned over the additional cost and reduced number of patrol units in service under two-person patrol systems. However logical it may seem to suggest that a patrol car containing two police officers is a safer arrangement than a unit with one, this conclusion does not appear to be supported by official data on the circumstances surrounding the death of police officers.[7] A surprising number of officers assigned to two-person units are killed in the line of duty each year. Just why this should be so is unclear. Two-officer patrol cars are, of course, routinely dispatched to situations that require the presence of more than one officer because of their seriousness. They may, therefore, be exposed to greater danger as a result. It has also been suggested that the two-officer patrol car sometimes creates a false sense of confidence and security in the officers assigned to it. Each officer may depend on his partner to be doing or watching certain things—such as the movement of a suspect at a crime scene or on a vehicle stop—when in fact the partner believes that the other officer has the situation under control. Such a condition closely approximates what sociologists call pluralistic ignorance, and may be especially likely to occur when, as often happens, patrol-car partners rotate frequently and find themselves working with partners whose particular methods of handling calls are unknown to them.

This is not to condemn the idea of two-officer patrol cars. To the contrary, their selective use may be called for by the nature of certain beats. For instance, in some city areas conditions of high population density and poverty result in officers handling a high incidence of calls in which the risk of assault and injury is significantly greater. The very nature of certain calls, such as domestic and bar disturbances, dictates the use of two officers—whether this is accomplished by means of assigning a two-person patrol car or by using two "solo" cars, one of which represents a backup unit. Beyond the use of two-officer cars to patrol certain selected problem areas and to respond to those types of calls known to pose either difficulty or danger to one-person units, the more common practice of utilizing single-officer patrol cars is suggested by considerations of both economy and efficiency.

AIRCRAFT PATROL

The growing use of fixed-wing aircraft and, especially, helicopters, by federal, state, and local law-enforcement agencies has become widespread in recent years. At the municipal police level, helicopters offer a number of distinct advantages when they are used as an integral part of the patrol operation. From the standpoint of the traditional practice of high-visibility for preventive patrol, the helicopter's conspicuousness is obviously far greater than that of either the foot-patrol or car-patrol officer. The noisy, chopping sounds and the lights of a helicopter on patrol duty serve to create the impression in the minds of criminals that "the cops are everywhere." Indeed, in a very real sense they are when a helicopter is in use, for its response capability is often measured in seconds rather than minutes. Even in downtown business districts during the most congested hours, the police helicopter can provide effective surveillance of an infinitely larger area than a number of officers on foot or in patrol cars. At the same time, a helicopter's high mobility enables it to move instantly to an altogether different and distant part of the city.[8]

The effectiveness of pursuit in situations involving fleeing felons is not only greatly increased through the use of helicopters, but the dangers to patrol-car officers and innocent citizens on the ground is reduced as well by eliminating the necessity for hazardous, high-speed auto chases. Once the observer in a police helicopter has spotted a suspect fleeing from a crime scene on foot or in a vehicle, there is literally noplace for the suspect to run or hide. In both criminal and emergency-rescue situations, the helicopter's communication and observation resources enable it to direct and coordinate even the most complex of ground activities. High-intensity floodlights carried by helicopters can instantly transform the darkened site of a burglary or street disturbance into day for police personnel attempting to deal with it. Helicopters can also provide the traffic division with valuable information on accidents and road conditions.

While other units within the police department (such as the investigation division) may make periodic use of the helicopter, its greatest single value is as a routine and vital part of the agency's patrol operation. In recent years the availability of large numbers of government-surplus helicopters at extremely low cost to police departments has made possible their purchase and use by many small and medium-sized communities. Thus, for instance, the Leon County, Florida, sheriff's department, a force of 180 personnel serving a community of about 100,000, was able to purchase two surplus helicopters from the Office of Civil Defense during 1977. Though each helicopter was worth $62,700, the department paid $500 for one and only a $25 transfer fee for the other. Because the actual maintenance and operation of helicopters may prove prohibitively expensive for very small departments, many of the latter have developed sharing arrangements with one another.

If it is true that the average citizen's sight of a uniformed patrol officer or a marked cruiser serves to increase her or his sense of psychological security, it seems reasonable to suppose that the police helicopter can accomplish this same function for a large number of people. Inevitably, however, there will be those law-abiding citizens who sincerely feel that the helicopter's advantages as a crime-fighting resource are offset by its noise, bright lights, and invasion of privacy. To a few, the "spy in the sky" contains the specter of "Big Brother" and an oppressive, totalitarian state in which every action on the part of citizens is carefully monitored and scrutinized. This notwithstanding, the use of the helicopter in police patrol work seems destined to increase as citizens and law-enforcement personnel alike recognize its value.

OTHER FORMS OF PATROL

The following represent other forms of patrol, whose use is determined by needs and conditions within a community:

- mounted horse patrol
- canine patrol
- boat patrol
- motorcycle patrol
- bicycle patrol
- patrol wagon

The physical features of a given area or the nature of a particular law-enforcement problem may call for the use of one or more of these patrol resources. For instance, in the case of a group of lost hikers in a mountainous region, radio-equipped officers on horseback or in jeeps may supplement the search activity being provided by fixed-wing aircraft and helicopters. Officers in a community whose parks have been plagued by a rapist may move quickly and quietly along footpaths on bicycles. The use of well-trained dogs in patrol work offers a number of advantages, including the tracking and apprehension of fleeing or concealed felons. The risk to police personnel is significantly reduced by the use of dogs in such situations. Cities surrounded by bodies of water, such as large lakes and harbors, may make regular use of patrol boats. The latter are operated by specially trained officers and may deal during a typical day's work with anything from narcotics smuggling to the enforcement of boating rules and the provision of emergency assistance to boats and swimmers in trouble.

The "paddy wagon," a specially equipped patrol van, has traditionally found its greatest use in deteriorated inner-city areas of the sort that usually attract a substantial number of hard-core alcoholics and transients. Picking up and transporting such individuals to jails, detoxification centers, and other facilities is a social service—as opposed to a law enforcement—responsibility which the police have inherited, along with many others, by default. They are traditionally the only resource in a community that can be mobilized on a 24-hour basis to provide help and service to people with pressing social and personal problems. In the past police patrol wagons have represented an essential service in core-city skid-row areas. By regularly cruising the streets and picking up alcoholics unable to care for themselves, patrol wagons have served to protect such individuals from becoming victims of such street crimes as robbery and assault, and have also saved many of them from the ravages of such natural elements as cold and hunger. While skid-row "winos" are often portrayed on television as street-corner philosophers and tipsters who provide valuable information to the police, they are more often a source of great frustration to officers who must regularly deal with them. The following experience, drawn from the senior author's first days as a criminology professor turned slum patrolman, illustrates the problems involved in encounters with such individuals:

> I guessed that he must be in his mid-sixties or even seventies from the look of him. He was thin and worn, emaciated looking. The Navy pea jacket he wore was soaking wet from the rain. Several days stubble of beard covered his face. "Mister . . . mister, wake up now," I said as I shook him harder. I bent closer. "Lemme 'lone," the figure suddenly growled. It abruptly turned over and bared itself to the rain. I recoiled as the smell of urine and vomit reached my nostrils. A wine bottle which had been nestled between his legs rolled into the gutter with a dull clunk.
>
> The bottoms of my uniform trousers were getting wet. My shoes made squishing sounds as I struggled to sit him up. "Come on now, old fellow!" I placed both hands under his armpits, held my breath, and pulled. "Lemme 'lone, goddamn ya!" he said drunkenly. He broke free of my grasp and fell back on the sidewalk, curled into a fetal position, and lay there motionless, still cursing to himself. A small crowd of people had gathered under the protective cover of an awning to watch the drama. I looked up at my partner. Beads of water were running off my uniform cap and dripping down my neck.[9]

The use of patrol wagons to pick up inner-city transients and drunks—and, indeed, police contact with them in general—may well decline steadily in the years ahead, with the growth of urban-renewal projects in such areas and a rise in the availability of other social-service resources to deal with them. Patrol wagons will doubtless always remain an important piece of backup equipment in large and medium-sized police departments, however—if only because of their utility in situations that require transporting a number of arrestees at one time, such as riots and vice raids. The use of patrol wagons on such assignments enables regular beat cars to remain in service and accomplishes the task of transportation with minimal risk to officers, since it is far easier to place combative and troublesome individuals in the back of a wagon than in the rear seat of a patrol car.

Patrol and Criminal Deterrence

Just how effective a deterrent to crime is the use of patrol? Do certain kinds of patrol programs and strategies appear to hold greater promise than others for future attempts to curb rising crime rates? It is possible to attempt at least tentative answers to these and other questions concerning the value of patrol, in light of experiments and research which have taken place in recent years.

THE VALUE OF PREVENTIVE PATROL

The use of high-visibility, random patrol has always been thought to represent the front line of defense in law enforcement's ongoing war on crime. Historically, the use of preventive patrol has rested on a basic— but largely untested—assumption: The greater the visible police presence within a given area, the lower the incidence of crime (or, at least, street crime) within it. Simply stated, the more police on patrol, the less crime. A great many police departments have, therefore, sought to increase the sheer size of their street forces in recent years, particularly within high-crime areas.

One of the first experiments involving a dramatically increased patrol force within a high-crime area took place in New York City during 1954. Labeled "Operation 25," this effort involved more than *doubling* the number of patrol officers assigned to East Harlem's Twenty-fifth Precinct for a period of four months, beginning September 1, 1954. Most of the additional officers were "rookies" fresh out of the academy, and were assigned to foot beats, although a small number of experienced officers were also added to the precinct's detective, narcotics, traffic, and juvenile units. Through the sudden experimental increase in work force, it became possible for the first time to cover every foot post within the precinct. Prior to the initiation of Operation 25, sometimes as few as one-third of the beats were covered. What were the results of this experiment? It was found that street crimes—particularly strong-arm robberies, burglaries, and auto thefts—dropped significantly below their 1953 levels in the precinct, a result which was attributed to the doubling of police personnel. This conclusion should be viewed in a very guarded way, since the claimed drop in rates of street crime was based on an analysis of official police records only. We know, on the basis of national victim surveys, that citizens report only about half of all the crimes that occur.[10] In other words, changes in the Twenty-fifth Precinct's *actual* crime rate may have been very different than changes in its *officially recorded* crime rate.

The findings of Operation 25 have been criticized on other grounds. Crime during 1954, the experimental year, was not compared with a number of other years, but only with the immediately preceding year. It is possible that crime during the year of the project declined (if it actually did) due to factors other than the increase in the police work force. There was no attempt to explore the possibility that crime, instead of being reduced in the Twenty-fifth Precinct, may have been merely-*displaced* into adjacent precincts.

Another, quite similar study was undertaken by the New York City Police Department in 1966, this time extending for a period of eight months. Because the earlier project had failed to consider the possibility that crime in the Twenty-fifth Precinct had only been displaced and not really reduced by the dramatic increase in personnel, the second study sought to remedy this deficiency. A new precinct, this time the Twentieth, was selected as the target area and given a 40 percent increase in numbers of police. Changes in crime rates were then examined not only within it, but within two nearby precincts as well, in an effort to discover whether crime was being displaced into them as a result of the Twentieth Precinct's energy increase. Basically, the findings of this study—which was conducted by the New York City Rand Institute[11]—were remarkably similar to the earlier Operation 25. Street robberies dropped 33 percent per week during the experiment, while auto theft was down by 49 percent and grand larcenies "visible from the street" were also down by 49 percent. Neither in this second project nor in Operation 25 was there much impact of increased patrol on so-called private crimes—acts such as murder and aggravated assault—which usually occur between friends or relatives in private places such as homes or apartments.

While the 1966 study, significantly, found that there was no apparent displacement or increase in the crime rates in the other two precincts studied, once again their data were based only on crimes officially reported to the police. If the actual incidence of street crime was truly down, it is possible that this was merely a short-run effect of the increased police presence. In other words, criminals might once again increase their incidence of offenses as they become accustomed to the increased number of police officers and find ways to work around it. This, of course, is exactly what is known to occur in the case of improved street lighting: Crime usually drops for a short time after better street lighting is installed, but then gradually returns to its earlier level.[12] Despite the very real possibility that the same thing might occur in the case of increased police personnel, and despite the numerous methodological weaknesses of the two New York studies, they served to greatly reinforce the traditional belief that large increases in preventive street patrol will invariably be accompanied by corresponding decreases in public crimes. Neither study, of course, recognizes the practical improbability of most departments being able to increase their patrol forces by anywhere near 40 to 50 percent.

At around the same time as the New York City Rand study was being conducted, the British police were also attempting to determine the value of increased patrol activity. A study conducted in four English cities by the Home Office varied the number of constables assigned to certain beats between zero and four during 1965. After examining changes in the incidence of reported crime on these experimental beats for a 1-year period, the British investigators emerged with somewhat puzzling results: When the number of constables assigned to patrol duty within a beat was increased from zero to one, the amount of reported street crime appeared to go down; however, when the number of patrol officers assigned to the beat was raised to two, there were no corresponding decreases in the volume of crime. There was only a slight indication in this study that jumping the number of officers from one to three or four on a beat would produce further reductions in street crime within it. As in the case of American police forces, personnel increases of this magnitude are simply not feasible. The British concluded on the basis of their "Beat Patrol Experiments" that increasing the number of patrol officers on a beat is not likely to significantly affect its crime rate.[13] As with the two New York projects, the English experiment was limited to examining increases in the number of foot-patrol officers. None of the studies tells us anything about the crime reduction likely to be achieved by an increased use of *patrol cars*—a significant failing in light of the fact that most patrol today is motorized patrol.

The longest evaluation ever conducted of the effects of increased patrol activity took place in New York City over an eight-year period.[14] In 1965 the city was experiencing a crime wave—consisting of both strong-arm and armed robbery—in its vast subway system. During the two preceding years, subway felonies increased at an annual rate of 50 percent. The casualties of this rise in subway crime were both passengers and change-booth workers. In order to combat the problem, it was decided to place a patrol officer on every subway train and in every station between 8 P.M. and 4 A.M., a decision that resulted in the addition of some nineteen hundred officers. The evaluation of this program over an eight-year period revealed that subway felonies during the hours of increased enforcement not only *declined* initially, but they remained low throughout the entire time period. Despite this obvious success in curtailing evening crime in the subways, however, the amount of daytime robberies began to soar after a short-run decline, so that by 1970 there were *six times more* robberies occurring in the subways than there were in 1965, when the project began.

Each of the four experiments on the impact of increased patrol just discussed involved changes only in the nationally fading practice of foot patrol. Three of the four experiments took place in New York City—a high-population-density city with a great many features, ranging from residential patterns to transportation and culture, that set it sharply apart from the rest of the country. There are, for example, many differences between a deputy sheriff on car patrol in a rural section of Columbus, Georgia, and a transit officer patrolling the subway system of New York City, with its tightly enclosed physical character and limited avenues of escape for criminals. The point of this is that we should be extremely careful in seeking to generalize the findings of any one patrol study in a single area to other communities with very different characteristics in their population, economy, geography, and crime problems.

Doubtless the greatest blow ever delivered to the historically assumed value of high-visibility, random patrol by uniformed officers in marked cars occurred in Kansas City, Missouri, between 1972 and 1973. During that time the Kansas City Police Department, with the assistance of a grant from the Police Foundation, designed an experiment intended to test scientifically the usefulness of preventive patrol as a deterrent to crime. The basic strategy involved in the project is reported by its authors:

> Briefly [the experiment] involved variations in the level of routine preventive patrol within 15 Kansas City police beats. These beats were randomly divided into three groups. In five "reactive" beats, routine preventive patrol was *eliminated* [italics ours] and officers were instructed to respond only to calls for service. In five "control" beats, routine preventive patrol was maintained at its usual level of one car per beat. In the remaining five "proactive" beats, routine preventive patrol was intensified by two to three times its usual level through the assignment of additional patrol cars and through the frequent presence of cars from "reactive" beats.[15]

Here was an experiment aimed at ascertaining the value of significant increases in *motorized* patrol, as opposed to the increases in foot patrol employed in the New York and British studies described earlier. The findings of this study were surprising—indeed, shocking—to law enforcement officers across the country. Briefly, it was found that after one year of utilizing the three different forms of preventive patrol, there were no significant differences between the three areas in either the amount of officially reported crime *or* the amount of crime informally reported by citizens in victim surveys. Further, there was no observed difference between the three groups in such things as level of citizen fear of crime and satisfaction with police performance. Ironically, citizens living on "proactive" beats—those with the highest level of preventive patrol— expressed more fear over the possibility of being robbed or raped. This is hard to explain in light of the fact that all of the beats were matched as closely as possible to eliminate the possibility that major differences in such factors as economic level and racial-ethnic status might influence citizen perceptions and responses.

Just what do these findings prove? Perhaps it is more important to indicate what they do *not* prove. As James Q. Wilson observes:

> The [Kansas City] experiment does *not* show that the police make no difference and it does not show that adding more police is useless in controlling crime. All it shows is that changes in the amount of random preventive patrol in marked cars does not, by itself, seem to affect, over

one year's time in Kansas City, how much crime occurs or how safe citizens feel.[16]

Clearly, this single study—important though it is—does not warrant either calling for the elimination of preventive patrol or reducing the amount of personnel within a police department. In its research design the Kansas City project neglected a number of important factors, which could well have influenced its findings and conclusions. Among these were the failure to collect detailed demographic data on the types of officers involved in the project and the quality of supervision they received during it. There were also a number of administrative changes and frictions between police and research personnel during the study, which could well have influenced its results.[17]

There has been increasing interest and experimentation in recent years with the idea of *target* or crime specific—as opposed to random— patrol. Very simply, this involves the strategic assignment of patrol officers to areas where data indicate there is a high probability of particular crimes occurring during certain hours. The use of target patrol is based on the ongoing collection and analysis of computer-based crime data on a day-by-day basis, and resulting changes in the patrol assignments of officers. Although target patrol, like the traditional practice of random patrol, may make use of uniformed officers in marked cars, it may also involve plainclothes officers and low-visibility vehicles.

A shift to a highly inconspicuous and carefully targeted patrol model may be dictated by the analysis of daily data on particular crime problems. An excellent example of this took place in New York City during 1971. Because of the extremely high incidence of street crime in certain areas, and the seeming inability of conventional patrol methods to effectively control it, a special anticrime unit was formed in 1971. The 1000 officers operating in this special patrol force were deployed in teams to conduct such activities as decoy and stakeout operations in areas selected as targets because of their volume of such crimes as robbery, burglary, and auto theft. Dressed as everything from little old ladies to cab drivers, derelicts, hippies, and average citizens, men and women of the New York Police Department's (NYPD) anticrime unit began quickly to score an impressive record of arrests. While officers within the unit comprised only 5 percent of the city's total precinct force, they accounted for over 18 percent of all felony arrests made by the department during 1973. The unit's most dramatic accomplishments were in the very categories of street crime they were formed to combat: robbery, burglary, and auto theft. During 1973 anticrime officers made over 50 percent of the NYPD's arrests for robbery and 40 percent of its arrests for burglary and auto theft. Moreover, their conviction rate—around 75 percent—was far higher than that of the department as a whole.

While the preliminary findings of this project are indeed encouraging, it will take some time to determine what—if any—long-range impact it will have on street crime. Certainly it does suggest that great value may lie in the future use of low-visibility patrol, at least on a selective basis and as a supplement to conventional patrol operations. Whatever the future of selective, low-visibility patrol, it seems unlikely that the historically dominant use of uniformed officers in marked cars will ever completely disappear—if only because of the basic sense of psychological security that their appearance affords a great many members of the community.

The success of both conventional and target patrol seems likely to be enhanced by efforts to involve citizens themselves in the business of law enforcement. Thus, for instance, the attempt of a police department to curb residential burglaries through the use of different patrol strategies may be greatly aided by citizen involvement in dealing with the problem. Police-operated "Help Stop Crime" programs can make residents aware of the kinds of suspicious individuals and situations to be on the watch for. The patrol officers of any police department cannot be everywhere at once, but citizens in the course of their everyday activity can almost be. A shopper or parent walking children down the street, a senior citizen taking the trash out to the curb, a trucker making routine deliveries— all are potentially invaluable and largely untapped resources for the officers of every department.

A recent craze sweeping the country that holds great promise as a tool to aid patrol officers is the ubiquitous citizen's band (CB) radio. CB clubs in many communities are already assisting local police by patrolling residential and commercial areas with the aim of alerting officers to suspicious circumstances. A CB radio in police communications, coupled with the organizing of citizen CB operators into volunteer patrol groups, can vastly extend the eyes and ears of a department's patrol division. It is, of course, important that such volunteer programs operate under close police supervision. No police administrator wants to unleash a band of vigilantes on the community, however well intentioned they may be. Mayor Thomas Bradley of Los Angeles has made a cogent proposal for the use of volunteer patrols as a supplement to regular patrol activity, which would not involve infringing the constitutional rights of citizens:

> Under my proposal we would formalize, refine and expand the
> Neighborhood Watch concept—and it matters little what we choose to call
> it. The police would, for instance, decide the pattern of patrol deployment

and would explain to the volunteers how they may be most helpful to the police.

In a typical operation, the volunteer patrol would log the license numbers, location and direction of travel of suspicious vehicles observed moving through the patrol area during certain hours. The police would be called when a vehicle, judging from these reports, appears to be on the prowl. These reports also would be useful to the police in follow-up investigations of crimes within the area. Since only the police have access to computerized vehicle-registration information, the volunteer patrols would not invade anybody's privacy.

The citizen patrols I suggest will not have police powers of arrest and detention, nor will they be armed: we do not need nor want vigilantes. Ideally, the volunteers should operate in cars, two to a car, equipped with citizen's-band transceivers. All patrol units would report to a base station in police headquarters where the liaison officer (a professional policeman) would decide which reports deserve police investigation.[18]

Beyond the invaluable assistance that the average citizen might provide, there are specialized groups of individuals whose observations during the course of their normal work activity might be of great help to a department's patrol division. For instance, a great many tradespeople—plumbers, electricians, television and telephone repair people, to name only a few—are constantly moving about the community in radio-equipped vehicles. Their inconspicuousness gives them an opportunity to observe a great many suspicious individuals and situations that a uniformed police officer in a marked car might never have the chance to see. To the extent that the sight of such workers and their vehicles becomes associated in the minds of criminals with a risk of detection and arrest, telephone trucks, taxicabs, and the like might serve a deterrent function very similar to that provided by high-visibility police patrol. Certainly the potential is worth exploring.

A major, recent development in the attempt to draw the police and the community they serve closer together in a common war on crime, and to improve the level of communication and understanding between them, has been the concept of *team policing*. As the expression suggests, the essence of this new police philosophy is teamwork. Municipal police agencies have tended over the years to become simultaneously overspecialized and increasingly remote from the community, with a resulting loss in both law-enforcement efficiency and public confidence. The well-established tradition of dividing every police department into the two basic units of patrol and investigation, and the creation of numerous subunits within each of these, often makes it difficult to solve crimes that follow a sequence or pattern.[19] In other words, each unit within the department typically handles a given crime problem in a highly fragmented, isolated manner. Often the units fail to share critical information on a case, sometimes out of ignorance and sometimes out of blatant rivalry. Where patterns of friction and overspecialization are well established, patrol officers may feel relegated to the role of organizational drones whose work is largely limited to filling out report forms and guarding crime scenes until the arrival of investigative personnel. They may accordingly experience a sense of alienation from the overall law-enforcement mission, which is comparable in many respects to the alienation of many modern industrial workers from the total product they are helping create. The resulting frame of mind—characterized by feelings of apathy, frustration, and despair—corresponds closely to what sociologist Emile Durkheim long ago called *anomie*.[20] Arthur Niederhoffer, applying the concept of anomie to police officers, observes, "The elements of this syndrome are loss of faith in people, of enthusiasm for the high ideals of policework, and of pride and integrity."[21]

Team policing may prove of great value in preventing the development of such attitudes. In place of the traditionally isolated, fragmented work of police, the essence of team policing is a cooperative, group effort in dealing with both crime and service needs. While the exact form of team-policing programs varies widely from community to community, such programs usually involve assigning a team of patrol officers and supervisors to a particular beat or area, and then making them responsible for the total enforcement and service task within it. Officers not only perform patrol activity within their assigned areas, but typically perform community service and often investigative work as well. It is the responsibility of each team of officers to become familiar with the unique character of their particular area—its people, crime problems, and service needs—and then evolve the best possible means of dealing with each.

Each team is highly autonomous and represents a kind of miniature police department, in the sense that it is expected to deal with all calls and problems within its assigned area. This includes at least the preliminary investigation of cases that would ordinarily be transferred to the detective division under traditional methods of policing. Teams of officers are given wide powers of discretion as to just how they wish to organize themselves to deal with particular problems in their neighborhoods, for instance, the needs of an area at a given time may dictate changes in work hours or a shift from uniform to plainclothes activity on the part of some members of the team.

Team policing is not only intended to combat the trend toward overspecialization and fragmentation of services [22]—and the resulting alienation of officers from the organization's total mission. It is also intended to restore a lost sense of community confidence in the police and to promote a strong identification on the part of officers with the areas in which they work. In contrast to the familiar figure represented by the beat cop of yesteryear, who came to know every nuance of the people and problems within his assigned territory, today's officer is apt to appear as a faceless, anonymous figure to the community. The modern replacement of foot patrol with motorized patrol (necessary though it has been), and the common practice of rotating officers to different beats, have conspired to leave both patrol officers and the communities they serve in the position of being virtual strangers to one another. Team policing, by identifying certain officers as responsible for totally serving a given area, may substitute a feeling of "our police officers" on the part of citizens and a feeling of "my beat" on the part of officers for the impersonality which too often seems to characterize police-citizen interaction today.

Although a number of team-policing experiments are currently under way in the United States,[23] the concept has been around for quite some years. Indeed, the first experiment with team policing took place in Aberdeen, Scotland, in 1948. Like so much of our modern police heritage in this country, we must credit the British with developing the practice of team policing. In 1966 the English began experimenting with a form of team policing which they called *unit beat policing.*[24] This involved combining patrol and investigative activity, by forming teams within each beat consisting of a one- or two-officer patrol car, two area constables, and a detective constable. Each group was intended to function as a unit within the area in question, with patrol-car officers, area constables, and detectives working closely together and constantly exchanging information on crimes and service problems.

While uniquely American variations of the English concept of team policing have taken place in recent years in cities ranging from Detroit, Los Angeles, and New York to Richmond, Charlotte, and St. Petersburg, the most extensive effort to date has been in Cincinnati. A program known as "COMSEC" (for Community Sector Team Policing) was begun in Cincinnati in March, 1973, and extended over an 18-month period. The program took place in a metropolitan, inner-city section designated on beat maps as District One. Under COMSEC, the number of officers assigned to District One was increased only slightly, but the officers within this area were given very different responsibilities from the rest of the force. Teams of officers within each sector of District One began handling virtually the entire scope of police activity within their assigned areas. For instance, instead of calling on the specialized services of such units as narcotics, crimes against persons, juvenile, and community relations, COMSEC teams began handling most situations which would normally have been passed on to these personnel.

Throughout the experiment teams of officers in District One did everything from routine patrol and criminal investigation to conducting community-relations meetings and crime-prevention programs. Seldom was outside help from other departmental units called upon; indeed, COMSEC officers dealt with approximately 91 percent of all service calls within their areas during the project period.

The preliminary findings of the Cincinnati project are quite impressive in the area of crime prevention, particularly with respect to burglary: Though reported burglaries increased by over 2 percent in the city as a whole during COMSEC, they *decreased* by 7 percent in District One, the area subjected to team policing.[25] Despite this apparent gain in police effectiveness in dealing with crime, however, there were, strangely, no parallel gains in either citizen perceptions of the amount of crime or in citizen attitudes toward the police. Thus the percentage of citizens who indicated that they felt unsafe when they were alone on the streets at night did not change in District One as a result of the team-policing program—even though the police were clearly able to decrease the incidence of at least some street crime: While the number of District One residents who reported seeing police activity in the area *increased* during the study, the visibility of these COMSEC officers apparently produced no corresponding increase in citizen feelings of security. Although this finding should be viewed cautiously, it clearly represents a challenge to the time-honored assumption that the sight of police officers helps allay citizen anxiety about crime. Perhaps the obverse is sometimes true, in a kind of boomerang effect. In other words, as citizens begin noticing more police officers in the areas where they live and work, they may assume that this is an indication that such areas must be infested with crime. It will be recalled that in the Kansas City patrol study cited earlier, citizens living on "proactive" beats (those with a doubling or better in the amount of patrol officers) were more frightened about the prospect of being robbed or raped than citizens of "reactive" and "control" beats. Heightened police visibility within areas may be counterproductive in terms of citizen security—or at least that is a conclusion which seems implicit in both the Kansas City and Cincinnati studies.

One of the supposed advantages of team policing is the expectation that having the same officers handle a case from beginning to end is likely to result in a greater success rate than compartmentalizing this effort. An attempt was made to examine this thesis in Rochester, New York, where a team-policing experiment combining patrol and investigative activity was undertaken. Several teams of officers were permanently assigned to certain areas and allowed to do follow-up investigations of crimes occurring on their beats, instead of turning cases over to the detective division for later, independent investigation. The track record of these teams proved substantially better than that of regular detective units operating in other areas of Rochester. One team, for instance, increased its robbery and burglary clearance rate from 18 percent before the project to 35 percent after it. The same team's clearance of larceny cases increased fivefold, while conventional police activity in similar areas produced no gains whatsoever.[26]

Team policing need not involve a merger of patrol and investigative activity. It may entail only a reorganization of patrol work in such a way as to increase its effectiveness. An example of this is the "basic car plan" operated by the Los Angeles Police Department.[27] Under this program, uniformed patrol officers are assigned in nine-person teams to areas designated as "basic car districts." Three officers from the team patrol the district during each of the day's three watches and are not dispatched on calls outside it except under emergency conditions. Every effort is made to assure that team officers remain within their assigned districts and become familiar with the people, crime problems, and service needs within them. To facilitate this process, each nine-officer team keeps a constantly updated file on relevant information on the district (e.g., wanted suspects to be on the lookout for, particular streets that are being plagued by crimes against persons or property). This file is kept current by a designated lead officer in the basic car team, and its contents are shared by the entire nine-officer unit. In order to promote rapport, communication, and the identification of a particular group of police officers as responsible for law enforcement and service within each basic car district, team members hold regular meetings with residents of their assigned areas, who are invited by mail to each session. These meetings consist of both formal presentations by team members on key police problems within the district, and informal discussion workshops where citizens have a chance to ask questions and raise law-enforcement issues which concern them. Specialized departmental personnel, such as community relations officers, stand ready to extend any requested services to members of basic car teams. Beyond the organization of patrol officers into unified area teams, the structure of patrol operations remains essentially unchanged under the basic car plan. Patrol sergeants maintain their normal responsibilities of supervision, in addition to functioning as advisors to basic car teams.

A number of other experiments involving changes in traditional methods of patrol and challenges to long-held but untested assumptions about how it should operate are currently under way in different parts of the country. Some of these are quite promising and may well help shape the future direction of police patrol. Thus, for instance, in light of the oft-mentioned distinction between that part of patrol which is devoted to order maintenance and service activity, and that part which involves law enforcement per se, the community of Wilmington is now operating a Split-Force Patrol experiment, which entails a separation of crime-prevention and citizen-service responsibilities within the patrol division.

Some police administrators have argued that the nature of the modern police role should give rise to two separate agencies, one oriented solely to law enforcement and the other entirely to community service.[28] Others have suggested that the police should remove themselves completely from any activity not directly involved with law enforcement and crime prevention,[29] although it seems unlikely that the police will be able to escape or transfer many of their traditional service roles in the near future—if only because there are few if any other agencies equipped to provide such services on a round-the-clock basis.

The future of patrol activity will doubtless continue to be greatly influenced by advances in law-enforcement technology. Thus, for example, patrol units in city after city will increasingly be deployed on the basis of sophisticated computer analysis of crime and service problems in different areas. Car computers are already being installed in a growing number of patrol vehicles across the country. Such technological creations will enable beat patrol officers to obtain instant TV-screen printouts of everything from criminal records to suspect photographs and fingerprints—all without leaving the front seat of their cruisers. Yet, while the growing use of computers appears to hold great promise for law enforcement, they seem also to hold certain dangers for the police and people of a free society. There seems to be an inherent wariness in the collective American psyche about the idea of transferring more and more law-enforcement responsibilities from people to machines. Much of this uneasiness is grounded in the fear that basic constitutional freedoms may be abridged in the process, and the entire society slowly propelled toward becoming an all-seeing police state along the lines of George Orwell's *1984.*

Such anxieties appear in the less than enthusiastic response of the American people so far to the idea of *electronic patrol.* Throughout major European cities today, remote-control television cameras mounted atop poles in weatherproof containers enable a small number of police officers seated at communications consoles to accomplish in the flash of an eye the work of a great many patrolling officers. Such cameras, many of them mounted in densely populated business and recreational areas, are capable of rotating a full 270 degrees in their surveillance, and can quickly zoom in to give a close-up picture of any suspicious individual or situation. Unquestionably, devices such as this could prove a valuable aid to patrol efforts in this country, from the standpoints of both efficiency and economy. However, the importance attached by Americans to individual privacy—even in the most public places—is such that they have reacted negatively for the most part to such uses of television equipment as a police tool. Indeed, large numbers of American football fans in some cities have become enraged in recent years upon learning that their spontaneous reactions at games were being monitored by TV cameras strategically located to detect trouble in the stands.[30] Whatever the future of such devices as electronic patrol may be in American law enforcement, certainly it is true that the crime-prevention potential of every police resource in a democracy must be carefully weighed against its potential for restricting individual liberty and privacy on the part of law-abiding citizens.[31]

Traffic

Many people argue that the police, if only because they represent a scarce resource in every community, should get out of the business of enforcing traffic laws altogether. Police time, it is said, is better spent on efforts aimed at apprehending felons and preventing crime than on such activities as directing traffic, investigating accidents, and issuing traffic citations to motorists. While such proposals are usually well intentioned, they invariably betray considerable ignorance of the nature of police work in modern society.

On the streets of every community in the country today, crime and the automobile are inextricably linked to each other. Cars are regularly used for every conceivable criminal purpose—to reach the location where a crime is to be committed and to flee from apprehension in its wake, to conceal and transport everything from narcotics, stolen furs, and television sets to human beings held for ransom. Cars themselves are a major theft target, and their ready availability has served to increase vastly the operation of modern criminals. From the mere 8,000 automobiles which existed in the United States in 1900, we have moved to a point where there are over 240 million cars, trucks, and buses in the country today.[32] A great many of what start out as "routine" traffic encounters between police officers and citizens turn out to involve serious criminal situations. The following example, drawn from the senior author's brief experience as a professor turned policeman, is an excellent case in point:

> Like so many patrolmen neither of us liked working traffic. We were both inclined to give a driver the benefit of the doubt in the majority of situations, let a man have ten miles over the speed limit on a good safe road, or sometimes even coast through a stop sign if he was careful. But this was too much; this was the kind of driver who caused accidents that left people dead or seriously injured.
>
> "Two Lima Ninety-Five to Headquarters, vehicle stop," Angie said . . . I flipped a switch on the dash and blue light bathed the car in front of us. The driver signaled and pulled over. "Listen, I'll catch this one. Just

run the plate, okay?" I said. I got out of the car and began walking toward the LeMans. A nice night for the end of June, I thought. There was a cool breeze starting to come out of the east, stirring bits of paper on the ground. The car window rolled down. "Can I see your driver's license, please?" I said. I looked at the person behind the wheel. He was white, with pale freckles dotted across his nose and red hair neatly combed back on his head. Nineteen or twenty, I guessed.

"Evening, Officer." He smiled . . . "Look, I know why you stopped me, sir. It's my own fault," he said. "I'm late to work. I work at the cannery over on Palmetto." "I'll need to see your license," I repeated. I pointed to his wallet. "Oh, sure! Sure! Let's see, it's here someplace," he said as he began rummaging through the billfold. The breeze had picked up now. I turned toward it, feeling the rush of wind on my face as I waited for the license. . . . "Freeze!" I started, turning abruptly back toward the car. Angie was standing on the passenger side with his gun pointed through the open window at the driver. "Wha--?" The man was bent over with one hand on the floorboard. "Angie, what is it?" "Car came back hot," he said without looking at me. I drew my gun and opened the car door. "Check under the seat," Angie instructed as he began searching the man. I took off my hat, knelt down and began groping under the front seat. My hand stopped as it came across checkered wood and cold metal. I pulled the object out and examined it. A .380 automatic. Full clip. Safety off. I pulled the slide back and watched a cartridge eject from the chamber and spin to the pavement. I felt weak, sick at my stomach. I leaned back against the car and started to tremble.[33]

Even where a formal, organizational distinction exists, between patrol and traffic, it is essential that every patrol officer realize that traffic-law enforcement—while it may not be the primary assignment, is nonetheless an inescapable part of a police officer's overall commitment to protect and serve the public. No patrol officer would hesitate for an instant to take action at the sight of an intoxicated person running down the street firing a revolver at random. Yet there are some officers who feel that getting drunk drivers off the road is not really part of their crime-fighting function. The fact is that several thousand pounds of metal hurtling down a public street may pose an infinitely greater danger to public safety than the discharge of a firearm.

It comes as a surprise to many people who are concerned about the incidence of violent crime in our society to discover that the amount of death and human suffering generated each year by traffic accidents is far greater than that produced by all forms of crime combined. Over 50,000 Americans die as a result of traffic accidents each year, and another 2 million are seriously injured. Beyond the immeasurable cost in human suffering, the economic toll in the form of damaged and destroyed automobiles, lost income, insurance claims, lawsuits, and hospital bills staggers the imagination. Estimates in recent years place the figure at nearly $14 billion per year.[34] Some perspective on just how costly traffic accidents are in our society may be gained by considering that the entire federal, state, and local budgets for *all forms* of criminal-justice activity (including police, courts, and corrections) presently runs around $17 billion.[35] Automobile-safety experts hope that the enforcement of lower speed limits nationwide in the wake of our recent energy crisis will serve to lower the soaring accident rates which have characterized the last two decades. Certainly the reduction of speed limits is a positive move, particularly when we consider that speeding and the related factor of drunk driving account for the highest percentage of automobile accidents. It is believed by some that the steadily rising gasoline prices which have also been generated by our fuel crisis will serve to keep more drivers off the road, thereby lowering the volume of traffic accidents. While there has been some slight downturn in accident rates in very recent years, it is simply too early to tell whether this marks the beginning of a long-range trend.

Doubtless the largest single problem confronting traffic-law enforcement in our society is the fact that large numbers of otherwise law-abiding citizens do not regard many traffic infractions as serious matters. They typically fail to make any connection between their own periodic disregard of certain traffic laws and the horrible carnage which takes place on the nation's streets and highways each year. The motorist pushing a gas pedal to the floor to make it through an intersection whose light has just turned from amber to red is unaware of this act, coupled with countless others like it helps give him or her a 1 in 200 chance of being killed or injured by an automobile during any given year, and results in a 50 percent probability that he or she will be involved in some kind of traffic accident sooner or later.[36]

The attitudes of police officers themselves toward traffic-law enforcement may limit its effectiveness. Encounters between officers and citizens in traffic situations have long been recognized as a major source of citizen hostility toward the police,[37] and are therefore studiously avoided by many patrol officers. The reasons for fairly widespread public resentment of traffic-law enforcement are varied and complex. For most citizens, traffic encounters represent their only contact with the police. Regardless of how diplomatic and skilled in interpersonal relations an officer may be in making a routine traffic stop, there are inherently negative features of such encounters which even an experienced clinical psychologist would find it difficult to surmount. Every traffic stop inescapably involves placing an adult momentarily in the status of an errant child who has been caught in wrongdoing and is therefore being disciplined in some way. Even where no citation is issued, the mortification of being stopped and detained in a public place by a uniformed officer is in itself an intrinsically unpleasant experience. The police car's rotating emergency lights seem to the distraught motorist to serve as a beacon which draws the entire community's attention to a mistake he has made. The minutes of such encounters seem like agonizing hours to the hapless driver, whose embarrassment may be compounded by the presence of a wife, children, or friends in his vehicle. Traffic stops are apt to be particularly unpleasant events for both officers and citizens when the latter have an audience of relatives, friends, or bystanders present. We all experience a greater need to save face and justify our actions in the presence of an audience.[38]

In attempting to understand why most traffic encounters have an inherently negative quality about them, it is important to bear in mind that the uniformed police officer is a highly visible symbol of governmental authority in a society whose people strongly value freedom from such authority. Our entire democratic structure of government is arranged in such a way as to minimize official interference with individual liberty. Every traffic stop an officer makes, however well intentioned or justified, represents an instance of temporary interference with an individual's freedom of action.

A kind of "why me?" attitude characterizes many motorists who, nevertheless, readily admit to having violated traffic laws. Because such infractions are widespread, and because most motorists witness many instances where they go undetected, there is a feeling of having been unjustly singled out for punishment. The officer is behind in his daily "quota" of traffic citations. He "has it in" for sports cars. He is prejudiced against blacks or whites, young or old. The list of such explanations for being stopped and cited is virtually endless. One recent survey in a West Coast city asked a cross-section of citizens the question, "What is the purpose of a traffic citation for a moving violation?" The responses reveal a disheartening lack of understanding of the basic reason behind every citation—the prevention of accidents.[39]

REASONS FOR ISSUING TRAFFIC CITATIONS

(Data derived from a citizen survey)

48%	To raise revenue for law enforcement
17%	To raise revenue for the city or state government
10%	To deter any further traffic violations on my part
9%	To give the traffic officer something to do besides investigate accidents
6%	To prevent accidents
3%	Other reasons

In small police departments—which is to say the majority of police departments in the United States—the enforcement of traffic laws is handled as one part of the overall patrol function. Police departments in larger cities, however, usually have a special traffic division which is organizationally separate from patrol. Where such units exist, they provide a variety of important services. These include not only traffic-law enforcement, but also control of vehicle and pedestrian traffic at congested intersections, accident investigation, operation of safety education programs, and ongoing analysis of accident statistics in an effort to determine the best deployment of traffic officers and equipment. Every traffic division maintains close liaison with the city or county engineer's office, in an effort to keep the latter advised of called-for changes in traffic-flow patterns, road conditions, and signal-light equipment.

Traffic-division officers are assigned to particular areas, rather than beats, on the basis of changing traffic and accident patterns, and are exempted from normal patrol responsibilities except under emergency conditions. Yet, just as every patrol officer must accept a secondary responsibility for traffic enforcement, traffic-division personnel must bear in mind that they are police officers first, and as such, must be alert to patrol problems and conditions in the areas they cover. Unlike other organizational bureaucracies where the handling of certain problems is automatically transferred to a designated unit, a police department can scarcely allow a traffic officer who comes upon a robbery or burglary in progress to refer the matter to the patrol division.

The key to every successful traffic division is the operation of a well-planned *selective-enforcement program*. Basically, selective enforcement involves a careful and ongoing analysis of traffic patterns and accident statistics by traffic-division personnel, and the resulting assignment of their officers and equipment to those locations with the highest incidence of moving violations and accidents. Selective enforcement is a valuable means of realizing the best possible use of a police department's resources, with the goal of minimizing accidents and the property damage and human suffering that accompany them. By their very nature selective-enforcement personnel must be highly flexible and capable of shifting their hours and areas of operation on a day-by-day basis as traffic problems within the community change.

In recent years the National Highway Traffic Safety Administration has undertaken studies of the effectiveness of selective-enforcement operations in a number of American cities. These have involved the experimental use of selective enforcement in certain high-accident areas of each city, and the coverage of other very comparable high-accident streets and intersections with ordinary (which is to say random and unplanned) enforcement coverage. Selective-enforcement officers sought to saturate their assigned areas during high-accident periods, making extensive use of such devices as radar, high-visibility patrol, and frequent citations for those moving violations most often associated with accidents. The results were generally quite impressive, with a substantially lowered number of traffic injuries and fatalities in those areas subjected to special-enforcement efforts, as well as a decline in the overall volume of accidents.

While selective-enforcement programs are the primary responsibility of the traffic division, it is important that the patrol division be kept constantly informed of particular areas in the community that are experiencing traffic or accident problems at any given time. Patrol officers can then seek to maintain high visibility in these sections of their beats in the course of their regular assignments, thereby supplementing the work of traffic-division officers.

Traffic enforcement often involves the use of specialized equipment, such as radar, helicopters, and motorcycles. The motorcycle is probably the most enduring symbol of traffic enforcement in the public mind, although its value as a police tool is presently the subject of widespread debate among law-enforcement administrators. Those departments that have continued to use motorcycles as the basic units of their traffic-enforcement operation point to such advantages as the motorcycle's superior mobility, a factor which is particularly important in view of the congested condition of many urban streets and highways during peak traffic hours. A motorcycle can thread its way with ease through long lines of bumper-to-bumper traffic to reach an assigned area or the scene of a serious accident, while a police car would be virtually immobilized. In heavy traffic, motorcycle officers can readily overtake traffic violators who would be lost to four-wheeled police vehicles. This same maneuverability makes the motorcycle extremely useful in keeping crowds of people within certain boundaries at parades and other public events.

From a purely psychological standpoint, the motorcycle officer's appearance is even more formidable and controlling to law violators than that of regular uniformed officers. The polished high boots, gleaming helmet, and bulky black leather jacket serve to exaggerate the image of authority and physical prowess—an effect which may be desirable in dealing with potentially troublesome or violent motorists, but which may also serve to alienate the authority-sensitive average citizen. Perhaps one of the most compelling arguments for the extensive use of motorcycles in traffic enforcement in our fuel-conscious times is that they cost very little to maintain and operate, compared to cars.

Police administrators who have either done away with or drastically curtailed the use of motorcycles, however, argue that such savings are more than offset by a number of hidden costs. Not the least of these is the duty time that is lost by motorcycle officers who are injured on duty, sometimes seriously. The use of motorcycles involves a far higher accident risk than police cars. While the greater maneuverability may enable the motorcycle officer to avoid some accidents more readily than an officer in a car, when an accident does occur, the former is utterly without the benefit of such safety factors as seat belts and a mass of metal to absorb the impact.

In addition to the substantially greater risk of injury which arises from operating a police motorcycle, the frequent exposure to harsh weather conditions gives "motor men" a far greater amount of such illnesses as colds and flu, with resulting time off work, than other officers. The very use of the motorcycle is limited by such conditions as rain and snow; where the police car is a 365-day-a-year piece of equipment. Finally, there is the expense of having to pay motorcycle officers special bonuses because of the hazardous nature of their work. A number of police administrators feel that these factors collectively make a strong case for the complete elimination of motorcycles in traffic enforcement.

The investigation of traffic accidents represents one of the most important responsibilities of the traffic division. Accident investigation consumes a substantial amount of a traffic officer's time and effort. Traffic officers handle a wide variety of different accidents on a routine basis. These range from minor "fender-benders," which involve minimal damage and can usually be handled in a few minutes, to major accidents involving injury, death, or the loss of thousands of dollars. This requires the application of highly specialized investigative skills that are seldom understood by the general public. In a very real sense, every officer investigating a serious traffic accident is a "detective" who must minutely scrutinize everything from skid-mark patterns to small bits of paint and metal for clues to their cause. The findings, carefully established and recorded, often prove to be of critical significance in court actions intended to ascertain the criminal and civil responsibilities of the parties involved in the accident.

Accident investigation is so complex and specialized an activity that some departments, usually quite large ones, maintain separate Accident Investigation (A-I) units within their traffic divisions. However, this is the exception rather than the rule. Most traffic accidents are investigated by regular officers assigned to the traffic division, or by patrol officers in the case of small departments without traffic sections.

In conclusion, it seems reasonable to state that people in our society fail to understand and appreciate the importance of the overall police traffic mission. We have come largely to take for granted the fact of safe, easy movement along our nation's streets and highways, with little thought to the continuing effort of the men and women who make this possible. The senior author recalls (with some embarrassment) his initial disdain for traffic assignments as simple, mindless, and unchallenging aspects of police work. He soon changed this perception—and substituted for it an appreciation of the complexity of even routine traffic work—by experiences such as the following (which occurred during his first day as a uniformed professor-policeman):

> "Two Lima Ninety-Five . . . check a report of a stalled truck in the westbound lane of Henessey Boulevard at Fourteenth Street," the dispatcher's voice said. "Ten-four," D'Angelo replied as he replaced the mike and changed our direction of travel. Traffic was still heavy. It took us a full fifteen minutes to snake our way along to the location of the stalled truck. "I can see it's gonna be a great night," D'Angelo said as we approached the tractor-trailer rig. It was sitting motionless, squarely in the middle of the road, like some giant turtle. Traffic was backed up in both directions as far as I could see. Horns honking. Motorists cursing and shouting at one another.
>
> D'Angelo parked the police car behind the truck and turned on the rotating blue lights on its roof. "Go over there and see if you can get them cars moving, while I see if I can find out where the hell the driver is," he said. Good, I thought to myself. This was something I knew I could handle . . . I walked to the roadway's double yellow line and surveyed the situation. A man came forward and told me that the driver of the truck had just parked the rig and walked off. I sent him over to tell D'Angelo while I addressed the traffic problem. I began giving hand signals to move forward. Gestures to halt. Something was wrong, I thought to myself. Only a few people were paying attention to my directions. Most of the motorists seemed to be ignoring me as they continued to struggle with one another for access to the only available lane leading around the truck.
>
> "Say, watch what you're doing," I shouted at one point, as I jumped back just in time to avoid having my foot run over by a sedan loaded with children and groceries. What on earth was I doing wrong? Now just keep calm and think it through, I thought as I stood there amid the honking horns and the occasional sound of jamming brakes. "What the hell you doing out there? Get them cars moving!" D'Angelo shouted from beside the patrol car, where he stood calling for a wrecker. The bulky form began jogging toward me, the keys and equipment on his belt jangling as he came closer. "Use your whistle!" he shouted. The whistle. Yes, of course. My mind flashed back to the academy. Was it one blast for stop and two for go, or two for stop and one for go? "No! No! Not that way! You gotta put something into it! Blow! Like this!" D'Angelo unleashed a piercing blast from his own whistle and held up both hands. Traffic screeched to a halt. "These people'll sit here all night long if you let 'em," he said as he smiled incongruously and gestured for an elderly woman in one lane to move ahead. D'Angelo spent the next several minutes demonstrating the finer points of traffic direction to me.[40]

SUMMARY   Patrol work represents the most vital and complex task within every police agency—large or small, urban or rural. The patrol division is in a very real sense the nucleus around which virtually every other function within the municipal law-enforcement agency revolves. It was seen that *patrol* is a simple and convenient label that masks a multitude of different activities. In addition to dealing with criminal activity (which, one estimate suggests consumes no more than two-tenths of 1 percent of the average patrol officer's time), patrol involves the performance of a wide variety of *service* and *crisis-intervention* activities. These range all the way from providing assistance to motorists who are locked out of their cars, reporting broken street lights, and transporting lost children home, to mediating difficult (and sometimes dangerous) disputes between husbands and wives, landlords and tenants, merchants and customers.

As virtually the only agency set up to deliver services to the entire community on a 24-hour basis, the police department, through its patrol division, becomes a convenient catchall for a vast number of human needs not specifically delegated to some other institution.

Recent years have witnessed a great many changes in actual patrol activity and the philosophy underlying it. Perhaps one of the most dramatic and impactful of these changes has been a challenging of the traditional practice of *preventive patrol*—the random and conspicuous movement of uniformed personnel throughout the community. Along with this has come a willingness to experiment with new modes of patrol activity, such as low-visibility *anticrime* units and the deployment of officers and equipment on the basis of computer-projected crime patterns. There is more awareness today than ever before in the history of American law enforcement that patrol is a scarce resource and must therefore be spent in the wisest possible way. Paralleling this has been a growing recognition of the complexity of the patrol function, with a resultant growth in the amount of preservice and in-service training time devoted to such subjects as crisis intervention and human relations. Experiments such as *team policing* symbolize an attempt on the part of law enforcement to become more closely integrated with the community as a whole, in an effort to more effectively "protect and serve."

NOTES

1. *Task Force Report: The Police,* The President's Commission on Law Enforcement and the Administration of Justice (Washington, D.C.: U.S. Government Printing Office, 1967), p. 7.
2. For a complete account of this project and the experiences and problems it involved, see George Kirkham, *Signal Zero* (New York: Lippincott, 1976).
3. Albert J. Reiss, Jr., *The Police and the Public* (New Haven, Conn.: Yale University Press, 1971), pp. 95–96.
4. *Ibid.,* pp. 101–102.

5. See Paul M. Whisenand, George M. Medak, and Bradley L. Gates, "The Four-Day, Forty-Hour Workweek," *1972 Municipal Yearbook* (Washington, D.C.: International City Management Association, 1972), p. 24.

6. Theodore Roosevelt, *An Autobiography* (New York: Macmillan, 1919), pp. 202–204.

7. See, for example, *Law Enforcement Officers Killed: Summary, 1975,* F.B.I. *Uniform Crime Reports* (Washington, D.C.: U.S. Department of Justice, 1975), p. 13.

8. Paul M. Whisenand and George M. Medak, "Police Helicopter Patrol," *Management Information Service* (Washington, D.C.: International City Management Association, October, 1971).

9. Kirkham, *Signal Zero,* pp. 56–57.

10. James Q. Wilson, *Thinking About Crime* (New York: Vantage, 1977), p. 97.

11. See S. J. Press, *Some Effects of An Increase In Police Manpower in the 20th Precinct of New York City,* Report No R-704, (New York: Rand Institute, 1971).

12. Wilson, *Thinking About Crime,* p. 94.

13. J. A. Bright, *Beat Patrol Experiment,* Report No.8/69 of the Police Research and Development Branch, Home Office, London, England (July, 1969).

14. Jan A. Chaiken, Michael W. Lawless, and Keith A. Stevenson, *The Impact of Police Activity on Crime in the New York City Subway System,* Report No. R-1424-NYC (New York: Rand Institute, 1974).

15. See *The Kansas City Preventive Patrol Experiment: A Summary Report,* George L. Kelling, Tony Pate, Duane Dieckman and Charles E. Brown (Washington, D.C.: Police Foundation, October, 1974).

16. Wilson, *Thinking About Crime,* p. 99.

17. For a critique of the Kansas City Study, see "I.A.C.P. Position Paper on the Kansas City Preventive Patrol Experiment" (September, 1975), pp. 16–20.

18. Thomas Bradley, "Citizen Patrol Urged to Help Fight on Crime," Los Angeles *Times,* September 5, 1972, Section B, p. 24.

19. See *Task Force Report: The Police* (Washington, D.C.: U.S. Government Printing Office, 1967), p. 53.

20. See Emile Durkheim, *The Division of Labor in Society* (New York: Free Press, 1965); also Emile Durkheim, *Suicide* (New York: Free Press, 1951).

21. Arthur Niederhoffer, *Behind the Shield* (New York: Doubleday-Anchor, 1969).

22. This is not to suggest that team policing is intended to completely eliminate the need for any specialized services. Thus, for example, any given team will—despite its basic autonomy—have to call upon the specialized resources of other units (such as homicide investigators and crime scene technicians) in certain situations.

23. For an overview of these, see *National Evaluation Program:* "Neighborhood Team Policing" (Phase I Report), William G. Gay, H. Talmadge Day, Jane P. Woodward (Washington, D.C.: U.S. Government Printing Office, 1977).

24. Eric Gregory and Peter Turner, "Unit Beat Policing in England," *The Police Chief* (July, 1968), pp. 42–47.

25. Reported in Wilson, *Thinking About Crime,* pp. 103–105.

26. *Ibid.,* p. 105.

27. "The Basic Car Plan," Los Angeles, California: Los Angeles Police Department Mimeograph (1971).

28. See, e.g., Bernard L. Garmire, "The Role of the Police in An Urban Society," pp. 1–11 in *The Police and the Community,* Robert F. Steadman, ed., (Baltimore: Johns Hopkins University Press), 1972.

29. See James F. Ahern, *Police in Trouble* (New York: Hawthorne, 1972).

30. Certainly there is considerable ambivalence on the part of the public regarding the use of such equipment. Juxtaposed with a sense of having one's privacy and personal

space invaded by "big brother" is the fact that the public has become increasingly accustomed in recent years to the use of closed-circuit TV monitors in banks and stores of all kinds.

31. For a discussion of the inherent conflict between "law" and "order" as basic concepts in a democracy, see Jerome Skolnick, *Justice Without Trial* (New York: Wiley, 1966).

32. American Manufacturers Association, "Automobile Facts and Figures (Detroit: A.M.A., 1970), p. 19.

33. Kirkham, *Signal Zero,* pp. 126–129.

34. See National Safety Council, *Accident Facts* (Chicago: National Safety Council, 1973).

35. *Law Enforcement Assistance Administration Newsletter* (Washington, D.C.: U.S. Government Printing Office, May, 1977, Vol. 6, No. 10).

36. Vern L. Folley, *American Law Enforcement,* 2nd ed. (Boston: Holbrook, 1976), p. 226.

37. See O. W. Wilson, "Police Authority in a Free Society," *Journal of Criminal Law, Criminology and Police Science* 54, June, 1964.

38. It should be noted that this is also true of police officers, whom studies show tend to be more aggressive in the presence of their peers than when working alone. For an interesting account of how people react to the presence of different audiences, see Erving Goffman, *Behavior in Public Places* (New York: Anchor, 1970).

39. This survey is reported in James R. Waters and Sheree A. McGrath, *Introduction to Law Enforcement* (Columbus, Ohio: Merrill, 1974), pp. 73–74.

40. Kirkham, *Signal Zero,* pp. 60–62.

SELECTED   James Q. Wilson, *Varieties of Police Behavior: The Management of Law and Order in Eight*
READINGS   *Communities* (Cambridge, Mass.: Harvard University Press, 1968).

O. W. Wilson, *Police Administration,* 3rd ed. (New York: McGaw-Hill, 1972).

G. D. Gourley and A. P. Bristow, *Patrol Administration* (Springfield, Ill.: Thomas, 1961).

P. Whisenand and J. L. Kline, *Patrol Operations* (Englewood Cliffs, N.J.: Prentice-Hall, 1971).

Richard L. Holcomb, *Police Patrol* (Springfield, Ill.: Charles Thomas, 1964).

Paul B. Weston, *The Police Traffic Control Function* (Springfield, Ill.: Thomas, 1960).

4
DETECTIVE, JUVENILE, AND OTHER POLICE FUNCTIONS

The Detective Business: Myths and Realities

No other police role in modern society is quite as surrounded with an aura of mystery and intrigue as that of the detective. The very mention of the word brings to the minds of most a trench-coat clad figure methodically following a trail of difficult clues which ultimately leads to the doorstep of a murderer or other culprit. Detective stories, chronicled each year in countless books and articles, movies and television shows, have long captured the imagination and interest of the American public in a way that no other aspect of police work has. While a television show dealing with the work of patrol officers appears from time to time, detective shows have been a nightly staple in American living rooms for quite some years.

Detectives—or *investigators,* as they are more commonly called in police parlance—are generally accorded greater prestige by the public because their work is assumed to demand a higher level of knowledge and skill than that of uniformed officers. While patrol officers are well aware that their own work is infinitely more complex and demanding than most citizens realize, they, too, usually attach greater prestige to the role of investigator. As Arthur Niederhoffer states, "Almost every cop dreams of the day when he will make the (detective) bureau. . . ."[1]

There are a number of good reasons why becoming an investigator is an important goal for most uniformed officers. Such an assignment oftens means a substantial salary increase, and perhaps even an increase in rank. At the very least, becoming an investigator means "getting out of the bag"—escaping the police uniform and all the behavioral restraints and frustrations which accompany it. Uniformed officers are tied to a radio and dispatcher nearly every working moment of the shift. The fact that they are readily identifiable to the public wherever they go gives them a feeling of having to work in a fishbowl, where they are constantly subject to the scrutiny and demands of others. More than one hungry patrol officer has experienced the frustration attendant upon having to get up from an unfinished hot meal to help a citizen who is locked out of car or to respond to an emergency call. Investigators, on the other hand, enjoy a low public profile as a result of the fact that they invariably work in plainclothes. They can melt in and out of the public view at will, thereby escaping most of the fishbowl sensations of patrol officers. Rather than being constricted by the boundaries of a patrol beat, investigators usually experience considerable freedom of movement in their daily handling of cases and are not subject to the subtle tension of having to be alert to radio dispatches on a minute-to-minute basis. Detectives also usually work hours that more closely approximate those of family and friends, therby easing some of the considerable strain on personal relationships that often goes along with a police career. Finally, investigators usually find themselves working in an occupational setting where there is at least some relaxing of the formal, paramilitary pressures of relationships with superiors. As Niederhoffer observes,

> Within (the detective division) democratic comraderie eliminates the social distance that ordinarily divides the various ranks of a bureaucratic hierarchy. A lower-ranking detective may call a detective captain by his first name without causing any surprise; he may walk arm-in-arm with a detective inspector (a very high superior officer), while discussing an important case.[2]

The special privileges and autonomy enjoyed by investigators, together with the tendency of both the press and the public to assume that their efforts are primarily responsible for the solution of serious crimes, often lead to considerable friction and resentment between officers of the patrol and detective divisions. Many patrol officers feel that they do all the real police work in the department while investigators receive all the credit. Detectives who assume an aloof and officious bearing when interacting with patrol officers do little to reduce such sentiments within a department. Conflict between patrol and investigative personnel is one of the consequences of the previously mentioned trend toward overspecialization in law enforcement.

The traditional cleavage between patrol officers and investigators is both artificial and unfortunate. In a very real sense, every uniformed patrol officer is necessarily also a detective. Indeed, a very large number of criminal cases begin and end with the patrol officer, who is usually first at the scene of a crime and who must conduct the preliminary investigation of it. The patrol officer's skill and knowledge in doing such things as, for instance, securing a crime scene until the arrival of evidence technicians and investigative personnel, and identifying and questioning victims and witnesses, often serves to either make or break a case. The patrol officer must decide, on the basis of his initial investigation, whether a given situation can best be handled informally and immediately by himself, or whether it should be referred to the detective division for a more thorough examination. As was true of the previously discussed traffic function, in small police departments the uniformed patrol officer often *is* the detective division, in the sense that the agency is simply too small to afford separate evidence and investigative specialists. In such departments every patrol officer becomes a "generalist," who assumes responsibility for everything from crime-scene photography and evidence collection to finger printing prisoners and follow-up investigation of cases which began as part of the patrol function.

Some criminal situations can be handled and resolved on the spot by a patrol officer, who perhaps comes upon a crime in progress and arrests the culprit or else develops sufficient information through preliminary investigation to identify the offender, who will be picked up at a later time and place. More commonly, however, essential information concerning the commission of a criminal act is still lacking after the patrol officer's initial investigation of it. In such cases it becomes impractical for the uniformed officer to suspend patrol activities in order to follow the case through to completion—except, as noted earlier, in departments that are so small that no other alternative exists. It is the complexity of certain crimes, and the sheer amount of time which must often be devoted to answering questions about their occurrence and perpetrators, that justifies the existence of detectives, the first of whom appeared in police service as early as 1750.

Investigators perform a wide variety of services. These include interviewing victims and witnesses, identifying and arresting offenders whose identity and location are initially unknown, collecting and preserving physical evidence linked to a crime, recovering and returning stolen property, and assisting in the successful prosecution of cases in court.

A detective may enter a case at a number of different points, depending on its seriousness. When a major crime is involved, such as a homicide, shooting, or kidnapping, the investigator may be contacted immediately and arrive at the scene to begin the investigation only minutes after the patrol officer's arrival. With most crimes, however, the detective's first contact with a case begins some hours after its occurrence—and perhaps even as long as four or five days later. Such delays are typically due to a combination of the heavy case loads being carried by many investigators and their hours of assignment. While many large departments provide 24-hour investigative coverage by assigning detectives to each shift, it is quite common for smaller agencies to place their investigative personnel on 8 A.M.-to-5 P.M., Monday-through-Friday shifts, and to designate certain officers to be "on call" for afterhours crimes too serious to be left until the next day. This responsibility for providing investigative services beyond the normal work day is usually rotated among detective-division personnel.

Because detectives usually enter a case on an after-the-fact basis, they must rely heavily on the initial investigative work of patrol officers. Often the key to their success or failure in following up a case is the accuracy and thoroughness of the patrol officer's written offense report, which is usually prepared immediately following the commission of a crime. The uniformed officer's notation of the details of the crime (such items as the offender's distinctive physical features, mannerisms, and clothing, and what was said to the victim) may provide valuable leads in the eventual solution of a case.

Working with the patrol officer's initial offense report, the investigator begins a systematic (and sometimes long and arduous) effort to enlarge upon the basic information it contains and pull together the facts of the case. This process usually begins with a recontacting of both the victim and any known witnesses the following day, in an attempt to elicit additional information about the crime. It is extremely common for both victims and witnesses to omit important facts about what happened in the tense, emotional atmosphere that follows the commission of a crime and its first reporting to police. Important bits of information may be recalled hours or even days later by victims who were initially too traumatized by the experience to give such details to patrol officers when the initial offense report was being prepared. Reinterviewing witnesses by investigators may also provide essential facts which had earlier been overlooked or regarded as unimportant. The same is true of a careful reexamination of the crime scene itself. Regardless of how thoroughly it may originally have been gone over by patrol officers and/or evidence technicians in a search for physical clues, some small particular—a piece of metal or fabric dropped some yards away, some aspect of the street lighting or shrubbery—may provide missing information that will ultimately lead to a conviction.

In addition to follow-up questioning of victims and witnesses and reexamination of the crime scene itself, investigators often rely on leads gleaned from reliable informants to give them direction in a case. While informants may take the form of friends, relatives, or enemies of an offender, or even concerned citizens who had not previously come forward with information bearing on a case, they more often consist of known criminals or "street people" with whom the detective has had extensive dealings in the past. Building and maintaining a sizable pool of such individuals often proves of major importance in the solution of certain crimes. The detective ferrets out informants on whom he has depended in the past in pool halls, flophouses, bars, jails—wherever they may be—in his handling of many cases. Who in the area is apt to be currently "fencing" the kind of jewelry taken in a particular residential burglary? Where is an armed robber who was recently released from prison and wanted for questioning on a case most likely to be located? Who are the suspects friends or "homeboys"? These and a myriad of similar questions are routinely put to street-level informants by detectives in an effort to clear cases.

Crimes that are not isolated, one-time occurrences tend, like most other forms of human behavior, to assume patterns which reflect the unique character of those committing them. A rapist may prey only on women in a certain age group or type of residence; a burglar may leave distinctive marks when entering buildings or take only certain things within them; an armed robber may unthinkingly make similar comments or use certain expressions with every victim. The particular characteristics displayed by each offender in the commission of crimes—the perpetrator's "trademarks"—comprise what is referred to in police parlance as a *modus operandi* (method of operation) or MO.

Each department seeks to maintain an extensive and up-to-date MO file on all reported crimes. Once the responsible party in a given type of offense has been identified on the basis of an MO, it becomes possible to readily link the same person to similar crimes in the future. Even if an habitual offender becomes consciously aware of aspects of his or her particular MO and seeks to alter them, he will usually betray other distinctive behavior patterns and personal characteristics. Arrest data show that most repeat offenders tend to establish a given modus operandi and continue operating on the basis of it.

In addition to developing leads on a case from the department's modus-operandi file, the investigator may also turn to a wide variety of other files at local, state, and federal levels to obtain important information about particular criminals and offenses. Most good-sized police departments maintain alphabetized records of all individuals and locations that have been connected with criminal activity in the past. Additional local files may provide the investigator with a detailed breakdown on where certain types of crime have taken place in the past, the time and date they occurred, and whether they are solved or unsolved.

A large and growing number of the records systems regularly utilized by investigators are computer based and therefore capable of retrieving and providing data instantly via teletype and other electronic means. An excellent—and most impressive—example of one such data-processing system on a nationwide scale is the National Crime Information Center (NCIC), based in Washington and operated by the Federal Bureau of Investigation. NCIC not only provides a vast and immediately accessible store of computer-maintained data on crime and criminals across the nation, but it also serves to link many thousands of law-enforcement agencies for purposes of criminal intelligence and information sharing— an accomplishment of no small proportions in a country with as many separate police entities as ours. Through this marvel of modern electronic technology, the computer terminals located in small and large police departments throughout the country are linked to one another as well as to NCIC's data bank. Thus, for instance, a burglary investigator in Sante Fe, New Mexico, who is seeking information on a .38-caliber revolver believed to be stolen simply enters the serial number into the NCIC computer through the department's local teletype. Moments later the teletype chatters out information revealing that the weapon in question was stolen in Chicago two weeks earlier. Patrol officers reap even more immediate advantages from NCIC during the frequently tense moments after a suspicious vehicle has been spotted and its license number passed through police communications to the computer. More than one patrol officer has been saved from death or serious injury by the computer's rapid discovery that a car about to be stopped and approached is a "hit"—that is, stolen. The various states have developed their own computer-based data systems in recent years to provide additional details on in-state crime and criminals, thereby supplementing the resource of NCIC.

Cooperation and coordination between law-enforcement investigators at all levels of government is fast becoming a reality in the United States today. In place of traditional patterns of rivalry and lack of communication between the detective divisions of some departments, a growing number of agencies within the same area are pooling their investigative resources in the form of major crime squads and crime-specific strike forces. Such cooperative enforcement efforts stem from a growing recognition that most crimes and criminals are no respectors of the artificial boundaries established by local units of government. Because many criminals alternate their crimes from community to community within the same general area, investigators in each agency come to acquire individual pieces of a puzzle which would lead to the arrest and conviction of an offender if they were pulled together. The chances of doing this become far greater when law-enforcement investigators voluntarily and systematically share their information on cases. Far greater resources can be mustered for the handling of complex cases through such teamwork than can possibly be obtained by an individual department.

Teamwork is also becoming an increasingly important aspect of investigative work within individual agencies. Some communities are experimenting with efforts aimed at eliminating the destructive, frictions which exist between many detectives and patrol officers. Some of these techniques, such as the use of patrol officers to conduct follow-up investigations of cases, were mentioned earlier during the discussion of team policing. Another recent extension of the team-policing idea intended to produce greater rapport between patrol and investigative personnel, as well as an increase in overall police effectiveness, is the assignment of detectives to patrol beats along with uniformed officers. Such investigators usually retain responsibility for handling cases in other areas when necessary, but focus their primary efforts within the designated beat. A likely positive effect of such an arrangement is a closer, more understanding level of interaction between investigator and patrol officers.

Detectives are usually assigned to the investigation of particular types of crime, although in very small agencies an investigator often functions as a generalist, handling everything from juvenile problems to burglary, rape, and even homicide. Investigators in very small communities increasingly call upon larger municipal agencies within their area for assistance when they face involved investigations of serious crimes. Many state agencies, such as the Florida Department of Law Enforcement (FDLE), stand ready to extend requested resources, in the form of specialized state investigators, equipment, and laboratory-analysis services, to local departments to assist them in their criminal investigations.

Larger municipal police departments usually organize their detective divisions into three major units, or details, intended to cover the spectrum of adult criminality: (1) crimes against persons, (2) crimes against property, and (3) a general assignment detail. Investigators in the persons unit handle all offenses where human beings have either been physically harmed, threatened with some form of violence, or otherwise abused as individuals. Crimes-against-persons detectives therefore deal with a wide variety of "persons" offenses, ranging from murder and assault to rape and armed robbery. Robbery, even when it is only of the "strong-arm" variety and involves no actual weapon or harm to the victim, is included within the persons category because it always contains an implicit threat of force or harm in obtaining the property of another.

Detectives in the crime-against-property unit deal with offenses involving some form of monetary or property loss. Property detectives thus deal with everything from "car clouters," who specialize in stealing the contents of parked cars, to auto thieves, shoplifters, and residential and commerical burglars.

The third unit, the general-assignment detail, functions as a kind of omnibus or catchall category for whatever crimes are not covered by one of the other two units. General-assignment officers deal with such specialized forms of crime as confidence games, embezzlement, and bad checks. Major urban police departments often further subdivide their detective divisions. In such agencies special details, each with their own investigators and supervisors, are assigned to handle particular major offenses such as robbery, homicide, burglary, missing persons, and sex crimes.

Such things as the work load and success rate as measured by crimes cleared vary considerably from one type of investigation to another. Predictably, homicide consistently shows the largest number of cases cleared by arrest—around 85 percent—which might be viewed as small consolation for the morbid scenes routinely witnessed by homicide detectives in the course of their work. The dramatic clearance rates of homicide units compared to other details within the detective division is to be explained by the fact that most killings of human beings are intensely personal matters, usually involving friends or relatives close to the victim. The crime is characteristically both emotional and spontaneous, with the result that the killer is relatively easy to locate, particularly when he or she is closely associated with the victim. Assault also tends to be a crime in which victim and assailant are linked to each other in some personal relationship, which gives it a clearance rate of close to 70 percent.

Most property crimes are far more difficult to clear than offenses such as assault and murder. The number of people well enough known to someone to be likely victims of an assault or homicide is relatively limited,[3] while the number of material objects that might be stolen at any given time is virtually infinite in our affluent society. In property crimes there is seldom the kind of personal connection between crime and criminal that one finds with persons offenses. Property crimes are more apt to be the end result of careful and quite rational planning by complete strangers, which makes them extremely difficult to solve. Not surprisingly, the burglary clearance rate—in sharp contrast to that of assault and murder—usually runs close to 20 percent. Even the most successful real-life detectives fail to come close, in their solution of crimes, to the accomplishments of their media counterparts. The latter can invariably be counted on to solve anything from murder to an elaborate counterfeiting operation within the confines of a 60-minute TV show (with time out for commercials). Doubtless the real-life detectives often become discouraged when watching the dramatic accomplishments of the television supercops, particularly when they stop to consider that their profession has for many years cleared an average of only about 25 percent of major reported crimes. Perhaps the public, too, is often inclined to evaluate their performance against the myth of TV detectives and to judge them woefully inadequate by comparison.

Detectives are most often selected from the ranks of uniformed patrol officers. Such a transfer usually represents a reward for successful performance as a patrol officer and may involve an increase in pay or rank, or the extension of permanent occupational tenure. This traditional practice of obtaining criminal investigators from the patrol division has come under increasing criticism in recent years. The skills required to be a good patrol officer may be quite different from the skills necessary to function successfully as a detective. Yet it has always been assumed by municipal police departments that success as a patrol officer is a good predictor of success as an investigator, despite the fact that there is no scientific evidence to support such an assumption.

Patrol officers typically operate within an *occupational time frame*, where decisions, some of them very grave, must be made within a matter of seconds or very few minutes: how best to approach a silent-alarm call or suspicious individual, what first-aid measures to use on a critically injured person until an ambulance arrives, whether to resort to the use óf chemical mace, the nightstick, or even the service revolver during an attack. Not only must patrol officers make these and other serious decisions affecting their own lives and the lives of others within an extremely tight time frame, but they must often do so in a climate of strong emotional pressure. Unlike their usually calm and collected television counterparts, real-life patrol officers often have the ability to make quick but rational decisions tested by the presence of a hammering heart, the rapid flow of adrenaline, and the knowledge that a wrong move may spell death or injury for themselves or someone else.

While investigators sometimes come upon situations that require quick decisions under emotionally provocative circumstances, they more often operate in relatively controlled settings and with greater amounts of time in which to decide on different courses of action. Danger is less of a pressing, unanticipated reality for the detective, who usually *plans* encounters with dangerous individuals, taking such assistance as seems likely to be necessary in effecting an arrest or serving a search warrant. The detective more often knows the kind of people and situations he is about to deal with in advance, whereas the uniformed officer simply faces far too many spontaneous events and unknown individuals to anticipate danger or other problems which may arise. In contrast to the detective's characteristic methodical, one-step-at-a-time analysis of problems, the uniformed officer must usually become adept at and accustomed to the process of *polyphasic activity*—handling multiple thought stimuli and different behavioral demands at the same time. Thus, for example, the uniformed officer responding to a prowler call at night may be simultaneously listening to his radio for other activity in the area, scanning the fronts of stores and businesses and the faces and appearance of people on the street, and checking the license plate of a car in front of him against his "hot sheet" list of stolen cars, reminding himself in the process to be sure to give extra patrol to a local clothing store whose burglar alarm is out of order. The patrol officer at the scene of a traffic accident is making a quick mental assessment of the damage to two vehicles, deciding how to answer the dispatcher's question as to whether the situation calls for a tow truck, listening to the excited and simultaneous statements of both drivers (and perhaps witnesses as well), and deciding whether or not to call for a back up unit to assist in traffic direction—all while walking the several yards that separate the police cruiser from the accident.

This is certainly not to say that patrol officers are usually more skilled or brighter than detectives, or vice versa. It is simply intended to emphasize the fact that each assignment has its own special demands and problems—which may require very different kinds of individuals. The police officer who is remarkably capable when it comes to divining the MO of a particular burglar or robber, or pulling together seemingly unrelated facts in a homicide case, may be a disaster attempting to mediate a landlord-tenant dispute or giving directions to an out-of-town motorist. A uniformed officer who is an excellent patrol officer with a high record of felony arrests on his beat may have no facility whatsoever for following up cases as an investigator. We presently know too little about the specific role skills required of patrol officers as opposed to investigators.

Some police departments engage in the process of rotating personnel through the detective division on a temporary basis, as needs and workforce conditions permit. In this case there is usually no change in either pay or rank, but simply the career-development goal of creating police generalists who are skilled in and capable of working in a variety of assignments, and who possess a greater understanding of the overall police mission in the community. Such a system serves to minimize the earlier mentioned tendency for officers to become overspecialized in one assignment, and thereby lose sight of the total "product" they are part of creating. Police personnel who have an opportunity to participate, however briefly, in the work of other organizational units are less likely to experience the kind of friction and rivalry that has become associated with specialized assignments in the past.

The exposure to new forms of knowledge and skills attendant upon a temporary rotation to the status of detective would doubtless serve to increase the morale and enthusiasm of officers. In place of the present rigid system of selecting detectives only from the ranks of patrol officers with several years experience, it would also be possible to transform the position of investigator into a professional-entry level intended to attract large numbers of bright, well-educated young people to police service. There is really no reason, short of the weight of tradition, that new officers who possess the necessary skills and educational background might not be hired directly as criminal investigators and assigned to the detective division upon graduation from the police academy. A department might stipulate, as an additional qualification for such employment, that the new officer spend an "internship" of between six months and one year working as a uniformed patrol officer before being assigned as an investigator. Unlike the military service and the police in some countries, where a career-oriented young person can enter directly as a commissioned officer, nothing approaching a professional-entry level has ever existed in municipal law enforcement in the United States. The status of detective could certainly be turned into such a position.

Youth Services

Police involvement with young people has steadily increased in recent years, as the volume of juvenile delinquency in our society has grown ever larger. Over half of all serious crimes in the United States today are committed by individuals between the ages of 10 and 17. In addition to accounting for about half of all arrests for the property crimes represented by burglary, larceny, and auto theft each year, juveniles are engaging in acts of violence as never before.[4] Indeed, during the last 15 years juvenile arrests for robbery, aggravated assault, forcible rape, and homicide have increased some 250 percent, the largest rise in history. Studies of juvenile-delinquency figures disclose some alarming trends, including a dramatic annual increase in juvenile arrests for narcotic and drug violations and a greater proportion of female juveniles arrested each year. Much to the surprise of police and parents alike, girls under the age of 18 are becoming ever more involved in violent crime. Between 1970 and 1975 the arrest rate of female juveniles climbed 40 percent—as opposed to 24 percent for boys. In 1975, 11 percent of all juveniles arrested for violent crime were female.[5] Today it is estimated that about 5 percent of all American children come to the attention of the police each year.[6] If present juvenile-delinquency trends continue, close to 27 percent of all male children in the country will have been arrested before they reach 18 years of age![7]

The sheer magnitude of juvenile delinquency in our society has necessitated the use of specialized police resources to deal with the problem. Most departments of any size maintain a juvenile or youth-services unit, either as a separate organizational entity or as a subunit within the detective division. The responsibilities of juvenile officers include not only dealing with juveniles as perpetrators of crime, but also as its victims. Thus, for instance, cases involving the abuse or neglect of children are investigated by juvenile-unit officers, as well as those in which children are runaways, missing persons, or incorrigible and beyond parental control.

The investigation of crimes committed by juveniles involves essentially the same kind of activity engaged in by other detectives—interviewing and reinterviewing victims and witnesses, examining crime scenes, scrutinizing available files and records, and working closely with other law-enforcement agencies in an effort to clear the case. Beyond this, however, juvenile officers face a number of added responsibilities— some of them extremely complex and demanding—which separate them from other investigators. These include the counseling of both juveniles and their parents as to the best ways to deal with the problems at hand as well as their relationship at home, a task which is certainly far closer to the activity of a social worker than a law-enforcement officer. While such personal qualities as sensitivity, insight, and compassion are important to the success of every modern police officer, they are especially essential to those charged with responsibility for working with young people on a regular basis. For this reason the selection of officers for the juvenile or youth-services unit is a matter of utmost importance.

Many states have steadily upgraded and increased their training requirements for juvenile officers, with an emphasis on assuring that personnel in this unit have a clear grasp of such subjects as human relations and adolescent and child psychology, as well as a strong interest in helping young people in trouble. Too often in the past, investigators have come into their new assignments directly from the uniform division, with no advance preparation or training whatsoever. On-the-job training has been relied on to provide new workers with whatever specialized knowledge they might require. While this practice is basically unsound and ill-advised for the detective division as a whole, it is especially hazardous in the juvenile unit. Unlike adult offenders, whose lives and criminal careers are likely to be well established, most juvenile delinquents, if only because of their age and lesser exposure to crime, are still capable of being influenced in the direction of leading law-abiding lives. An adolescent's first encounters with juvenile officers as authority symbols and representatives of the "straight" life may be of critical significance in determining whether he continues his involvement in crime. Therefore all juvenile officers need to come to their work possessed of as much interpersonal skill and knowledge of human behavior as possible.

In additon to providing counseling services, juvenile officers work closely with the juvenile court and probation department in the handling of individual cases. Juvenile officers play a vital role in determining whether a given child is referred to the court for formal handling, referred to some public or private agency in the community for assistance, or released to her parents or guardian. The department's juvenile unit works closely with schools and other community agencies in the operation of delinquency prevention and assistance programs. Often individual officers are assigned as resource persons at particular schools for the purpose of counseling students and building police-youth rapport.

Such activity on the part of juvenile officers arises from a conception of delinquency that is fundamentally and legally different from the police conception of adult criminality. By definition such as burglary, auto theft, and armed robbery—which would constitute crime if they were committed by an adult—are labeled juvenile delinquency if committed by a person between the ages of 7 and 16.[8] Even the most serious forms of crime— offenses such as rape and murder—do not normally result in the handling of a juvenile delinquent as an adult offender unless he or she has attained a certain age (usually 16 or 18 depending on the jurisdiction). Cases that involve exceptional forms of brutality and violence, however, may result in the adult prosecution of juveniles under the age of 16.

Some forms of behavior that would not qualify as crimes were they to be committed by adults are classified as delinquency and accordingly handled by the police. Examples of such offenses include curfew violations, school truancy, consumption of alcoholic beverages, running away from home, and incorrigibility. The concern with these and other relatively minor forms of misconduct on the part of the juvenile justice system stems from the philosophy that its entire reason for being is to provide help and guidance for young people, whose small acts of deviance from society's rules may mark the beginning of a criminal career if left unchecked. For this reason all proceedings involving juveniles are civil and nonadversary in nature. Their purpose is to diagnose and prescribe, not to adjudicate and punish. The decision whether to commit a youth to a detention center or return him or her to the community is based not on the nature of the offense, but on an assessment of his or her overall character and a consideration of what will most likely be in the best interest of the youth and those of the community.

Despite our society's belief that juvenile offenders should be handled differently from adult criminals, a combination of high juvenile recidivism rates and growing numbers of unusually vicious acts committed by young people in recent years has led to public demands for sterner forms of juvenile justice. The all-too-frequent appearance of juvenile atrocities and their lenient handling by officials, has been partly responsible for this change.

In many large cities elderly and handicapped citizens live as virtual prisoners in their own homes out of fear of marauding young criminals, often in gangs, who terrorize the streets by day and night. Even when they are apprehended for the most serious crimes, many of these youthful offenders adopt a "so what" attitude, expecting to hide successfully from punishment by virtue of their status as juveniles. As one New York teenager explained his robbing of elderly women, "I was young and I knew I wasn't gonna get no big time. So, you know, what's to worry? If you're doin' wrong, do it while you're young, because you won't do that much time."[9]

Frequent abuses of the juvenile justice system by hardened youthful offenders have led to two responses: (1) a call to reduce the maximum age of coverage provided by juvenile laws and to subject those who commit serious crimes to penalties of the adult system; and (2) the increasing segregation of seriously delinquent youth from children who are either victims of some sort themselves or who are not yet deeply involved in delinquent behavior. To the police juvenile unit, this last development means that it will most likely be divided into two separate sections in the future: One will handle the investigation of juvenile offenders and their acts, while the other will devote itself entirely to delinquency-prevention programs and to helping children who are either victims of crime and neglect or in need of guidance relating to less serious forms of misconduct. In some departments the investigation of juvenile offenses is simply being transferred to the detective division, leaving the youth-services or juvenile division free to concern itself largely with the business of prevention.

In the past, police contacts with juveniles were usually of a highly informal nature, even when a youth was suspected of serious crime. The protective philosophy of juvenile law and the courts involved in administering it resulted in little concern with extending the constitutional rights accorded adult offenders accused of crimes to juveniles. A series of Supreme Court cases extending from 1948 to 1967, however, changed this. In the most famous of these cases, *In re Gault* (1967), the Court affirmed that juveniles also are entitled to such basic constitutional protections as the right to counsel, the right to confront and cross-examine witnesses, and the privilege against self-incrimination. Today, juveniles involved in delinquency proceedings are entitled to the same constitutional protections as adults charged with crime—something that obviously makes police-juvenile encounters more legally problematical and formal in nature whenever suspected criminal conduct is involved.

Despite this, police officers continue to have far more discretion in their dealings with juveniles than any adults they have contact with. The range of possible responses is greatest for uniformed patrol officers, who are more apt to initiate juvenile contacts themselves than to do so in response to citizen requests or complaints. Most often, patrol officers handle juveniles on a very informal basis, citing or arresting them in only a minority of cases. It was noted earlier that over 5 percent of the country's children have some contact with the police each year; yet only about 1 percent are formally brought to the attention of juvenile courts.[10] Studies show that the most important determinant of whether an officer elects to handle a juvenile informally or draw him into the juvenile justice system is the child's *demeanor*, not the nature of his misconduct.[11] Officers tend to make on-the-spot assessments of a juvenile's overall character and potential for further crime or law abidance on the basis of such things as manner of speech and dress, and whether or not the youth displays what the officer regards as appropriate respect and sorrow for the offending behavior. Given the same kind of misconduct, those defined as "basically good kids" are more likely to released or taken home to their parents after a verbal reprimand, while juveniles whom officers regard as disrespectful or unrepentant are apt to be handled formally by arrest and referral to the department's juvenile division.

Patrol officers come to anticipate more trouble and disrespect from their encounters with juveniles. As Albert J. Reiss observes,

> Patrol officers commonly regard juveniles as the most difficult class of citizens to police and the most leniently handled in the system of justice. . . . They show less respect for law and authority, are more aggressive and defiant, and rebellious, and are more aware of restrictions on police conduct.[12]

One study revealed that officers regarded contact with large-sized teenagers as the most stressful of all citizen interactions.[13] Since dealing with juveniles is regarded as stressful by officers, and because the formal processing of youthful offenders is likely to be both extremely involved and unproductive from the standpoint of what officers regard as justice, they are inclined to avoid making arrests whenever possible.

Much of the friction existing between the police and juveniles as a group must be related to the fact that the police are inescapably perceived as strong authority symbols. A large percentage of the youthful offenders whom police officers deal with harbor strong feelings of resentment or ambivalence toward authority in general, as a result of unpleasant experiences with parents, teachers, and other significant adult figures. Such feelings are readily transferred to and acted out against society's ultimate authority figure—the police officer.

It has been proposed in recent years that the police and other agencies involved in the juvenile justice process should disengage themselves from handling forms of misconduct that, while they are perhaps undesirable, do not pose a major threat to society. Given the growing commission of such serious crimes as murder, robbery, and rape by juveniles, and the resultant strain on already limited juvenile justice resources, it is argued that it is both impractical and unwise to continue committing vast amounts of money and personnel to the processing of "kiddie crime"— such problems as incorrigibility, curfew violations, and school truancy, none of which would be classified as even the most minor of misdemeanors were they to involve adults. It is suggested that such forms of behavior on the part of juveniles be viewed as social and psychological problems which can best be dealt with by public and private agencies that are not part of the juvenile justice system.

Another strong impetus toward diverting youth who have not yet become involved in serious misconduct away from the juvenile justice system is the belief that formal processing by police and courts may do more harm than good. Basically conforming and well socialized juveniles who happen to be funneled into the juvenile justice mill are more likely to be stigmatized and traumatized than helped by the process. The informal labeling of a child as a juvenile delinquent by relatives, teachers, peers, and others in the wake of formal handling by the justice system may lead to indelible social scars that may pave the way for adult criminal careers. There are many other agencies in most communities far better equipped to deal with the emotional and behavioral problems of youth than the police and juvenile courts.

Vice and Narcotics: "Victimless Crimes"

In small police departments the enforcement of laws pertaining to vice and narcotics activity necessarily falls to "generalists," who pursue assignments in these areas right along with their investigations of crimes against persons and property. In agencies serving larger communities, however, the magnitude of vice and narcotics offenses is usually such that a special division exists to enforce laws pertaining to them. Organizationally, the vice section may represent a separate unit within the detective division, or it may be completely independent and operate directly under the department's chief administrator. Because of the increasing complexity and specialization surrounding the enforcement of narcotics laws, many departments maintain a narcotics unit which is organizationally separate from the vice division, although the traditional practice has been to combine the two.

Vice-law-enforcement embraces a variety of different offenses, usually consisting of the following: homosexuality, prostitution, illegal gambling, liquor law violations, pornography, and narcotics abuse. All these areas differ from other crimes dealt with by the police in one important respect: Each involves the interaction of offenders with *willing victims*. Homosexuals voluntarily seek out other homosexuals for illegal sexual activity; "johns" willingly pay prostitutes for the services they offer. Many otherwise law abiding citizens wish to place illegal bets, purchase alcoholic beverages after legally prescribed hours, or read literature defined as obscene or pornographic by prevailing community norms, and no one forces the average narcotics user to ingest the prohibited substance.

The voluntary nature of such acts has given rise in recent years to the social labeling of them as "crimes without victims" and the attempt by some to abolish the laws underpinning them. Individuals, so the argument typically goes, should be free to engage in any behavior they wish—providing such conduct does not demonstrably injure others or infringe on their rights in some way. The sole reason for creating any law and enforcing it is to protect the public from clear and identifiable harm, and "crimes without victims" involve no such threat, it is said. Laws regulating such things as sexual conduct and narcotics use unnecessarily stigmatize basically harmless behavior and individuals and only serve to tax the resources of our already overburdened criminal justice system.

As persuasive as the logic of such arguments sounds, the fact is that a great deal of so-called victimless crime involves quite tangible harm both to individuals and society, most of it of a hidden and indirect nature. Some examples may serve to illustrate this point. Homosexuality is often assumed to be one of the most innocuous of victimless crimes, involving as it does the action of consenting adults. Yet elements of both crime and offense to the public often surround it. While most male homosexual activity presumably occurs in private, a substantial amount of it takes place in public places—such as parks, restrooms, and darkened streets and alleys—which usually become well known as meeting places for those interested in homosexual gratification. The senior author spent a brief stint as a vice officer assigned to one such location during his period as a police participant-observer:

> "Behold the Friendly Fountain," my partner said as he pointed to a large basin in the park where a jet of water shot high into the afternoon sky. . . .We followed the winding cement path we were on until it snaked into a raised mound of grass and bushes. From where we stood, we could see the fountain, the parking area and a row of buildings just below us surrounded by benches. The building closest to us had the word *MEN* painted in large black letters on its door. Kupiszewski pointed to the benches which were perhaps twenty yards in front of and below us. We knelt on the damp grass and peered through the bushes. "Now that's what's known as the meat rack out here," he said. "A queer will usually walk over from either the fountain or the parking lot and just sit around waiting to score. Other fags will come by and check the merchandise to see if there's anything they like. Sometimes the crazy bastards'll hang around for hours, following different guys inside the can, until they finally find somebody that's willing to make it with them. . . .[14]

If such locations are well known to homosexuals themselves, they are unfortunately equally well known to muggers, blackmail artists, and other criminals who frequently prey upon them. It is impossible to know the actual number of homosexuals who are assaulted, robbed, or victimized by other crimes as a result of their attempts to solicit sexual contacts in such places as public parks and restrooms. Most such crimes are never reported because of the embarrassment and possible social damage that might result; indeed, a surprising number of those arrested by vice officers in such places prove to be otherwise upstanding citizens, many of them professional people.

> My initial shock [at having arrested a bank vice-president] would diminish in the days ahead as we arrested other businessmen, teachers (one of them a teacher of retarded children), an architect, a minister, a certified public accountant, even a psychiatrist. Indeed, I would leave my short tour of duty as a vice officer never really understanding why people who had spent their lives struggling for economic and social success would risk it all for a few moments of perverse gratification in a public toilet.[15]

It seems unlikely that "decriminalizing" homosexuality will do much to protect homosexuals from the depredations of those who would rob, beat, blackmail, or even murder them. It is not the illegality of homosexuality itself that enables such criminals to operate, but the fact that it is sufficiently surrounded by a social aura of shame and rejection that homosexuals are unwilling to risk public disclosure of their behavior by reporting crimes they have suffered. Even states that have legalized homosexual activity, such as California and Illinois, do not extend such legalization to cover the practice of homosexuality in public places such as parks and restrooms. Clearly, the community has a right to be protected against public displays of conduct—whether homosexual or heterosexual—that offend its collective sense of decency. Adults and children alike should be able to use such facilities as public parks, restrooms, and streets without having to witness offensive sexual activity. For children, whose identities are still in the process of formation, such sights may be especially undesirable or even traumatic. Today, vice officers have far too much work and too little time to engage in harassment of homosexuals and the places they frequent, allegations to the contrary notwithstanding. Such enforcement contacts as they do have are largely linked not only to protecting society from offensive public displays of sexuality, but also to protecting homosexuals themselves from becoming victims of crime.

Many people view the continued existence and enforcement of laws dealing with prostitution as a meaningless waste of criminal justice time and effort, as well as an expression of our society's unrealistic and lingering Puritan attitudes toward sex. Why should we not allow completely willing adult patrons to purchase sexual favors when they wish, just as so many other goods and services are freely bought in our society? As harmless as prostitution may appear to some on the surface, the fact is that it is often linked to more serious criminal activity. Thus, for instance, more than one "john" has been lured to a dark apartment or alley in anticipation of sex with a prostitute, only to be met with the violence of a pimp or other accomplice intent on robbery. In addition to strong-arm robbery, more serious assaults and even homicide are sometimes associated with prostitution. Often referred to as the oldest profession, prostitution affords numerous opportunities for the operation of organized criminals, many of whom dovetail their control of prostitutes with such activities as corruption of public officials, extortion, gambling, and narcotics.

Prostitutes range from "streetwalkers," many of whom are drug addicts who "trick" for very little money, to sophisticated "high rollers," who command large sums and are well organized and skilled at recognizing vice officers. Once such high roller is described by a senior vice officer:

> These are broads that trick for maybe a hundred, hundred and fifty bucks a shot. Really sharp looking. You'd never think one of them was a whore if you ran into her on the streets. Most of these gals work a regular circuit around the country. They'll hit, say, Memphis, New Orleans, Dallas, Jacksonville, Atlanta, then shift to another part of the country. Some of them just free-lance, but most of them work with pimps. They usually plan to arrive at a hotel about the same time as a big convention, maybe a legislative session. . . . Most high rollers keep trick books like Sally here," he continued. He opened a small, brown leather address book and showed it to me. "See, it lists regular tricks in each city and how much they're worth. A lot of it is in code. Like this one here." He pointed to the initials *CB-1* just above an address on one of the pages. "This means that this cat CB is good for a hundred bucks. . . . Here's a two-fifty. The girls usually won't give each other the names of their johns, but they will trade information on which hotels are best to work, which bellboys to see and so on.[16]

While the proponents of legalized prostitution often argue that the ready availability of such women would likely serve to produce a decline in the incidence of crimes like rape and child molestation, available scientific evidence suggests that the kinds of offenders who commit such acts would not be likely to be dissuaded from them by the availability of prostitutes. Rape, for instance, is primarily an act of anger and aggression directed against women, not an act intended to afford sexual gratification.[17] It is also often heard that legalized prostitution coupled with some system of required medical inspection would probably reduce the amount of venereal disease that presently results from uncontrolled prostitution; yet there is no way to assure that a prostitute inspected at a given time and found to be free of disease will not acquire and begin transmitting a venereal disease a few minutes or hours later.

Probably the most impressive case for continued police involvement in the area of so-called victimless crime can be made with respect to narcotics, particularly heroin. Heroin addicts, rather than conforming to stereotypes of passive withdrawal from the world around them, are often actively involved in victimizing others in an effort to support their habit. Such victimization most often takes the form of property crime, such as burglary and shoplifting, although many assaults, armed and strong-arm robberies, and sometimes even homicides are drug-related. It is estimated that over one billion dollars is lost each year in drug-related shoplifting alone.

An addict's habit can quickly and easily escalate to the point that he or she needs several hundred dollars a day—a level which requires an enormous amount of criminal activity to support, particularly when one stops to realize that the average addict can expect to receive from a "fence" only between one-fifth and one-third of the actual value of stolen merchandise. Not surprisingly, it is estimated that somewhere between 25 and 67 percent of all property crime is committed by drug addicts. In addition to the chronic problems posed by heroin use, law enforcement in recent years has found itself faced with a variety of other forms of drug abuse, including the use of such chemical substances as amphetamines, barbiturates, and hypnotics. Certain of these drugs, such as barbiturates, are also addictive, and their use can lead to serious forms of mental and physical illness, even death in some instances.

The business of enforcing narcotics laws is both difficult and dangerous. The difficulty arises from the fact that investigations are typically long and involved, often requiring coordinated effort between local, state, and federal enforcement agents. With the arrest or identification of a given user or small-time pusher, narcotics officers must begin the tedious process of trying to trace the drug in question back to its source, something that may involve the surveillance and careful observation of a number of different individuals and places over a period of days, weeks, or even months. Because organized crime is heavily involved in the importation and wholesaling of narcotics as a major economic enterprise, it usually becomes a formidable task to cut through the maze of intermediaries that ultimately links the street-level sale of heroin to the activities of organized crime figures.

The sale of narcotics is organized like a legitimate importing-wholesaling-retailing business. The distribution of heroin, for example, requires movement of the drug through four or five levels between the importer and the street peddler. Many enforcement officials believe that the severity of mandatory Federal narcotics penalties has caused organized criminals to restrict their activities to importing and wholesale distribution. They stay away from smaller-scale wholesale transactions or dealing at the retail level. Transactions with addicts are handled by independent narcotics pushers using drugs imported by organized crime.[18]

As severe and mandatory prison sentences for the sale of hard drugs become ever more common, the risks assumed by undercover officers who seek to penetrate narcotics operations understandably become much greater. The calculatedly scruffy looking "narc" who moves about the netherworld of drug pushers each day does so with the knowledge that many of the latter are armed and would not hesitate an instant to kill an officer should his or her true identity become known. In addition to living with such pressures, narcotics officers involved in street-level undercover work also face severe strains on their personal lives. Long and unpredictable hours, coupled with the frequent necessity to approximate the appearance and mannerisms of the criminals they stalk, often prove too much for even the best marriages. When this happens, reassignment of an officer may be the only realistic way of averting separation or divorce.

The work of vice officers in enforcing laws dealing with illegal gambling thrusts them into another major dimension of "victimless crime." Gambling is usually identified as the single largest source of revenue for organized criminals in the United States, with some estimates ranging as high as $50 billion in gross annual revenue! Illegal gambling operations range from the playing of "numbers" to "bolita" to lotteries, off-track horse betting, dice games, bets on sporting events, and operation of illegal casinos. Even Nevada, which has legalized gambling, experiences serious problems with the abuse of existing laws. Many criminals, who are ineligible for licenses because of their past records, operate a variety of illegal gambling activities, such as bookmaking and floating card games. A great many of those who naively participate in illegal gambling are cheated by the use of such devices as "loaded" dice and marked cards.

The enforcement of gambling laws is made especially difficult by a combination of apathy and tolerance on the part of the public. Citizens who vigorously press for full enforcement of laws pertaining to prostitution and narcotics often fail to see anything intrinsically wrong or harmful in illegal gambling. Many otherwise law abiding citizens place occasional bets with local bookies or play numbers games in their neighborhoods. Certain groups of citizens, including some churches and civic groups, have in the past sometimes expected and received exemptions from gambling laws in order to operate such things as lotteries and bingo games for charitable and recreational purposes.

Illegal gambling is closely related to many other forms of crime, some of them quite serious and damaging to society. Because most illegal gambling in the country is tightly controlled and efficiently managed by organized crime groups, the vast revenues that it generates are regularly poured into other criminal enterprises in the form of new investment capital. Mob monies derived from gambling are used for such things as the infiltration and takeover of legitimate businesses, corruption of public officials at all levels of government, and narcotics wholesaling. Much gambling is directly linked to "loan-sharking" operations, the second largest source of organized crime revenue. For many people, including some prominent business people and public officials, gambling often assumes the proportions of a personal compulsion or sickness leading to losses in a single evening which are far greater than the individual has on hand. In the case of gambling operations run by organized criminals, those heavily in debt are offered usurious personal loans, which range as high as 150 percent interest per week. The alternative to accepting such an illegal loan may be broken bones or worse. For the businessperson who is unable to pay the interest on the money a loan shark has given him, a partnership with organized criminals or a complete takeover of the business by the latter may be the only out. Organized criminals eagerly extend gambling credit to politicians in the hope of exacting payment in the form of political favors. Illegal gambling operations go hand in hand with other forms of vice. Thus, for instance, the bar or nightclub with a "back room" game may also be involved in the sale of liquor after legal hours, the use of prostitutes to entice players, and sometimes the selling of narcotics and "hot" merchandise as well.

To be certain, police involvement in some areas of vice enforcement is highly controversial and difficult to justify in the form of tangible benefits to society. Laws relating to pornography represent a classic illustration of this point. The latter are invariably vague and the subject of heated political debate. Some groups feel strongly that the law should function as a guardian of public morality, while others claim that it has no business setting itself up as the arbiter of what citizens can read or view. Court decisions that seek to define pornography in terms of such criteria as "redeeming social value" do little to settle the issue, which is one that finds the police caught in the middle as they attempt to interpret both the law and prevailing community sentiments on the subject. The recent escalation of pornographic content in some magazines and the growth of an illicit industry commonly referred to as "kiddie porn"—the dissemination of films and pictures involving obscene acts on the part of children—seems certain to further inflame the present controversy over pornography.

Support and Auxiliary Services

Just as the military effectiveness of combat troops depends heavily on the logistical support of personnel located well behind the front lines, so does the success of every police operation, from patrol and traffic to investigations and juvenile work, depend upon the existence of a great many support services and resources within the organization as a whole. We would do well at this point to consider briefly the most important of these back up facilities and the ways in which they relate to accomplishing the overall police mission.

CRIMINALISTICS

The role of physical evidence looms large in many criminal cases, ranging from vehicular hit-and-run to robbery, burglary, rape, and murder. Indeed, in some cases bits of circumstantial evidence such as clothing fibers, paint residue, pieces of glass, hair, and cartridge casings may form the entire basis for prosecution because of the unavailability of witnesses or other forms of evidence. In such cases the services provided to investigators by the crime laboratory become invaluable. Many larger departments maintain their own full-service crime laboratories, which are staffed by well-trained *criminalists*. The criminalist is a scientist who brings knowledge of such disciplines as physics, chemistry, biology, and medicine to bear on studying the physical evidence of a crime. The province of criminalists is limited to the analysis of physical factors, and therefore stops short of any consideration of the social and psychological factors that concern investigators, lawyers, and others involved in a case. Criminalists utilize the scientific equipment and laboratory facilities at their disposal in the analysis of everything from blood stains and semen to forged documents and murder weapons, making their findings available to the investigators assigned to a case and offering testimony in court as expert witnesses. Because laboratory criminalists move in a complex technical realm replete with such expressions as "neutron activation analysis," "chromatography," and "X ray diffraction," they face the difficult task of presenting their findings in a case in such a way that they are clear and understandable to lay jurors.

Police departments which are too small to provide their own crime laboratories make use of either regional, state, or federal resources within a given area to deal with routine evidence-analysis needs, while depending on either regional or state laboratories to handle highly technical situations.

The effectiveness of a laboratory criminalist in providing evidence-analysis services depends heavily upon how well the patrol officer or evidence technician accomplishes the task of safeguarding a crime scene and carefully collecting and preserving the evidence it contains. Some police departments train all patrol officers in the basic techniques of collecting and preserving evidence, while others rely upon the specialized services of evidence technicians, who often operate out of mobile crime-lab vehicles. Whether the responsibility of identifying and collecting criminal evidence falls to the beat patrol officer or to an evidence technician, it is essential that great care be exercised to avoid contaminating or destroying pieces of physical evidence that may later prove to be of major importance in a case. Too often the area immediately surrounding a serious crime is inundated by onlookers eager to catch a glimpse of what happened. Even police officers, who certainly know better, sometimes "beehive" at the scene of a crime—picking up objects and walking in and out of the area with little thought to the damage they may be doing. A skilled evidence technician arriving at the scene of a crime minutes after a patrol officer has supposedly secured it can do little good if such evidence as tire marks, footprints, and fingerprints have already been destroyed or damaged by people or other officers who have carelessly been allowed to enter the area. Even where nothing at a crime scene is consciously touched or moved in any way, officers and citizens may unwittingly contaminate evidence by tracking material in and out of the area on the bottoms of their shoes. Many otherwise promising criminal cases have been lost at the outset because crime scenes were improperly secured or evidence carelessly handled.

COMMUNICATIONS

The majority of order maintenance as well as criminal situations handled by patrol officers involve a chain of events which usually begins with a citizen's phone call to the police communications center and ends with the dispatching of the appropriate units, passing along in the process essential information about the call's location and nature and the circumstances surrounding it. The crisp, clipped transmissions of the radio dispatcher assume important—indeed, sometimes life-and-death—proportions to the patrol officer, who must be prepared to deal with unknown people and events entirely on the basis of the messages emanating from a radio. Inaccurate description of a fleeing robbery vehicle or suspect, a wrong address or direction of travel, delay in obtaining and transmitting information on a suspect stopped for questioning, failure to determine if an enraged husband arguing with his wife has a weapon—any of these and many other errors on the part of communications personnel can result in anything from failure to apprehend a dangerous felon to serious injury or death of a police officer. Accurate, clear, and rapid radio communication forms the life blood of every police department on a 24-hour basis.

Patrol officers often fail to appreciate both the complexity and the range of tasks performed by communications workers, who are usually civilian employees. Those assigned to handle incoming telephone calls, some of which involve dire emergencies and confused, hysterical callers, must remain calm and controlled while quickly eliciting the information necessary to send help. During peak activity periods, workers receiving incoming complaints operate under enormous emotional pressure. Frequently they find themselves forced into the role of social worker or psychiatrist while listening to the problems of neurotic, depressed, or suicidal callers.

Perhaps the least understood of all communications workers is the radio dispatcher, whose tasks and responsibilities often result in levels of emotional pressure not unlike those experienced by air-traffic controllers. Not only must the dispatcher assume primary responsibility for quickly sending officers to the scene of criminal and service situations with as much information as possible, but he or she must also handle an often dizzying array of requests from patrol units for special information on everything from stolen cars and property to wants and warrants, vehicle registration, and the like. A number of such requests are often received within seconds of each other, with each officer pressing to receive the information as fast as possible. ("Headquarters, anything back on that plate yet?") In addition to the volume of transmission work generated by requests for patrol units coming from workers on the complaint board, the dispatcher must also keep up with the barrage of activity being generated by officers in the field ("Headquarters, 2Mary45 will be on a vehicle stop at Main and Carswell . . ." "Headquarters, 2Mary30 . . . be out with a suspicious person at 1816 Vermont . . .").

Not surprisingly, dispatchers often become a favorite target of grumbling on the part of patrol officers as well as the victims of a process that psychologists label *displaced aggression*—the venting of anger and frustration on a handy object that really had nothing to do with evoking such feelings in the first place. The senior author found himself reflecting on the sometimes strained relations between patrol officers and dispatchers during his period of police participant–observation:

"New dispatcher," I said. Griffin nodded and smiled. I guessed that the girl on the other end of the radio was probably manning the Zone Three communications console for the first time tonight under the watchful eyes of a supervisor. The invisible women, I thought. They were our eyes in a very real sense, for we had to depend on them time after time each night to tell us everything possible about the kinds of calls we were about to walk up on. We accordingly blamed them, bitterly denounced them to each other, when the information they gave us proved to be wrong or incomplete or when they were too slow to respond to our requests. . . Hapless females. We took it all out on them so many times, all the tension and anger we built up handling other people's problems. Perhaps we did so because the alternative was to begin venting aggression against each other, and men who have to depend on each other night after night for their very lives can't afford to do that.

Looking back, I suppose we were so often hard on the faceless women just because of the fact that they were women and we were men. The inescapable truth was that here was a goddess who held our fate in her hands every night, who decided when we could or could not eat dinner or stop for coffee, who nightly ran us around the small grid of our beat like some schoolmistress sending boys on errands. If men generally resent being supervised and controlled by members of the opposite sex, this is doubly true in police work, for it represents perhaps one of the last bastions of traditional masculinity in American society.[19]

Some departments expose their officers to brief periods of work in communications, either during the orientation period or while they are in active service. An officer who logs even a few hours handling telephone complaints, dispatching other patrol officers, running teletypes, receiving incoming warrants and records, monitoring silent alarm systems, and the myriad other items routinely handled by communications workers is likely to come away with a newfound appreciation of the complexity and importance of their role in the department. The other side of the coin, of course, is to allow dispatchers to spend at least some time riding with patrol officers in order to generate a better understanding of their work and problems. Some departments are following this practice.

Modern law-enforcement technology is having a major and positive effect on radio communications systems in a growing number of cities. Computer-assisted dispatching, for instance, provides the dispatcher with such information as the best available unit to send on a call once the type of call and location are entered into the system. Patrol cars in a number of communities are now equipped with electronic systems that enable them to place requests for information on suspects, vehicles, and stolen property directly into the computer, without the necessity of going through the intermediate step of passing the request verbally to a dispatcher, who must then teletype it into the computer. Under traditional communications systems officers will sometimes refrain from running a wanted check on an individual or automobile simply because they sense that the dispatchers are too burdened with other work or because they realize that the vehicle in question will probably be well beyond the boundaries of the beat by the time they receive a reply. Direct access to the computer data base by patrol units means that officers can make any number of inquiries without tying up dispatchers and other communications workers, who in the past have had to stop other activities to manually enter information requests into the computer. It also means that valuable air time is not taken up with lengthy oral transmissions regarding suspects, vehicles, and stolen property. Seated behind the wheel of a patrol car, an officer merely presses designated buttons on a small piece of equipment and receives instant printouts of the requested information on a minature TV screen in the car. Such modern systems hold great promise from the standpoint of officer safety. Aside from the time delays in obtaining critical information through manual means in the past, many officers have sought to use the radio in an emergency only to find the frequency blocked by another unit receiving or transmitting detailed information on a suspect or vehicle. Another modern technological boon to both officer safety and efficient dispatching is the growing use of location transmitters in patrol vehicles. Such equipment serves to keep communications personnel constantly aware of changes in any unit's position by quickly glancing at a status map mounted in front of the dispatch console.

RECORDS

Every police department accumulates a vast store of information on everything from its own personnel, operating costs, and equipment to data on crime and criminals, traffic accidents, citations, arrests, fingerprints, and stolen property. Such data form the basis for evaluating the effectiveness of existing operations and charting new directions for change, as well as for dealing with the pressing problem of solving crimes and safeguarding the community. The essence of every records operation is the existence of highly efficient system for recording, storing, and retrieving information for ready use by departmental personnel. Whether the research and planning unit is trying to evaluate the success of a new pattern of beats on a given watch, or an individual investigator is seeking information about a suspect's modus operandi, the data requested must be readily accessible to be of use.

As the business of storing and retrieving records has become increasingly involved, many departments have moved from manual files to computerized data systems of the sort employed in modern business operations. The use of computers in the records section of a police department to store and retrieve data of all kinds makes it possible, for instance, for a detective to obtain such details as the time a crime occurred as well as the exact location and day of the week, in a fraction of the time it would take to search the relevant files manually. Even small departments are increasingly entering into time-sharing arrangements with other agencies, which gives them access to computer services they would be unable to afford on their own. As time goes on, the work of records specialists takes on an ever more important role as the foundation of virtually all departmental operations. There is every indication that records work will become much more of a civilian operation in the future, with clerical, business, and computer specialists appropriately taking the place of sworn police personnel.

However the records section of a department is staffed, and regardless of whether it makes use of manual or computerized files, its ability to provide requested information rapidly and accurately will have a major impact on both the morale and effectiveness of the department as a whole.

RESEARCH AND PLANNING

The best records system in the world is of little value unless the wealth of data it contains is somehow synthesized and analyzed for the purpose of evaluating the success of existing operations and making whatever changes seem to be indicated. It is here that the research and planning staff of a department plays a vital role, albeit one which often goes unrecognized or unappreciated by other personnel. The research and planning unit exists to help the police administrator intelligently evaluate the effectiveness of everything from management procedures to anticrime and traffic-safety programs to different types of physical equipment, report forms, and departmental regulations.

Its personnel are also involved in the administration and operation of various research grants from public and private sources, the nature or findings of which may result in dramatic changes in the way such divisions as patrol, traffic, and investigations operate. Perhaps one reason for the frequent unpopularity of research and planning staff has to do with the fact that they are so often catalysts of change and critics of well-established departmental traditions. This notwithstanding, their role is essential in making certain that the agency has constantly available to it the best possible information on every aspect of its operation. The patrol division, for instance, must depend on research and planning to give it data on patterns of crime occurrence by area and time in order to assure the best possible use of the work force and stay current with changing conditions. The same is true of traffic personnel seeking to identify the best possible use of a selective-enforcement program at a given time. The performance of individual officers as well as entire departmental programs must constantly be related to established standards and goals of the organization as a whole. Research and planning personnel are assuming an ever more important role in determining the future direction of law-enforcement agencies at every level of government.

INTELLIGENCE

In contrast to criminal acts which are highly individualistic and opportunistic, or which stem from such emotional factors as rage and jealousy, a certain amount of crime in every community is the direct result of often sophisticated organization and planning by those intent on realizing profit from the economic enterprise represented by crime. Today, organized criminal groups—structured along the same lines as modern business operations—are engaged in illegal activities ranging from bribery of public officials to extortion, narcotics importation, gambling, labor racketeering, and loan sharking. Such groups, and the individuals behind them, must be carefully monitored by law enforcement at all levels of government, with an aim to their eventual prosecution. This poses an extremely difficult task, because of the covert nature of most organized criminal activity and the fact that its leaders are effectively insulated from association with such street-level operations as narcotics sales and bookmaking.

It is primarily because of the threat to the community posed by organized crime that special intelligence units have been created within many municipal police departments. Intelligence personnel, working closely with their counterparts at both the state and federal levels, seek to develop both *tactical* and *strategic* information concerning the scope and operation of organized crime in the community and the individuals behind it. Tactical intelligence is aimed at such short-run goals as the immediate identification and prosecution of organized criminals, whereas strategic intelligence seeks to amass information on the overall structure, capabilities, weaknesses, and plans of organized criminal groups. Gathering both kinds of intelligence data is typically a tedious and time-consuming process, requiring the specialized skills and efforts of personnel set apart from the rest of the organizational structure. Most often, intelligence units work directly under the chief of police or sheriff. Because a great deal of organized crime is centered upon such vice operations as narcotics and gambling, intelligence units are often located within the vice division. The overarching purpose of every intelligence unit is to keep the chief administrator and his staff constantly informed as to the status of organized criminal activity at any time, through careful surveillance and analysis of information.

INTERNAL AFFAIRS

There are few occupations that provide as many opportunities for deviant, immoral, and illegal conduct as law enforcement. Indeed, police work may be described in sociological terms as a *deviant opportunity structure,* in the sense that most officers have available to them a seemingly limitless variety of illegal or unethical goods and services during the course of an average workday. There are countless opportunities to violate not only the criminal law and the ethical code of the police profession generally, but a myriad of departmental rules and regulations that relate to both. Instances of deviant behavior on the part of police officers range from accepting relatively minor gratuities, such as free meals, cigarettes, and liquor, to receiving sizable sums of money from gamblers, pimps, and narcotics dealers in return for allowing their illegal operations to continue. The risk of such forms of corruption occurring is far greater in such enforcement specialties as vice and narcotics work, if only because of their low public visibility and the frequent contact with known criminals which they involve. The wonder is not that police corruption is a problem in many communities, but that it is not a far greater problem than it is. Of the approximately 420,000 people employed in American law enforcement, only a tiny fraction ever becomes involved in unethical or corrupt practices of any kind, which must be interpreted as mute testimony to the dedication and integrity of most police officers. Yet the existence of even that tiny fraction, and the omnipresent potential for corruption even in the most professional agency, necessitates the existence of some individual or group charged with responsibility for "policing the police."

The task of investigating allegations of police misconduct may be handled by a separate internal-affairs or internal-investigations unit operating directly under the chief of police or sheriff, or—as is often the case in smaller departments—it may be delegated to a designated division head or staff officer on a rotating basis, as the need arises. The work of internal affairs is singularly unpopular even among the most ethical police officers. While the latter usually recognize the necessity of conducting such investigations in order to protect the integrity of the department as a whole, most officers nonetheless feel that the ferreting out of isolated instances of corruption exacts a heavy toll in the sense that it damages the standing of all officers. For this reason some officers have in the past failed to report instances of corrupt behavior. Evidence of such behavior in other cases has been concealed by basically honest officers out of a misguided sense of loyalty and responsibility to corrupt peers.

The work of an internal-affairs unit in a given case may be generated either by complaints on the part of other police officers, or by citizen allegations. However it actually begins, the sequence of steps is usually well established: a careful investigation of the complaint and the facts surrounding it, followed by a submission of findings to the chief of police for review and disposition. In some cases a review panel or trial board of other officers is also involved in examining the case, although responsibility for determining appropriate disciplinary measures is ususally left to the chief of police or sheriff. The seriousness of misconduct in some cases may warrant dismissal and referral for criminal prosecution.

COMMUNITY RELATIONS

The work of community-relations personnel has been much maligned and misunderstood by other police officers in the past. Often it is equated with the business of political image-making and is regarded as having little if anything to do with "real police work." In fact, community relations is an integral part of the overall police mission, and its success or failure will largely determine the success or failure of the department as a whole. It was pointed out earlier in this chapter that such developments as motorized patrol, the frequent rotation of officers to different neighborhoods, and the high degree of specialization in modern law enforcement have often served to isolate officers from the community they serve. The purpose of community-relations units is basically to close the gap which has appeared between the police and the public in recent years, with the important qualification that true "community relations" must remain the basic responsibility of every member of the department in each contact he or she has with the public. A citizen's positive or negative feelings about an entire law-enforcement agency and its personnel can often be traced to single encounters with a particular patrol officer, traffic officer, investigator, communications worker, or record clerk. In the final analysis, good community relations is the business of every employee of the department.

Community-relations units engage in a wide variety of activities, each of them intended to increase the level of understanding and communication between the police department and the public it serves. Basic to its operation is a recognition that the police represent an extremely scarce resource, and that they can accomplish their goals only with the active support and cooperation of the community. Thus, for instance, large numbers of police departments are currently engaged in "Help Stop Crime!" and neighborhood block-watch programs as part of their community-relations effort. Such programs seek to familiarize citizens with ways they can help the police curb such crimes as burglary, auto theft, and rape, while reducing their risk of victimization at the same time. Community-relations officers meet regularly with citizen groups for the purpose of giving them practical information about such things as proper locks and lighting and the identification of valuables in such a way as to increase the chance of recovering them in the event of a burglary.

Community-relations officers regularly speak before religious and civic groups, youth organizations, and schools. They also form a vital resource in many of the team-policing programs discussed earlier in Chapter 3, appearing at meetings along with beat officers to listen to citizen comments and complaints and help devise solutions to neighborhood problems. Such officers often assume responsibility for maintaining liaison with the media, and regularly sponsor such plans as "ride-along" programs for citizens and youth, tours of the department and its facilities, and demonstrations of equipment. Some community-relations efforts may be directed at improving police-citizen interaction in minority areas, or in other parts of the community where special needs and problems exist.

County Sheriff

Chapter 2 showed that the office that was to evolve into our modern-day position of sheriff was first brought to America in 1634 by English colonists. Since that time the position has gradually assumed most of the responsibilities that are characteristic of municipal police departments. The organization of most contemporary sheriff's departments closely parallels that of their city police counterparts, with several important exceptions, including responsibility for operating and maintaining all county jail facilities and taking charge of all persons housed in them— whether temporarily, as in the case of individuals awaiting arraignment and trial, or as a result of postconviction sentences of anywhere from several days to a year.

Some police departments maintain their own jail facilities, but most often these are limited to situations requiring extremely short-term detention and usually consist of little more than holding, or detention, cells where prisoners can be safely contained while the arresting officers complete the procedures necessary to remove them to the county jail. Responsibility for operating everything from maximum-security jail units to minimum-security rehabilitation centers and honor farms falls to the elected county sheriff in most areas. Unlike the city police department, the sheriff department's area of responsibility extends beyond enforcement of the criminal law to include a great many civil matters as well. Because the sheriff is an officer of the county court system, his duties include such services as provision of court bailiffs and handling a wide variety of court documents. Deputies, for instance, engage in such activities as serving witness subpoenas in civil and criminal cases, collecting court-ordered fees, and arresting individuals for whom outstanding court warrants exist.

Beyond these specialized duties, the official responsibility and legal authority of county sheriffs vary widely from one area to the next. In some communities, for instance, the sheriff—like his historical predecessor, the English *shire-reeve*—is the chief law-enforcement officer of the entire county, with authority far exceeding that of chiefs of police. Under such an arrangement, by law, the sheriff has the final say in all law-enforcement matters within the county, even in incorporated towns with their own full-time police departments. As might be imagined, friction, political conflict, and duplication of effort not infrequently result from such overlapping jurisdiction. Even where the sheriff is the chief law-enforcement officer of the county, his activity is often confined primarily to unincorporated areas in the interest of avoiding conflict and duplication of city police services. Often the sheriff represents a resource person to whom smaller police agencies can turn for assistance or for the assumption of a leadership role in the face of particular law-enforcement problems. As was noted in the last chapter, county sheriffs have historically been most powerful in the southern part of the United States, while in the north their role has often been limited to such duties as maintaining jail facilities and serving the courts. In some communities sheriffs have no general police or law-enforcement responsibilities to speak of.

State, Federal, and Private Agencies

STATE

Chapter 2 noted that state law-enforcement agencies first began to appear just after World War I, largely in response to such problems as auto theft, increased physical mobility of criminals, and corruption and inefficiency on the part of local police charged with responsibility for enforcing state laws. Over the years, law-enforcement activity at the state level has steadily expanded to take on an ever-increasing number of services and responsibilities.

The very words *state police* are synonymous in the minds of most citizens with "highway patrol." While the work of state law enforcement actually encompasses far more than this, the highway-patrol organization within most states is usually one of their largest and most visible law-enforcement operations. Although highway-patrol agencies are often thought of exclusively in terms of the enforcement of state traffic laws in unincorporated parts of the state and the investigation of accidents which occur in them, they typically perform a great many other services as well. These include, for instance, conducting statewide research on traffic accident and enforcement problems, as well as operating traffic safety programs, inspecting school buses and automobile safety equipment, operating weighing stations for commercial vehicles, and providing traffic-enforcement training for local police agencies.

Every state in the union—with the sole exception of Hawaii—presently has some form of state police organization, although the range of services provided by each varies considerably. About half the states limit the enforcement responsibility of state police agencies primarily to the area of traffic-law enforcement and vehicle regulation, while the remainder assume a variety of other duties as well. In some states this includes full authority for conducting statewide criminal investigations and providing requested services to local agencies that lack the resources to deal with particular cases and enforcement problems on their own. Some state police agencies provide to police and sheriff's departments such statewide facilities as central crime laboratories to receive and process evidence, computerized records-information systems, and specialized training programs for officers at the local level.

The enforcement of state laws pertaining to such things as narcotics, alcoholic beverages, fire prevention, fish and game, and labor practices, often involves the operation of highly specialized state agencies whose authority is limited to a particular problem area. In some states, however, a single agency may be charged with enforcement responsibility for such seemingly disparate fields as fire prevention and fish and game regulation. Certain areas of state law-enforcement activity, such as narcotics and beverage operations, require especially close liaison and coordination with local police agencies if they are to be effective.

FEDERAL

The last chapter discussed how federal law enforcement gradually evolved as a result of situations which neither local nor state jurisdictions were equipped to handle. Federal law-enforcement agencies have historically developed on a piecemeal basis to deal with highly specific problem areas. Beginning with the Revenue Cutter Service in 1789, which was established to combat smuggling, and continuing through to the 50 agencies which today make up the spectrum of federal law enforcement, no single enforcement entity has ever been allowed to acquire anything approaching broad police powers or unlimited jurisdiction. The establishment of basic controls on the scope of every federal law-enforcement operation has always been deemed essential to the preservation of a free society.

Of all the federal law-enforcement agencies that exist today, doubtless the Federal Bureau of Investigation (FBI) is most often regarded as symbolizing police activity at the federal level. Yet the FBI is *not* a police agency, but rather an investigative body organized to look into violations of specific federal laws. Today the FBI's area of enforcement responsibility encompasses some 170 different federal statutes and includes all laws not specifically assigned to some other federal agency. Operating under the attorney general within the Department of Justice, the FBI investigates such crimes as robbery and burglary of banks insured by the Federal Deposit Insurance Corporation, interstate transportation of stolen vehicles and property, kidnapping, assaults and homicides involving federal officers, mail fraud, espionage, and civil-rights violations, to mention only a few of its areas of responsibility.

Aside from its investigative efforts, the FBI also provides such services to local law enforcement as training officers, maintaining a national crime laboratory for analysis of evidence, compiling and publishing national crime statistics through its annual *Uniform Crime Reports,* and providing the most exhaustive records available on fingerprints, criminal arrest histories, and stolen vehicles and property. The National Crime Information Center (NCIC), discussed earlier in this chapter, which is operated by the FBI represents an invaluable means of communication and computer-based information sharing for the over 40,000 agencies, large and small, that make up American law enforcement today.

In addition to the FBI, the following agencies, although they are perhaps less well known to the public, make equally important contributions to the overall federal law-enforcement effort.

Drug Enforcement Administration (DEA). Once known as the Bureau of Narcotics and Dangerous Drugs (BNDD) and formerly located within the Treasury Department, the Drug Enforcement Administration has as its basic responsibility the task of enforcing all federal drug laws. Rather than becoming involved in street-level narcotics transactions, the DEA focuses its attention primarily on large-scale national and international trafficking in such drugs as heroin and cocaine, with particular concentration on those narcotics operations that are linked to organized crime. DEA agents work closely with local law-enforcement officials, providing everything from intelligence information and technical assistance to the funds necessary to effect large narcotics purchases. Personnel of the Drug Enforcement Administration deal with the regulation of legally controlled drugs as well as the enforcement of laws relating to such illegal substances as heroin.

Immigration and Naturalization Service (INS).   Officials within this agency are basically concerned with controlling the entrance of aliens into the United States, with the aim of preventing the illegal entry of such individuals. This responsibility falls to some 1700 border patrol officers, whose monumental task it is to continuously watch the nation's geographically vast borders and monitor points of entry for aliens seeking to enter the country illegally.

Bureau of Alcohol, Tobacco, and Firearms (ATF).   Historically, agents of this organization were primarily concerned with enforcement activities directed at the owners and operators of illegal "moonshine" stills, most of which were located in the southeastern part of the United States. While the regulation of liquor production and the collection of taxes due the government on it is still a concern of the ATF, the colorful moonshine era that produced the image of the federal "revenuer" (and which, incidentally, also produced a large number of fatalities among agents charged with enforcing federal liquor laws) has largely passed, owing to a combination of factors ranging from the prohibitively high costs of sugar today to successful federal efforts both to shut down moonshine operations and to make the public more aware of the physical risks of consuming unregulated alcoholic beverages. Today, the ATF's area of enforcement responsibility has expanded to include regulation of firearms and explosives, by virtue of federal legislation beginning with the Gun Control Act of 1968 and followed by the Explosives Act of 1970. ATF agents provide extensive assistance to state and local agencies in everything from bombing investigations to training personnel and providing laboratory services. Tracing firearms for local and state agencies represents yet another vital law-enforcement service of this federal agency.

Secret Service.   The last chapter showed that the Secret Service was originally formed to deal with the problem of counterfeiting, and was remarkably successful in its efforts. Largely because of the agency's success in suppressing counterfeiting and arresting counterfeiters, Secret Service agents were often borrowed by other governmental organizations to assist in their investigations. Over the years the responsibility of the Secret Service has steadily expanded. Today it not only investigates the counterfeiting of government currency, checks, securities, bonds, stamps, and other documents, but also has responsibility for protecting the president of the United States and his immediate family, as well as the vice-president, former presidents, and all presidential and vice-presidential candidates. Given the frequent public appearances of modern presidents, the task of providing them with adequate protection and security is both complex and anxiety-provoking. The Secret Service also oversees and supervises the Executive Protective Service, formerly the White House Police. The Executive Protective Service today not only guards the White House, but also provides security for foreign embassies in the Washington, D.C., area.

Bureau of Customs.   Whereas the Immigration and Naturalization Service is primarily concerned with preventing the movement of illegal aliens into the United States, the U.S. Bureau of Customs has as its basic concern controlling the smuggling of illegal merchandise into the country. Such material ranges from narcotics and firearms to gold, and necessarily involves close liaison between customs personnel and other federal agencies as well as local police. Customs patrol officers monitor points of entry at airports, seaports, and border crossings throughout the country in an effort to detect smuggling of contraband of all sorts.

Internal Revenue Service.   The IRS consists of three basic divisions: intelligence, audits, and collections. The intelligence division, while the smallest of the three in staff, has responsibility for investigating all violations of federal tax laws, and works closely with other agencies and the U.S. attorneys in preparing cases for prosecution. As a result of a concerted federal effort to identify and prosecute large-scale narcotics traffickers which was begun in 1971, the intelligence and audit divisions of the IRS are today engaged in a coordinated attempt to use existing tax laws as a means of disrupting major narcotics operations across the country. The prosecution of narcotics financiers, the imposition of stiff penalties, and the collections of taxes on unreported and drug-related income represent promising devices in the attempt to curb drug traffic. In addition to investigating tax frauds and other violations of federal tax laws, the IRS is involved in the massive task of providing the public with sufficient assistance and information to assure voluntary compliance with tax regulations.

This brief discussion of the most prominent federal law-enforcement agencies leaves untouched the efforts of a vast number of other equally important agencies, ranging from the office of United States Marshal to the Office of Naval Intelligence, the Air Force Office of Special Investigations, and the Military Police units of the various armed forces. Each of the 50 agencies that make up the business of federal policing plays a vital role in the success of the overall mission of law enforcement in our society.

PRIVATE AGENCIES

With the growth of crime in our society, private policing has become a major industry. Indeed, in 1969 over $8 billion was spent on security services and equipment in the United States. Today, of over 800,000 public and private security workers in the nation, only about half are public police officers. As a generic term, *private policing* denotes a wide variety of different activities. These extend, for example, from the work of private guards or watchkeepers at industrial plants and warehouses to private patrol officers in certain residential areas, armored-car services, and burglar alarm and investigative services on a fee or contract basis. Ordinarily, private police do not have peace-officer status and exist only to supplement the work of regular law-enforcement agencies where special problems or needs exist that are plainly beyond the scope and resources of regular police agencies. For example, despite the availability of regular police patrol on a limited basis, certain firms may wish to supplement this resource with private policing—both to minimize the risk of crimes such as burglary and vandalism and to lower the insurance premiums they must pay. In-house investigators may be retained to perform specialized services extending from preemployment background checks to the investigation of industrial espionage. Frequent criticism of some forms of private policing, such as guard and watchkeeper services, is sometimes voiced on the grounds that personnel employed in these areas are often poorly trained and therefore may constitute a menace to public safety. This notwithstanding, all indications are that public security will remain a multibillion-dollar growth industry for some years to come.

SUMMARY

Like a soldier on the front lines whose activities are made possible by the logistical support of other personnel, the patrol officer's work is inextricably tied to the work of countless others. This chapter sought to go "beyond the uniform," examining the contributions to the overall municipal police mission made by criminal investigators, vice and narcotics officers, youth-services bureaus or juvenile units, and records, communications criminalists, and other personnel who fall within the amorphous but important category of "support and auxiliary services." We attempted to penetrate the irrational mystique that surrounds the detective of television and motion-picture fame, and explored the work-a-day activities of the real-life investigator. It was accordingly seen that such things as tedious records examinations and a team approach loom much larger than the revolver and trench coat of the fictional media detective. The traditional cleavage and friction that often exists between patrol officers and investigators was explored, and basic differences between the two roles were considered.

Vice work, involving, as it typically does, the enforcement of laws about which the public is ambivalent at best, was discussed as posing special pressures and problems for those assigned to it. The juvenile or youth-services bureau was described as being unquestionably one of the most difficult and challenging of all assignments within the police department, insofar as it requires of those within it the skills of both a police officer and a counselor.

NOTES

1. Arthur Niederhoffer, *Behind The Shield* (New York: Doubleday, 1969), p.82.
2. Ibid., p. 83.
3. It is interesting to note, however, that these traditionally "personal" crimes tend to become increasingly anonymous and impersonal under conditions of modern urban life. The New York City Police Department, for instance, reports that of the 1554 people who were killed there in 1974, 34 percent were total strangers to their assailants. From 1965 to 1975 the incidence of felony murder—killings which occur in the course of some other felony—increased over 300 percent nationwide.
4. Federal Bureau of Investigation, *Uniform Crime Reports* (1971), pp. 122–123.
5. *Time,* "The Youth Crime Plague," July, 1977, p. 19.
6. John P. Kenny and Dan Pursuit, *Police Work With Juveniles* (Springfield, Ill.: Thomas, 1962), p.10
7. Alfred Blumstein, *Systems Analysis and the Criminal Justice System,* American Academy of Political and Social Sciences 374 (1967), pp. 92–100.
8. See Task Force Report: *Juvenile Delinquency,* President's Commission on Law Enforcement and The Administration of Justice (Washington, D.C.: U.S. Government Printing Office), p. 26.
9. Ibid., p. 19.
10. Kenny and Pursuit, *Police Work,* p. 10.
11. Irving Piliavin and Scott Briar, "Police Encounters With Juveniles," *American Journal of Sociology* 70 (September, 1964), pp. 206–14.
12. Albert J. Reiss, Jr., *The Police and The Public* (New Haven, Conn.: Yale University Press, 1971), p. 137.
13. See Daniel Cruse and Jesse Rubin, *Determinants of Police Behavior: A Summary* (Criminal Justice Monograph) (Washington, D.C.: U.S. Government Printing Office, June, 1973).
14. George Kirkham, *Signal Zero* (New York: Lippincott, 1976), p. 176.
15. Ibid., p. 180.
16. Ibid., p. 187.
17. See, for example, Susan Brownmiller, *Against Our Will: Men, Women and Rape* (New York: Simon and Schuster, 1975).
18. President's Commission on Law Enforcement and Administration of Justice, *The Challenge of Crime in a Free Society* (Washington, D.C.: U.S. Government Printing Office, 1973), p. 189.
19. Kirkham, *Signal Zero,* pp. 133–134.

SELECTED READINGS

Paul B. Weston and Kenneth M. Wells, *Elements of Criminal Investigation* (Englewood Cliffs, N.J.: Prentice-Hall, 1970).

John P. Kenny and Dan G. Pursuit, *Police Work With Juveniles and The Administration of Juvenile Justice,* 4th ed. (Springfield, Ill: Thomas, 1971).

Edwin M. Schur, *Crimes Without Victims* (Englewood Cliffs, N.J.: Prentice-Hall, 1965).

George Kirkham, *Signal Zero* (New York: Lippincott, 1976).

Two

THE POLICE IN A SYSTEM OF SYSTEMS

Part Two shifts to a setting of the police as a system within other systems. Chapter 5 begins with a review of the activities of the police, as the "long arm of the law," that control the quantity and quality of the cases that enter the pipeline of criminal justice by way of the intake valve of the police phase. But the police are shown to be more than that: They have direct relationships throughout the criminal-justice system, participating actively at some points (as in the trial itself when they give testimony) and less directly at other points (as when consulted by probation officials preparing reports for judges determining sentences).

Beyond the criminal-justice system the police have relationships of two kinds, which Chapter 6 explores. First is their relationship with those systems, institutions, groups, and individuals handling aspects of criminal justice that help serve the police—such as prevention and detection of crime, tasks for which the agencies of criminal justice would seem to have primary responsibility. Criminal justice, however, will be seen as far from monopolized by the formal members of the criminal justice system; indeed, criminal justice is a widely shared responsibility with a significant amount of responsibility borne by the private sector. Second is the connection of the police with the systems they serve— agencies that have primary responsibility for the support services the officer deals with, such as the agencies that service the alcoholic, the lost child, the injured motorist, the stray animal, the fallen power line, the abandoned vehicle. Thus, the police are in a reciprocal relationship: The nonpolice systems perform criminal justice tasks for the police and the police provide services for the nonpolice systems.

Beyond these directly related systems are other auxiliary systems in which the police are involved. The police relate to other parts of the executive branch of government, and the executive branch relates in special ways to the legislative and judicial branches. In addition, the municipal police, on which this text focuses, who are at the local level of government, relate to the state, national, and even international levels of government, with special problems posed by the American system of federalism which dictates that governing powers be divided between national and state governments.

Chapter 7 continues the exploration of the environment of the police by looking first into the political context of public opinion, political parties, and interest groups, and then beyond the political system to the even wider environment of society as a whole, which includes the influences of ideas and spiritual values at one level and material conditions of geography and climate at yet another level.

5
THE POLICE AND THE CRIMINAL-JUSTICE SYSTEM

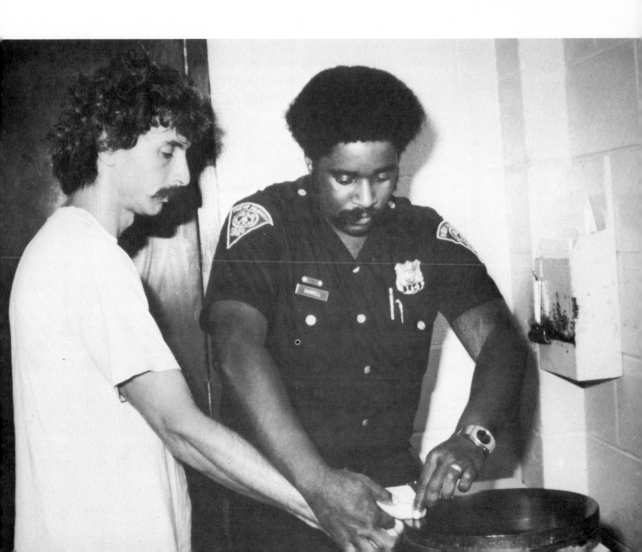

This chapter and Chapters 6 and 7 will discuss five levels or conceptions of the relationship of the police to their environment: (1) as the "intake valve" of the "pipeline" of criminal justice, (2) as a participant in or influence on many of the decisions made in the criminal-justice system along the pipeline, (3) as sharer of the functions of criminal justice with institutions beyond the criminal-justice system, (4) as an agent sharing in the functions of systems beyond criminal justice, and (5) as an element of other systems beyond the community but directly related to criminal justice—that is, in the wider environment of government, politics, and society. The first and second conceptions of the relationship of the police to their environment are discussed in this chapter; the third and fourth levels are taken up in Chapter 6, and the fifth level in Chapter 7.

The Police As Intake Valve

At the first level, the police are seen as the first phase in the flow of cases into the criminal-justice system, as an intake valve serving up suspects to be processed by prosecutor, court, and corrections. In this conception the police appear to have little if anything to do with what follows down the pipeline, other than controlling the volume that flows into it. This is a useful conception of the relationship of the police and the criminal-justice system, because there *is* a flow of cases and the police *do* bring most of the cases into the system. And the police have less to do with what happens later than do the district attorneys, judges, prison officials, and parole commissioners who more directly influence the movement of offenders through—and out of—the system. But this picture is limited because, even if it reveals the *qualitative* as well as the *quantitative* control the police have in their filtering function, it does not reveal the connections between the police and those other parts of the system which seem so far removed from the intake function. In addition, this picture obscures the other systems that relate to the police and the other elements of criminal justice. It gives rise to an impression of the police as isolated gatekeepers of criminal justice.

In the most elementary conception of the place of the police, they are at the beginning of the entire process of criminal justice. The President's Crime Commission put it simply:

> The popular, or even the lawbook, theory of everyday criminal process oversimplifies in some respects and overcomplicates in others what usually happens. That theory is that when an infraction of the law occurs, a policeman finds, if he can, the probable offender, arrests him and brings him promptly before a magistrate. If the offense is minor the magistrate disposes of it forthwith; if it is serious, he holds the defendant for further action and admits him to bail. The case then is turned over to a prosecuting attorney who charges the defendant with a specific statutory crime. This charge is subject to review by a judge at a preliminary hearing of the evidence and in many places if the offense charged is a felony, by a grand jury that can dismiss the charge, or affirm it by delivering it to a judge in the form of an indictment. If the defendant pleads "not guilty" to the charge he comes to trial; the facts of his case are marshaled by prosecuting and defense attorneys and presented, under the supervision of a judge, through witnesses, to a jury. If the jury finds the defendant guilty, he is sentenced by the judge to a term in prison, where a systematic attempt to convert him into a law-abiding citizen is made, or to a term of probation, under which he is permitted to live in the community as long as he behaves himself.[1]

The flow chart presented in the commission's report (Figure 5.1) clearly reproduces this understanding of the system as a pipeline, with the police placed distinctly at the beginning, and crime (observed by or reported to the police) flowing through the police to the criminal-justice system beyond it. Thereafter, the flow diminishes as cases make their exit from the pipeline, passing into other pipelines (such as juvenile justice) or back into the pool of the citizenry as a whole. A thin pipe represents nonpolice referrals to the juvenile-justice system, but nothing represents nonpolice referrals to the adult justice system. (This, of course, does not mean there are none, for some, such as public corruption cases, originate with the prosecutor's investigations.)

The metaphor of pipeline suggests, correctly, that the police are the intake valve controlling the quality and quantity of cases entering the

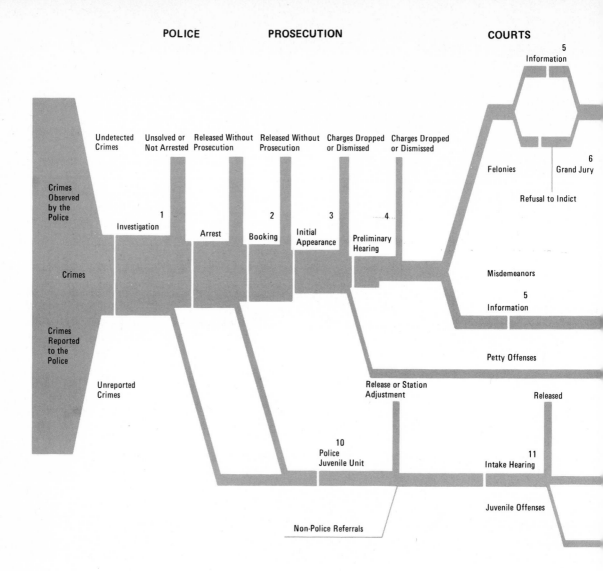

POLICE **PROSECUTION** **COURTS**

5
Information

Undetected Crimes

Unsolved or Not Arrested

Released Without Prosecution

Released Without Prosecution

Charges Dropped or Dismissed

Charges Dropped or Dismissed

Felonies 6 Grand Jury

Crimes Observed by the Police

Refusal to Indict

1 Investigation

Arrest

2 Booking

3 Initial Appearance

4 Preliminary Hearing

Crimes

Misdemeanors

5 Information

Crimes Reported to the Police

Petty Offenses

Unreported Crimes

Release or Station Adjustment

Released

10 Police Juvenile Unit

11 Intake Hearing

Non-Police Referrals

Juvenile Offenses

---

1 May continue until trial.

2 Administrative record of arrest. First step at which temporary release on bail may be available.

3 Before magistrate, commissioner, or justice of peace. Formal notice of charge, advice of rights. Bail set. Summary trials for petty offenses usually conducted here without further processing.

4 Preliminary testing of evidence against defendant. Charge may be reduced. No separate preliminary hearing for misdemeanors in some systems.

5 Charge filed by prosecutor on basis of information submitted by police or citizens. Alternative to grand jury indictment; often used in felonies, almost always in misdemeanors.

6 Reviews whether Government evidence sufficient to justify trial. Some States have no grand jury system; others seldom use it.

Figure 5.1 A General View of the Criminal-Justice System. This chart seeks to present a simple yet comprehensive view of the movement of cases through the criminal-justice system. Procedures in individual jurisdictions may vary from the pattern shown here. The differing weights of line indicate the relative volumes of cases disposed of at various points in the system, but this is only suggestive since no nationwide data of this sort exists.

Source: President's Commission on Law Enforcement and the Administration of Justice, *Challenge of Crime in a Free Society.* [Washington, D.C.: U.S. Government Printing Office, 1967], pp. 5–9)

CORRECTIONS

Charge Dismissed   Acquitted

Probation

7
Arraignment   Trial   Sentencing

Revocation

Penitentiary

Out of System

Guilty Pleas

8
Reduction of Charge

Appeal

Parole

Revocation

9
Habeas Corpus

Charge Dismissed   Acquitted

Probation

7
Arraignment   Trial   Sentencing

Revocation

Out of System

Guilty Pleas

Fine   Jail

Nonpayment

Released

Probation

Adjudicatory Hearing

Revocation

Juvenile Institution

Out of System

12
Nonadjudicatory Disposition

Parole

Revocation

7   Appearance for plea; defendant elects trial by judge or jury (if available); counsel for indigent usually appointed here in felonies. Often not at all in other cases.

8   Charge may be reduced at any time prior to trial in return for plea of guilty or for other reasons.

9   Challenge on constitutional grounds to legality of detention. May be sought at any point in process.

10   Police often hold informal hearings, dismiss or adjust many cases without further processing.

11   Probation officer decides desirability of further court action.

12   Welfare agency, social services, counselling, medical care, etc., for cases where adjudicatory handling not needed.

system. The patrol officer has wide-ranging discretion and can decide whether something should be done about an incident, whether it is the police who should do something about it, and if so, whether someone should be entered in the pipeline. The alternatives are to do nothing, to see that someone else does something, or to see that someone goes into some system other than the criminal-justice system, such as the mental-health system.

The styles of policing described by James Q. Wilson as "watchman" (emphasizing order maintenance), "legalistic" (emphasizing law enforcement), and "service" (bridging both styles but responding informally) indicate that the flow of cases into the system can vary in kind and amount by the case-selection and case-handling policies of the police departments, depending upon which style they follow.[2] For instance, a legalistically run department is likely to treat a "public drunk" the same regardless of where he or she is, and to handle the situation with an arrest. A department using the watchman style is more likely to take into consideration the situation of the subject (for example, the neighborhood) and the visibility or disorderliness of the offense, and to either ignore it or deal with it informally by referral (diversion) to an agency outside the criminal justice system. A department using the service style is likely to do something other than ignore the situation, but will not do something "heavy-handed" like arresting the alcoholic.

Moreover, the pressure on the police to increase their "clearance rates," or the ratio of solved crimes to known crimes, can be influenced by a department's policy on recognition of crimes. For instance, Jerome Skolnick, in his classic study, *Justice Without Trial,* an account of this process, shows that the police can place cases in two categories that remove them from the "uncleared" or "unsolved" categories: These are "unfounded" and "suspicious circumstance." By categorizing a rape complaint as unfounded, the department avoids putting it in the records as uncleared or unsolved. Skolnick's comparison of major cities, called "Westville" and "Eastville" in his study, indicates that one department was strict about labeling complaints as actual offenses, while the other was lax and used the nonoffense categories, thus altering the appearance but not the reality of their effectiveness.[3]

Skolnick described a more serious aspect of this power of the police to control the flow of cases: They can "reverse the hierarchy of penalties." This means that a defendant who "cops a plea" to one charge may admit to several other crimes, thus "clearing" them as far as the police records are concerned. Yet the defendant is penalized for the one crime to which he or she pleads guilty, and is neither held accountable for the greater criminality implied by the commission of other crimes (a consideration of importance in a parole hearing) nor liable in future arrest for the "cleared" crimes. The effect is that, in the interest of efficiency (a high rate of crime-clearance), an offender is punished much less severely than the accumulation of crimes would otherwise require.[4]

The power of the police to judge how crimes should be classified affects the totals they send to the Federal Bureau of Investigation in Washington for compilation into the *Uniform Crime Reports (UCRs)*, the annual reports of the volume and rate of crime in this country. Until a decade ago the *UCRs* were virtually the only data on crime, so scholars as well as the public and their politicians were dependent on the police for this vital statistic. The power of the police to distort the figures gives them great influence over how crime and police work are evaluated.

Donald J. Black, in his study of the "official recognition of crimes" in his "Production of Crime Rates," found several influences on the recognition of deviant behavior: seriousness of crime (legally serious crimes are recognized more than legally minor crimes); complainant's preference for disposition of one sort or another (crimes are recognized by the police more if the complainant wants the police to act); relational distance between offender and victim (the closer the relationship the less likely, the further the relationship the more likely the police will recognize the offense); complainant's deference to the police (the more deferential to police the more likely that the police will recognize the offense). Black found that racial status of the offender makes no difference, while white-collar status makes only slight difference in the likelihood that police will recognize an offense. As Black points out, these findings challenge the reliability of official crime rates; they also indicate distortions in the subsequent workings of the rest of the system, from investigation through arrest and conviction. The police are the pivotal point in this filtering of complaints from the public, hence in what society officially recognizes as crime.[5]

Armando Morales has shown another effect of this intake function: how police department attitudes toward minorities dramatically influence the arrest rates. According to his comparison of two precincts in Los Angeles, one a poor, Mexican-American precinct and the other a middle-class, Anglo-Saxon neighborhood, the police department assigns more patrol officers to the Mexican-American community, apparently based on the department's anticipation that more crime will occur there. Because there are more patrol officers there to observe and hear about such crimes as drunkenness and drunk driving, more of those crimes are recorded by the police; hence, more of those crimes are attributed to the Mexican-American community—when reports of other, more serious crimes were in fact lower there than in the Anglo-Saxon community! Thus Morales

BECAUSE THERE WERE MORE COPS IN THE AREA TO OBSERVE CRIME ⟶

concludes that police attitudes lead to a policy that, as if by a self-fulfilling prophecy, increases crime rates accordingly, thereby "proving" the initial, erroneous supposition.[6]

The Police as an Influence on Criminal Justice

The second level of understanding reveals a number of ways in which the police influence the decisions of the other institutions of the criminal-justice system, and even participate in many of them. Patrol officers can be observed walking about in the corridors of prosecution, adjudication, and corrections institutions; they are directly involved in these operations. These links are important in establishing the full extent of police activity and responsibility. This conception, however, focuses attention on the criminal-justice system alone; it does not trace the police officer's activities in the other systems to which she or he also relates. These connections constitute a complex network of relationships within what can be understood as a system of systems, of linkages of interdependency among the systems of the community, with the police in the very middle of them.

The conception of the police as an intake valve, as the starting point and an important controlling point in the criminal justice system is limited by its suggestion that police involvement in the system ends with the deposit of defendants at the doorstep of the courts. In reality, the police are involved at many other points. So the conventional division of the system of criminal justice into police, courts, and corrections as a process that carries an offender from one to the next in strict succession should not be allowed to obscure the connections between the police and critical decision points in the operations of other parts and processes of the system.

PRETRIAL PROCEDURES

Pretrial Detention. Pretrial detention is accomplished not only by jails, as discussed in Chapter 6, but also in other ways. For example, the bail bondsman "ties" the accused by a financial commitment to the subsequent appearances he or she is obliged to make. Today this function of detention is increasingly the responsibility of the police, but in many cities it remains in the hands of the professional bondsman. The police relate closely to the bondsman at two levels: One is that of sharing information on the whereabouts of the accused; the other is that of collusion. Paul B. Wice has stated the charge this way:

> This illicit relationship [between police and bondsmen] supposedly begins with the arresting officer or someone in the stationhouse recommending a particular bondsman to the defendant. At the end of the month, the policeman can expect to receive a kickback from that bondsman, based on the number of clients referred.[7]

This practice is declining, but it continues to exist in some agencies.

When the process shifts away from the police phase into the prosecution and court phases, one expects a decline in police involvement and influence. But that is not always so. Rosett and Cressey answer the question of "Who runs the courthouse?" this way:

> In some cities, the police department is very stong politically, and its officials do much of the selecting [of offenses and charges]. . . . In some cities the complaint officer [who drafts charges under which arrest warrants are issued] is a senior policeman. He sits in a courtlike room and is addressed by lawyers, who presumably know his true status, as "Your Honor."[8]

Preliminary Hearing. Following the arrest and booking steps comes a preliminary hearing. This is the point at which the process begins to develop in its formality and its adversary quality. It is more formal because the process depends less on the subjective factors of personality and police dominance and more on the objective factors of legal authority and status.[9] In addition, the process begins to resemble the carefully prescribed trial (discussed below), with almost ritualistic movements. The preliminary hearing is closer to the adversary process because it is no longer, at least in theory, a bureaucratic disposition of a disturbance. The "subject" of police action emerges as the "accused," entitled to (and usually represented by) counsel, protected by an array of rights, and empowered to stand up to the state as an equal.[10] It is important to note, however, that this is the "theory" rather than the "practice" of criminal justice, because the reality, which Abraham Blumberg describes in *Criminal Justice,* is often closer to an informal, cooperative process. This is indicated by the President's Crime Commission:

> In direct contrast to the policeman, the magistrate before whom a suspect is first brought usually exercises less discretion than the law allows him. He is entitled to inquire into the facts of the case, into whether there are grounds for holding the accused. He seldom does. He seldom can. The more promptly an arrested suspect is brought into magistrate's court, the less likelihood there is that much information about the arrest other than the arresting officer's statement will be available to the magistrate. Moreover, many magistrates, especially in big cities, have such congested

calendars that it is almost impossible for them to subject any case but an extraordinary one to prolonged scrutiny.[11]

The preliminary hearing also involves the setting of bail (except in minor cases, where it is set according to a schedule administered by the police in the booking process). If the magistrate determines that the case is one with sufficient evidence or reasonable grounds to believe the crime has been committed and that the accused committed it, the accused will be held for grand-jury indictment (or "bound over" to the grand jury, in the parlance of many jurisdictions). In such cases the magistrate will also set bail if the offense is "bailable"; that is, if it is less than the most serious offenses (usually the capital crimes), for which bail is not mandatory under the Eighth Amendment. The issue in setting bail is, officially, what amount of money set as bail will induce the accused to appear at the subsequent procedural steps, but unofficially, in many cases, the issue is whether the accused is dangerous and what amount of money set as bail will be too large for her or him to obtain, thereby preventing release. On both of these questions the magistrate will rely heavily on the arresting officer for the information that goes into this decision.

The judge, magistrate, or justice of the peace (according to local terminology) who holds the preliminary hearing in cases of felonies may actually conduct the trial in cases involving misdemeanors. *Trials* (discussed more fully below) are proceedings in which guilt or innocence are determined; whereas *preliminary hearings* determine whether there is sufficient evidence to go to trial. In many cases of trials at this level, the police officer is the principal witness; in traffic trials, the officer is usually the only witness, unless an accident has occurred. In some "J.P.," or justice of the peace trials, the police officer is virtually the prosecutor of the case. Likewise, in the more serious felony cases, the preliminary hearing features testimony of police officers on the issue of whether there are reasonable grounds to believe that the accused committed the offense. The preliminary hearing is less formal than the trial itself, so the full array of witnesses available to the prosecution is not necessary to establish reasonable grounds, and defense witnesses ordinarily are not heard. Thus it is often sufficient for the police officer alone to testify, not only because he or she is more readily available than other prosecution witnesses, but because it saves other witnesses the inconvenience of a double appearance, then and later at trial.

The authority of the system to detain a person is sometimes tested in a hearing that may come before or after the preliminary hearing, if a magistrate or judge issues a *writ of habeas corpus* based on the prisoner's petition, or request. This means the police must bring the prisoner into court and explain to the judge why he or she is being held. They must be able, then or soon after, to demonstrate that there are legal reasons to support the charge or, if there has been no charge at all, they must make a formal accusation. The burden of meeting the system's obligations at this point is on the police.

The *grand jury* is a group of citizens (traditionally with 23 members) who formally accuse a person of a felony, the next step in serious cases. Whether or not the magistrate has found reasonable grounds to believe a crime has been committed and that the accused has committed it, the grand jury may take up the issue and hear evidence presented only by the prosecution and favorable to its side. This one-sided affair, however, is a protection of the accused because it passes the accusation through a filter of judgment reflecting the citizenry as a whole; without it there can be no trial (except in those states that have substituted the "prosecutor's information" for the indictment). (The *prosecutor's information* is a formal accusation and is, for all purposes, equivalent to an indictment.) The prosecutor's evidence in the grand jury typically relies heavily on testimony of law-enforcement officers, for much the same reason that the preliminary hearing does: convenience and, in many cases, the pivotal importance of an officer's contribution of information on the issues involved. Like other citizens, the police officer will be subpoenaed to appear and give evidence; an officer cannot refuse to appear except by paying the penalty for "contempt," which is imprisonment until he changes his mind and testifies or the term of the grand jury comes to an end.

Some states have done away with the grand jury; there and in other states that permit some crimes to be charged without indictment, accusation is by means of the prosecutor's information or word (like the grand jury's word), that reasonable grounds exist for the accusation. Prosecutors, who dominate grand juries anyway, will rely heavily on police information for their own decisions, much as they would present police information for a grand jury's decision.

Arraignment. The arraignment, or the defendant's appearance before a judge with jurisdiction to try such cases, follows the formal accusation (indictment or information) in felony cases. The charges are announced to the defendant, who is given a choice of pleas: guilty, not guilty, no plea (which is equivalent to not guilty), or *nolo contendere* (which is equivalent in federal courts to a plea of guilty). If the defendant pleads guilty (or *nolo* in federal cases), the judge may sentence the accused immediately, but will usually take further time to study the case. If the defendant pleads not guilty, then (or soon after) the judge sets a date for the trial. This step, the arraignment, is one of the few in which the police have virtually no role to play. Even at the arraignment, however, if a guilty plea is expected and sentencing will take place immediately, the police

officer may be called upon for information that may be pertinent to the
sentencing decision.

The formal charging decision, which involves the grand jury and the
prosecutor's information, reflects one of the most critical and complex
judgments in the criminal process. The responsibility for it rests mainly
with the prosecutor, as the President's Crime Commission points out:

> The key administrative officer in the processing of cases is the prosecutor.
> Theoretically the examination of the evidence against a defendant by
> a judge at a preliminary hearing, and its reexamination by a grand jury,
> are important parts of the process. Practically they seldom are because a
> prosecutor seldom has any difficulty in making a prima facie case against
> a defendant. In fact most defendants waive their rights to preliminary
> hearings and much more often than not grand juries indict precisely as
> prosecutors ask them to. The prosecutor wields almost undisputed sway
> over the pretrial progress of most cases. He decides whether to press a
> case or drop it. He determines the specific charges against a defendant.
> When the charge is reduced, as it is in as many as two-thirds of all cases
> in some cities, the prosecutor is usually the official who reduces it.[12]

This is an awesome responsibility, and it is ordinarily exercised with
careful regard for a multitude of considerations, among which is the
interest of the police. Many of the factors influencing the prosecutor's
charging decision closely resemble those influencing the police officer's
arresting decision (which will be taken up in detail in Chapter 6). Such
factors as attitude of the victim, cost to the system, and harm to the
suspect, which weigh on the decisions of both police officer and prosecutor,
indicate that the two share (without necessarily agreeing on) their perception of the participants and the needs, interests, and values operating
within the system. In a study by Frank W. Miller in the American Bar
Foundation's Survey of the Administration of Criminal Justice in the
United States, many of these factors are presented, lending support to
his observations of the ways in which the police exercise informal influence on the prosecutor:

> The police may affect the charging decision both negatively and positively.
> Most simply, if the police do not think that prosecution is warranted
> despite adequate evidence, they release suspects without calling them to
> the attention of the prosecutor at all. Less simply, they may request
> a warrant, but may make obvious to the prosecutor that they do not
> believe that prosecution is desirable. In many cases prosecutors agree with
> the police assessment, but in others they simply defer to it. Sometimes
> this reflects recognition of particular expertise in some classes of cases. . . .
> In other instances, a negative charging decision reflects awareness of

the need for cooperation to permit police to carry out enforcement objectives. . . . Frequently, the issue is not whether to charge at all, but which charge to select. Here, too, the prosecutor frequently cooperates with the police. Police requests for undercharging to avoid extra court appearances are sometimes treated sympathetically by prosecutors.

The influence on charge selection is perhaps greatest when the police report which accompanies a warrant request also contains a recommended charge. . . . When, in addition, the police officer is permitted to "shop around" for an assistant prosecutor whom he believes will be more receptive to police suggestions than would other assistants, police influence on the charging decisions increases. . . .[13]

Those influences clearly indicate the important role of the police in the charging process. This influence carries over into the criminal process, affecting not only the charging phase itself but subsequent stages of trial, sentence, and corrections.

Pretrial Motions.   Pretrial motions, or requests for a ruling or order of the judges, are very important to the prosecutor in the period between arraignment and trial. The star witness at some of the more important motions is the police officer; the consultant in preparing for many motions is likewise the police officer. For instance, one kind of pretrial motion, for the *bill of particulars,* attempts to gain more detailed information for the defense about the charges. A prosecutor who is ordered to provide more particulars can often do so from information in his or her own file; sometimes, however, the prosecutor must turn to the police officer for such information. In addition, the prosecutor discusses with the police what information must be withheld (e.g., the identity of an informer), even at the cost of losing the case.

The most common pretrial motion made by the defense is a motion to suppress evidence because it was illegally obtained in violation of constitutional rights (which will be taken up in Chapter 6). The principal witness in such hearings is the police officer who made the arrest and search or handled the investigation. The officer is not only the main witness in such hearings, but because the defense is on the offensive, the officer is on the defensive, justifying his actions as if he himself were on trial. Preparation for such hearings involves delicate judgments of what can and cannot be revealed, sometimes to protect informers, to protect other information, to protect practices of the department, or even to protect the officer whose conduct might otherwise be challenged in a costly suit. There is often a spirit of teamwork between prosecutor and police in these matters: The prosecutor directs the strategy and tactics, to be sure, but often consults and sometimes defers to the needs of the police in deciding the objectives. In any case, the police officer must be prepared—sometimes even coached by the prosecutor—in the testimony he will give.

TRIAL

The trial is the formal process, highly refined and thoroughly adversary in nature, by which the issue of the defendant's guilt is resolved. It involves the presentation of evidence by the prosecution to prove *beyond a reasonable doubt* that the defendant committed the acts which constitute the crime; the defense presents evidence aimed to counter such evidence or brings into question certain elements of the defendant's capacity to commit a crime, such as sanity, after which the prosecution must prove sanity.

The *trier of fact* or fact-finder in the trial is, in the popular view, the jury; but the judge may find the facts without a jury in a so-called bench trial, if the defendant *waives*, or forgoes, the right to trial by jury. A substantial portion of all criminal trials, particularly of the less serious offenses, are nonjury trials because they are simpler (no jury has to be selected). They can be scheduled earlier and are less costly, especially in attorney's fees. In jury trials the job of the judge is to umpire the competition between the prosecution and the defense by ruling on questions of procedure and evidence, much as if it were a game, with one side or the other "off sides" or in "illegal procedure."

Sooner or later most police officers will be witnesses in a trial; they undergo the ordeal many times during their careers. As witnesses, they are asked questions by the prosecutor that elicit information to prove some proposition involved in the case against the accused. The prosecutor, after some questions to put the witness at the place and time of the occurrence, will be permitted to ask no more *leading questions,* which suggest their answers. The prosecutor will then ask questions that permit the officer to give a narrative statement of what he observed or to respond with yes or no answers.

The lawyer for the defense will interrupt from time to time with objections of various kinds: that the question calls for (or the answer promises to give) information that is *irrelevant,* or not *probative of the point at issue;* that is *immaterial,* or not closely connected to the point; that is *cumulative,* or *redundant* (15 or 20 witnesses already testified to the same thing). A number of other reasons also bar an answer, including its *incompetence,* meaning its origin in an unconstitutional search or some other reason that makes it inappropriate for introduction, even if it is relevant and material. When the prosecutor finishes examining the witness, the defense counsel takes over for *cross-examination.* The police officer, under cross-examination, will often experience a withering scrutiny of his experience as an observer, his powers of perception, his possible interest in the victim or defendant or in the outcome of the case *(bias)*. After this ordeal the prosecutor may question the witness again to "rehabilitate" him and his testimony, that is, to overcome any "bad light" resulting from the cross-examination.

Judges rule on objections, overruling some, sustaining others. They tend, however, to err in favor of the defense for the understandable reason that they can avoid appellate-court scrutiny of erroneous rulings if the defense wins, because verdicts of acquittal are ordinarily not appealable. By sustaining the defense objections to prosecution testimony and overruling prosecution objections to defense testimony, a judge helps the defense make the police witness look worse rather than better.

Observing all this is the *jury,* which will decide which side's evidence is sufficient (the prosecution's to a level of persuasion *beyond a reasonable doubt,* the defense's to a level making for reasonable doubt). The jury is traditionally a body of "twelve good men and true"—now including women, too—selected from among the citizens of the jurisdiction. In some jurisdictions there is no right to a jury trial for misdemeanors; in other jurisdictions the number of jurors has been reduced to six and nonunanimous verdicts are permitted, rather than the traditional unanimous verdict.

At the beginning of the trial, before opening statements are made by either side, the jury is selected in a process called *voir dire,* by which each juror reveals factors that might bias her or him. All *veniremen* (people drawn from the community, from whom the jury itself will be selected) are asked questions, and if anything is revealed that is likely to produce bias, such as a relationship with a defendant, or employment by a law-enforcement agency, or inability to function adequately as a fact-finder (e.g., deafness), the venireman will be excused "for cause." In addition to excusals for cause, both sides have a certain number of what are called *peremptory challenges,* by which veniremen may be excused without any stated reason.

There is a great deal of lore involved in jury selection, most of it having to do with supposedly prejudicial factors. For instance, northern European types are said to favor the prosecution because they are cool, law-abiding, orderly; conversely, Mediterraneans are thought to favor the defense because they are passionate, rule-flaunting, disorderly types. There may be some truth in such stereotypes, but surely not so much as justifies the lengthy (sometimes months long) process of selecting juries. Some lawyers opt for the first 12 to come into the box, and the experience of England, where prolonged *voir dire* does not occur, would suggest that there is no need for the American style of jury selection.

Once the jury is selected, the two sides make opening statements, although it is common for the defense to waive its right to make its opening statement at the beginning, waiting until after the close of the case for the prosecution. The prosecution presents *testimonial evidence* in the manner indicated above, any *physical evidence* that may be useful (guns, contraband, footprint casts, and so forth), and *expert testimony* (on fingerprint comparisons, for example) aimed to prove beyond a reasonable doubt that the defendant is guilty. At the close of the case for the prosecution, the defense may—and usually does—make a motion for a *directed verdict,* arguing that the evidence for the prosecution, taken as favorably for that side as it can be, does not meet the standard of persuasion, "beyond a reasonable doubt." If the judge agrees, he or she will grant the motion and direct the jury to bring in a verdict of acquittal (or not guilty)—about which the jury has no choice.

It is uncommon, though, for a judge to direct the jury's verdict, so the defense then presents its case, answering the evidence of the prosecution with evidence of its own. The prosecution is permitted to rebut such testimony and, sooner or later, there will be no more evidence for either side to present, *cumulative* evidence being objectionable and excludable. At that point the defense ordinarily makes a motion for a directed verdict once again, with the answering evidence they have presented to be taken into consideration as detracting from what the prosecution might have established with its evidence. Once again the judge may—but most do not—direct a verdict; instead, most let it go to the jury.

The two sides then make their closing arguments, both summarizing their own evidence and attempting to persuade the jury to believe their presentations. Here again the police officer is likely to be put in a good light by the prosecution but in a bad light by the defense. Then the judge instructs the jury in carefully chosen language, putting the issues in words drawn from legal definitions of crime and other elements of the case, such as presumption and standards of proof.

The jury then retires to the jury room to deliberate in secret, and stays until they all agree (or as many agree as is necessary, in jurisdictions that do not require unanimity). If the jury fails to reach agreement, the judge can send it back for more deliberation—and can do so again and again—until it clearly appears that it, as a *hung jury,* will never reach agreement. If this happens the judge will declare a *mistrial* and force the process to begin again with the selection of another jury.

The integrity of the jury is one of the most critical aspects of the fairness of the criminal process; hence, *jury tampering* is a crime. The police and the prosecutor have a keen interest in protecting jurors from being influenced, and the case for less-than-unanimous verdicts is increasingly compelling as the offense grows more common, given the ease of intimidating or corrupting at least one member of a jury. A mistrial may also be declared for reasons that "spoil" it, such as the revelation of inflammatory information which goes beyond what the judge can instruct the jury to disregard. For this reason police witnesses must be especially guarded in their testimony, responding only with the essential information a question aims to draw out.

During trial the police play an inconspicuous role, except as witnesses. Their role as witnesses is very important, however. A famous study of jury deliberations by Harry Kalven, Jr. and Hans Zeisel of the University of Chicago Law School revealed that prosecution evidence involved police in 78 percent of all cases, compared with the complainant in 57 percent, eyewitnesses in 25 percent, experts in 25 percent, and other kinds in lower percentages.

The effect of police activities on the jury is also important. Kalven and Zeisel found that in some cases of resisting arrest,

> It comes as something of a surprise to find that, in this situation, the jury at times shows a special indulgence for the defendant. It is tempting to see in this sequence a trace of the jury's once classic role of protecting the citizen against official tyranny.[14]

During the trial sudden developments, such as an alibi defense, which asserts that the defendant was elsewhere when the crime was committed, may send the police back into action for further investigation; or inadvertent disclosure of certain information or the need to produce an informant may cause the police to reconsider further prosecution.

PLEA NEGOTIATION

Plea negotiation or plea bargaining, rather than trial, is the way most cases are resolved: nearly 90 percent are settled by a compromise worked out by the prosecution and the defense, rather than battled out in the courts with their adversary character and win-or-lose results. The jury, too, may effect a compromise by finding a defendant guilty of *lesser included* offenses, such as trespass rather than burglary, robbery rather than armed robbery, or manslaughter rather than murder. In the relatively unstructured process of plea negotiation, the prosecutor and the defense counsel have much more leeway. It is not absolute, however, but conditioned by the probabilities of the outcome of such cases if they should go to trial, by the imperatives of ongoing relations between counsel (requiring a high level of trust and dependability), and by the acceptability of their decisions to higher-ups in the prosecutor's office, the client of the defense lawyer, and the judge.

Within the framework of negotiation, the prosecutor—as in the charging decision—is able to take into consideration the interests and inclinations of the police. So the terms of the disposition of the case will be shaped, in part, by the wishes of the police. The influence of the police can be very great, as Donald J. Newman indicates in another of the American Bar Foundation's studies:

> The role of the police in influencing the charge complicates the fixing of responsibility for the negotiation process. Police may request a warrant for an offense less than the one reflecting the defendant's actual conduct or, to insure that the more serious offense will not be charged, may withhold some evidence. Where this is done purposely to induce a guilty plea, the conviction decision is functionally if not formally made by the police.[15]

The agreement reached by negotiation between prosecutor and defense counsel is ordinarily accepted by the judge, although he may reject it. In some jurisdictions the judge also enters into the bargaining process. The plea-negotiation process involves some of the same considerations that influence charge selection (youth and inexperience of the offender; status of the offender; and disrepute of victim, complainant, or witness, among other reasons), and some of these will be asserted by the police, especially if the prosecutor had not taken them fully into account or deferred to the police evaluation in the charge-selection stage. Considerations of concern to the police may emerge in the pretrial stage (e.g., willingness of the offender to trade information for leniency), and changes of mind along the way will be communicated to the prosecutor, who often will accede to police needs even at an advanced stage.

In any discussion of plea negotiation, it is important to call attention to some of the wider aspects of nonadversary alternatives in criminal justice. The criminal process in its entirety and the criminal court as an institution may be conceived as bureaucratic, dedicated to the administration of justice by negotiation rather than trial. Abraham S. Blumberg has given this a most complete analysis in his book *Criminal Justice*. He describes the "twilight of the adversary system," the court as "organization and communication system," the lawyer as "agent-mediator," and the judge as "bureaucrat." He concludes that there is a convergence of the adversary model of criminal justice ("couched in constitutional ideological terms of due process and rule of law") and the bureaucratic model ("administrative, ministerial, rational-bureaucratic").

While we continue to express our preference and reverence for the constitutional ideology, it is the perfunctory and efficacious system of justice that we implement. In large measure we do so because of its value and utility for each actor in the system.

SENTENCING

Sentencing practices vary from state to state. In most the jury is limited to a finding of guilt or acquittal; the judge has sole responsibility for sentencing. In other states the jury may make a recommendation. In some states, for some crimes, the jury's finding of guilty carries with it a mandatory sentence set by the legislature, as in Massachusetts's mandatory one-year sentence for possession of a handgun. In most states there is a statutory, or legally set, minimum and maximum period of time for misdemeanors, felonies, capital cases, and certain special offenses—and for all of these the judge may set a sentence of "not more than, and not less than" certain years within that statutory range. In such sentencing systems there is usually a period of time which must be served, ordinarily a third or a fourth of the minimum sentence.

In the sentencing function the police play a limited role, although they may be consulted by probation officers preparing a presentence investigation report. At sentencing, especially in misdemeanors handled by a magistrate, police officers may be asked for information about the defendant and even to make a recommendation as to the penalty itself. Such information or recommendation can be influential in the judge's decision to release the offender, to suspend the sentence, or to put the defendant on probation. In such cases there will be some degree of supervision by probation officers and certain conditions that must be fulfilled by the defendant, such as complying with a curfew, making restitution for the loss he or she caused, or not associating with the "bad company" that got him or her in trouble. If the conditions of a suspended sentence are violated, the sentence may go into effect; if the conditions of probation are violated, probation may be revoked and a jail sentence imposed. In either case, the decision is within the discretion of the judge. A police officer will often trigger this process by detecting a violation and reporting it to the probation official. Additional information from the officer may strongly influence the judge's decision.

CORRECTIONS

The police play no part in the corrections process insofar as prisons are concerned, because state prisons ordinarily are operated by a state department of corrections. But the police run the *jails*—the sheriff runs the county jail, the municipal police run the city jail—where a substantial number of persons receive their punishment. State prisons are ordinarily reserved for convicted felons whose sentence is a year or more; jails are for incarceration of less than that, up to the maximum for a misdemeanor, which is ordinarily no more than a year. But in 1965 there were 201,220 adults in state facilities, 141,303 in local jails and workhouses. For index crimes in 1965 (murder, forcible rape, aggravated assault, robbery, burglary, larceny-theft, and auto theft) 63,000 people were sentenced to prisons, 35,000 to jails.[16] (Index crimes are discussed in Chapter 9.)

What occurs within the institutional phase is thus of interest to the police. In the penitentiary there are vocational training, counseling, education, and other programs of rehabilitation. But virtually no rehabilitative effort is even attempted in the jails. This is causing increasing concern, especially because the jails suit the trend toward shorter periods of incarceration, and because they are better situated for community-based or community-oriented programs. Thus jails are among the last frontiers in criminal justice—and responsibility for them rests with the municipal and county police.

Near the end of a convict's sentence, he is likely to be paroled. Parole today comes earlier in the corrections phase than it used to. Many states, as well as the federal government, establish eligibility for parole after some portion of the minimum term. Thus, in a sentence of 5 to 10 years, after a fourth or a third of the 5-year minimum has been served (depending on the jurisdiction), the convict is eligible for parole—in this case after 15 or 20 months. Sometime after that point the convict will be paroled. As with probation, the convict will be under the supervision of an official—this time a parole officer rather than a probation officer. And, also as with probation, the police officer is likely to be the one who initiates the process of parole revocation by detecting or reporting a violation to the parole officer.

SUMMARY   This chapter has presented two conceptions of the relationship of the police to their environment. The first level of understanding is that of the police as the first phase in the criminal-justice system, the point (or intake valve) at which most criminal cases make their entry into the pipeline of criminal justice. By their handling of incidents on the street, at intersections, and in homes, taverns, and other settings, the police control the quantity and quality of the cases that enter the system. Practically all cases are brought into the criminal-justice system by the police.

But the police are not only important in the beginning phase, as "gatekeepers," to use another concept: They have direct influence over other elements of the criminal-justice system, such as the bail bonds-person, the prosecutor, and the jury. Indirectly, their influence extends even further, as in the information they can provide to the parole decision.

These concepts, as they have been developed in this chapter, are limited, because their outer reaches are the boundaries of the criminal-justice system as it is ordinarily understood. The next two chapters pursue the intermingling of the police with other systems within our society.

NOTES

1. The President's Commission on Law Enforcement and Administration of Justice, *The Challenge of Crime in a Free Society* (Washington, D.C.: U.S. Government Printing Office, 1967), p. 7.
2. James Q. Wilson, *Varieties of Police Behavior* (New York: Atheneum, 1975), pp. 140–226.
3. Jerome H. Skolnick, *Justice Without Trial,* 2nd ed. (New York: Wiley, 1975), pp. 164–173.
4. Ibid., pp. 174–176.
5. Donald J. Black, "Production of Crime Rates," *American Journal of Sociology* (August, 1970), pp. 733–748.
6. Armando Morales, *Andos Sangrando: A Study of Mexican American Police Conflict* (La Puente, Calif.: Perspectiva Publications, 1973).
7. Paul B. Wice, "Purveyors of Freedom: The Professional Bondsman," *Society* 11: 5 (1974) in Jerome H. Skolnick et al., *Crime and Justice in America* (Delmar, Calif.: Publishers' Inc., 1977), pp. 244–246.
8. Arthur Rosett and Donald R. Cressey, *Justice By Consent* (Philadelphia: Lippincott, 1976), p. 44.
9. For a discussion of formal and informal organization, see Robert Bierstedt, *The Social Order,* 3rd ed. (New York: McGraw-Hill, 1970), pp. 313–318.
10. The variations on this theme are stated by Abraham S. Goldstein, "Reflections on Two Models: Inquisitorial Themes in American Criminal Procedure," *Stanford Law Review* (May, 1974) in Jerome H. Skolnick, *Crime and Justice in America* (Delmar, Calif.: Publishers' Inc., 1977), pp. 204–211.
11. President's Commission, *The Challenge of Crime,* p. 10.
12. Ibid., pp. 10–11.
13. Frank W. Miller, *Prosecution: The Decision to Charge a Suspect With a Crime* (Boston: Little, Brown, 1969), pp. 338–340.
14. Harry Kalven, Jr., and Hans Zeisel, *The American Jury* (Boston: Little, Brown, 1966), pp. 236–237.
15. Donald J. Newman, *Convictions: The Determination of Guilt or Innocence Without Trial* (Boston: Little, Brown, 1966), p. 95.
16. President's Commission, *The Challenge of Crime,* pp. 172, 263.

SELECTED READINGS

Abraham Blumberg, *Criminal Justice* (New York: New Viewpoint, 1974).
George F. Cole, *Politics and the Administration of Justice* (Beverly Hills, Calif.: Sage, 1973).
Louis B. Heller, *Do You Solemnly Swear?* (Garden City, New York: Doubleday, 1968).
Morton Hunt, *The Mugging* (New York: Atheneum, 1972).

R. M. Jackson, *Enforcing the Law* (Pelican Books, 1967).

Delmar Karlen, *Anglo-American Criminal Justice* (New York: Oxford, 1967).

Frank W. Miller, *Prosecution: The Decision to Charge A Suspect with a Crime* (Boston: Little, Brown, 1969).

David W. Neubauer, *Criminal Justice in Middle America* (Morristown, N.J.: General Learning Press, 1974).

Donald J. Newman, *Conviction: The Determination of Guilt or Innocence Without Trial* (Boston: Little, Brown, 1966).

John W. Poulos, *The Anatomy of Criminal Justice* (Mineola, N.Y.: Foundation Press, 1976).

Ernst W. Puttkammer, *Administration of Criminal Law* (Chicago: University of Chicago Press, 1953).

Arthur Train, *From the District Attorney's Office* (New York: Scribner's, 1939).

6

FUNCTIONS, SYSTEMS, AND POLICE RELATIONSHIPS

In this chapter we will survey how far the criminal-justice functions have been penetrated by other institutions. Particularly important is the extent to which the private sector participates in functions closely associated with the state. This implies that a closer relationship might be established in a cooperative effort to control crime.

This chapter looks also to the other side of that coin and examines how the police are involved in the functions of other institutions and systems, such as mental health. The police serve the clients of those systems and therefore those systems themselves. The complex network of connections between the patrol officer and those other systems indicates that the police function as a system in the midst of those other systems. This system of systems is the basis of a new conception of the police, as Herman Goldstein has argued, as an agency of municipal government involved in many functions in addition to those of criminal justice. The police are involved in functions customarily identified with courts and corrections, as indicated in Chapter 5. Less well known, yet of potentially more importance, is the involvement of others from outside the criminal-justice system in the functions associated with police, courts, and corrections. This appears to be part of a trend toward the involvement of an "outside" institution in matters traditionally "staked out" as being the monopoly of another institution. It is revolutionary in the "privatization" of traditionally public functions or functions dominated by government, such as education. It is related to other recent trends such as the "civilianizing" of institutions such as the military and the church which have formerly drawn on "their own" for staffing virtually all positions, and the "paraprofessionalization" of professions such as law and medicine, which have formerly permitted only certified members to perform the tasks and skills officially defined as the practice of the profession.

These developments are occurring throughout the criminal-justice system, and in the police departments in particular. They need to be scrutinized carefully so that sound decisions are made on whether to prevent or resist such developments, support or speed them up, or simply leave them alone. For instance, it takes more than knee-jerk reactions to soundly endorse or condemn an innovation such as citizen patrols: It takes a thoughtful analysis of how to promote citizen involvement in law enforcement, its potential development, what, if any of it, is legitimate, how, if at all, it can be accommodated within the existing police organization and operation, and so forth.

The Functions of Criminal Justice

An analysis of the functions of the criminal-justice system is helpful in reviewing some of the incursions being made into law enforcement. These newly developing functions are more numerous than the traditional three functions of law enforcement, order maintenance, and public service. Yet the functional analysis attempted here is concerned mainly with those activities generally subsumed under the function of law enforcement. Presumably such an analysis of the remaining two (order maintenance and public service) would yield an equally complex set of functions along with a variety of nonpolice involvement.

The "what" of criminal justice includes those things that must be done if the community is to maintain control over its members. These functions of criminal justice include detection of the offense and the offender, accusation of the detected offender, apprehension of the accused offender, detention of the apprehended offender, protection of the offender, prosecution of the case against the offender, adjudication, or trying, of the case, disposition of the case and offender, and finally, reintegration of the offender into the community. All are aspects of the broader "functional prerequisites of society," by which society meets its need to endure. These include such basics as (1) role differentiation and role assignment—the identification and assignment of essential tasks, "otherwise everyone would be doing everything or nothing," and (2) communication, which is fundamental to socialization, role differentiation, and defense. Also among the "functional prerequisites" is "the effective control of disruptive forms of behavior," with crime being the disruptive behavior and law enforcement and order maintenance serving as the effective control.[1] Thus the police participate in the fulfillment of this most basic functional prerequisite.

Each of the functions of criminal justice can be fulfilled informally as well as formally. When a husband discovers his wife and her lover in bed together, he may shoot the lover (usually not the wife), thereby detecting, accusing, deciding, and disposing of the offender in one quick shot. The functions can be performed unofficially as well as officially. A group not long ago caught a burglar, "tried" him in a charade of adjudication, and executed him by dropping him off a two-hundred-foot cliff, thereby performing several functions of the criminal-justice system—formally but quite unofficially. In a primitive society the functional prerequisites are usually informal, although some of them may be ritualistic, ceremonial, and very formal. But in such societies there is usually no clear-cut distinction between the official and the unofficial.

The most familiar functions of modern law enforcement and criminal justice are both formal and official; the vigilante mode of "justice" offends not because it is ineffective—for it is all too often quite effective—but because it is informal and especially because it is unofficial. A good many of the functions of law enforcement are informal and unofficial. Virtually all crime detection, for instance, is not the result of police activity. Later we shall consider the increasing variety and the arguable legitimacy of some of the emerging social-control methods which are informal and—as yet, for the most part—unofficial.

DETECTION OF OFFENSE AND OFFENDER

The functions of criminal justice begin with the detection of the very existence of a crime, then the detection of the criminal—both "alleged" at this point if one cares to be technical, because it is customary to use "crime" and "criminal" as official designations only after conviction.

If an offense goes undetected, it has not much disrupted society. The taking of a mislaid wallet is theft but is hardly disruptive even to the owner, who would probably have given up recovering it anyway. In such a case there is no need for the function of controlling the behavior because there has been no disruption. Most offenses, however, are disruptive to some extent, hence noticeable in that somebody is troubled by them, even though many offenses (about half) are not reported to the police. Some of these detected but unreported offenses are dealt with informally, as when a passenger scolds a driver for running a red light in the middle of the night on an untraveled road, which is disruptive only to those who are fastidious about obedience to the law. Many offenses are not reported because they are considered too trivial for any formal, official action. Patrol officers see thousands in a year without issuing more than a verbal reprimand to drivers, jay-walkers, and so on.

Detection of an offense is ordinarily not difficult: The corpse is found with knife in heart, the safe's door is blasted wide open, the infant is missing from the crib, the hubcaps are gone. Detection of the offender, too, is ordinarily a simple thing: The gunman stands over the victim, smoking pistol in hand; the car thief sits at the wheel of someone else's car; the shopper stands at the door holding goods that have not been paid for; the teenager runs down the street with the purse. Now and then the appearance belies the reality: A bypasser comes upon the victim and picks up the smoking pistol; the driver is a joyrider, not really a thief; the shopper has entered the store to return something and finds he has forgotten the receipt; the teenager has picked up the purse while in pursuit of the real thief.

The vast majority of crimes and criminals are detected unofficially. Complex crimes in commercial fields are ordinarily detected by the businesses involved as victims. Sometimes collaboration between business and police investigators takes place, but it is an uneasy relationship. The role of insurance investigator is often very important. The investigative journalist has drawn attention in recent years as yet another detective of crimes. "Whistle-blowers" inside organizations sometimes bring crimes to the attention of the police. The private detective, a staple of crime fiction, is also important in the development of information to prove that someone has been involved in criminal activity. Thus the role of nongovernmental agents in discovering, investigating, and preparing cases of crime is very important. It is not known, however, just how extensive and significant the private sector is in crime detection.

What is known is that cases of investigative detection—when police detectives put together the puzzle—are relatively rare. Instead, most detective work is case preparation—the assembling of evidence to confirm the elements of a crime and the links of the accused to the crime. Research by the Rand Corporation, a West-Coast research firm that has extended its work from defense studies to criminal justice, indicates that when cases were solved, it was as a result of information gathered by the first police officer on the scene—the patrol officer, in most instances.[2] Some people draw the inference that, on a cost-benefit basis, the detective bureau is not worthwhile. A futher inference is that the detective function, now formally lodged in local policing agencies, might well be shifted to regional or state levels, to be called in locally for particularly difficult jobs. This way human energy would not be dedicated to—and wasted on—the improbable detection of offenders. The detective function at the local level is more than merely difficult—in most cases it is all but impossible, as most robberies, burglaries, and auto thefts go unsolved. Perhaps recognition of that should be reflected in the allocation of departmental resources.

ACCUSATION

Once the offense and the offender are detected, accusation follows. Often, especially informally, accusation is implicit: The witness points to the offender and both identifies and accuses with the same finger. More formally, however, especially in the official system, the function of accusation is a serious matter that is not undertaken lightly. A grand jury of 23 men and women hears evidence and decides if a formal accusation, or indictment, should be made. If an indictment is "returned," the grand jury states the accusation in ponderous, portentous language.

> The Jurors for the State upon oath present, That Hubert Greer, late of the County of McDowell, on the nineteenth day of January, in the year of our Lord one thousand nine hundred and fifty-three, with force and arms, at and in the County aforesaid, unlawfully, wilfully and feloniously offered a bribe to D. C. Safriet, Jr., he being a State Highway Patrolman, with the corrupt intent to influence the said officer in the performance of his official duties; and did unlawfully, wilfully and feloniously send to the said D. C. Safriet, Jr., he being a State Highway Patrolman, the sum of $100.00 through the United States Mail, as a bribe with the corrupt intent to influence said officer in the performance of his official duties against the form of the statute in such case made and provided against the peace and dignity of the State.[3]

The prosecutor's *information,* as a simpler substitute for the indictment, is equally weighty in its language and effect. Even a traffic ticket is not issued lightly, although it may seem so to the recipient.

Accusations of crimes are made outside the criminal-justice system, too, as in civil complaints (trespass), labor grievances (battery), and procedures in schools (vandalism), stores (pilfering), and even churches (embezzlement). Many of these result in private or noncriminal handling of the matter, often with the knowledge—sometimes even with the encouragement—of the police. But this is uncharted territory of criminal and law-enforcement activity, not only in its kinds and amounts, but in the extent of official complicity in the private disposition of what is normally viewed as a public matter. It would be very useful to know exactly how much crime—and criminal justice—completely bypasses the criminal-justice system.

APPREHENSION OF THE OFFENDER

After detection and accusation comes apprehension, a function which often is instantaneous but which may be prolonged and dramatic—the chase has inspired hundreds of stories and miles of Hollywood film. Usually the offender gives himself up or turns himself in. The role of the police is minimal. In many cases a police officer or citizen "collars" the offender on the spot. But the chase takes place often enough, and at breakneck speed over miles of highway, into mountains, across tenement rooftops, even from country to country. Sometimes the chase goes on for years. Often the chase is undramatic, as when pursuit takes the form of post office "wanted" notices issued by the FBI, enlisting the aid of citizens who might recognize the fugitive (and sometimes the chase has warmed when someone spots a face on such a poster). In these as well as the quick-and-easy apprehensions, the effort is collaborative, with many citizens assisting the agents of criminal justice.

The arrest is simply the taking of a person into custody; *apprehension* literally means "taking hold" of the person. Unless a substitute for arrest is used, such as a *summons* (which, like a traffic ticket, orders the recipient to appear in court at a specified time), apprehension results in custody for a limited period of time while certain procedures are followed, such as taking the person to the police station, *booking* and *printing* and *mugging*—or taking down name and address, fingerprinting, and photographing.

In this country, with 50 states and a highly mobile population, often there is a "hold" on an arrested person, indicating that he or she is "wanted" in another jurisdiction, in which case the time of custody is extended for the *extradition* process, in which the governor of the "wanting" state requests "rendition" by the governor of the holding state, followed by the transfer of custody to officials of the state wanting the prisoner. It will be a police officer who goes to get the prisoner in the extradition process.

DETENTION OF THE OFFENDER

The detected, accused, and apprehended offender must be detained beyond the initial custody which accompanies arrest until subsequent functions are fulfilled. This, too, is a near-monopoly of the police. Detention may or may not be physical. Physical detention traditionally was by means of the duke's dungeon. Today it is accomplished at the sheriff's jail or the police department's "lockup." But the device of bail was developed centuries ago; through it an amount of money was put in the hands of the jailer, to be held until the released offender showed up for later proceedings. The idea was that offenders would be sufficiently attached to the money—their own or a relative's or friend's—that they would show up rather than forsake or "forfeit" it to the jailer. The effect of the deposit of money was a nonphysical detention until those later steps could be taken. A variation on this in modern times is the deposit of a driver's license as bail in traffic cases. This is handled by the police, too.

Along the way, the device of *bail bond* was developed, which worked for centuries to permit the accused to go free on the basis of a bond or contract under which the "bail bondsman" agreed to pay to the court the full amount of the bail if the accused failed to appear when required, in exchange for the accused's payment to the bondsman of an amount considerably lower than the total amount of bail *and* the bondsman's right to sue the fugitive for the full amount. The bondsman was also given by statute the power to arrest the fugitive, whose appearance would entitle the bondsman to the return of the forfeited bail. This was a strong incentive for the bondsman to seek and find the fugitive.

The tie that bound the accused to appear was therefore financial. At the same time, the financial ability which made release possible—the more easily the money could be produced, the more likely the accused could "make bail" and be released—meant some hardship on the poor, who could not "make bail" and were forced to undergo detention in jail or release at grievous financial sacrifice by family or friends who might put up the money or its equivalent, usually a house or some other security. Even modern reforms such as the Illinois system, which requires a deposit of only 10 percent of the amount of bail (or its equivalent in some security, such as a residence), made for some hardship, even though it put the bail bondsman out of business—along with some of the oppressive factors that went along with that system, such as the bondsman's power of arrest and the exploitation of needy prisoners and their relatives.

These hardships have led to a bail-reform movement in recent years, one result of which has been the widespread use of *release on recognizance*—or release of the accused on the basis of his recognition of his obligation to appear, coupled with his further obligation to pay the court the amount of the bail in case he fails to appear, as well as to suffer the further consequences of flight (a distinct offense with severe penalties). Release on recognizance (ROR) is granted to offenders who have jobs, family in the community, or other ties which are presumed to "detain" or hold them in the community; the accused must agree to appear in court at a specified time. The New York law on ROR takes the following information about the accused into account:

1. character, reputation, habits and mental condition
2. employment and financial resources
3. family ties and length of residence, if any, in the community
4. criminal record, if any
5. previous record, if any, in responding to court appearances when required
6. weight of evidence in the pending criminal action and any other factor indicating probability of conviction
7. sentence which may be imposed upon conviction

Thus there is a shifting of considerations away from the fact of accusation, away from exclusive concern for the charge and the likelihood of conviction, toward considerations of ties to where the trial will take place if it occurs. Increasing emphasis on the accused's personal qualities and community ties indicates that the *private* rather than the *public* aspect of the matter is critical if not determinative.

Another private consideration in detention is becoming obvious as a hidden purpose of detention comes close to open acknowledgment. The purpose of detention has been not only to assure that the offender will be in court at the appointed time for hearings or trial. It obviously has served—and continues to serve—another purpose as well: protection of the community, especially the victim and witnesses, from dangerous offenders. This function, however important it may be, is not recognized officially, because incarceration is said to be reserved for detention to assure appearance at trial or for punishment, which can come only after conviction. Those who can post bail or qualify for ROR must be released. However, it has been customary to set bail astronomically high in order to prevent the release of presumably dangerous offenders or of those accused of especially heinous offenses. The perceived need of the community poses a dilemma that can be resolved in principle only by acknowledging that "preventive detention" is legitimate and constitutional, then by spelling out its conditions and limitations in law (or by mitigating its hardships by speeding up the proceedings to minimize the time spent in pretrial preventive detention). Such a reform was enacted in the District of Columbia in 1970 but it was rarely used, mainly because of the stringent requirements of demonstrating dangerousness and the disinclination of judges to "punish" an offender before conviction. Preventive detention will take critical judgment of psychiatric experts, rather than police intuitions, to be fully effective in its predictions.

PROTECTION OF THE OFFENDER

Physical detention of offenders has another secondary function, in addition to the primary function of assuring their appearance for court proceedings and the secondary function of protecting the community from the prisoner: It protects the prisoner from the community. Many a prisoner has been spared a beating or a lynching by being locked up by courageous or clever sheriffs brave enough to stand off a mob or cunning enough to convince them they have the prisoner and justice will be done, when in truth the prisoner has been spirited off to a safe haven, such as a neighboring county's jail.

In terms of the "functional prerequisites of society," harm done to an accused person is "disruptive behavior" on the part of those in the community who would shortcut the regular processes established to fulfill the criminal-justice function. In addition, such vigilante behavior tends to escalate and continue, as in family feuds like the Hatfields and McCoys in Kentucky and in organized-crime vendettas like the gangland reprisals in modern American cities, which widen and deepen the disruption of the community. Thus society must provide protection even of those who have themselves offended society by disruptive behavior, lest that disruption be compounded by further disruptions. For the same reasons offenders must be protected even from the officials of the community, whose offenses against the accused may be far less than lynchings—beatings, deprivation of necessities like food and water, or more subtle denials such as rights to counsel and other constitutional rights, because all of these threaten further disruption (to say nothing of their betrayal of basic ideals).

This function of protecting the offender is in theory that of the judiciary. But in practice the immediate responsibility for assuring that constitutional guarantees are fully realized is that of the police. The responsibility is shared, however, by the legislative branch of government, the legal profession, the press, organizations like the American Civil Liberties Union (which have on going concern for rights), ad hoc organizations that spring up to protect groups like the Chicago 8 and the Wilmington 10, and of course the family and friends of the accused.

PROSECUTION OF THE CASE

The next function of criminal justice is carrying the case against the accused from accusation toward adjudication. Up to this point the functions are personalized: who did it, where is he, is she dangerous, does he need protection, will she appear for trial? But as the adjudication function is approached, the questions come to be in terms not only of the personal characteristics of the offender (was he responsible for his action, was it indeed she who did it), but also of the crime and its elements. No one is accused, in theory, of being a *criminal*. Instead, one is accused of a *crime*, and the community proceeds against the accused in terms of a case, which involves (1) an underlying legal definition of the offense, (2) a charge spelled out, with some indication of what acts constitute the offense, (3) a body of rules governing the manner and means of proving the charges, and (4) standards of weighing the evidence. These constitute the framework of the trial or the negotiation which yields the decision in the case. But they begin in the prosecution phase, in which the police are participants.

It is important to note, however, that what a person *is* may be important. There are so-called crimes of status, such as juvenile delinquency (e.g., a young person is "incorrigible," even though he committed no specific criminal act) or public drunkenness or narcotics addiction or vagrancy, all of which have to do with the nature of the person or the overall pattern or style of behavior. These "crimes" are being eliminated from the criminal law. There are sometimes added penalties having to do with prior conduct, such as prior convictions, which, under "habitual criminal" statutes, result in increased penalties for convictions of current crimes. There are also programs under which law-enforcement efforts are focused on persons because of what they are, such as "career criminals," organized crime figures, or terrorists.

The programs that concentrate on career criminals of one kind or another are likely to proliferate, because emphasis is shifting to incapacitation of dangerous offenders by detention in prison, as it is discovered that a handful of such offenders do a disproportionate amount of damage to society. The career-criminal programs involve very close teamwork between prosecutors and police personnel, focusing on the target criminals. This fusion of police and prosecutors, focused on violent criminals and others (some burglars, for instance) who do great damage, resembles the integration of investigation and prosecution that occurs in cases of complex corporate and governmental crime, with investigators attached to the prosecutor's office working under the direction of the prosecutor. There are other teamwork systems developed by the federal government, such as "Strike Forces," or interdepartmental teams of investigators and prosecutors headed by an Assistant United States Attorney, for combatting organized crime. There are also intergovernmental teams in the narcotics field, under the federal Drug Enforcement Administration, in which federal, state, and local personnel team up in a functional integration. These developments suggest that the investigative phase, long the realm of the police, is likely to be dominated (at least in significant, complex cases) by prosecution personnel and higher governmental levels of law enforcement. It also suggests that sooner or later there will be some integration of private investigators into the combined police-and-prosecution function of preparing cases for trial (insurance investigators, as in arson cases; investigative journalists, as in government corruption cases; social workers, as in cases of child abuse or spouse abuse; accountants, as in commercial embezzlement cases; computer technicians, as in cases of fraud by computer).

The function of carrying this investigation forward on behalf of society is the responsibility of the prosecutor. There are varying degrees, however, in the extent to which this function can be made the responsibility of an official called the prosecutor, or district attorney, or county attorney, or state's attorney. At one extreme a judge might formulate the charge and present the case before a jury as if he were a paternalistic figure governing every step, much as a parent oversees a dispute between children (the "children" in this instance being the state and the accused), stepping in to support both sides so neither will be hurt. Or a judge might stand aside, as if she were an umpire, and allow the two sides to fight it out within the limits of the rules, letting the chips fall, giving no second chances.

Our system is closer to the latter end of the spectrum and is, accordingly, called an *adversary system* of criminal justice. This means the prosecutor is balanced, in theory, by counsel for the accused. Their clash is supposed to yield a fair amount of truth, which will resolve the dispute by the judgment of the jury that the prosecution has presented enough truth to satisfy, "beyond a reasonable doubt," that the state has proved the case against the accused. This has been called, rather caustically, the sporting theory of justice.

ADJUDICATION OF THE CASE

The function that follows prosecution is adjudication, or the decision of the case, in terms of whether the prosecution succeeded or not, as determined by the judgment of the judge or jury that the accused is guilty or not guilty. Our system presumes that the accused is innocent until the prosecutor proves, and the jury (or judge in a bench trial) finds, that the accused is guilty "beyond a reasonable doubt." Another system could be one—and there have been such systems—in which the accused is presumed to be guilty until he himself proves, and the jury finds, that he is innocent. In either way, the adjudication function is fulfilled by the trial, an elaborate process familiar in some respects from television dramatizations.

Contrary to the impression of many television viewers, adjudication results from trial in only about 10 percent of all cases. The other 90 percent are handled in a very different way: by negotiation between the prosecutor and defense counsel, leading to a compromise. The compromise is based in part on their anticipation of what the outcome of a trial would be should one take place. It is also based in part on the convenience which results from avoiding trial. But *plea bargaining* is highly controversial—not because it does not fulfill the function of adjudication, for cases are just as much decided by discussion and compromise as they are by a verdict. The accused and the state (represented by defense counsel and prosecutor) strike a bargain, and the accused enters a plea of guilty in lieu of a jury's finding of guilt. The accused hopes to exchange the uncertainty of a trial-and-jury verdict for the certainty of an agreed conviction on a lower charge, say robbery instead of armed robbery, for which the penalties are lower. And in some jurisdictions the penalties also are subject to negotiation, with the judge accepting the entire "package."

Plea bargaining is controversial because the adversary mode of adjudication by trial is thought to be a superior way of making such a crucial decision than the more or less amiable mode of decision-making by agreement between two integral parts of a system. It is feared that neither one—given their involvement in a bureaucracy administering justice—is fully committed to the principle of fighting for justice, the rights of the individual, and the security of the public. Moreover, in the negotiation mode of adjudication, the police play a much greater part. Also, all parties are likely to be more influenced by unofficial considerations, such as what will happen in the private realm to punish the offender. "He has suffered enough," is a common—and often a determinative—consideration.

Even in jury trials, which are not supposed to involve negotiation and compromise, a degree of it occurs. The jury only seems to be of "one mind" when it reaches a verdict. In the process of reaching a verdict, in many cases the jury members divide into two camps, then compromise on a verdict of not guilty to the more serious charges, guilty to the less serious ones.[4]

The adjudication function ends after the jury (or judge in a bench trial) comes to a verdict of guilty or not guilty in the trial mode, or the accused enters a plea of guilty resulting from a bargain in the nontrial mode. The judge then pronounces *judgment* that the defendant is or is not guilty of certain charges, either specified in the verdict of the jury or agreed to by the defendant in the plea of guilty.

The adjudicatory process in its trial mode has caused misgivings on the part of many observers of criminal justice. It is costly, complex, and prolonged; it emphasizes areas of disagreement rather than agreement; and it evokes hostility and makes reconciliation more difficult. This has stimulated the development of alternatives to the conventional criminal-justice modes of disposition. Pretrial diversion of offenders from the pipeline is now a well-established alternative: accused persons, particularly young and first-time offenders, are shunted from the usual path to other institutions where they are not exposed to the ordeal of the trial and the counterproductive influences of jail, reform school, or penitentiary. Instead, under intensive supervision in halfway houses and rehabilitative programs outside rather than inside the prisons, in the hands of "civilian" rather than correctional personnel, it is expected that they will do better—or at least not as bad as if they were thrown into the bad company and alienating experience of official, institutional punishment. This emphasis on diversion is an interesting testimonial to the promise of the private sector for the performance of this function of criminal justice.

Another problem with the adjudicatory process in its adversary style is the tendency toward formality. The ideal appears to be the "capital" case—the trial that may conclude with a death sentence. Precautions are added to precautions to ensure that mistakes are minimized, as they should be when the stakes are so high. But the ideal commands such respect that the trial of less serious crimes is driven to emulate the ideal, even when the stakes are much lower than life itself. Gradually the rights and protections accorded the accused in capital cases have been extended to virtually all types of criminal trial. The elimination of the justice-of-the-peace court represents the realization of the goals of modernization, professionalization, and formalization in the criminal process. But with the disappearance of simple, informal criminal trials in a neighborhood setting (often in a "store-front" forum), there has been a loss of certain good qualities that accompanied informality and simplicity, such as directness, spontaneity, accommodation, personalization, and a kind of fine-tuning of equity or justice to fit concrete circumstances well known to the participants rather than an abstraction of a case. This loss has been aggravated by the sordid, assemblyline character of big city courts. Hence, a reaction has occurred in which the ideal of "a day in court" is coupled with a sense of decency, a mode of informality, and a yearning for the values of community. The result has been experimentation with neighborhood courts for the resolution of less serious offenses. These resemble, ironically, the justice-of-the-peace courts and they provide more leeway for community sentiment, and even for the police officer, than the more stilted procedures of the full-fledged courts "downtown."

DISPOSITION OF THE CASE

Following the judge's pronouncement of judgment comes the sentence, which the judge usually announces at the same time, although often after an adjournment for presentence investigation by others and by his or her own deliberations upon it. Then comes implementation of the sentence. This can be execution as it has come to mean figuratively, that is, the death of the convict, or it can mean incarceration or some form of release. Immediate release, in the form of probation, depends on a presentence investigation, which is based in part on reports from police officers for insight into the likelihood of release to accomplish more good (and less harm) than some form of incarceration.

Following sentence, and conceptually part of the entire disposition function, is adjustment of the sentence by the chief executive. A governor may adjust a sentence by *reprieve,* which delays the sentence; by *commutation,* which lessens the sentence (e.g., from death to life, from 10 to 20 years to 5 to 10 years); by *pardon,* which forgives the offense and releases the offender; or by *parole,* which releases the convict before the formal end of the maximum time specified by the judge in the sentence, at a time when the convict is deemed ready for release. These adjustments are often influenced strongly by public opinion. Executive clemency in forms other than parole is fairly uncommon, but parole has become basic to the correctional phase of disposition function. Such decisions are assigned to a parole board, which is advised by prison officials, whose decisions—in the form of recommendations to the chief executive—are ordinarily accepted. Few sentences today are not shortened by parole. The "clemency" decisions in their various forms often rely heavily on reports from law-enforcement agencies, especially on recommendations from police officers who have personal knowledge of the inmate.

REINTEGRATION OF THE OFFENDER

When punishments were swift and physical—death, mutilation (branding, nose slitting, ear notching), or public humiliation (stocks, ducking stools)—there was no need for the function of reintegration of the offender back into the community, because it was impossible in the case of death or virtually impossible in the case of *transportation* (to penal colonies in Australia, or Devil's Island, or Georgia) or because the convict was not removed from the community for very long, but quickly returned to it, albeit with a brand, amputation, or stigma (e.g., "scarlet letter" for adultery). With the use of prisons, however, convicts were removed from the community, but usually not forever. Little thought was given, however, to the problems of "ex-cons" upon reentry. They were given a new—but cheap and ill-fitting—prison-made suit, a few dollars, and a ticket somewhere—and then they were on their own, scarcely more equipped than before to cope with problems of illiteracy, lack of vocational skills, and so forth, to say nothing of the unfriendly attitude of the community toward ex-cons.

Today, however, reintegration of the offender has come to be a function necessary to minimize the disruption of the ex-con's reentry into society. This function arises in part out of the community's recognition that *recidivism* (or the subsequent criminal activity, or relapse, of the offender) is not so much the ex-con's problem as it is the community's problem. The reappearance of an ex-con under the best conditions may be disruptive, both to himself and to the community, unless both are prepared for the occasion. So the community, through elements of the criminal-justice system, has come to recognize the function of reintegration of ex-cons into the community as undisruptively as possible. Formerly communities did this in limited and usually ineffective ways. Now ex-cons are prepared for liberty by stages of reintegration, with emphasis on the community's ability to receive them by reducing the handicaps imposed on ex-cons, like outright bans on certain kinds of employment, membership in certain professions, voting, and the like. Effective reintegration is more likely to occur with halfway houses, work-release programs, study-release programs, furloughs, and so forth.

As society places more reliance on the jails for punishment, there will be pressure on the police (unless jails are transferred to the jurisdiction of corrections departments) for them to take a greater interest in ways of making incarceration a more constructive, less destructive experience. The "cop-a-con" idea (which substitutes intensive one-on-one surveillance outside of prison in place of continued detention inside) captures the concept of the fusion of corrections and police functions and symbolizes the interpenetration of police and other functions of criminal justice.

But perhaps more important than the fusion of policing with the probation and parole functions are the implications of pretrial diversion and reintegration functions: The private sector does better by the offender than the public correctional institutions and their programs. This is likely to come to mean that more of the private sector, especially the business community, will become involved in the correctional function. Insofar as the less serious offenses are involved, this means the jails will be affected—for which the police are responsible. Hence, it means that the law-enforcement community can become responsible for the important alternatives to jail. This connection of the police to the private sector promises to be an exciting, uncharted territory of development of mutual responsibility.

The Privatization of Criminal Justice

Breaking criminal justice into several functions reveals a variety of participants and influences from outside the criminal-justice system. The modern tendency appears to be for more and more private individuals and organizations to become involved in public functions—and not only in criminal justice. For example, in the field of education, which became a public responsibility only during the last century, there has been a rapid trend toward variety in the private sector. There is even a significant growth in the personal education system, as it might be called, in which parents individually or in cooperation with other parents educate their children outside of the private as well as the public schools—that is to say, outside of school altogether.

Having observed some instances of this overlapping of functions in the field of criminal justice (and more of them to be discussed in Chapter 10's review of the individual and communal response to crime), the question arises as to whether this trend should be fostered or discouraged. The answer depends in part on what *is* happening, but also on what *should be* happening, and that requires recourse to political philosophy to settle the issue of the legitimacy of the nongovernmental performance of responsibilities traditionally monopolized by government. One writer who suggests that the movement be encouraged is Peter F. Drucker, a widely read commentator on business and social problems and changes:

> It would rather be a systematic policy of using the other, nongovernmental institutions of the society of organizations, for the actual "doing," i.e., for performance, operations, executions.
>
> Such a policy might be called "reprivatization." The tasks which flowed to government in the last century because the original private institution of society, the family, could not discharge them, would be turned over to the new, nongovernmental institutions that have sprung up and grown these last sixty to seventy years.
>
> Government would start out by asking the question: "How do these institutions work and what can they do?" It would then ask: "How can political and social objectives be formulated and organized in such a manner as to become opportunities for performance for these institutions?" It would also ask: "And what opportunities for accomplishment of political objectives do the abilities and capacities of these institutions offer to government?"
>
> This would be a very different role for government from what it plays in traditional political theory. In all our theories government is *the* institution. If "reprivatization" were to be applied, however, government would become *one* institution albeit the central, the top, institution.[5]

The application of this approach to criminal justice would involve establishing the role and responsibility of the police and other institutions as selectors and definers of the functions of their institutions, in a relationship to be discussed in Chapter 11. It would require that the institutions of criminal justice (the police chief, as far as law enforcement is concerned) and the institutions of community leadership decide what will be the responsibilities and tasks of criminal justice institutions and of family, schools, churches, business organizations, recreational agencies, and so forth—all orchestrated, as it were, as an ensemble of organizations engaged in the performance of a symphony of criminal justice functions.

The Police and the Systems in Their Environment

The environment of the police includes many systems beyond criminal justice. The first of them to be taken up are those in the immediate environment of the police—the systems the police serve in many ways by exercising the police responsibility for maintaining order and providing service. The other systems taken up in Chapter 7 (governmental, political, and social) comprise the wider environment that has the police in the midst of an ecology of systems, in which everything—including the police—relates to everything else.

LAW ENFORCEMENT IN A SYSTEM OF SYSTEMS

Recent studies of policing confirm what a reading of earlier chapters indicates: that the tasks of the police are many and varied. This is clear from the classification of incidents in a New York City precinct (Tables 6.1 and 6.2). Of the top ten types of incident, only two are clearly criminal—and one of them is not of the serious variety. Herman Goldstein makes this a central point of his analysis:

> What do police do with their time if they are not working on matters related to crime? The studies report the large numbers of hours devoted to handling accidents and illnesses, stray and injured animals, and intoxicated persons; dealing with family disturbances, fights among teenage gangs, and noisy gatherings; taking reports on damage to property, traffic accidents, missing persons, and lost and found property. They cite the amount of time devoted to adminstering systems of registration and licensing; to directing traffic; to dealing with complaints of improper parking; to controlling crowds at public events; and to dealing with numerous hazards and municipal service defects that require attention.[6]

The American Bar Association's Advisory Committee identified a wide range of responsibilities in what it called the "complex task" of the police:

1. To identify criminal offenders and criminal activity and, where appropriate, to apprehend offenders and participate in subsequent court proceedings.
2. To reduce the opportunities for the commission of some crimes through preventative patrol and other measures.
3. To aid individuals who are in danger of physical harm.
4. To protect constitutional guarantees.
5. To facilitate the movement of people and vehicles.

TABLE 6.1.
Incidents in the 20th Precinct, New York City Police Department, Ranked in Order of Total Time Spent per Incident, 1967–1968

Incident Type	Number of Incidents	Total Time (in minutes)	Average Time (in minutes)
1. Sick	4,552	202,143	44.4
2. Other	5,629	162,310	28.8
3. Other misdemeanors	1,190	106,034	89.1
4. Dispute	3,582	106,016	29.6
5. Burglary	2,518	104,881	41.7
6. Unfounded	5,132	102,881	20.7
7. Dead on arrival	402	60,126	149.8
8. Injured	1,170	46,063	41.1
9. Intoxicated person	1,555	41,830	25.9
10. Disorderly groups	1,693	37,780	22.3
11. Robbery	512	33,476	65.4
12. Auto accident	547	32,943	60.2
13. Alarm of fire	1,013	30,483	30.0
14. Felonious assault	309	26,982	87.3
15. Auto accident-injury	286	25,334	88.6
16. Larceny from auto	514	17,579	34.2
17. Malicious mischief	435	16,261	37.4
18. Utility trouble	378	14,502	38.4
19. Narcotics	59	13,582	230.2
20. Auto larceny	104	12,556	120.7
21. Grand larceny	235	11,598	49.4
22. Other felonies	64	9,559	149.4
23. Motor vehicle recovered	73	7,221	98.8
24. Traffic violation	270	7,201	27.1
25. Vehicles mechanical trouble	201	7,201	35.8
26. Accidental alarm	264	6,873	26.0
27. Grand larceny-pocketbook snatch	130	6,366	48.9
28. Auto safety check	126	4,175	33.1
29. Prowler	121	3,549	29.3
30. Dangerous condition	81	3,510	43.0
31. Found persons	46	2,802	60.9
32. Auto accident-serious injury or death	13	2,587	199.0
33. Arrest-serving summons	81	2,480	30.6
34. False alarm of fire	86	1,865	21.7
35. Property recovered	35	1,848	52.8
36. Homicide	6	1,744	290.6
37. Rape	29	1,622	55.9
38. Weapons	9	1,298	144.2
39. Missing persons	24	1,096	45.7
40. Prostitution	7	1,090	155.7
41. Attempted suicide	13	1,056	81.2
42. Gambling	7	813	116.1
43. Traffic court warrants	40	713	17.8
44. Suicide	6	607	101.2
45. ABC violation	5	160	32.0

Source: U.S. Department of Justice, National Institute of Law Enforcement and Criminal Justice, *Police Training and Performance Study* (Washington, D.C.: GPO, 1970), p. 15.

6. To assist those who cannot care for themselves.
7. To resolve conflict.
8. To identify problems that are potentially serious law enforcement or governmental problems.
9. To create and maintain a feeling of security in the community.
10. To promote and preserve civil order.
11. To provide other services on an emergency basis.[7]

(In Chapter 8 it will be argued that most of these seemingly noncriminal matters have a criminal dimension, in their potential if not in the strict legalistic sense, that makes their nature and meaning for the police somewhat different than the designation "noncriminal" would ordinarily suggest.)

Just as the police are concerned not only with crime but with the entire criminal-justice system, so they are concerned not only with this wide variety of problems but also with the systems for which those problems are the central concerns. The police officer's concern with them is temporary, transitional, and emergency-based rather than extended, as it is for the criminal matters as they are processed through the criminal-justice system. Even though the relationship of the police to those systems is not so far-reaching, it is a close, regular, working relationship.

A police officer relates to so many "sister sytems" that law enforcement can be viewed as a member system, not only of the criminal-justice system itself as a whole, but also of several other systems as well; many overlaps of police and such systems, resulting from a shared concern for common problems, involve the police in approaches which are in some ways radically different from the conventional methods of criminal justice. For instance, the alcoholic who is abusive is treated differently (in purpose, at least) if taken to a detoxification center for a "cure" rather than to jail for punishment. Many of the events and persons, such as the public drunk, engaging the police have "criminal dimension," as noted earlier, but "belong" more clearly to systems other than criminal justice because some other characteristic is dominant, such as age, mental condition, or military status. The police involvement comes in part because of the criminal dimension or potential, but much more because of the availability of the police for service to the other systems on a 24-hour-a-day basis.

The implication of all this is that law enforcement (the police) is not *congruent* with criminal justice or with any of the other systems to which law enforcement relates; instead, it *overlaps* them all. Hence, it is useful to view the law-enforcement system not as a component of any one of the other systems nor even of criminal justice of which it is only a part, but

TABLE 6.2.
Incidents in the 20th Precinct, New York City Police Department, Ranked in Order of Frequency of Occurrence, 1967–1968

Incident Type	Number of Incidents	Total Time (in minutes)	Average Time (in minutes)
1. Other	5,629	163,310	28.8
2. Unfounded	5,132	102,881	20.0
3. Sick	4,552	202,142	44.4
4. Dispute	3,582	106,016	29.6
5. Burglary	2,518	104,881	41.7
6. Disorderly groups	1,693	37,780	22.3
7. Intoxicated person	1,555	41,830	25.9
8. Other misdemeanors	1,190	106,034	89.1
9. Injured	1,170	46,063	41.1
10. Alarm of fire	1,013	30,483	30.0
11. Auto accident	547	32,943	60.2
12. Larceny from auto	514	17,579	34.2
13. Robbery	512	33,476	65.4
14. Malicious mischief	435	16,261	37.4
15. Dead on arrival	402	60,216	149.8
16. Utility trouble	378	14,502	38.4
17. Felonious assault	309	26,982	87.3
18. Auto accident injury	286	25,334	88.6
19. Traffic violation	270	7,201	27.1
20. Accidental alarm	264	6,873	26.0
21. Grand larceny	235	11,598	49.4
22. Vehicle mechanical trouble	201	7,201	35.8
23. Grand larceny-pocketbook snatch	130	6,366	48.9
24. Auto safety check	126	4,175	33.1
25. Prowler	121	3,549	29.3
26. Auto larceny	104	12,556	120.7
27. False alarm of fire	86	1,865	21.7
28. Arrest-serving summons	81	2,480	30.6
29. Dangerous condition	81	3,510	43.0
30. Motor vehicle recovered	73	7,211	98.8
31. Other felonies	64	9,559	149.4
32. Narcotics	59	13,582	230.2
33. Found person	46	2,802	60.9
34. Traffic warrants	40	713	17.8
35. Property recovered	35	1,848	52.8
36. Rape	29	1,622	55.9
37. Missing persons	24	1,096	45.7
38. Auto accident-serious injury or death	13	2,587	199.0
39. Attempted suicide	13	1,056	81.2
40. Weapons	9	1,298	144.2
41. Prostitution	7	1,090	155.7
42. Gambling	7	813	116.1
43. Homicide	6	1,744	290.6
44. Suicide	6	607	101.2
45. ABC violation	5	160	32.0

Source: U.S. Department of Justice National Institute of Law Enforcement and Criminal Justice, *Police Training and Performance Study* (Washington, D.C.: GPO, 1970), p. 15.

as a conceptually and institutionally distinct governmental agency having multiple purposes and functions shared with other agencies.

Systems Processing People. Some of the systems to which law enforcement relates are concerned primarily with people who can be classified according to some characteristic for which each such system has the principal concern. The juvenile system is concerned with young people, the drug-abuse system with persons dependent on alcohol or other drugs, the health system with people who are physically sick or injured, the mental-health system with people who are mentally ill, the welfare system with people who are needy, the military system with young people capable of combat or already in service, the education system with those in school or educational programs, the religious system with the spiritual aspect (which gets translated into many material programs), the business system with the employment of people.

The *juvenile system* involves both public- and private-school systems; facilities for battered children, neglected children, truant or runaway children, "incorrigible" children, children in need of supervision; mental-health facilities for retarded children or mentally disturbed children; reform schools for children who are delinquent. A major component of the juvenile system, as far as the police are concerned, is of course the so-called juvenile-justice system, which involves special police units and officers, special courts, special procedures, and special correctional components, to each of which police officers are likely to relate at one time or another. They may call in juvenile officers to handle a youngster, they may have to testify in a juvenile facility. But police officers may also decide, when they deal with a young person, that the youngster should be taken to some nonjustice facility rather than another—back to the schoolhouse, for example, rather than to the jail.

The *drug-abuse system* involves the alcohol and narcotics sides of the drug problem. The police are regularly picking up "public drunks" who are making nuisances of themselves or are in danger, passed out in a gutter somewhere or reeling about in a busy intersection. Ordinarily the police take them to jail to sober up (or "dry out") overnight. But many cities are setting up facilities especially for alcoholics.

Likewise, narcotics addicts are taken in by the police, to face criminal charges if they are involved in unlawful possession or sale of narcotics or other crimes, but sometimes simply because of physical difficulties, such as having overdosed. There are other facilities than jails in the case of drug addicts, too. For instance, if an addict is from a "halfway house," the police officer may choose to return the addict there rather than take her to jail (unless, of course, a serious crime is involved).

The *health system,* mainly the hospitals, is another system to which police officers relate frequently. Officers are often the first to come upon traffic accidents and must meet the emergency need for first aid until an ambulance arrives, and often an officer takes the sick or injured person to the emergency room. Some police departments even operate ambulance services. The police also relate to the public-health portion of the health system, in some places being involved in communicable-disease quarantine operations (especially with prostitutes, where the police may have an incidental, tactical aspect: uncooperative prostitutes are held in quarantine ostensibly for a venereal disease check, but in truth for some other purpose, such as hassling them). Some police departments even have water and food inspection responsibilities.

The *mental-health system* involves the police because the mentally ill are sometimes violent, sometimes physically or emotionally trying beyond the abilities of their families to cope, and sometimes dangerous to themselves. Retarded children and senile persons may stray beyond the neighborhood they know and get helplessly lost. The mental-health facility is sometimes a police officer's best recourse in such cases, as an alternative to jail.

The *welfare system* comes into play when the police have to deal with families that have been evicted with no place to go, with people who are hungry (the police often feed the hungry, because most police departments have a food-service function connected with their detention facilities). The senile now and then wander around unable to tell who they are or where they belong. Missing persons are a responsibility of the police, some departments having enough need for a missing-persons section. Dependent children, who are not delinquent or in need of supervision, sometimes come within the purview of the police. Welfare agencies often meet the police officer's need for someplace to turn in such cases—other than to the jail.

Now and then a person in military service will get into trouble. The police officer may call a counterpart in the *military system* (M.P., Shore Patrol) to take the drunk and/or disorderly soldier or sailor to the barracks or base for military rather than civilian punishment. There are usually well-established relationships between the civilian and military law-enforcement authorities in major cities and in cities such as Norfolk, Virginia, and San Diego, California, where there are large military installations with thousands of personnel. In the days of the draft (and even today, to a much lesser extent), entry into the military was an alternative to the criminal-justice system's processes: young people were given the option of enlistment in place of further prosecution.

The *education system* has school-age youngsters in its programs until age 16, more or less. The influence the schools and their administrators have is often sufficient to induce police officers to return truants to school, even if they are involved in disorderly behavior (fights) or petty offenses (vandalism, gambling, underage drinking). In addition, the police have programs ("Officer Friendly") in which they attempt to educate young people in schools.

Many churches (preeminently the Salvation Army) provide services in what might be called the *religious system* that are alternatives to the criminal-justice system for the old, the incapacitated, the drunk. Many of the clergy work closely with the police in law-enforcement programs, especially in the probation and juvenile aspects.

Even the *business system* is involved. Businesses victimized by their own employees may handle some criminal matters on their own, by forgiving the errant worker and giving him or her another chance, or by firing and no second chance. The police often consult with the management in deciding which course to follow and whether to pursue it in the criminal-justice system as well—or instead. Many business people will "take in" as an employee a young person in trouble or one diverted formally or informally from the criminal-justice system—often with the advice of the police.

These aspects of police work are bound to increase as the emerging identities of classes of people with special characteristics lead to the development of specialized systems for handling them. An "elderly" system is emerging in many communities, with programs, services, shelters, and so forth that are available now to the police as alternatives to jail for care and treatment of such persons. A "battered spouse" system is responding to recognition of that problem.

An outgrowth of these developments is that police departments are encouraging their officers to learn about such systems and refer or deliver persons to them rather than to the police station. This promises, as time goes on, to involve police officers even more deeply in those systems.

Nonpeople Systems. There are many systems not officially part of law enforcement to which the police relate regularly, receiving support from them and giving them support in a reciprocal relationship. These include the animal-welfare system, the parks and recreation system, the utilities system, the fire-protection system, the transportation system, the regulatory system, the communications system, the information system, the education system, the business system, and a system that might be called the criminal-justice community.

The dog pound plus the groups concerned with stray and maltreated animals (e.g., the SPCA) constitute what might be called the *animal-welfare system*. The police find themselves concerned not only with the kitten in the tree and the lost dog, but with cattle, horses, livestock of all kinds, alligators, unusual pets—the lost boa constrictor, the huge rat-like South American cayman—which terrorize a neighborhood for a while, and so on.

Special police agencies sometimes having the responsibility for policing *parks and recreation system,* but usually not. Police patrol by car is not fully sufficient, so horses and bicycles have come to be used. Such areas involve special problems, as do the libraries, museums, art galleries, and zoos.

The *utilities system* involves the power system; the water-supply system, which is perennially threatened with poisons; the sanitation system—the police get called because of uncollected garbage, and in a few cities during sanitation workers' strikes the police have had to collect the garbage. The police are usually the first on hand when power lines fall, when streets cave in, when street-repair warnings signs are down, and when fire hydrants leak or burst.

The *fire protection system,* too, is linked closely to the police, often under the same official in the city government. The police have special problems of traffic control and other problems when fires break out. Arson, the deliberate setting of a fire, joins the police and fire departments together in the investigative aspect. The police have to protect the firefighters, who have come in recent years to be the target of assaults such as rock throwing and even sniping as they go about their job. There is even the idea, inspired by some European systems, of combining police and fire departments so the same person would do both kinds of work.

The *transportation system* involves the police in many ways. The control of traffic is primarily a police responsibility. Certain highways have their own police departments. In addition to the streets, the transportation system includes the rapid-transit systems, the airports, and the harbors and waterfronts, each having its own police in some cases, but often not. The close connection between law enforcement and the transportation system is illustrated by the new Washington, D.C., Metro subway system: It is probably the first subway system to be designed with careful attention to the protection of its users from criminal activity and to the special needs of the police for handling instances of crime in the system. Many technological devices are employed for the discouragement and surveillance of crime, and great care was given to assuring prompt police response and access.

The *regulatory system* is predominantly governed by agencies other than the police. Federal agencies such as the Federal Communications Commission, state agencies such as a Department of Mines and Minerals, and local agencies such as the Bureau of Motor Vehicles have the lion's share of regulatory responsibilities. But the police departments have their share, too, with the licensing of guns, explosives, parades, taxicabs, parking garages, and numerous other enterprises, and the inspection of buildings for code compliance, liquor store and saloon operations, elevators, tow truckers, and the like.

The *communications system* is conceived broadly here to include any manner of communication. Police operations have been revolutionized by communications of the electronic variety; law enforcement without telephone or radio is all but unimaginable. In addition, recently the citizens-band radio has come upon the scene to aid the police, as when CBers report problems to the police, even using the system here and there as an auxilliary to the police patroling function; but now and then frustrating the police as well, when CBers report that "Smokey Bear" or "County Mountie" is ahead with radar.

The media is an extremely important communications system: Not only does crime constitute a major component of the news, but crime, detective, and police serials have been a staple of the comics and radio and television, shaping the image of the public about the police function, even shaping the police officers' image of themselves, partly because such programs glamorize them and they want to live up to that image, and partly because they know that the image is nothing less than the public expects. In addition, the media have some effect on crime itself, as we will see in Chapter 8.

Just as we are in the midst of a communications revolution, so we are in the midst of a revolution that is rapidly changing the *information system.* The day is long past when the police could do their business on the basis of remembering who was who and who did what and when. Today there is paperwork, from the traffic ticket through the patrol officer's daily diary or log and field notebook, to the reports he must write up on the offenses he handles. Infomation is collected and must be reported elsewhere. Central offices gather, hold, retrieve, and disseminate information. Finally, the computer has made it possible to do these things electronically, as well as summon up and transmit information instantly. All the states are now linked in a system by which they can transmit information to each other. The information revolution is not without its drawbacks, however; the police find themselves embroiled in controversy about what kind of information should be gathered, how and for how long it should be stored, who should have access to it, and so forth.

The *education system* has a "nonpeople" side which is of direct interest to law enforcement because it produces knowledge. Most of the researchers who study law enforcement are located in universities. The resulting research information is transmitted through hundreds of criminal justice programs, especially in community colleges. The study of law enforcement to develop better policies, strategies, and tactics is of growing concern, as Chapter 9 will indicate. Law enforcement has begun to be taught in most universities; at the community-college level, there are hundreds of criminal-justice programs that draw on police for instructors and, in turn, instruct them.

Business, too, lends its resources to law enforcement in many ways. The *business system* provides public-service advertising with law-enforcement themes, underwrites the costs of educational programs, and lends its leaders to local and state crime commissions. Business is the model for the rational, bureaucratic approach and management science provides law enforcement with many techniques of planning, budgeting, and so forth. Business security needs have sensitized business to the urgency of greater involvement of law enforcement in its day-to-day operations, such as improved surveillance for shoplifting and devices for signaling an attempted removal of an unpurchased item from a store. It has also sensitized business to the crime-prevention aspects of building design. And, of course, many police moonlight as security guards for business.

The information, education, and communication systems serve what might be called the *criminal-justice community,* which is made up of journalists commenting on matters of law enforcement, scholars studying crime and criminal justice, and groups that are one or two removed from the system itself and therefore unlike, say, the American Civil Liberties Union, which has lawyers directly involved, or the Police Benevolent Association, which is made up of police officers and deals directly with police leadership. Organizations like the American Bar Association take an interest in law enforcement, sponsoring among other things the important studies referred to in Chapters 10 and 11. The National Council on Crime and Delinquency takes an interest in the reform of criminal justice, especially corrections, and it has proposed several "model" statutes. Most commentators—Reston, Lewis, Reisel, Buckley, Von Hoffman, Horne—become interested in law enforcement; some even become personally involved, like Jimmy Breslin's receipt of messages from Son of Sam.

THE POLICE AS AN AGENCY OF MUNICIPAL GOVERNMENT

The realization that the police relate to several systems, not just to the criminal-justice system, gives rise to a fresh understanding of policing. This has been stated well by Herman Goldstein:

> To analyze the *totality* of police functioning and the police *as an institution*, it is essential to break through the confining criminal justice framework, for it is now clear that it is not sufficiently comprehensive to encompass all that goes on in the daily operations of a police agency. The bulk of police business, measured in terms of contacts with citizens,

takes place *before* invoking the criminal justice system (for example, checking suspicious circumstances, stopping and questioning people, maintaining surveillance), makes use of the system for *purposes other than prosecution* (to provide safekeeping or to investigate), or occurs in its entirety *outside* the system (resolving conflict, handling crowds, protecting demonstrators).[8]

The upshot of this new conception of the police is that it can be best understood as an agency of municipal government rather than as a part of the criminal-justice system. Goldstein, the "father" of this idea, states its value this way:

> Viewing the police—first and foremost—simply as an agency of municipal government, elementary as this concept may seem, serves a number of important purposes. It puts to rest the argument that police functioning should be viewed solely within the context of the criminal justice system. It rids us of the notion that the police are a legal institution created with a function strictly defined by statute, and substitutes in its place a more flexible concept of the police as an administrative unit of local government. And it contributes toward challenging the widely held belief that dealing with crime is the sole function of the police; that all other tasks are peripheral or ancillary.[9]

Some of the significance of this new conception will be developed in Chapter 11, which addresses the dissonance of the legal and the legitimate, or the inappropriateness of conventional powers (e.g., arrest), that are suitable for criminal justice but not the full range of noncriminal police tasks.

The relationships of the police to other systems is important for an additional reason: The significant recent development of civilianization implies the subsequent development of paraprofessionalization—a combination that promises to change the nature of the responsibilities of the police officer. In the last generation there has been a steady increase in civilianization, or the use of persons other than sworn police officers ("civilians") for many tasks in the police department. Initially civilians performed clerical, janitorial, and other simple, routine chores for which police officers were overqualified. Although at first an economy measure, the employment of civilians was extended to law enforcement specialties such as communications (many dispatchers are civilians now), fingerprinting, photography, various investigative and detention tasks, and some community relations work. This hiring practice parallels a similar development in other fields, such as the military, where civilians are now performing many tasks that enlisted men exclusively handled before, and in the parochial schools, where the teachers were exclusively members of teaching orders, the proportion of nuns teaching is declining.

A related movement, *paraprofessionalization,* is occurring in the professions. Increasingly the work of doctors and lawyers is being done by persons without professional training but with enough skills to do many of the tasks formerly done exclusively by the professionals. For example, in medicine there are numerous things that only doctors used to do (much of the physical examination, for instance) that others, such as nurses or paramedics can do just as well—and perhaps even better, since it represents a "high skill' for them rather than a "low skill" for a doctor. This suggests that many of the tasks police officers have traditionally performed might well be done by others. Specifically, if "social work" is what police officers do with much of their time, it can be done by social workers in the police agency; traffic work can be done as well by specialists in its various fields, just as "meter maids" have supplanted the patrolman issuing parking tickets in most cities. Likewise, the juvenile officer might as well—or better—be someone with training and experience in youth work. Police officers can, of course, be given this training and many do acquire such experience. But their time and effort, given the qualifications for which they were originally recruited and selected, might better be put into work involving serious crime rather than the usual juvenile delinquencies.

One implication of the paraprofessionalization of the police is that an assessment of the full range of police tasks and the skills required to perform them (as reviewed in this chapter), would reveal an array of competencies calling for specialized paraprofessionals—even for fully professionalized specialists. Such specialists would strengthen the union of police and other systems and improve the bridge of services the police provide to these systems. The police officer would be a "generalist" in a position of directing the specialist; the patrolman would coordinate the police and other systems through the "bridging" work of the specialists. This is yet another unexplored frontier in law enforcement.

SUMMARY   This chapter has surveyed the interpenetration of other institutions and systems into what is traditionally associated with the criminal-justice system. It looked into identification, detection, accusation, apprehension, detention, protection, prosecution, adjudication, disposition, and reintegration. It noted the variety of institutions outside the criminal-justice system that participate in these functions, aiding and sometimes displacing the police, courts, and corrections institutions. It was suggested that this was part of a general movement to *privatize* functions of government.

The survey then turned outward from criminal justice to look at the many systems to which the police also relate, such as the juvenile system, the drug-abuse system, the health system, the mental-health system, the welfare system, the military, education, religious, business, and "elderly" systems, to mention those mainly concerned with people. In addition, we also considered the systems of animal welfare, parks and recreation, utilities, fire protection, transportation, regulation, communications, information, and the "nonpeople" aspects of education, business, and the criminal justice community. This leads to a new conception of the police as an agency of municipal government. Thus conceived, the police constitute a system within a system of all these other systems. This requires a rethinking of much of the functions, systems, and institutions of law enforcement. Out of this may come a redefinition of responsibilities, powers, and authority.

NOTES

1. D. F. Aberle et al., "The Functional Prerequisites of a Society," *Ethics* (1949–1950), vol. 60, pp. 100–111.
2. Peter W. Greenwood and Joan Petersilia, *The Criminal Investigation Process, Vol. I: Summary and Policy Implications* (Santa Monica, Calif.: Rand Corporation, 1975).
3. Monrad G. Paulsen and Sanford H. Kadish, *Criminal Law and Its Processes* (Boston: Little, Brown, 1962), p. 994.
4. Harry Kalven, Jr. and Hans Zeisel, *The American Jury* (Boston: Little, Brown, 1966).
5. Peter F. Drucker, *The Age of Discontinuity* (New York: Harper & Row, 1968), p. 234.
6. Herman Goldstein, *Policing a Free Society* (Cambridge, Mass.: Ballinger, 1977), pp. 24–25.
7. American Bar Association, *Urban Police Function,* 2nd ed., tentative draft (approved February 12, 1979), p. 12.
8. Goldstein, *Policing a Free Society,* pp. 32–33.
9. Ibid., p. 33.

SELECTED READINGS

Donald W. McEvoy, *The Police and Their Many Publics* (Metuchen, N.J.: Scarecrow Press, 1976).
Norval Morris, and Gordon Hawkins, *Letter to the President on Crime Control* (Chicago: University of Chicago Press, 1977).
George O'Toole, *The Private Sector* (New York: Norton, 1978).
Albert J. Reiss Jr., *The Police and the Public* (New Haven, Conn.: Yale University Press, 1971).

7
THE WIDER ENVIRONMENT OF THE POLICE

The survey in Chapters 5 and 6 carried the police from the initial point in a process of moving offenders along the pipeline of criminal justice, to an institution with many connections to other parts of the criminal-justice system, to a system sharing its responsibilities for criminal justice with other institutions as well as sharing some of the responsibility for the functions of these institutions. The survey now turns further outward to the wider environment that influences and is influenced by the police. This chapter explores the governmental, political and social environments of the police and the outer reaches of the problems and policies of policing.

A brief look at *systems thinking* sets the stage for a style of analysis that has everything related to everything else. It questions the conventional understanding of the criminal-justice system (a) as a nonsystem with its purposes confused and its parts uncoordinated, and (b) as a self-contained system—or nonsystem—like an unmovable rock about which the troubled waters of the community swirl. In the alternative view pictured here, the police are enmeshed in a system of governmental levels and branches, a political network, and a broader social context.

A "Systems" View of Law Enforcement

The tasks of the police officer indicate that policing is much more than initiating the flow of offenders from arrest through conviction and into corrections. The police have connections throughout the criminal-justice system. In addition, the police have much to do with other systems, and other systems have much to do with the police. Moreover, "out there" are additional influences on the functions, purposes, institutions, and processes of criminal justice in general and law enforcement in particular. This suggests the value of viewing criminal justice and law enforcement in the "systems" mode.[1] As in an ecology, the elements have become differentiated into distinct units, which interact together as a system so everything relates to everything else, as the saying goes. Nothing can be done to one part of the system without something happening in another part. In other words, those of a poet (with slight poetic license), "Thou canst not stir a flower without troubling of a star."

A *system* has come to be conceived of in the social sciences as a process sometimes so mysterious in its workings that its center is called a *black box,* into which go "inputs" from the environment and out of which come "outputs." These act upon the environment, causing things to happen in reaction. Through a "feedback loop," data about the reaction are fed back into the system once again as fresh input. The usefulness of this kind of analysis can be seen in the business world, where people, through systems thinking, have become sensitive to a complex environment of shareholders, customers, employees, suppliers, community, regulating agencies, press, and intellectual atmosphere (e.g., consumerism). This aids in fashioning appropriate strategies for responding to the needs, claims, demands, and support of those parts of its environment on which depends so much of "the bottom line" of profit. Law enforcement, too, has a complex environment which it needs to get to know—and respond to, and perhaps even manipulate.

A Note on Criminal Justice as a Nonsystem. The criminal-justice system has sometimes been viewed as a nonsystem[2] because it is thought to be too "unsystematic" to conduct any kind of business without its major components having an obligation to coordinate their activities, and without a central body having the power to require such coordination. By contrast the police, courts, and corrections systems have no such obligations and no such common head for supervision and control. Each is responsible to a different constituency—the municipal police to the mayor or the voters of the city, the sheriff and prosecutor to the voters of the county, the judge to the voters of the city, county, or another elected official, and corrections to the governor and the voters of the state. There is no single commanding unit, as in a military or business organization. There is no overall hierarchy, no chain of command, except within the separate elements, and nothing to bind the elements together in a system.

But that is to insist on an administrative model of a system, rather than on the conception of a system as something in which everything is related, responsive, and mutually dependent.[3] As *system* is used here, there ordinarily is no head managing the body deliberately to do as it demands; instead the blood flows, the stomach digests, and so on, as the result of a physiological system governed by the brain but not by conscious thought. Criminal justice can be conceived of as such a system, because things happening in one part have an effect on other parts. More crime ordinarily means more convictions; more convictions mean more prisoners or shorter sentences; and earlier releases mean earlier and perhaps more recidivism; hence, earlier or more recidivism means more crime—and so forth. There is a good deal of information flowing throughout the system. Judges are not unaware of the prison population when they sentence prisoners; parole boards are not unaware of community sentiment when they consider an application for parole; prosecutors and defense counsel communicate with each other. Thus it is not true that the criminal-justice system is a nonsystem (except in the administrative sense of *system*). Indeed, criminal justice is at the center of a complex system of systems, which in turn is surrounded by an environment of influences working upon the elements of criminal justice, which in its turn works upon them.

Thus the police are a system within this system of interrelated systems. The environment provides input into law enforcement's interrelated systems. Three systems in that enviornment—the governmental, the political, and the social—provide a context of profound and powerful forces to which law enforcement responds.

THE GOVERNMENTAL CONTEXT

Law enforcement is first of all a part of the government. It cannot be fully understood apart from the broader system of government of which it is a part. The governmental system as a whole involves (a) a *constitution,* which is at the foundation of law enforcement, as it is of the rest of the government; (b) three *branches of government,* each of which influences it deeply; and (c) the *levels of government* in a "federal" system.

The Constitution.   A constitution provides the framework of government. It is the underlying statement of governmental powers and limitations to which the people of the nation or state have agreed. The Constitution of the United States delegates powers to the national government, some of which are implemented in ways and by agencies with law-enforcement aspects. The Constitution also contains specific limitations on the states, hence on their police agencies, mainly in the ways the Bill of Rights protects the accused (which will be discussed in Chapter 10).

The state constitutions provide many of the same protections, and in some cases, even more. The state constitutions also provide the powers of state and local law-enforcement agencies. Technically this is the concept known as the *police power,* which means the power to deal with matters of "health, safety, morals, and welfare." This authority enables states to legislate in almost any way they please, subject only to the rights of individuals as they are protected in state and federal constitutions.

The "constitution" of a city is its municipal charter, granted by the state legislature. The powers of cities, under the typical state constitution, are entirely derivative: They have only the powers granted by the state legislature—and those are strictly construed. The power of cities to provide for law enforcement, however, is ordinarily quite broad, so that there is no question but that cities may have police departments. They must operate them, however, within the limits of the power spelled out in the city charter.

Branches of Government. A special feature of the American constitutional system is its three-fold division of government. At the time of the founding of the United States, it was thought that there were but three functions of government—the legislative, the executive, and the judicial—and that they should be lodged in separate parts of the government, each to be a check on the other. This has come to be known as the *separation of powers* and *checks and balances,* the latter being accomplished by deliberate overlaps in which each branch has some function more or less in the nature of that of another (like the legislature's power to deny consent to the executive's appointment of officials, which enables it to participate in the personnel function of the executive). The checks and balances help block what the founding fathers feared was a tendency of one branch to become a tyrant over the others, hence over the people.

The legislature is the sole source of written laws. No crime can be "created" except through definition by a legislature in the form of a statute, even though some states still permit (theoretically) prosecution of the so-called common-law crimes, which are declared by courts in the case-by-case fashion of legal definition so characteristic of the Anglo-American legal system. This applies at the national and state levels, and at the county and city levels as well, where a statute is usually called an *ordinance.* Crimes cannot be created by the police or other parts of the executive branch. Sometimes, however, the legislature delegates to an executive agency the power to make rules and regulations (e.g., to punish fraud) in the implementation of a broad legislative scheme (e.g., a welfare program). Some of the rules and regulations may be backed up by criminal sanctions which the law-enforcement agencies are obliged to enforce, although the main responsibility is often limited to the law-enforcement unit of the agency that has administrative responsibility for the program (e.g., the Internal Revenue Service's investigative unit for violations of income-tax laws).

The representative function of the legislature is one reason for the authority of its laws: Its members are elected by the people; it is a deliberative body thought to be, among the three branches of government, the one best suited for thoughtful policy decisions of a very broad sort. The narrower policy questions, as in the decision about specific ways of implementing a program, are often of a technical nature and best left to the executive branch. The legislature, however, has investigative powers to aid it in the supervision of the executive branch; it can summon before its investigative committeee the members of the executive agencies and compel them to explain their actions and provide information for further legislative deliberations. And the judiciary has the power, in deciding cases by interpreting statutes and regulations, to refine those rules. Thus the police are responsible for the enforcement of rules that evolve through the process of legislative enactment of statutes, executive promulgation of regulations, and judicial "fine-tuning" through "case law."

The executive (president, governor, mayor) is responsible for executing the laws, that is, for administering or enforcing them. It is by this authority that police agencies are created. And it is by the limitation of the separation-of-powers doctrine that the executive (therefore the police) does not itself legislate, that is, create new crimes—except insofar as agencies do as they implement legislation through the rule-making power delegated to them by the legislative authority, as indicated above. This gives rise to a serious problem of police discretion discussed later in Chapter 11: Patrol officers, at the lowest level of enforcement, typically select what laws they will enforce and how they will do so, according to their own set of values, experiences, and preferences, without much guidance from above, either from the legislature or their own department.

More generally, the executive occasionally clashes with the legislature over policy for two reasons: first, the executive, too, is a representative, being elected by the people, even if usually not quite the same constituency; second, the executive, because of the complexity of modern life and the difficulties of formulating policies, has gained the initiative in policy-making. Indeed, the chief executive enjoys the role of legislative leader, especially when he or she is of the same party as the legislative majority. The police officer must likewise be seen as a policy-maker in criminal justice, having similar qualities of representativeness (albeit not of the elected variety) and expertise. These qualities go far toward legitimizing the policy-making responsibilities the police have come to exercise.

The judicial branch settles disputes and "establishes justice" in its decisions, by interpreting and applying the law to the cases and controversies that arise in a complex and litigious society. Initially this is done in a trial court, where both sides to the dispute present evidence in support of their contentions. The decision of the trial court can then be appealed up through the hierarchy of courts. Most states, like the federal government, have an intermediate appellate court and an even higher, or Supreme Court, for final decisions. Some decisions of the highest state court can be appealed even further to the federal court system.

These processes are subject to complicated rules of jurisdiction, venue, and also to informal rules of "judicial self-restraint." Much of the self-restraint of the judiciary arises out of the recognition that the judges are not representative (in the elected sense) and not involved in the political process in the way and degree legislators are, so judicial decisions should go contrary to public sentiment only in unusual and compelling cases, or the public's generous view of the courts will be eroded. The result is a careful filtering of issues up through the hierarchy of courts to decision by the highest courts, which cautiously define and further refine the very foundations of the constitutional system, its separation of powers among the branches of government, its distribution of powers between national and state governments, and its balance of power and liberty between state and individual. This responsibility adds to the judges' sense of restraint. It also gives reason to the opposition to activist encroachments by the courts, as in certain decisions of the Warren Court (such as the *Miranda* case), into areas of policy acceptable to the legislative and executive branches and to public sentiment. (This dimension of the constitutional balancing will be discussed further in Chapter 10.)

The administration of government is accomplished in part by independent agencies sometimes collectively called the fourth branch. It is not a branch in the strict sense, but an extension of the legislative branch for delegated lawmaking, an augmentation of the executive branch for administering it, and a displacement of the judicial branch for deciding cases. Its independence comes from the creation of administrative boards and commissions by the legislature, with members appointed by the chief executive, who are thereafter largely independent of the influence of either branch because members' terms are fixed and neither the legislature nor the executive can remove them. In such commissions, such as the Securities and Exchange Commission, the legislative, executive, and judicial functions are combined, although they are carried out with some internal separation, in keeping with the principles of separation of power. The commissions have authority delegated to them by the legislative body to enact regulations pertaining to the general legislative program, to enforce those regulations through investigations and other policing activities carried out by their staff, and to conduct hearings before "hearing officers" in procedures that are quite like trials but whose decisions can be "appealed" to the commission itself, sitting much like an appellate court, after which the issue may go to the court system for further appellate consideration. The violations of administrative regulations frequently involve criminal sanctions, and this field of law enforcement is one of great importance, even though it is somewhat remote from the sort of law enforcement the public has in mind when they think of the police.

Levels of Government.   Another principle of American government that is important in its application to law enforcement is *federalism* or the division of governmental power among levels—national, state, and local. This contrasts with the unitary system of government, as in Great Britain or France, where there is one government divided into regional units for administrative purposes.

The concept of sovereignty is the controlling idea here. In a unitary system there is undivided sovereignty, lodged in a central government which has ultimate control over the workings of its administrative sub-divisions—just as Sears Roebuck controls each of its stores throughout the country. In a federal system, by contrast, sovereignty is divided be-tween the national government and the constituent governments, which, in most federal systems, came together at one time to create a national government to serve selected, collective purposes such as national de-fense, foreign policy, regulation of interstate commerce, and those other things a central government can do better than its parts can do even by cooperation.

A federal system is a difficult one to maintain, in part because the delicate balance between the national and state governments is main-tained by the courts, institutions that are vulnerable to political power. From time to time issues arise, like desegregation, over which some states will rise up in the name of their sovereignty and insist, as if they were as fully sovereign as independent nations in a confederation, that they can do what they please about the matter. Throughout our history those risings have been unsuccessful because the national interest came to prevail, through military force in the case of the Civil War. Force is usually avoided through the interpretations of the courts, which walk a tightrope between the competing claims of nation and state, working out adjustments that accommodate each other. Today the Supreme Court's balancing act involves criminal justice especially. The cases of *Mapp, Escobedo,* and *Miranda,* discussed in Chapter 10, are symbols of the Supreme Court's insistence on national standards of fairness to be fol-lowed by each and every state. Other cases, however, have permitted variety among the states, as in the case of *Terry* v. *Ohio,* which permits the states to adopt a more relaxed standard for "stop-and-frisk" than probable cause (one of the constitutional issues to be taken up later in that chapter).

International. Beyond the borders of a nation, law enforcement runs into problems because the powers of the nation end at its borders, beyond which it must depend on the cooperation of other nations. Most nations have entered into agreements pertaining to extradition, so fugitives cannot escape the nation seeking them. But the agreements are incomplete; some crimes are not included, and some nations do not have agreements. So there are havens from some prosecutions, such as the Dominican Republic, where Robert Vesco, an American financier, has resided for several years beyond the reach of the United States.

In recognition of common problems of law enforcement, many nations support international organizations such as Interpol, which maintains records and facilitates the efforts of nations to apprehend international fugitives, and the United Nations, which is beginning to turn its attention to problems of crime. There are many cooperative efforts between nations to deal with criminal activity of an international character, such as narcotics, which begins with poppy production in Turkey, Mexico, or the Far East; continues with transportation of its syrup to laboratories in France and elsewhere for production of heroin; then shipment into the United States and other countries for wholesale and retail distribution. There is a brisk international traffic in stolen, forged, and counterfeited securities; in art works; in archeological treasures; and in many other items of value. Terrorism has recently come to have a distinct international flavor, with terrorists headquartered in one country striking in another; skyjacking usually involves international flights.

To cope with foreign aspects of law enforcement, six federal agencies (Drug Enforcement Administration, Federal Bureau of Investigation, Immigration and Naturalization Service, Customs Service, Internal Revenue Service, and the Secret Service) have foreign operations.[4]

National. The "police power" to make laws about health, safety, morals, and welfare is lodged in the states, not in the national government. Under the U.S. Constitution, the powers of the national government are enumerated rather than general, so it addresses crime in selective rather than general ways. The constitutional rationale of modern federal programs in labor relations, welfare, agriculture, housing, and the like could, nevertheless, be made the basis for a general, national law-enforcement program, a national police force, and all that conceivably might go with it. But the tradition of state and local responsibility for law enforcement's general concerns is strong, so it will no doubt be many years, if ever, before crime reaches a point of such urgency or of such difficulty or expense of enforcement, that the federal government would take over the law-enforcement function of the states and cities.

There are important law-enforcement functions vested in several of the cabinet departments of the national government.[5] The Attorney General is the leading law-enforcement official of the land, heading all efforts of the Department of Justice. Its Solicitor General selects and manages the federal government's appeal of criminal cases argued before the United States Supreme Court. The Criminal Division handles the bulk of the department's criminal business through its specialized sections, such as the one on organized crime. The United States Attorneys, one for each federal judicial district, prosecute the federal cases all over the country. The Federal Bureau of Investigation (FBI), the best-known federal law-enforcement agency, has several parts providing services to state and local agencies, such as its Identification, Training, General Investigation, Domestic Intelligence, Special Investigating, Criminal Records, and Laboratory divisions—all serve state and local law-enforcement agencies in various ways.

The Drug Enforcement Administration, likewise part of the Justice Department, aids state and local law-enforcement and deals directly with a subject (the narcotics laws) that overlaps state and local jurisdiction even more than the FBI overlaps it. The Immigration and Naturalization Service of the Justice Department also has law enforcement-responsibilities, which grow with the influx of illegal aliens. The Department also has a Civil Rights Division which enforces the Civil Rights Act under which cases of deprivation of civil rights, such as police brutality, may be investigated and prosecuted.

The Law Enforcement Assistance Administration, also in the Justice Department, has grown in prominence in recent years, reaching a spending level of nearly a billion dollars a year in 1975. Much of its expenditure flows directly to the states, whose planning agencies put the funds into specific agencies for their improvement. The administration's National Institute for Law Enforcement and Criminal Justice puts money into research and development rather than purchases of equipment and other subsidies of police operations.

Outside of the Justice Department, the Department of the Treasury has its well-known Internal Revenue Service (IRS), which includes Intelligence, Inspection, and Internal Security units, each of which has law-enforcement functions that are especially important, given the ability of the IRS to successfully prosecute for tax evasion many of the prominent figures in organized crime who have eluded the efforts of the government to prosecute them under conventional criminal laws. In addition, there is the Customs Service, which is involved in detection of illegal items from abroad; the Bureau of Alcohol, Tobacco and Firearms, which has important functions in the gun-control and explosives area. The Secret Service is the arm of Treasury which provides protection to the president and investigative functions pertaining to counterfeiting of money, bonds, and other federal instruments. Finally, the Treasury Department administers the Consolidated Law Enforcement Training Center, which provides training for many federal law-enforcement agencies.

Other cabinet departments with law-enforcement responsibilities include Transportation, whose Coast Guard is involved in smuggling protection; Defense, whose military branches have law-enforcement arms (the army's Military Police Corps, the navy's Shore Patrol, and the air force's Security Police); Interior, with policing function in the Fish and Wildlife, Indian Affairs, Mines, and National Park Services; Agriculture, with law enforcement programs concerned with preventing and detecting violations of laws about food stamps, meat and poultry regulations (processing, labeling, shipping), farm mortgages, as well as the Forest Service, which patrols the national forests; Health, Education and Welfare with Medicare and other welfare programs. The Postal Service, until recently a cabinet department, has its Postal Inspection Service, which provides mail-fraud investigations, which is especially important because few large-scale frauds are conducted without some use of the mails.

Independent agencies are also important in law enforcement. The Central Intelligence Agency (CIA) conducts foreign intelligence operations. The Civil Service Commission, the Federal Communications Commission, the Federal Trade Commission, the Interstate Commerce Commission, the National Transportation Safety Board, the Securities and Exchange Commission—all have connections with law-enforcement functions.

A recent survey conducted by the President's Office of Management and Budget reveals extensive police and investigative activities by agencies of the federal government. In addition to 12 organizations with direct law enforcement missions (Bureau of Alcohol, Tobacco and Firearms, Bureau of Indian Affairs, Coast Guard, Customs Service, Drug Enforcement Administration, FBI, Immigration and Naturalization Service, Marshall's Service, National Park Service, Postal Service, and Secret Service), some 101 other agencies that engage in law-enforcement related activities were surveyed. Nine of the 12 major agencies and 22 of the 101 other agencies have programs concerned with organized crime. Seven of the 12 and 67 of the 101 are involved in combatting white-collar crime. Eleven of the 12 and 35 of the 101 others have programs aimed against terrorism.[6]

In addition, there are hundreds, perhaps thousands, of federal statutes and regulations making something illegal and providing criminal penalties. These are enforced in a wide variety of ways but prosecuted almost exclusively by the United States attorneys in the district having jurisdiction. In each session of Congress, like each session of a state legislature, there is pressure to enact new prohibitions with criminal penalties attached, and many are enacted each term.

States.   The law enforcement powers of the states differ markedly from those of the national government. This is because the states have general rather than selected jurisdiction over crime, which means that the states and their subdivisions are responsible for the ordinary crimes rather than the specialized crimes, which are subject to federal law enforcement. Despite this difference in theory, the federal government has power in certain limited jurisdictions like the power of a state. So it has a criminal code covering crimes similar to those the states are concerned with (these will be discussed in Chapter 8, using the proposed revision of the federal criminal law as the model).

Governors are constitutionally responsible for administering the laws of their states, but so much of the operational responsibility which is theoretically theirs has been removed by the legislature that they have few responsibilities for the enforcement of ordinary laws. The attorney general, on the other hand, may be vested with responsibility for certain kinds of crimes such as consumer fraud, securities fraud, and organized crime.

At the state level there are various agencies and officials with law-enforcement responsibility.[7] The National Guard is the state's military arm, existing now mainly as a training and readiness operation for national defense. But it has riot-control responsibilities, along with its other civil emergency duties, and has been involved in some of the well-known law-enforcement operations in recent years, such as the Kent State affair. In the last decade, in recognition of its lack of preparation for such things as the riots of the 1960s, the National Guard has paid a good deal of attention to riot control.

The state's alcohol control agency is involved in policing the liquor business. A civil-defense agency has potential law-enforcement responsibilities. A fire marshal is involved in the criminal aspect of fires, such as arson investigation. The fish, game, and wildlife agencies have law-enforcement responsibilities—the game warden is an ancient and familiar figure in rural law enforcement.

The highway patrol is the best known, seemingly omnipresent law-enforcement agency of the state, and often its best-trained police agency. Some have long and proud traditions, like the Texas Rangers, which is not strictly a highway patrol agency but, like several other "highway patrols," has several additional law-enforcement responsibilities. State police departments, often beginning as highway-patrol agencies, keep expanding in their responsibilities for law-enforcement assistance to other state-level agencies and in their services to local agencies (e.g., laboratory analysis).

Several states have narcotics agencies paralleling the Justice Department's Drug Enforcement Administration, providing direct investigation as well as services to local agencies. Professional certification agencies (licensing occupations and professions) and racing boards (horse and dog racing) have law-enforcement duties. The state's labor-relations agency and its mines and minerals agency have law-enforcement dimensions. The motor-vehicle administration has enforcement responsibilities involving its inspection, licensing, and record-keeping functions. Finally, like their federal counterpart, the state legislatures have committees concerned with law enforcement and now and then create commissions for continual or occasional investigation of criminal conditions.

Local. At the local level the county sheriff is the oldest of the law-enforcement officers, going back a millenium into medieval English history for its origins. The sheriff is still, in most counties, a vital element of law enforcement, even in counties like Cook County, Illinois, where most of the county is urbanized and each municipal agency has its own police agency.

The municipal police department, the most common, best known of the local agencies, has already been dealt with in its organizational aspects. There are other local officials, however, related closely to law enforcement. There is a constable in some parts of the country, a marshal in others, and specialized public police here and there for parks and parkways or special protective functions (e.g., the Executive Protection Service in Washington, which guards embassies, consulates, and the like). In addition, most jurisdictions have a coroner or medical examiner responsible for investigation of uncertain causes of death. Skilled medical examiners like Milton Halperin of New York City have been able to identify homicides which would otherwise have gone undetected.

Intergovernmental Cooperation. The 50 states were created many years ago in circumstances that were very different from today's complex urbanized, mobilized society. Borders were and remain more accidental than not, rivers being a typical dividing line. This has given rise to many efforts to bring about cooperation among the states with respect to common problems in metropolitan areas. The *interstate compact* is a device by which two or more states agree to deal cooperatively with a problem. Law enforcement, too, has become complex over the years, and crime and criminals have never respected the boundaries between states. In many metropolitan areas (Chicago, Philadelphia, St. Louis, Louisville, Pittsburgh), organized crime—and unorganized crime, for that matter—covers multiple jurisdiction, most of which spread over two or more states. Modern communications and transportation have made things even more complex. The Beltway, or the circumferential expressway of the Washington, D.C., area, made possible the Beltway Bandits, who could commit robberies or burglaries in Maryland or Virginia and be miles away in another jurisdiction in minutes. But cooperation among jurisdictions has been slow to develop. The federal government has contributed to cooperative ventures with its "strike forces," which in varying degrees have involved local police agencies and the "task forces" of DEA, which were designed to involve federal, state, and local agencies under federal leadership. The growing movement toward interagency cooperation among local and state jurisidictions leaves a long way to go toward meeting the interjurisdictional challenge of crime.[8]

Consolidation Movement.   The inefficiency of small, local police departments has led to some experimentation with more drastic solutions. Where with urban development, a city spreads to fill out a county, it ceases to make much sense to maintain separate police agencies, with a sheriff and police chiefs often at odds over common problems. This has led to consolidation plans. More often these have been for specialized functions other than law enforcement (such as sanitation), but increasing attention is being given the consolidation of all law-enforcement agencies, as in Jacksonville, Florida, where the city and county police agencies have been combined.[9]

THE POLITICAL CONTEXT

If the constitution is the framework of government, politics is its foundation. The governmental context is part of a broader political context to which law enforcement is related. If politics were only a matter of political parties, it would be safe to say that politics has little to do with law enforcement. But law enforcement relates to politics in many ways if politics is understood as political scientists understand it—including not only political parties but other political phenomena such as political culture, public opinion, interest groups, elections and voting behavior, and many institutions—including legislatures, courts, and executive agencies.

Politics.   Politics is not merely the activities of politicians, which include many of the activities of political parties that were so offensive in the early decades of this century, such as graft and corruption. Politics is the art or science of governing the community, of dealing with the very purposes of the polity (political community)—and law enforcement is involved in that. In recent decades the study of politics has focused on "the state" and its activities, and law enforcement is fundamental to that. Some political scientists focus on "power" and there is clearly a "power relationship" between the police officer and the offender and between law enforcement and minorities, especially "deviant" minorities of the community. Thus, the police—the very term comes from *polis,* which meant "polity or political community" in ancient Greek—are clearly involved in politics.

Political Culture.   An important part of the environment of criminal justice and law enforcement is the political culture.[10] Political culture, in addition to partaking of the broader social culture (which will be discussed in the next section, consists of specifically political aspects which relate in particular to political institutions. The political culture is the source of many inputs of the political system, such as the support, the expectations, and the demands that flow into the "black box" of politics, (see page 179) or of criminal justice in particular. Emerging are the policies, decisions, and actions which constitute the output of the system. For example, Americans exhibit a high level of support for political and governmental institutions, but less support for the incumbents, that is, for the politicians who are the flesh and blood of the abstractions to which the people are loyal. Blacks and young people rank somewhat lower than the population generally in terms of their support for institutions, but in neither cases is the level of support generally much lower. This reflects the broad loss of authority of institutions in our time, which Robert Nisbet called the "twilight of authority."[11] As it goes on and deepens, it would seem likely to affect the levels of respect for law and its enforcement as well as for the police officers who do so.

Expectations exhibit both consensus and conflict. The public expects full, even zealous enforcement of laws against violent crime, but expectations divide sharply on "moral" or "victimless" crimes (which will be discussed in Chapter 8). Demands have to do with both content and manner of policy. There are some things the public demands of government, like crackdowns of certain kinds; other things it does not, like full, sustained enforcement of law. As for the method of expressing demands, most of the public chooses the nonviolent over the violent, clearly preferring ballots to bullets. So elections, lobbying, and political parties are accepted ways of expressing demands, rather than terrorism, extortion, and intimidation.

Elements of culture in the American character, political scientist Stephan V. Monsma points out, are competitiveness for the good (that is, material) things of life, emphasis on religious/moral values, antiauthoritarianism, optimism, common sense, but also racism (and sexism) and Americanism.[12] These are reflected in law enforcement, as in the slow opening up of its ranks to blacks and women, the moralistic approach to criminal law, and the suspicion of law enforcement's power.

Public Opinion. The expressed political consensus on issues is what is meant by public opinion.[13] It can be found by polls and measured by the extent to which people hold various views. Public opinion expresses the sense of the community on an issue, thereby lending support to the political and governmental institutions, or indicating lack of support. The sources of public opinion include opinion shapers such as family, class, ethnic groups, coworkers, and any influence which socializes people or shapes their opinions, such as school and church. Vehicles for the expression of public opinion are the so-called primary groups (family, friends, coworkers) within which views are expressed by word of mouth; the political process (platforms, candidates, parties, elections), which crystallizes issues and opinion; and the mass media, which articulate and influence as well as express opinion.

Opinion is communicated to the political system in all these ways, to the black box of political decision, wherein legislative, executive, and judicial officials formulate the policies which emerge from the system as outputs of law, administrative decision, and judicial opinion. The police, as part of the executive branch, are directly influenced in all these ways by public opinion; they sense the public mood. In addition, they respond to changing opinion indirectly as it influences legislatures and courts. For example, as opinion on the seriousness of the use of marijuana shifted, some police agencies and officers let up somewhat on their investigative and apprehension activities; later their letup was sanctioned or legitimized in some jurisdictions by "decriminalization."

Interest Groups. The pluralistic character of the American people, resulting from the freedom to join groups combined with a propensity to do so (America is a nation of joiners), yields a diversity of interest groups. These are organized aggregations of people banded together on the basis of a common interest or shared attitude. Unlike many groups, however, which have purely social, financial, or recreational aims, the aim of interest groups is to influence public policy. They influence public opinion through the media, and they directly "lobby" the legislature, the executive, the courts, and other groups. Interest groups are in disrepute these days because some have sought to "buy" influence with political contributions or outright bribes. But there is much to be said for them: They have a representative function which is crucial in a democracy; they negotiate among each other, aiding in the sharpening of proposals in the policy-making process; they—paradoxically—restrain the particularism of American democracy, its disintegrative, centrifugal force of factionalism, by balancing interests, by overlapping memberships, by forming coalitions.

Law enforcement is influenced by interest groups or "pressure groups," and not only through their influence on the legislature, executive, and judiciary branches, which trickles down to the police. There are interests which attempt to reach the police directly. Some do this in subtle ways, and are usually (but not always) turned away. Racketeers, gangsters, professional thieves, organized criminals, prostitutes, and gamblers are each organized in a loose sense (without the dues-paying memberships, newsletter, and other trappings of formal organization), and seek to gain in direct dealing with police. On the other side are the churches, good-government groups such as the League of Women Voters, local organizations such as the Chicago Crime Commission, the police rank-and-file itself (Patrolman's Benevolent Association, the unions), the militants, the NAACP, the ACLU—all representing more or less distinct interests, each with a membership of sorts, some dues-paying, some not, and all transmitting their messages to the police.

Not many years ago political scientists thought interest groups held the key to policy, that the positions of the interest groups could be represented as if by vectors reflecting the force and direction of policy preferences of the interest group. Hence, as in the vector-analysis of the physicist, they thought they could calculate the resultant policy as the product of the combined directions and forces of the interests involved in the shaping of a particular policy. It is no longer thought possible to do it quite that way. Nonetheless, the combination of interest groups makes for some predictability of policy outcomes. To put it very simply, when the American Civil Liberties Union and Americans for Effective Law Enforcement lock horns on an issue, the outcome is likely to reflect the stalemate: either nothing will happen or the difference will be split.

Political Parties.   The police have been wary for decades of political parties and their associated evils, such as political bosses, corruption, graft, party machines, and the like. Reformers have sought to separate the police from political-party influence. But political parties, like politics, are basic to American democracy: The two-party system is thought to be a key to stability and continuity in American democracy because both parties attempt to gain the support of a majority of the voters by building a consensus that moderates divisive extremes. That may be overdrawn and it may be threatened by the proliferation of interest groups, but political parties continue to enable the electorate to shape its views in the party's "platform" and its less formal positions, and through the party to influence its members in the legislature and at the highest levels of executive branch.

Reformers successfully eradicated partisan politics from many city governments—at least in a formal way—early in this century. Many city governments were made nonpartisan, meaning their candidates for office ran on a nonpartisan basis, with no formal party identification as Republicans or Democrats or whatever. This went a long way toward removing the police from party connections and obligations. Even in cities that did not have such reforms, the spirit of reform was strong enough to cause the city fathers to keep politics out of consideration in law-enforcement matters such as selection of a police chief. The politics of picking a chief, however, only shifted to another level and kind—the informal kind of politics among ethnic groups, classes, and other groupings—which is what realists would have predicted. One could hardly expect otherwise, given the ubiquity of politics. Today, policing is still not much involved in politics of the partisan sort, yet it responds to political influences in other ways.

Elections and Voting Behavior. Removal of the police from partisan politics has had the effect of removing them from electioneering, political campaigning, solicitations (of the overt sort), and other aspects of partisan politics. The civil-service reforms of the late nineteenth century, launched by the 1883 Pendleton Act, which brought civil service to the federal government, restrained the police in state and city systems from partisan activity—principally financial contributions and other direct support for political parties and candidates other than the casting of a vote.

Every now and then, however, a law-enforcement issue can be decisive in an election, with the police involved mightily—and permissibly so, as long as the issue is not colored in terms of Republican or Democratic sides. The civilian review board in New York City in 1966 is an illustration. Moreover, law enforcement generally has become a public issue in the last decade, championed by Barry Goldwater, the conservative Republican candidate for president in 1964. After Richard M. Nixon used the "law-and-order" issue effectively in 1972, virtually every candidate has taken up the issue. The most dramatic evidence of the change was in the 1977 mayoral primary in New York City, where all the candidates, most of them of various liberal persuasions, were speaking out strongly for stern measures they once would have had little use for.

One aspect of elections continues to be a sore spot in law enforcement—and perhaps inevitably so. Financial contributions from private sources continue to be necessary for most politicians, even for those whose personal wealth enables them to campaign with less concern for money.

Few contributions are made without a concomitant obligation on the part of the politician, usually implicit but well understood on the giving and receiving ends of the contribution. Thus it is difficult for an elected official to refrain completely from using influence over the police and prosecutor to gain favor for interests or persons close to a contributor.

THE SOCIAL CONTEXT

Beyond the governmental and political systems is yet another, broader and more inclusive system: society as a whole, which provides law enforcement with yet another important context of its nature and activities. The social context includes demography, culture, social organization, and social institutions.

Demography. The people of a society are the starting point of social analysis. In the United States the people are heterogeneous, urbanized, and mobile. There is a mixture of peoples but not nearly the blend of racial, ethnic, and national types our "melting pot" once promised. Thus in most large cities—and in many smaller ones, too—there is a significant degree of difference among the peoples of the city, often reflected in distinct neighborhoods, each having characteristics that must be met by the police with slightly—or sometimes greatly—differing responses, strategies, and tactics. For example, the Chinatowns of New York City, San Francisco, and elsewhere have traditionally been very law-abiding, whereas the black and Puerto Rican neighborhoods have been less so— calling for heavier patroling and other police involvement than in the Chinese communities.

The American people are urbanized, living in the cities and suburbs in increasing numbers, and are only recently beginning to shift back into small towns and rural areas. The crowding of the cities has been thought to have bad effects for centuries. For example, rural Southern culture, black and white alike, appears to be prone to violence that is of manageable proportions in a rural setting, where there is less frequency of engagements between people with such propensities. But when members of that culture move into the city and into much more frequent confrontations, their propensity to violence has more occasions for eruption.

Beyond this, there is thought to be a change from friendliness to hostility accompanying a move to a city. Also, the mobility of the people— the average American moves several times—from countryside to city, from inner city to suburb, from town to town, has an unsettling effect on many as it sunders the bond that holds people to people in a community.

The composition of the population is important, too. Much of the violence of the 1960s appears to have been the result of the coming of age of the children born in the postwar baby boom. Conversely, the generation coming along now is relatively smaller in proportion to the population as a whole. So demographers expect a decline in violence in the 1980s.

Social Institutions. The police is a social institution, which shares with other institutions its concern for law enforcement and social control. The family, education, and religion are also fundamental institutions in society. They function in part to control their members. In addition, there are political and governmental institutions, some of which are law-enforcement agencies, and economic institutions such as business and labor, which have social-control functions in addition to their principal functions. So firmly established is the family and so highly respected is it as an institution, even with its troubles today, that law enforcement defers to it in many ways. For instance, if the police come upon a fighting couple, it makes all the difference in the world whether they are family members: If they are merely two men, or two boys, or a boyfriend and girl friend, a man and his mistress, an employer and employee, a foreman and a laborer, a man and the wife of a neighbor—or any number of combinations—the police are likely to intervene and arrest one or both, but not if it is a fight between husband and wife or members of a family unit or close relatives residing together. Family fights, dangerous as they may be to the combatants, let alone to anyone who dares to interfere and find the combatants joined together against the outsider, are left uninterrupted to a far greater extent than other kinds of fights, which may be statistically much less dangerous. Saloon brawls, for all the slugging and cutting, lead to fewer homicides than family quarrels.

Education is a fundamental institution rooted in the capability of young people to learn and the need to transmit the culture to them through the learning process. Education would always occur in a society, but not necessarily in an organized, institutionalized way. Americans place great emphasis on education, often arguing that it is the key to the success of our democracy. Thus vandalism when it is aimed at school buildings is more shocking than vandalism aimed at subway trains or bus seats—except perhaps vandalism aimed at churches and synagogues. One result of this esteem of education is that students are given breaks that dropouts are denied. In addition, the police look to higher education, perhaps naively, for a better quality of police officer; and higher education itself, perhaps even more naively, believes it can supply that officer, as well as an educated citizenry better able than in the past to shoulder the responsibilities of shaping and guiding law enforcement.

Economic institutions, mainly business and labor, are deeply influential, too. Radicals have long argued that the legal system, including the criminal law and the police, is in the service of capitalism. There is much evidence of relationships between business and law enforcement, although they are not necessarily as supportive of "the establishment" as the radicals insist. The labor side of the American economic system has been influential, finally winning the right to "organize" police departments into labor unions in some cities.

Law enforcement is subject to a multitude of influences beyond the social, political, and governmental systems, although it is through those systems that many influences find their way to law enforcement. These influences can be considered to be elements of the culture in its broadest sense, hence they fall into such categories as material conditions and ideas.

Among the *material conditions,* geography and climate set limits on the social system, hence on the political and governmental systems, that influence law enforcement. For example, policing a mountainous area differs from policing a semitropical coastal area: Vehicles, clothing, and even the kinds of crime will differ according to the geography and climate—jeeps and horses rather than boats; heavy clothing rather than light clothing; mountain rescue gear rather than scuba gear; crimes relating to mining rather than fishing; relationships with the Forest Service rather than the Coast Guard; theft of snow skis rather than water skis; tourists in winter rather than summer.

The differences could be extended indefinitely; the sum of the differences would be two policing enterprises with many levels and kinds of differences between them. Sociologist Robert Bierstedt says these are negative, limiting factors, whereas culture is a positive, shaping factor, determining the nature of the social, hence the political, governmental, and law-enforcement system.[14] Among the cultural influences are *ideas:* "Ideas have consequences," Richard Weaver argued in a book of that title. This affects law enforcement. Sir Robert Peel's idea of a military style of municipal policing has powerfully influenced law enforcement to this day and will no doubt continue to—our grandchildren will speak of police sergeants and lieutenants and will probably see them in uniform (perhaps different, but uniforms nonetheless). The reformers of rehabilitation have been as much influenced in recent years by the argument of philosophers that the community has no right to intervene in the life of a prisoner against her or his will as they have been influenced by the discovery that rehabilitation techniques do not produce the effects intended. Like the inventory of material conditions, the catalog of ideas and their consequences could be multiplied many times. These conditioning factors (biology and geography) and this shaping factor (culture, especially its intellectual dimension) are indispensable to the study of the social factors that surround and influence law enforcement.

IMPLICATIONS OF SYSTEMS ANALYSIS OF POLICING

Seeing, as we have in these last three chapters, some of the many connections between the police and other elements of the criminal-justice system, other systems, and the wider environment gives rise to a picture of a network of relationship's in the law-enforcement system. In this context three developments or ideas begin to make more sense than they did in the abstract or on first hearing.

First, a situational analysis of "turfs" of law enforcement, or settings of particular kinds of crime, promises to make possible a more discriminating kind of prevention and reaction, based on a more sophisticated understanding of criminal behavior and its circumstances. Second, the structures and strategies of police-community relations (PCR) can be strengthened by systems analysis: it can aid in developing "PCR" from its early emphasis on public relations through today's more fundamental and constructive approaches of liaison between police agency and community leadership to a more far-reaching establishment of many relationships of mutual influence and support. Third, the privatization of criminal justice, suggested earlier in Chapter 6, can be appreciated best as part of a complex structure of associations in which the police and other institutions collaborate in carrying out the community's responsibility for social control.

The Situational Approach.   In Chapter 9 there will be some discussion of criminal behavior systems and a crime-specific analysis that promises to be helpful in law enforcement. It is worthwhile to anticipate that discussion by noting here that the systems approach brings into focus aspects of crime that might be overlooked if one concentrated only on the criminal act itself. Just as mountains differ from the seaside, with implications for policing, so the city differs from the countryside and the many parts of the city from one another. Railroad yards, high-rise housing projects, "Bohemian" neighborhoods, industrial parks, heavy construction sites, docks, airline terminals, "tenderloins" (or high-vice areas), and other territories must be known in detail for effective patrol and investigation. The university campus, for example, differs in some important ways from other areas. Donald Goodman and Arthur Niederhoffer, in their analysis of the relationship of police and campus, note that campus criminality tends toward victimless crime, the mood is one of tolerance of various behaviors of young people passing uncertainly from adolescence to adulthood, the style *is* one of discussion and persuasion rather than authority and directives.[15] One can add that the campus sensibilities are attuned to individual civil rights and to freedom of speech in particular, the actions are highly symbolic of independence, self-realization, and principle rather than aimed instrumentally at specific gains, such as a stolen car or purse. The police officer who does not appreciate these characteristics will be an alien in academic territory—and will provoke rather than pacify trouble.

A "holistic" analysis that attempts to see the totality of the situation (the many influences by which everything relates to everything else) would be useful in studying criminal activity in the figurative sense of geography as well as the literal sense: "Wall Street" for finance, "Madison Avenue" for advertising, "Fifth Avenue" for the shops catering to the "carriage trade," "Times Square" for pornography and prostitution. The police officer who works one "street" may well be out of his or her element on another—and none will be in their element if content only to observe from the sidewalk or patrol car. Each setting has important characteristics for criminal activity; each needs careful systems analysis for identification of relationships behind the building fronts, through and beyond the immediate setting of crime to the incentives, opportunities, transactions, and dispositions that make crime "happen" in its special ways under certain circumstances.

This approach would be useful in preventing and investigating other kinds of crimes that are set in complex systems, such as computerized accounting, welfare-payment procedures, insurance compensation systems, wholesale distribution channels, and the like. A better understanding of one's turf, hence better policing, would result from more systematic study than from the intuitions of shrewd but ignorant Columbos.

Police-Community Relations (PCR). Since the tumultuous mid-1960s there has been a keen interest on the part of the police and community leaders to establish and develop what has come to be known as "PCR." Its aim has been the minimization of disturbances—ranging from vandalism to riot—which are thought to be expressions of class, ethnic, or generational discontentments (lower class versus middle- and upper class, blacks and Hispanics versus whites, teenagers versus everyone else) rather than psychological disorders, marital discords, and other causes of violent behavior. This once meant little more than public relations or image-enhancing tactics. But many soon recognized, as did the President's Crime Commission in 1967, that more was needed:

> Community relations are not the exclusive business of specialized units, but the business of an entire department from the chief down. Community

relations are not exclusively a matter of special programs, but a matter that touches on all aspects of police work. They must play a part in the selection, training, deployment, and promotion of personnel; in the execution of field procedures; in staff policymaking and planning; in the enforcement of departmental discipline; and in the handling of citizens' complaints.[16]

Police-community relations units in the department, citizen advisory committees, programs of education, organizational liaisons, tours, institutes, school programs, crime-prevention programs, community service programs, and recreation programs were among the measures identified by the commission. The emphasis of the commission (and of most of those measures) was on responsiveness of the police to the community. But the problem—and the continuing shortcoming of PCR programs—may be only partially due to the closed nature of the police. So opening up the department and its members to outside influences may be only part of the answer. The rest of the answer is likely to be found in a more thoroughgoing analysis of the system's variety, to reveal precisely what and where connections exist or can be created so that the police can design proactive, not merely reactive, measures that go straight to the source of the problems, conditions, and circumstances that interfere with or upset the potential relationships that might be cultivated between police and community.

The Privatization of Criminal Justice. The third implication of systems analysis relates to the idea of privatization: it helps to overcome the resistance to the idea that law, police, courts, prisons—the criminal justice system, in short—can do it alone, that they stand like "the thin blue line" of police, between social order and chaos, between civilization and the jungle. That view overestimates criminal justice and underestimates the rest of society as a means of socialization and control. The traditional institutions—family, church, school—have no doubt declined in importance as social control mechanisms. But it is not clear just how far they have declined or that other institutions (the juvenile gang, the television series) have not taken up some of the slack, albeit with aims that may be somewhat misguided. The "mediating structures," both old and new, are likely to be more vital than they are credited with being in this age of attention to the larger structures of government and economics. To the extent they are more vital, the criminal justice system has partners in the enterprise of social control. How, and how well, they can work together remains to be seen, with systems analysis being the major means of determining how much of the burden of criminal justice can be shared and with whom.

SUMMARY   This chapter looked beyond the police to the wider environment—government, politics, and society, each extending further from the institutions with which the police are immediately associated. The police are influenced by the legislative, executive, and judicial branches of national, state, and local governments; the culture, opinions, interests, parties, and elections of politics; and the broader elements of society. This wider environment of the police accounts for much of the nature of American law enforcement.

Systems analysis provides an important technique for identifying influences in that environment and tracing them, as input, into the system of the police, then out again as output. The reciprocal relationship of the police to the elements of their environment suggests that an analysis of the situation, including the elements of the environment, may be a way for the police to develop policies and programs for dealing with crime, as well as their other concerns. Chapters 10 and 11 will take up some of these implications.

NOTES
1. C. West Churchman, *The Systems Approach* (New York: Dell, 1968), pp. 1–78.
2. Richter H. Moore, Jr., "The Criminal Justice Non-System," in Richter H. Moore, Jr., et al., eds., *Readings in Criminal Justice* (Indianapolis: Bobbs-Merrill, 1976), pp. 5–13.
3. Jim L. Munro, "Towards a Theory of Criminal Justice Administration: A General Systems Perspective," *Public Administration Review* (November/December 1971), pp. 621–631.
4. Office of Management and Budget, *Federal Law Enforcement, Police and Investigative Activities: A Descriptive Report* (Washington, D.C.: President's Reorganization Project, 1978), pp. 88–89.
5. U.S. Dept. of Justice, *Federal Law Enforcement and Criminal Justice Assistance Activities* (Washington, D.C.: U.S. Government Printing Office, 1972).
6. U.S. Department of Justice, *Criminal Justice Assistance Activities*, pp. 68–70.
7. National Criminal Justice Information and Statistics Service, *Criminal Justice Agencies* (Washington, D.C.: Law Enforcement Assistance Administration, 1975).
8. Office of Management and Budget, *Federal Law Enforcement*, pp. 70–71.
9. National Advisory Commission on Criminal Justice Standards and Goals, *Police* (Washington, D.C.: U.S. Government Printing Office, 1973), pp. 108–116.
10. Stephen V. Monsma, *American Politics: A Systems Approach* (New York: Holt, Rinehart and Winston, 1969), pp. 23–47.
11. Robert Nisbet, *Twilight of Authority* (New York: Oxford, 1975).
12. Monsma, pp. 35–42.
13. James Garofalo, *Public Opinion About Crime* (Washington, D.C.: Law Enforcement Assistance Administration, 1977).
14. Robert Bierstedt, *The Social Order*, 3rd ed. (New York: McGraw-Hill, 1970), p. 63.
15. "Universities and the Police," Arthur Niederhoffer and Abraham Blumberg, eds., in *The Ambivalent Force*, 2nd ed. (New York: Holt, Rinehart and Winston, 1976), pp. 210–217.
16. President's Commission on Law Enforcement, *The Challenge of Crime in a Free Society* (Washington, D.C.: GPO, 1967), p. 100

SELECTED READINGS

Russel L. Ackoff, *Redesigning the Future: A Systems Approach to Societal Problems* (New York: Wiley, 1974).

Walter Buckley, *Sociology and Modern Systems Theory* (Englewood Cliffs, N.J.: Prentice-Hall, 1967).

C. West Churchman, *The Systems Approach* (New York: Delta, 1968).

N. Gary Holten, and Melvin E. Jones, *The System of Criminal Justice* (Boston: Little, Brown, 1978).

Stephen V. Monsma, *American Politics: A Systems Approach* (New York: Holt, Rinehart and Winston, 1969).

Richter H. Moore, Jr., "The Criminal Justice Non-System," in *Readings in Criminal Justice,* Moore, Marks, and Barrows, eds. (Indianapolis: Bobbs-Merrill, 1976), pp. 5–13.

Jim L. Munro, "Towards a Theory of Criminal Justice Administration: A General Systems Perspective," *Public Administration Review* (November-December 1971).

Robin M. Williams, Jr., *American Society: A Sociological Interpretation* (New York: Knopf, 1960).

Three

COPS, CRIMES, AND CRIMINAL LAW: PURPOSES AND PRINCIPLES OF LAW ENFORCEMENT

Part Three takes up the purposes and principles of law enforcement. Chapter 8 opens with an unorthodox suggestion that most, rather than little, of what concerns the patrol officer involves crime, not necessarily in the essence of an event (as in a rape or robbery), but as one because of the circumstances and elements of such events (as in the trespass or assault or battery typically involved in a domestic dispute) or in the potential of volatile situations to erupt unpredictably into violence. The chapter then proceeds to a discussion of crime, with some general definitions and distinctions of criminal law by which offenders are classified for processing and punishment. The discussion of criminal law concludes with the troublesome relationship of law and morality, with special attention to the problem of "victimless" crimes.

Chapter 9 turns to the events and people categorized as crime and criminals. It shifts from the abstractions of criminal law to those of criminological theory, with a brief survey of the causes of crime. Also presented are statistics on crime rates, types of crime and criminals, and specific descriptive material. After tracing the impact of crime on its victims and the community, the chapter winds up with a "crime analysis," or the police study of crime, which promises to bridge the practice of law enforcement and the science of criminology.

Chapters 10 and 11 come to grips with some of the special problems inherent in the purposes and principles of law enforcement. Chapter 10 describes the balancing of conflicting values, and authority versus liberty in particular, with some historical background on constitutional liberties. The chapter then discusses the rules of arrest procedures and search and seizure. Two "models" of the criminal process are presented by which the balance between police power and individual liberty might be judged, and finally some cases of constitutional law which demonstrate the balancing process in the Supreme Court. Chapter 10 ends with a discussion of the exclusionary rule—the rule by which the trial courts attempt to keep police practices within the boundaries set by the Supreme Court.

Chapter 11 deals with the lesser-known problems of discretion and "dissonance" in police authority. Discretion (the range of choice open to the police to do what they do and by what means) is reviewed with special attention to the approaches to controlling discretion. The approach gaining favor in recent years, rule-making by the police in consultation with the community, is studied in light of the political realm in which the police would find themselves. The political role of the police is explored (along with the political hazard of police corruption) as the foundation of an approach to the problem of dissonance, or lack of harmony, between legality and legitimacy in police authority. This is the problem of the police lacking the power to perform appropriate services and, conversely, the problem of the police having powers that are used inappropriately.

8

CRIME AND CRIMINAL LAW: THE LAW ENFORCEMENT MISSION

This chapter challenges the popular notion that little of the police officer's time and energy is devoted to crime. Most of what engages the patrol officer does, in fact, have to do with crime: If it is not crime in the usual sense, it at least includes crime as one of its elements (in a sense sufficient for a "legalistic" police officer) or it threatens to erupt into crime or disorder.

This chapter explores the concept of crime and its definitions, especially those contained in the law of crimes, because coping with crime is an important (if not the most important) responsibility of the police. After sketching the more general aspects of criminal law, this chapter sets forth several definitions of specific crimes. It concludes with a discussion of the relationship between law and morals, which is the basis of the controversy over decriminalization of certain kinds of conduct.

Crime animates the enterprise of law enforcement even if patrol officers (supposedly preoccupied with rescuing kittens in trees) spend much of their time on matters not clearly or directly criminal in nature. It is crime that patrol officers have in mind as they walk or drive the beat. It is the pursuit of the criminal that shapes the organization, management, strategies, and tactics of law-enforcement agencies, even as their front-line personnel give directions to tourists and aid motorists with car trouble. Thus crime and the criminal must be focal points of study in law enforcement. The seemingly noncriminal matters that police officers attend to during most of their time have a criminal dimension, which makes the formal definitions and elements of criminal law essential in the study of law enforcement.

Theories of criminology, too, have more relevance to police officers than they ordinarily think is so. And as one moves from the causes and conditions of crime to the rates and the richness of its variety, one comes to appreciate the compulsion of the police to "fight crime." The realities of crime, seemingly so far removed from the abstractions of theory but experienced (actually or vicariously) by so many, give rise to the response of the community. The consequent shifts of perception and interest, hence of values and priorities, translate into shifts in policies, procedures, and other aspects of law enforcement.

The Criminal Dimension of Policing

For some time now it has been widely taught that much of the time of the police, certainly of the patrol officers, is involved in activities not directly engaged in criminal matters: Patroling (when "nothing" happens), writing reports, getting one's gear ready, and so forth. And it is true, of course, that the human condition consumes the individual in comings and goings, in getting to and from rather than grappling with the central concerns of life. Even in a football game, the players are mostly "passing time" rather than "playing," even when time is "in" rather than "out." But even the "action" of police officers, when they are "doing something real" (as opposed to writing reports or eating lunch) is supposed to be concerned often with noncriminal matters. They are not criminal, however, only if *criminal* is understood to mean only serious crime which has happened or is about to, or minor crime which is actually happening. If *criminal* is understood to mean minor as well as serious crime, potential as well as actual crime, and crime embedded in an event in which other "noncriminal" aspects weigh more importantly, then the police engage in it most of their time, with the truly noncriminal matters being a very small part of their activities.

For example, suppose a manhole cover is missing from a manhole on a dark street. Is that a criminal problem or a utilities problem? It may involve theft of the cover (which these days is probably grand larceny). If a vehicle stops abruptly enough to cause damage and injury, is that a health problem or a traffic problem? It may make the motorist prey to a thief or worse. Is that a criminal problem? Even clearer is the family dispute: Often resulting in nothing, it is still a very dangerous situation for participants and police alike—a high percentage of homicides grow out of family disputes; these homicides involve family members *and* police officers (indeed, more of the latter than in other kinds of situations). These conflicts ordinarily involve the commission of a crime (assault, battery, aggravated battery, homicide, trespass, property damage) and even more often the threat of or probability of eruption or escalation into something worse, even if no crime has actually been committed in a strict sense. Even the cases that seem clearly noncriminal, like the proverbial kitten in the tree, have, in the police officer's experience and understanding, a dark, threatening edge to them. (Not long ago a boy climbed a neighbor's tree to retrieve a frisbee—and was shot dead by the neighbor.) The kitten (or frisbee) in the tree marks the purely non-criminal end of the spectrum of criminality of acts or events the police deal with. The police officer cannot ignore the criminal dimension of the most insignificant-appearing activity even though the criminal dimension is much greater toward the other end of the spectrum.

Even if the activities of patrol officers were mostly noncriminal in the purest sense, it would make little difference for the police department as a whole, for most of these activities are handled by the officers and concluded by them, without involving the sergeant or even the dispatcher. Criminal matters (or a few noncriminal matters treated as criminal, such as the drunk who is arrested for his own protection) come to the attention of the department when patrol officers bring the subject into the station house. This means that the rest of the department can be concerned almost entirely with crime, diverted from it only by the things that take up time in a bureaucracy (and make "Barney Miller" such an entertaining television program for the police officer).

The Definitions of Crime

The definition of crime varies from culture to culture and from time to time. Crime is not everywhere and always the same. Variations can be found from state to state in the United States and from time to time within a state, even within a community. The formal definitions, however, tend to be basically the same in the statutory and case laws of several American states. Where differences occur they tend to reflect differences in the dominant morality. And this dimension of criminal law is steadily changing and controversial.

A crime is a wrong. "Frankie and Johnny were lovers . . . but he done her wrong." That *wrong*, immortalized in the ballad, happened to be a murder in St. Louis in 1899. But not every wrong is a crime. An insult, a broken promise, a deadline forgotten—these and many other wrongs are not crimes. Yet it might be wrong *not* to commit a crime to accomplish a *right*, as when one must trespass or take property to save a person's life, for example, to get to the river's edge with a lifeline.

Arthur Train, an attorney, said, "A crime is any act or omission to act punishable as such by law."[1] *Black's,* the standard law dictionary, puts it this way: "A positive or negative act in violation of penal law; an offense against the State." *Black's* goes on to deal with distinction within the concept of crime:

According to Blackstone, the word "crime" denotes such offenses as are of a deeper and more atrocious dye, while smaller faults and omissions of less consequence are called "misdemeanors." But the better use appears to be to make *crime* a term of broad and general import, including both felonies and misdemeanors, and hence covering all infractions of the criminal law. In this sense it is not a technical phrase, strictly speaking (as "felony" and "misdemeanor" are), but a convenient general term. In this sense, also, "offense" or "public offense" should be used as synonymous with it.[2]

Train presents some important distinctions with concentric circles (Figure 8.1), the innermost representing crimes, the next ring representing torts, for which one may seek compensation in a civil suit, and the outermost ring including other wrongful acts for which there is no legal corrective. *Torts* are wrongful acts that violate private rights, for which the remedy or redress is usually financial, to restore the victim to some semblance of her or his earlier position. The lawsuit occurs in the civil courts rather than in the criminal-justice system.

The concentric circles suggest an overlapping of crimes and torts. Some wrongful acts, such as slander or battery, may be both criminal and tortious. Other wrongful acts, such as negligent operation of an automobile which causes death or injury (so long as recklessness or intoxication are not the cause), may be torts but not crimes. Some crimes, such as treason or pornography, are not torts because there is no specific,

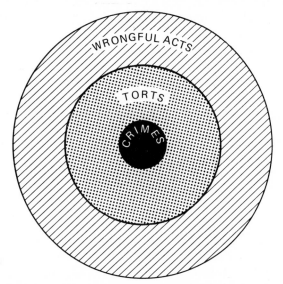

Figure 8.1 The Relation of Crime to Wrongs. (*Source:* Arthur Train, *From the District Attorney's Office* [New York: Scribner's, 1939], p. 2. Reprinted by permission.)

identifiable victim, hence no one is entitled to sue individually for compensation or injury.

Train's outermost ring includes less serious wrongs such as violations of rules of etiquette, taste, morals, or even religious strictures. For instance, working on Sunday may violate the "Sunday closing" law of a community but not the rules of a religious denomination which observes Saturday as the Sabbath; while working on Saturday may be legal but a breach of the denomination's "sabbatarian" rules. In certain circumstances or cultures the seemingly less serious wrongs can be taken very seriously, as when an insult leads to a challenge to a duel (as in older American times) or a "loss of face" leads to suicide, as in certain oriental cultures.

Sins are viewed in religious quarters as extremely serious matters, and have often been criminalized when the religious element of the community had enough influence to see that its notions of right and wrong were backed up by the state and the sanctions of its criminal punishments. Suicide, which is a sin in the Roman Catholic religion for example, used to be a crime, and still is in some states. Blasphemy, another religious wrong, was a crime in England until recently.

Such cultural variations from civilization to civilization, nation to nation, state to state, even neighborhood to neighborhood, have meant that very few if any behaviors have not been criminal at some place or time and noncriminal at some other place or time. Incest seems to be the only universal taboo, and even this varies in its extent from first cousins on outward in consanguinity. This is of interest not only to anthropologists for their comparisons and contrasts of culture, but to police officers who encounter different rankings of offenses according to cultural variations within the community and even within the beat. An officer may cross a street from a black neighborhood, where gambling is enthusiastically pursued, to a Jewish neighborhood, where it is not.

From time to time legislative changes have abruptly reversed criminal coverage. For instance, a man on a certain date in 1933 with a sack of bottled whiskey in one hand and a bag of gold in the other was a criminal for what he had in one hand but not the other in one year but not the next, when the Volstead Act was repealed to permit private possession of alcoholic beverages and when the private possession of gold was prohibited.[3]

In addition to cultural variations, there is far more extensive criminalization than one might think. It is not much of an exaggeration to say, with Arthur Train, "almost everything becomes a crime, depending upon the arbitrary act of the legislature." Train makes his point with this catalog of crimes from the 1930s:

It is a crime (in New York State) punishable by a year in the penitentiary for a person driving a vehicle upon any highway to permit his horses to run; to advertise as a divorce lawyer; to "hunt" or to "play" on the first day of the week; to have band music at a military funeral in a city on Sunday; to arrest or attach a corpse for payment of debt; to own a "slot machine"; to do business under any name not actually your own name without filing a certificate with the county clerk (as, for example, if being a tailor, you call your shop "The Two Little Tailors"); to ride in a long-distance bicycle race more than twelve hours out of twenty-four or to dance in a "Marathon" more than eight; to shoe horses without complying with certain articles of the Labor Law; to fail to supply seats for female employees in a mercantile establishment; to steal a ride in a freight car, or for a would-be passenger to board a car or train while in motion; to walk on a railroad track, to run a ferry without authority, or having contracted to run one, to fail to do so; to neglect to post ferry rates in English; to induce the employee of a railroad company to leave its service because it requires him to wear a uniform; to wear a railroad uniform with authority; to fish with a net in any part of the Hudson River (except where permitted by statute); to loiter secretly about a building with intent to overhear discourse therein, and to repeat the same to vex others (eavesdropping); to plant oysters (if you are a non-resident) inside the State without the consent of the owner of the water; to enter an agricultural fair without paying the entrance fee; to go out on the street having your face painted, discolored, covered, or concealed or being otherwise disguised, or to assemble two or more such persons indoors save at a fancy-dress ball for which permission has been duly obtained from the police; or to wear the badge of the "Patrons of Husbandry" and of certain other orders without authority. These illustrations are selected at random from the New York Penal Code.[4]

The content and other aspects of law will be taken up shortly. Here a few sociological concepts help set the stage for further discussion of criminal law. The law is both an *institution* and a *norm*. Robert Bierstedt has defined the former as "an organized procedure . . . , a formal, recognized, established, and stabilized way of pursuing some activity in society."[5] Law is indeed formal, not informal: It is not merely known "in the bones" as one knows customs or "written on the heart" as one knows morality, it is spelled out with great care by legislatures in the form of statutes, and it is written by courts in judicial opinions, such as the landmarks of constitutional law which we will study in Chapter 10. Law is unavoidably recognized, even when it is defied—and perhaps especially then, for defiance is a tribute to the existence and effect of law. It is established, not tentative; stabilized, not spasmodic. Although statutes are sometimes repealed and judicial precedents overturned, this is difficult and uncommon; hence, when a rule is made into a law, it is truly as if it were "engraven in granite."

Law is also a norm. Bierstedt defines it as:

> . . . a rule or a standard that governs our conduct in the social situations in which we participate. It is a societal expectation. It is a standard to which we are expected to conform whether we actually do so or not. It is a cultural specification that guides our conduct in society. It is a way of doing things, the way that is set for us by our society. It is also . . . an essential instrument of social control.[6]

Norms are also expressed by customs, taboos, even fashions and etiquette, but mainly by *folkways* ("to which we conform because it is customary to do so in our society," as Bierstedt says[7]), and by *mores* (because it is moral to do so). Laws are distinguished from folkways and mores (a) by their comprehensive application to all persons within a state, (b) by their special punishments (fines, prison sentences, even death), and (c) by their supporting organizations. Laws do not depend on the support of groups or on the entire community (which actively support the folkways and mores). Laws rely on associations—specifically on police departments, courts, and prisons. This aspect of the law as a norm and an institution, as "institutionalized norms," is explained by Bierstedt:

> The folkways and mores are sustained and sanctioned by unorganized groups within a society and by entire communities. Institutions, on the other hand, always require specific associations to sustain them. Wherever we find an institution, therefore, we find also at least one association— and usually many more—whose function it is to pursue the institutionalized activity.
>
> . . . Institutions and associations are thus concomitant and correlative phenomena. Folkways and mores are uninstitutionalized norms and require no associations to support them. Laws, on the other hand, are institutionalized norms that appear only in the political organization of society and that require an association called a government for the enactment and enforcement. Government, incidentally, is an institution; *a government is an association.*[8]

The conceptual clarity of these ideas (and in the discussion toward the end of this chapter) helps one to understand what is going on in criminal law. But it is important to understand that clearcut distinctions are rarely found in the "real world" of lines that are blurred and colors that are mostly gray. There is an area of overlap among norms: As time passes, folkways and mores that enjoy widespread support are enacted into law, but as more time passes the folkways and mores change and begin to conflict with laws that once reflected them. The associations supporting the law, mainly the police, are divided between their duty to support law-as-institution and their allegiance to the people, whose folkways and mores are law-as-norm.

In addition, in the modern community many folkways and mores are no longer left entirely to the support of groups and the community as a whole. The sentiment that "there oughta be a law" is strong in American society. So many who believe that a certain way is the best, either because it is their own way (folkway) or the right way (a more), will not hesitate to back up such rules with the special powers of the state. If one believes strongly enough that the monokini, let us say, is inappropriate attire on public beaches, one will not be content to lift an eyebrow, frown, shun, or ostracize if the offending bather can be forcibly removed from the beach by arrest. As nongovernmental sanctions lose their authority, moralists are tempted to preserve proprieties by enacting the rules in statutory form so the supporting associations of the law can make good its threat by using the "heavy artillary" of punishment.

THE LAW OF CRIMES

Criminal law, or the law of crimes, as one finds it gathered into a criminal "code"—a systematically arranged body of laws—ordinarily is divided into two parts: (1) the so-called "general part," often literally "Part I" of the code, made up of provisions that apply generally to all criminal conduct (such as the capacity to commit an offense), and (2) the so-called "special part," often labeled "Part II," which defines the dozens of specific crimes in the code. In addition to the "Part II" offenses, each state has hundreds of crimes scattered throughout the rest of its statutory or written law.

Certain traditional definitions and distinctions must be covered first, such as that of *substance* or substantive law versus *procedure* or procedural law (sometimes also called adjective law). Substantive law is the definition of the wrongs that constitute crimes; procedural law prescribes the process by which the state deals with those whose conduct comes within the terms of substantive law. *Malum in se* is Latin for something bad in itself, such as homicide or incest; *malum prohibitum* is something bad not because of intrinsic qualities of wickedness but rather because it has been declared to be bad by law and its prohibition makes it so. The classic illustration is the rule against driving on the left side of the highway: There is nothing inherently wrong with that (indeed, in Europe it is required); it is simply that safe, orderly movement of traffic requires an arbitrary decision that the cars drive on one side or the other but not on either side at the driver's choice. Another distinction separates *felonies* from *misdemeanors,* or more serious from less serious crimes. Today felonies ordinarily involve a year or more of incarceration in a state prison; misdemeanors involve punishment by fines or imprisonment in a county or city jail for less than a year. The movement to decriminalize minor offenses and to "civilize" or treat them more like civil than criminal offenses has led to the development of a third class, the *offense* or *infraction,* which carries a penalty of a fine but no imprisonment.

The General Part. The students of law enforcement would do well, as the patrol officer must, to look at the criminal code of their own state for its statement of general principles and specific definitions of crime. But it will do for introductory purposes to look at one code, the proposed revision of the federal criminal law, which can be expected to have a good deal of influence on future revisions of state laws. The federal criminal laws have been the subject of intensive study for over a decade, beginning with a national commission headed by former governor Edmund Brown of California in the late 1960s. Later, simultaneous studies in the U.S. Senate and in the Department of Justice led to proposals which were consolidated in "S.1" in 1975, the Senate bill which has drawn a good deal of attention, and a later revision of 1977 (§1437), from which passages below are taken along with their numbering of sections.

The general principle of criminal liability, under the proposed federal criminal law reform, is as follows:

> A person commits an offense . . . only if: (a) he directly or indirectly engages in conduct, or . . . is responsible for conduct [of another] described as an offense in a section set forth in part II . . . ; (b) the circumstances, if any, described in [that] section exist at the time of the conduct; (c) the results, if any, described in [that] section are caused by the conduct; (d) the states of mind described in [that] section, or required by the provisions [on culpable states of mind] exist with respect to the described conduct, circumstances, and results; and (e) a defense or an affirmative defense . . . described in [that] section, described in [the chapter on bars and defenses], or otherwise recognized by law, did not exist at the time of the conduct (§ 102).

Conduct means "any act, any omission, and any possession" involved according to the definition of the offense (§ 111).

State of mind means "the mental state required to be proved with respect to conduct, an existing circumstance, or a result set forth in a section describing an offense" (§ 301). The proposed federal code uses the terms *intentional, knowing, reckless,* and *negligent* for the mental element of crime, rather than the many terms, such as *malice aforethought,* now employed in the federal law.

The general principle that a person may be criminally liable not only for directly or indirectly engaging in conduct, but for the conduct of another, is elaborated in the chapter dealing with *complicity*:

A person is criminally liable for an offense based upon the conduct of another person if: (1) he knowingly aids or abets the commission of the offense by the other person; or (2) acting with the state of mind required for the commission of the offense, he causes the other person to engage in conduct that would constitute an offense if engaged in personally by the defendant or any other person.

One may also be criminally liable as a coconspirator if:

(1) he and the other person [engage in a conspiracy]; (2) the other person engages in the conduct in furtherance of the conspiracy; and (3) the conduct is authorized by agreement or is reasonably forseeable that the conduct would be performed in furtherance of the conspiracy (§ 401).

In addition, an organization can be liable for conduct of an agent (§ 402) and an agent can be liable for conduct of an organization (§ 403).

These general principles of liability would lead to convictions of crimes (defined in the next section) that many observers would think were inappropriate. For example, Smith shoots Jones for the purpose of protecting himself and his family, fully intending to kill him. The injustice of convicting Smith of murder, when he protected himself and others from being killed, has resulted over the years in the development by courts of several *defenses* to crimes. The writers of the proposed federal criminal code have chosen to let that case-by-case development continue. So the revision does not include sections spelling out defenses. Instead a single section deals with defenses in this way:

Except as otherwise required by the Constitution or by a federal statute, the existence of a bar to a prosecution under any federal statute, or the existence of a defense or affirmative defense to a prosecution under any federal statute, including a defense or an affirmative defense of mistake of fact or law, insanity, intoxication, duress, exercise of public authority, protection of persons, protection of property, unlawful entrapment, and official misstatement of law, shall be determined by the courts of the United States according to the principles of the common law as they may be interpreted in the light of reason and experience (§ 501).

Later in this chapter we will indicate some of the defenses "otherwise required . . . by a federal statute," namely by the criminal code itself (when it is enacted), such as the scholarship defense to the crime of disseminating obscene material. Here we will present briefly some generally applicable defenses and bars. One *bar* (or "ground for terminating a prosecution in favor of a defendant on a ground irrelevant to guilt or innocence") is commonly called the *statute of limitations.* It results in the dismissal of a case if the prescribed time has passed, no matter how guilty the defendant may be. The period of limitations for most felonies and misdemeanors is 5 years after commission of the offense, with the exception of the crime of espionage, for which there is no time limitation. There are extensions of the time limit for prosecution in crimes involving fraud or breach of a fiduciary obligation (meaning a duty of trust on behalf of another, such as a trustee or a banker might have). In such cases, the prosecution may begin within 1 year after the facts are known by a federal officer who is not an accomplice (§ 511). The reason for the extension in such crimes is that perpetrators design such crimes to be inconspicuous, so the facts are likely to have been obscured. The other bar in the proposed code is immaturity: The defendant cannot be prosecuted for a federal crime other than murder if he or she was under 16 years of age when the offense was committed (§ 512), although a juvenile-delinquency proceeding might still be possible, however. (Other bars will be taken up in Chapter 10.)

Of the defenses mentioned in the general principle quoted earlier, some are technical and rare, such as "mistake of law," "official misstatement of law," and "exercise of public authority" (which prevents the prosecution of a police officer for battery when he arrests someone forcibly, or of an executioner for murder when he administers the death penalty). The more familiar defenses differ from each other in their reasons. For instance, *duress* is based on a lack of volition or will to commit the criminal act, as when one is forced to steal. This defense requires that the defendant have believed that serious harm was inevitable and inescapable (e.g., "our guns are trained on you and if you try to get away before you come out of that store with the jewels, we'll shoot you—and we can see whatever you do through the window, so don't try to call for help or have anyone do it for you!"). This defense does not apply, however, when the defendant got himself or herself into such circumstances knowing what was involved, and it does not apply in cases of murder—the defense or protection of persons (to be discussed later) does not permit one to kill anyone other than those threatening life.

Some defenses are based on *justifiable conduct*—the required criminal state of mind is present (intention, knowledge) and no force overrides the defendant's will, yet, there is some reason to permit the act. *Protection of persons,* including self-defense, rests on the right to resist attack; otherwise, marauders and other assailants would enjoy a privilege of attacking and the peaceable citizen would forever be in flight. So long as the defender did not provoke the attack, he may respond to it with a reasonable amount of force: fists against fists, knife against knife, gun against gun. Even one who provokes an attack, as in a fight, may protect himself if, after he has indicated his wish to withdraw, the other person persists with the attack in spite of the withdrawal. Retreat, as indicated earlier, is not required but will be considered among the factors determining whether the protective measures were reasonable. *Protection of property* is also a defense, but with a difference: the value of property is less than that of life, so deadly force may not be used to defend property (e.g., spring guns or other deadly traps on unoccupied property).

Another defense, based on "official action," or governmental involvement in a crime, is *entrapment,* but only if it is *unlawful entrapment.* This defense is available if government agents induce an action beyond merely providing an opportunity or a means for the action. For example, if a narcotics dealer sells drugs to an undercover agent, just as he might sell to another customer in the regular course of business, the entrapment is not unlawful; but if an agent concocts an involved scheme, persistently persuading the seller to make a sale, especially if the seller is not predisposed to sell to him or her anyway, the entrapment goes over the line between legitimate and illegitmate government activity and becomes unlawful entrapment. Examples of lawful entrapment are:

1. Decoy letters soliciting the mailing of obscene material;
2. Using a decoy letter containing money to trap an embezzling postal employee;
3. Undercover purchase of contraband;
4. Supplying the essential ingredient or facility, which may be difficult to obtain, for the commission of an offense;
5. Feigning interest in a bribe offer;
6. Offering a bribe to an officer suspected of corruption in an amount not exceeding the degree of temptation to which he or she would normally be exposed;
7. Use of a contingent fee arrangement to pay informers;
8. The mention by an informer to a defense counsel of his or her relationship with a prospective juror, precipitating the suggestion that a juror be corruptly approached;
9. Allowing the completed delivery of intercepted contraband or incriminating evidence, where a defendant set the chain of events in motion;
10. Failing to remove a corrupt officer so as to preclude a bribe offer.[9]

Examples of unlawful entrapment are:

1. Repeated solicitations of narcotics by addict informers claiming to be suffering from withdrawal; and,
2. Informer supplying contraband (heroin) to a defendant to sell to an undercover agent.[10]

The other defenses to be discussed involve lack of *culpability* or blameworthiness, when one's mental state itself, rather than some overriding consideration, is at fault. *Mistake of fact* is another defense if a mistake prevented the defendant from having the state of mind required for a crime. Murder, for instance, requires intentional killing, so a motorist mistakenly driving the wrong way on a one-one street would not be convicted of murder for a killing resulting from a collision, but such driving might well be reckless—and recklessness is an acknowledged state of mind in manslaughter.

The *insanity* defense—the most complex and controversial of the defenses—arose out of recognition that some acts result from a fault in the mind itself. The defense began in *M'Naghten's Case* in England in 1843:

> To establish a defense on the ground of insanity, it must be clearly proved that, at the time of the committing of the act, the party accused was labouring under such a defect of reason, from disease of the mind, as not to know he was doing what was wrong.[11]

This statement did not take into consideration the person who knows what he or she is doing but cannot help doing it. So the rule was broadened to include one who knows what he or she is doing and even that it is wrong, but whose act springs from an "irresistible impulse." These two aspects of the insanity defense—the emphasis on knowledge and on control—caused psychiatrists a great deal of trouble. As far as the knowledge aspect is concerned, they concluded that all but the feebleminded or psychotic lack such knowledge. They were also troubled by having to testify as experts on right and wrong because these are legal matters, whereas their expertise is medical and concerned with health and sickness. Concerning the control aspect, psychiatrists (like other scientists) assume that the human being (like the universe as a whole) is deterministic—that every action is the result of a cause; hence all criminal action, not merely the insane act, is the result of an inability to control one's behavior as it corresponds to the rules of criminal law.

The United States Court of Appeals for the District of Columbia, met these difficulties in the *Durham* v. *United States* case (1954) with a shift from the traditional knowledge/control test of the *M'Naghten* case to one more congenial to psychiatrists: "[A]n accused is not criminally responsible if his unlawful act was the product of mental disease or mental defect."[12] This permitted psychiatrists to deal with the causes of behavior without having to fit them into a legalistic formulation. But this guideline proved to be too broad: the issue of mental disease or defect involves the consideration of wide-ranging biographical factors going far beyond the act for which the accused is on trial, and it results in the acquittal of persons who are dangerous to society. It also complicates and prolongs the criminal trial.

In 1972 the same Court of Appeals overruled the *Durham* decision in the *United States* v. *Brawner* case, which bridged the traditional and modern views:

> [A] person is not responsible for criminal conduct if at the time of such conduct, as a result of mental diasease or defect, he lacks substantial capacity to appreciate the criminality of his conduct or to conform to the requirements of law.[13]

This form of the insanity defense focuses the trial on the facts of the criminal act, the defendant's knowledge and control with reference to that act, and the relationship of his or her mental state to mental disease or defect.

The Special Part.   The special part of the proposed federal code revision, or Part II, differs from the typical state code because it includes provisions on offenses involving national defense, international affairs, governmental processes, taxation, and individual rights which are more explicit than the provisions touching some of those subjects in state codes. Beyond those subjects, the federal code revision deals with offenses involving the person, property, and public order, safety, health, and welfare—the subjects covered by the "police power" discussed in the last chapter as the basis of the general power of state governments. This is because, in certain jurisdictions (the District of Columbia, territories, Indian territories, military bases, vessels, aircraft, and other special jurisdictions), the government of the United States has fully sovereign powers. Hence its code is as broad in its coverage of offenses as state codes.

The *general offenses* are attempt, conspiracy, and solicitation, sometimes called inchoate offenses or anticipatory offenses because they are beginnings or unfinished phases of crimes which would have been achieved.

Attempt: A person is guilty of an offense if, acting with the state of mind required for the commission of a crime, he intentionally engages in conduct that, in fact, contributes a substantial step toward the commission of the cime (§1001).

Conspiracy: A person is guilty of an offense if he agrees with one or more persons to engage in conduct, the performance of which would constitute a crime or crimes, and he, or one of such persons in fact, engages in any conduct with intent to effect any objective of the agreement (§1002).

Solicitation: A person is guilty of an offense if, with intent that another person engage in conduct constituting a crime, and, in fact, under circumstances strongly corroborative of that intent, he commands, entreats, induces, or otherwise endeavors to persuade such other person to engage in such conduct (§1003).

It is an affirmative defense to each one of the inchoate offenses if "under circumstances manifesting a voluntary and complete renunuciation of his criminal intent . . ."

> [the attempt defendant] avoided the commission of the crime attempted by abandoning the criminal effort and, if mere abandonment was insufficient to accomplish such avoidance, by taking affirmative steps that prevented the commission of the crime . . . [the conspiracy defendant] prevented the commission of every crime that was an object of the conspiracy . . . [the solicitation defendant] prevented the commission of the crime solicited. . . .

The offenses involving national defense include *treason* and related offenses such as armed rebellion, insurrection, engaging in paramilitary activity; *sabotage* and related offenses, such as impairing military effectiveness, violating an emergency regulation, evading military or alternative civilian service, obstructing military recruitment or induction, inciting or aiding mutiny, insubordination, or desertion, or aiding the escape of a prisoner of war or an enemy alien; and *espionage* and related offenses, such as disseminating national defense information, disseminating classified information, receiving classified information, failing to register as a person trained in a foreign espionage system, failing to register as, or acting as, a foreign agent (§§1111–1126).

The offenses involving international affairs include offenses involving *foreign relations,* such as attacking a foreign power, conspiracy against a foreign power, entering or recruiting for a foreign armed force, violating neutrality by causing departure of a vessel or aircraft, disclosing a foreign diplomatic code or correspondence, engaging in an unlawful international transaction; and offenses involving *immigration, naturalization, and passports,* such as unlawfully entering the United States as an alien, smuggling an alien into the United States, hindering discovery of an alien unlawfully in the United States, unlawfully employing an alien, fraudulently acquiring or improperly using evidence of citizenship, or fraudulently acquiring or improperly using a passport (§§1201–1216).

The offenses involving the government processes include *general ob-*

structions of government functions, such as obstructing a government function by fraud, obstructing a government function by physical interference, or impersonating an official; *obstructions of law enforcement,* such as hindering law enforcement, jumping bail, prison escape, providing or possessing contraband in a prison, or flight to avoid prosecution or appearance as a witness; *obstruction of justice,* such as witness bribery, corrupting a witness or an informant, tampering with a witness or informant, retaliating against a witness or an informant, tampering with physical evidence, improperly influencing a juror, monitoring jury deliberation, or demonstrating to influence a judicial proceeding; *contempt offenses,* such as criminal contempt, failing to appear as a witness, refusing to testify or to produce information, obstructing a proceeding by disorderly conduct, or disobeying a judicial order; *perjury, false statements,* and related offenses, such as false swearing, making a false statement, or tampering with a government record; and *official corruption and intimidation,* including bribery, graft, trading in government assistance, trading on special influence, trading in public office, speculating on official action or information, tampering with a public servant, or retaliating against a public servant (§§1301–1358).

The offenses involving taxation include *internal revenue offenses,* such as tax evasion, disregarding a tax obligation, or alcohol and tobacco tax offenses; and *customs offenses,* such as smuggling, trafficking in smuggled property, or receiving smuggled property (§§1401–1413).

The offenses involving individual rights include offenses involving *civil rights,* such as interfering with civil rights, interfering with civil rights under color of law, interfering with a federal benefit, unlawful discrimination, or interfering with speech or assembly related to civil rights activities, or strikebreaking; offenses involving *political rights,* such as obstructing an election, obstructing registration, obstructing a political campaign, interfering with a federal benefit for a political purpose, misusing authority over personnel for a political purpose, soliciting a political contribution as a federal public servant or in a federal building, or making an excess campaign expenditure; and offenses involving *privacy,* such as eavesdropping, trafficking in an eavesdropping device, possessing an eavesdropping device, intercepting correspondence, or revealing private information submitted for a government purpose (§§1501–1525).

The laws of the states include many of these provisions, even some of the ones concerning national defense. But they tend not to be gathered together into a code and they are cast in language appropriate to the difference between national and state government (e.g., revenue provisions in states typically speak of property and sales taxes rather than income taxes).

Much more familiar are the offenses involving the person: the homicide offenses, assault offenses, kidnapping and related offenses, hijacking offenses, and sex offenses. The *homicide* offenses include murder, manslaughter, and negligent homicide. A person is guilty of murder if:

> (1) he engages in conduct by which he knowingly causes the death of another person [*first degree*]; (2) he engages in conduct by which he causes the death of another person under circumstances in fact manifesting extreme indifference to human life [*second degree*]; or (3) in fact during the commission of [certain separate offenses, including escape, maiming, kidnapping, aircraft hijacking, rape, arson, burglary, and robbery] that he commits either alone or with one or more other participants, he or another person engages in conduct that in fact causes the death of a person other than one of the participants in such underlying offense [*third degree*] (§ 1601)

This third kind of murder is *felony-murder,* in which a participant in a nonhomicidal crime may be convicted of murder if someone else participating with him or her actually does the killing. This is not uncommon in robbery: the trigger man's partner is equally guilty of murder.

In addition to the general defenses mentioned earlier, such as insanity and self-defense, there are special defenses to the first and third degrees of murder. The defense to the first degree is that "the death was caused under circumstances, for which the defendant was not responsible, that: (1) caused the defendant to lose his self-control; and (2) would be likely to cause an ordinary person to lose his self-control to at least the same extent." In other words, in the traditional law-school illustration (which may be old-fashioned now), a man walks into his bedroom, finds another man making love to his wife, and promptly kills him on the spot. The provocation, which would make this a so-called "crime of passion," reduces this from a premeditated murder to manslaughter.

The defense to third-degree murder is that "the death was not a reasonably foreseeable consequence of neither: (1) the underlying offense; nor (2) the particular circumstances under which the underlying offense was committed." In other words, a "felony-murder," for which one robber would be held responsible even though his partner did the killing, is not reasonably foreseeable in the case of an auto thief deliberately driving into the owner who happens to walk onto the driveway, while his fellow thief rides beside him. The killing is considered probable in the armed robbery but improbable in the auto theft.

If this seems complicated, it should be noted that the code revision actually simplifies the federal law. For one thing, it combines first- and second-degree murder. The former is a killing that results from some planning, however brief, as defined in the present federal statute, which includes "every murder perpetrated by poison, lying in wait or any other kind of willful, deliberate, malicious, and premeditated killing. . . ." The reason for dividing murder into first and second degrees was the death penalty, which was mandatory at one time, yet not appropriate for those cases in which juries had difficulty finding *malice aforethought,* or premeditation to kill or to do great bodily harm. As a result, legislatures divided murder into first-degree, or premeditated, murder for which the death penalty was still mandatory, and second-degree murder for which it was not. Second-degree murder included all other unpremeditated homicides unless they fell into the category of manslaughter. The code revision addresses second-degree murder in its phrase "extreme indifference to human life," which covers the case of someone taking potshots into a crowd of people.

Manslaughter is traditionally divided into two categories: (1) *voluntary manslaughter,* or a homicide resulting from passion, provocation, or unreasonably excessive self-defense, and (2) *involuntary manslaughter,* or homicide resulting from recklessness or negligence. Another variety of manslaughter is *misdemeanor-manslaughter,* or a homicide committed in the course of a misdemeanor: it parallels felony-murder. The provision in the proposed revision of the federal criminal code is as follows. A person is guilty of manslaughter if:

> (1) he engages in conduct by which he causes the death of another person; or (2) he engages in conduct by which he knowingly causes the death of another person under circumstances that would constitute an offense under [murder of the first variety] (§1602).

By reason of some technical rules of interpretation of the proposed code, the first kind of manslaughter (which corresponds to voluntary manslaughter) requires that the defendant have a state of mind of knowingly causing the death by conduct which is reckless.

Three things are notable about manslaughter under the proposed revision. First, the provision combines voluntary and involuntary manslaughter, although it reflects both of them. Second, it eliminates the offense of misdemeanor-manslaughter. Third, it illustrates a legal concept known as *lesser, included offense.* The first kind of manslaughter (1) is a lesser, included offense with reference to second-degree murder; that is, where the defense to second-degree murder applies, the result is manslaughter. Likewise, the second kind of manslaughter (2) is a lesser, included offense wither reference to first-degree murder. This is important in the adjudication of guilt because indictments typically charge lesser, included offenses as well as greater, inclusive offenses (both manslaughter and murder), so juries—and bargaining lawyers—can opt for the lesser offense if the evidence does not enable them to agree upon the higher level of guilt.

Finally, a third kind of homicide is covered by the proposed revision. Involuntary manslaughter traditionally included not only reckless conduct but negligent conduct. Juries, however, have been reluctant to find persons guilty of manslaughter because of negligent conduct, even if the negligence involved was gross negligence. As a result, many states have enacted negligent-homicide statutes carrying lesser penalties than manslaughter. The code revision does likewise in providing that a person is guilty of *negligent homicide* "if he engages in conduct by which he negligently causes the death of another person" (§1603).

The *assault offenses* include maiming, aggravated battery, battery, menacing, terrorizing, communicating a threat, and reckless endangerment. Among the more familiar and common are the following: *Maiming:* "... if, by physical force, he intentionally causes serious bodily injury, that is permanent or likely to be permanent, to another person" (§1611). *Serious bodily injury* is defined as "bodily injury which involves (a) a substantial risk of death; (b) unconsciousness; (c) extreme physical pain; (d) protracted and obvious disfigurement; or (e) protracted loss or impairment of the function of a bodily member, organ, or mental faculty" (§111). *Aggravated battery:* "... if, by physical force, he causes serious bodily injury to another person" (§1612). This is a "lesser included offense" of maiming. A lesser included offense of aggravated battery is *battery:* "... if, by physical force he causes bodily injury to another person" (§1613). *Bodily injury* is defined to include "(a) a cut, abrasion, bruise, burn, or disfigurement; (b) physical pain; (c) illness; (d) impairment of the function of a bodily member, organ, or mental faculty; and (e) any other injury to the body no matter how temporary" (§111). Similar to common-law assault is the proposed offense of *menacing:* "... if he engages in physical conduct by which he intentionally places another person in fear of imminent bodily injury" (§1614).

Terrorizing is defined as follows:

> ... if he communicates: (1) a threat to commit, or to continue to commit, a federal, state, or local crime of violence or unlawful conduct dangerous to human life; or (2) information, that he knows is false, that the commission of a federal, state, or local crime of violence is imminent or in progress or that a circumstance dangerous to human life exists or is about to exist; and thereby causes any person to be in sustained fear for his or another person's safety; causes evacuation of a building, a public structure, or a facility of transportation; or causes other serious disruption to the public (§1615).

Kidnapping is defined as follows:

. . . if he restrains another person with intent to:
(1) hold him for ransom or reward;
(2) use him as a shield or hostage;
(3) commit a felony; or
(4) interfere with the performance of a government function (§1621).

The penalty for kidnapping is higher "if the actor does not voluntarily release the victim alive and in a safe place prior to trial."

The *hijacking* offenses include aircraft hijacking and commandeering a vessel. *Aircraft hijacking* is involved ". . . if he seizes or exercises control over an aircraft by force, threat, intimidation, or deception" (§1631).

The *sex offenses* include rape, sexual assault, sexual abuse of a minor, sexual abuse of a ward, and unlawful sexual contact.

Rape is committed:

. . . if he engages in a sexual act with another person and
(1) compels the other person to participate in such act:
   (a) by force, or
   (b) by threatening or placing the other person in fear that any person will imminently be subject to death, serious bodily injury, or kidnapping;
(2) has, with intent to engage in a sexual act, substantially impaired the ability of the other person to appraise or control conduct by administering or employing a substance that he knows is a drug or intoxicant, or by other means, without the knowledge or against the will of the other person; or
(3) the other person is, in fact, less than twelve years old (§1641).

The third kind of rape (3) is the offense commonly known as *statutory rape,* in which age alone, not force or threat, renders the perpetrator liable. The traditional defense of reasonable mistake as to age has been eliminated because the age of 12 makes it unlikely that a minor will be mistaken for an adult. All these kinds of rape may be committed by a male upon a male, or even a female upon a male.

Sexual assault is committed

. . . if he engages in a sexual act with another person and
(1) knows that the other person is incapable of understanding the nature of the conduct;
(2) knows that the other person is physically incapable of resisting, or of declining consent to, the sexual act;
(3) knows that the other person is unaware that a sexual act is being committed;

(4) knows that the other person participates because of a mistaken belief that the actor is married to the other person; or

(5) compels the other person to participate by any threat or by placing the other person in fear (§1642).

Sexual act is defined to mean "conduct between human beings consisting of contact between penis and the vulva, the penis and the anus, the mouth and the penis, or the mouth and the vulva; for purposes of this [definition] contact involving the penis occurs upon penetration, however slight" (§1646).

Unlawful sexual contact is involved ". . . if he engages in sexual contact with another person who is not his spouse, under circumstances that would constitute [rape, sexual assault, sexual abuse of a minor, or sexual abuse of a ward] if such contact involved a sexual act." *Sexual contact* is defined as "a touching of the sexual or other intimate parts of a person to arouse or gratify the sexual desire of any person" (§1646).

The *offenses involving property* include arson and other property-destruction offenses; burglary and other criminal-intrusion offenses; robbery, extortion, and blackmail; theft and related offenses; counterfeiting, forgery, and related offenses; commercial bribery and related offenses; and investment, monetary, and antitrust offenses. *Arson* is involved ". . . if, by fire or explosion, he: (1) damages a public facility; or (2) damages substantially a building or a public structure" (§1701).

Burglary and other criminal-intrusion offenses include criminal entry, criminal trespass, stowing away, and possession of burglar's tools. Burglary is involved ". . . if at night, with intent to engage in conduct constituting a federal, state, or local crime, other than [the other intrusion crimes indicated above], and without privilege he enters, or remains surreptitiously within, a dwelling that is the property of another (§1711). *Criminal entry* is the same thing during daytime though not necessarily a dwelling (§1712). *Criminal trespass* is the same thing as criminal entry, except that it does not require the intent to commit a crime (§1713).

Robbery is involved ". . . if he takes property of another from the person or presence of another by force and violence, or by threatening or placing a person in fear that any person will imminently be subjected to bodily injury (§1721). *Extortion* is involved ". . . if he obtains property of another: (1) by threatening or placing another person in fear that any person will be subjected to bodily injury or kidnapping or that any property will be damaged; or (2) under color of official right." The difference between extortion and robbery is that the extortionist takes property not just from the victim's person or presence and does so by a wider range of force or threat.

Blackmail is involved

. . . if he obtains property of another by threatening or placing another person in fear that any person will:

(1) engage in conduct constituting a federal, state, or local crime other than [extortion];
(2) accuse any person of a federal, state, or local crime;
(3) procure the dismissal of any person from employment, or refuse to employ or renew a contract of employment of any person;
(4) improperly subject any person to economic loss or injury to his business or profession;
(5) expose a secret or publicize an asserted fact, whether true or false, with intent to subject any person, living or dead, to hatred, contempt, or ridicule, or to impair his personal, financial, professional, or business reputation; or
(6) take or withhold official action as a public servant, or cause a public servant to take or withhold official action (§1723).

Blackmail differs from extortion in that threats employed may be other than force or its threat. There are important defenses to blackmail. It is a defense to all but (1) above that the defendant "(1) reasonably believed his conduct to be justified; and (2) intended solely to compel or induce the other person to take lawful and reasonable action to prevent or remedy the asserted wrong that prompted the defendant's conduct," and as to (2) in the definition of blackmail, in addition to the foregoing, that the defendant "reasonably believed that the threatened accusation was true."

Theft and related offenses include trafficking in stolen property, receiving stolen property, executing a fraudulent scheme, bankruptcy fraud, interfering with a security interest, fraud in a regulated industry, and consumer fraud. Theft is involved ". . . if he obtains or uses the property of another with intent (1) to deprive the other of a right to the property or a benefit of the property; or (2) to appropriate the property to his own use or to the use of another person" (§1731). *Trafficking in stolen property* is involved ". . . if he traffics in property of another that has been stolen" (§1732). *Traffic* is defined to mean "(a) to sell, pledge, transfer, distribute, dispense, or otherwise dispose of to another person as consideration for anything of value; or (b) to buy, receive, possess, or obtain control of with intent to do any of the foregoing" (§111). *Receiving stolen property* is involved ". . . if he buys, receives, possesses, or obtains control of property of another that has been stolen" (§1733). The theft revisions eliminate complexities of common-law crimes such as larceny, embezzlement, fraud, and false pretenses.

Consumer fraud, a "new" crime, reflects the need to specify some of the wrongful actions victimizing consumers in an age of "consumerism." It is committed

> . . . if, with the intent to deceive or defraud a purchaser, he:
> (1) offers or advertises property for sale to a purchaser, knowing that such property will not be sold as so offered or advertised; or
> (2) makes a material statement that is false, concerning property that he offers or advertises for sale, sells, or has sold to a purchaser, with respect to:
> (a) the purchaser's need for the property;
> (b) the nature of the property, including its origins; its age; its grade, quality, style, or model; its ingredients or components; its quantity; its performance or safety characteristics; or its uses or benefits;
> (c) the sponsorship or approval of the property;
> (d) the comparison between the price or quality of the property and that of similar property offered or advertised for sale by the same or another person;
> (e) the prior ownership of the property;
> (f) the purchaser's need for the repair or replacement of the property;
> (g) the person's completion of the repair or replacement of the property; or
> (h) the purchaser's rights, privileges, or remedies with regard to the property (§1738).

Counterfeiting, forgery, and related offenses include criminal endorsement of a written instrument, criminal issuance of a written instrument, and trafficking in a counterfeiting implement. *Counterfeiting* is involved ". . . if, with intent to deceive or harm another person or a government, he makes, utters, or possesses a counterfeited written instrument" (§1741). The technical terms, which inevitably appear in legal writing, despite the intentions of the drafters to keep the language as simple as possible, are used because they are well understood and do not have undue complications and confusions (as does "malice aforethought"). *Counterfeited written instrument* is defined to mean a written instrument "that purports to be genuine but is not, because it has been falsely made or manufactured in its entirety" (§1746). *Utter* means "to issue, authenticate, transfer, publish, sell, deliver, transmit, present, display, use, certify, or otherwise given currency to." *Forgery* is involved ". . . if, with intent to deceive or harm another person or a government, he makes, utters, or possesses a forged written instrument" (§1742). This is exactly the same as counterfeiting except for the term *forged written instrument,* which is defined to mean "a written instrument that purports to be genuine but is not because it: (1) has been falsely altered, completed, signed, or endorsed; (2) contains a false addition thereto or insertion therein; or

(3) is a combination of parts of two or more genuine written instruments" (§1746).

The *bribery* offenses include commercial bribery, labor bribery, and sports bribery. *Sports bribery* is involved

> . . . if, with intent to affect the outcome, result, or margin of victory of a publicly exhibited sporting contest: (1) he offers, gives, or agrees to give anything of value to a participant, official, or other person associated with the contest; or (2) as a participant, official, or other person associated with the contest, he solicits, demands, accepts, or agrees to accept anything of value (§1753).

The offenses involving *public order, safety, health, and welfare* include organized-crime offenses; drug offenses; explosives and firearms offenses; riot offenses; gambling, obscenity, and prostitution offenses; public health offenses; and miscellaneous offenses. The *organized crime offenses* include operating a racketeering syndicate, racketeering, washing racketeering proceeds, loansharking, and facilitating a racketeering activity by violence. *Racketeering* is involved ". . . if, through a pattern of racketeering activity, he acquires or maintains an interest in, or controls, or conducts, an enterprise" (§1802). *Racketeering activity* is defined to mean conduct constituting several of the federal felonies, such as witness bribery, graft, murder, maiming, terrorizing, arson, extortion, blackmail, bribery; and state felonies of similar sorts. *Washing racketeering proceeds* is involved ". . . if, by using or investing proceeds from a pattern of racketeering activity, he acquires or maintains an interest in, or establishes or conducts, an enterprise" (§1803).

Drug offenses include trafficking in an opiate, trafficking in drugs, possessing drugs, and violating a drug regulation. *Explosives and firearms offenses* include using a weapon in the course of a crime and possessing a weapon aboard an aircraft. The foregoing offenses involve extensive reference to other statutes for their content, such as "controlled substances" under the Controlled Substance Act.

The *riot offenses* include leading a riot, providing arms for a riot, and engaging in a riot. *Leading a riot* is involved ". . . if (1) he causes a riot by incitement or during a riot he invites participation in the riot; or (2) during a riot he leads, or gives commands, instructions, or directions in furtherance of, the riot" (§1831). *Riot* is defined as "a public disturbance (a) that involves 10 or more persons or participants; (b) that involves violent and tumultuous conduct on the part of the participants; and (c) that causes, or creates a grave danger of imminently causing bodily injury to a person or damage to property." (§1834). The commentary in the Judiciary Committee Report elaborates on this:

> The distinguishing factor in a riot is the agitation of the rioters. Physical acts are committed violently and tumultuously when they are furious,

extreme, sudden, vehement, passionate, or otherwise characterized by intense movement or feeling, so as to appear out of control or to threaten indiscriminate injury.[14]

Gambling, obscenity, and prostitution offenses under the proposed federal law are limited to engaging in a gambling business, disseminating obscene material, and conducting a prostitution business. *Gambling business* is defined to mean "a business involving gambling of any kind that, in fact: (a) has five or more persons engaged in the business; and (b) has been in substantially continuous operation for a period of thirty days or more, or has taken in $2,000 or more in any single day" (§1841). *Disseminating obscene material* is involved ". . . if he (1) disseminates obscene material: (a) to a minor; or (b) to any person in a manner affording no immediately effective opportunity to avoid exposure to such material; or (2) commercially disseminates obscene material to any person (§1842). *Obscene material* is defined to mean material that

(a) sets forth in a patently offensive way:
    (1) an explicit representation, or a detailed written or verbal description, of an act of sexual intercourse, including genital-genital, anal-genital, or oral-genital intercourse, whether between human beings or between a human being and an animal; of masturbation; or of flagellation, torture, or other violence indicating a sadomasochistic sexual relationship; or
    (2) an explicit, close-up representation of a human genital organ;
(b) taken as a whole, appeals to the prurient interest of:
    (1) the average person, applying contemporary community standards; or
    (2) the average person within a sexually deviant class of persons, if such material is designed for dissemination to such class of persons; and
(c) taken as a whole, lacks serious artistic, scientific, literary, or political value (§1842).

One of the defenses to this is dissemination limited to "a person associated with an institution of higher learning, either as a member of the faculty or as an enrolled student, teaching or pursuing a bona fide course of study, or conducting or engaging in a bona fide research program, to which such material is pertinent."

The *miscellaneous offenses* include disorderly conduct, failing to obey a public safety order, and violating state or local law in an enclave—that is, in federal territories to which state and local law has been permitted to apply.

Law and Morals. Police power traditionally implies the power of a state to provide for or protect the "health, safety, morals, and welfare" of its people. The missing element, in terms of the traditional purposes of police, is the protection of society's morality. To protect the public morals, many kinds of conduct and practices have been criminalized by state criminal codes. Among these are *adultery* (consensual sexual intercourse between a married person and a partner of the opposite sex not his or her spouse), *fornication* (consensual sexual intercourse between unmarried partners of the opposite sex), *sodomy* ("abnormal" sexual intercourse or activity, usually between persons of the same sex, sometimes between a person and an animal), *bestiality* (sexual intercourse between a person and an animal), *bigamy* (marriage in which one spouse is still married to another), *incest* (sexual intercourse between closely related persons), *abortion* (unlawful expulsion of the fetus from the womb), *patronizing a prostitute, possession of obscene materials, possession of narcotics for personal use, drunkenness,* and *gambling*. Statutes, concerning these activities have been omitted from the revision of the federal criminal laws and left to the states to enact, where virtually all such activities are now defined as crimes in the state criminal codes.

Most of these acts, behaviors, or relationships have historically been considered morally offensive (called *mala in se,* or things bad-in-themselves), unnatural, or a violation of what philosophers call the "laws of nature." Punishing violators of the moral code has troubled few people for most of history, perhaps not even very many of the violators themselves, because it was assumed that the laws of the state should correspond to the laws of nature—especially if the laws of nature were thought to correspond to the laws of God.

Three things happened late in the eighteenth and early nineteenth centuries to unsettle the assumption that the laws of the state should correspond to the laws of nature. First, scholars in the field of law began to analyze the concept of law. Led by John Austin in England, they concluded that law was the command of the sovereign—no more, no less. *Legal positivism,* as this view came to be called, insisted that law did not necessarily correspond to folkways, mores, the laws of nature, or the laws of God. Although the term *law* might be used in connection with any of those norms, it should be reserved, they argued, for the various forms in which the commands of the sovereign might be expressed, such as statutes and court decisions. The effect was that the laws of nature and of God lost some of their authority. It would no longer "go without saying" that the rules prescribed by nature or God should be synonymous with the laws of the state, applicable to man and backed up by the agencies of government.

Second, a philosophy of *utilitarianism* developed under the leadership of Jeremy Bentham in England, in which the policies of the state, hence the laws, were evaluated by the good that they did. The good of something, in Bentham's utilitarianist view, was measured by an excess of pleasure over pain. And in an age of increasing skepticism, the goodness of a law had less to do with spiritual things than material things. In addition, the utility or value of a law depended in large part on how well it could be administered, and the utilitarians took a dim view of laws that required policing the bedroom.

Third, a disciple of Bentham, John Stuart Mill, lead the movement known as *liberalism,* which was concerned in its early years with freeing men and women from intrusions of the state upon their liberty. Their concern was initially with freedom of speech and press, but later their attention shifted to limiting government intrusions into the privacy of sexual preferences and activities. These three movements—legal positivism, utilitarianism, and liberalism—combined to produce a foundation of principle for the politics of *decriminalization.* It has had some effect: Some states have relaxed their laws against possession of narcotics, and many laws against "victimless crimes" are not enforced, such as those against fornication and sodomy.

The movement to decriminalize victimless crimes has not gone unopposed. Sir Patrick Devlin, a British judge, has argued that a moral code is essential to the community's survival because it binds the members of the community together and prevents its disintegration into atomistic individualism and its eventual collapse. So, he concluded, conventional morality should be supported, especially by the law, whether it is right or wrong. Devlin used drunkenness as an example:

> . . . while a few people getting drunk in private cause no problem at all, widespread drunkenness, whether in private or in public, would create a social problem. The line between drunkenness that creates a social problem of sufficient magnitude to justify the intervention of a law and that which does not, cannot be drawn on the distinction between private indulgence and public sobriety. It is a practical one, based on an estimate of what can be safely tolerated whether in public or in private, and shifting from time to time as circumstances change. The licensing laws coupled with high taxation may be all that is needed. But if more is needed there is no doctrinal answer even to complete prohibition. It cannot be said that so much is the law's business but more is not.[15]

Sociologist Jerome Skolnick has replied with a general objection to "coercion to virtue" (Can one be forced to be good?) and specific objections to Devlin's argument:

> How do we find the "width" or the "spread" of drunkenness; what is meant by "drunkenness" for these purposes; how do we know that measures taken to suppress "drunkenness," prohibition for example, will not only be effective in achieving the non-use of alcoholic beverages—if that was what was intended—but will also not produce socially undesirable side-effects?[16]

Other problems with Devlin's position emerge in Skolnick's analysis: Are the state and society more or less congruent in their scope? If not, is the influence of the state on society positive and liberating or negative and repressive? Is legislation a "natural embodiment" of social sentiments, as though folkways and mores naturally evolve into statutes? Or is the state a distinct and rational instrument that does—or should—respond (or be made to respond) more critically and carefully to such sentiments? And what, precisely (for legislation demands precision), are the customs and conventions that should be reflected in law? When one comes down to moralities, are they not often the result of what has been called the moral entrepreneur, who fashions and leads a moral crusade (which may be humane, but which may merely be meddlesome)? And, as if all this were not enough, are not legislative enactments of a moral code often intended by crusaders to shore up or reassure a declining class? As Skolnick puts it:

> For those who affirm a strong moral position, the capacity to regulate public morality may document their status in society. In contrast to conventional politics, power is required to achieve status, not to achieve wealth. . . .
> The greater the committment to a declining way of life, the more important is validation of public recognition through public power. Genuine custom requires less state support than mere convention, which is spurious custom.[17]

With reference to marijuana, Professor John Kaplan of Stanford Law School points out several "costs" of criminalization: Criminalization of large numbers of marijuana smokers; administration of the law against it; disruption of the lives of those arrested for it; inefficiency of programs aimed against it; inequality in the enforcement of the law (light on campuses, heavy in ghettos); use of intrusive investigative practices (informers, surveillance); and, potentially, the entry of organized crime and the further breakdown of law enforcement as citizens decline to support the system.[18]

Herbert L. Packer adds another, perhaps the most ominous, effect:

> If the criminal sanction is widely used to deal with morally neutral behavior, law enforcement officials are likely to be at least subconsciously defensive about their work, and the public will find the criminal law a confusing guide to moral, or even acceptable, behavior.[19]

On the other side is a deep concern, too—indeed a number of concerns. Are we not our brother's keepers? Have we no obligation to sustain virtue, to make it tough-going for vice? Can we relax our standards without stepping onto "the slippery slope" down which we must slide, once the brakes of principle are removed? First marijuana, then cocaine, then heroin? or abortion allowed in the first trimester, then the second, then the third, and finally infanticide? These are truly, as Kaplan says, "some of the most emotion-laden issues confronting the United States today":

> The issues include the proper place of pleasure in our lives; the threat of radicalism, not only to our society but also to our values; the question of permissiveness and the proper degree of subordination of personal desires necessary to ensure survival of a civilized society; the necessity of obedience to authority, whether or not there is personal agreement with its commands. . . .[20]

The conflict between law and morals is far from easy to resolve because much of the difficulty is a result of society's desire to have its cake and eat it, too. Society wants things both ways: many want liberation from constraints, others want constraints, and some, oddly, want both. At the very least, society wants something done about the immediate effects or excesses of freedom (e.g., the drunk in the gutter, the overdosed addict), and it usually falls to the police officer to take care of these problems. There is likely to be some slight decriminalization (e.g., of small amounts of marijuana for personal use), but most of the victimless crimes "on the books" in the criminal codes around the country will remain. This is largely for the symbolic value of the statutory denunciation of behaviors considered immoral. While the community cracks down rhetorically, it does so with a wink, to indicate its understanding that the criminal justice agencies will crack down in practice only on the most extreme, the most obnoxious instances of formally forbidden behaviors.

The dilemma of choice in theory and in practice, between "law on the books" and "law in action" will be resolved mainly by the cop on the beat. But the burden of the police officer can be eased greatly by more involvement of his or her department and the community in the establishment of law enforcement policies. This will be taken up again in Chapter 11 where it will be treated in the context of the discretion to select which laws to enforce, the extent of enforcement, the means of enforcement, and the alternatives to enforcement.

SUMMARY

This chapter presented an argument for the centrality of crime in the concerns of the patrol officer. It defined crime, made some distinctions among related concepts such as crime, torts, and etiquette, and surveyed some cultural variations in the criminalization of conduct.

The chapter gave major attention to the legal dimension of crime: the general aspects of criminal law, such as principles of liability, defenses.

and bars to prosecution; liability for the acts of others; and the special aspects of criminal law, such as liability for uncompleted conduct, and the definitions of the elements of numerous crimes.

The chapter concluded with discussion of the relationship of law and morals and the controversy over decriminalization.

NOTES

1. Arthur Train, *From the District Attorney's Office* (New York: Scribner's, 1939), p. 1.
2. *Black's Law Dictionary* (St. Paul, Minn.: West, 1951), p. 445.
3. Gwynn Nettler, *Explaining Crime*, 2nd ed. (New York: McGraw-Hill, 1978), p. 2.
4. Train, *From the District Attorney's Office*, pp. 8–9.
5. Robert Bierstedt, *The Social Order*, 3rd ed. (New York: McGraw-Hill, 1970), p. 320.
6. *Ibid.*, p. 209.
7. *Ibid.*, p. 214.
8. *Ibid.*, p. 322.
9. (United States Senate, *Report of the Committee on the Judiciary*, 95th Congress, 1st Session, Report No. 95-605, Part 1), Washington, D.C.: GPO, pp. 118–119.
10. *Ibid.*, p. 119.
11. *Ibid.*, p. 87.
12. *Ibid.*, p. 87.
13. *Ibid.*, p. 88.
14. *Ibid.*, p. 829.
15. Quoted in Jerome H. Skolnick, "Coercion to Virtue," *Southern California Law Review* 41 (1968), p. 590.
16. *Ibid.*, p. 590.
17. *Ibid.*, pp. 610–611.
18. John Kaplan, *Marijuana—The New Prohibition* (1970), in Skolnick et al., eds., *Crime and Justice* (Del Mar, Calif.: Publisher's Inc., 1977), pp. 173–174.
19. Herbert L. Packer, *The Limits of the Criminal Sanction* (Stanford, Calif.: Stanford, 1968), p. 262.
20. Kaplan, *Marijuana*, p. 172.

SELECTED READINGS

Macklin Fleming, *Of Crimes and Rights* (New York: Norton, 1978).

Gilbert Geis, *Not the Law's Business? An Examination of Homosexuality, Abortion, Prostitution, Narcotics, Gambling in the United States* (Washington, D.C.: Center for Studies of Crime and Delinquency, 1972).

Stuart L. Hills, *Crime, Power, and Morality: The Criminal-Law Process in the United States* (Scranton, Pa.: Chandler, 1971).

Wayne R. LaFave, and Austin W. Scott, Jr., *Criminal Law* (St. Paul, Minn.: West, 1972).

Arnold H. Loewy, *Criminal Law* (St. Paul, Minn.: West, 1975).

Herbert L. Packer, *The Limits of the Criminal Sanction* (Stanford, Calif.: Stanford University Press, 1968).

Jerome Michael, and Herbert Wechsler, "A Rationale of the Law of Homicide," *Columbia Law Review*, 37 (1937), p. 701.

Herbert Wechslar, "The Challenge of a Model Penal Code," *Harvard Law Review* 65 (1952), p. 1097.

9

CRIMES, CRIMINALS, AND THE POLICE RESPONSE

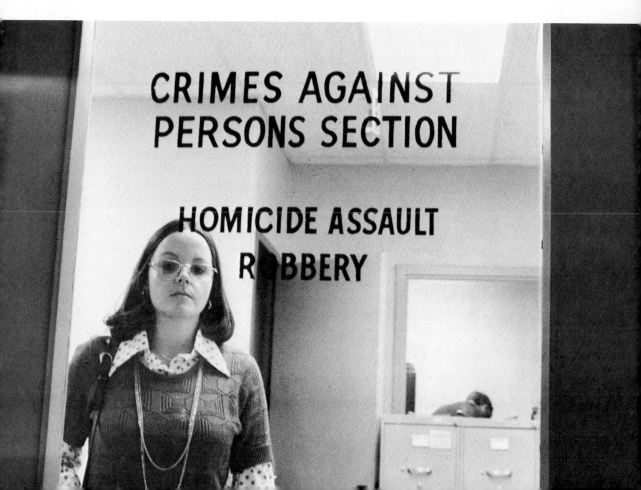

CRIMES AGAINST
PERSONS SECTION

HOMICIDE ASSAULT
ROBBERY

This chapter shifts from criminal law to criminology. After a brief discussion of the levels of explaining crime, it surveys many explanations that have been offered from time to time. It shifts to the quantitative aspects of crime with a presentation of various measures of magnitude of crime, then to some qualitative aspects of criminals and the crimes they commit. Victimology follows, with a look at some of the consequences of crime. This leads to a section on the development of "crime analysis," as the law enforcement response to the foregoing studies of crime.

The Causes of Crime

The definitions of crimes in the criminal code are legal abstractions. They are important in law enforcement because they provide the police with categories for classifying the conduct that comes to their attention. But criminal law lacks the flesh-and-blood of the police officer's day-to-day concerns. This is true, too, of the scientific abstractions of criminology. Theories of crime causation are important to law enforcement because theory—despite its weak reputation in the "real world" of practitioners—can and does guide the design of effective practices in the prevention and detection of crime. Thus, it is worth reviewing criminology before shifting in the balance of this chapter to some realities of crime and its rates, criminals and their activities, and their impact on victims and the community.

Criminology is worth reviewing also because its speculations and findings on the puzzles of behavior are fascinating. Cops are in the midst of a mix of passions, motivations, conditions, and circumstances producing criminals and crimes. They observe firsthand much of what engages those who study crime scientifically from a distance—traditionally the sociologists, psychologists, and psychiatrists; more recently the economists, political scientists, and geographers; and now the operations researchers, systems analysts, even architects; and once again, after long absence, the biologists. Even if conclusive answers continue to elude the scientists, and even if some of their best answers (like Sutherland's theory of "differential association") seem like truisms of curbstone wisdom (bad company corrupts), the quest for insight, perhaps even for truth, is absorbing.

The student of law enforcement, like its practitioner, must appreciate, however (and it comes more easily for the latter than the former), that the value of criminology to the enterprise of law enforcement is not in the satisfaction of intellectual curiosity but rather in its payoff for law-enforcement policy, strategy, and tactics. On this front there is much to be gained from a partnership of theorists and practitioners.

This suggests an added dimension in the review of criminology which is of interest to the student and practitioner of law enforcement: The law enforcement community, police officers in particular, have not yet been tapped for data in the quest for causes of crime. The officer's own information and insights may be useful to the criminologist in the search for definitive answers to the question of why people commit crimes. A productive partnership of police officers and theoreticians in the development of criminological theory has not yet been developed. It may depend upon the police community coming forth with contributions of its own, mainly in the production of useful data by which the criminologist may develop theories. This, however, probably can happen only if the student of policing has some appreciation of criminological theory.

EXPLANATIONS OF CRIME

The causes of crime involve a number of puzzles of human behavior. "Why Do Men Kill?" is the title of a chapter in Arthur Train's *From the District Attorney's Office*. He answered,

> There can be practically but one motive for theft, burglary, or robbery. It is, of course, conceivable that such crimes might be perpetrated for revenge—to deprive the victim of some highly prized possession. But in the main there is only one subject—unlawful gain. . . . The usual motive for crimes against the person—assault, manslaughter, mayhem, murder, etc.—is the desire to punish, or be avenged upon another by inflicting personal pain upon him or by depriving him of his most valuable assest—life. And this desire for retaliation or revenge generally grows out of a recent humiliation received at the hands of the other person, a real or fancied wrong to oneself, a member of one's family, or one's property.[1]

The quest for understanding leads the scholar and the student to three levels of explanation: (1) description, (2) patterns of correlation, and (3) theory. A *description* merely provides the who, what, where, when, and how, or the formula for good reporting, and journalists have provided most of the factual accounts of crime. It is what Sgt. Joe Friday gets when he is "Just getting the facts, ma'am." For example, a woman steps from the elevator into the hallway of her apartment building, a young man standing there grabs her, muffles her screams, pulls her into the stairwell, rapes her, takes no money, and leaves quickly. That describes a crime but it explains nothing.

The next level necessary in explaining crime establishes correlations in patterns of behavior: Of the hundreds of rapes in the city, a significant number involve upstairs hallways in apartment buildings, young men, and no theft of property. This provides some pattern for a crime analysis: there may be meaning in the unwatched circumstances, the age and sex of the perpetrator, and the omission of theft. An analysis does not, in and of itself, provide an explanation, but it moves from the particulars of who, what, where, when, and how to some generalities from which the theorist can begin to draw inferences. This level of analysis is very important but dangerous: the association of factors in the pattern (for example, youth and "maleness" associated with rape), sometimes leads the analyst to a hasty conclusion—that youthfulness or "maleness," or the combination of the two, are causes of rape. A good illustration of both the importance and the danger of identifying patterns is the imaginary map Ramsey Clark invites his readers to "mark" in this passage from his *Crime in America:*

> You have marked the areas where there are slums, poor schools, high unemployment, widespread poverty; where sickness and mental illness are common, housing is decrepit and nearly every sight is ugly—and you have marked the areas where crime flourishes. Behold your city—you have marked the same places every time. Poverty, illness, injustice, idleness, ignorance, human misery and crime go together.[2]

Clark hastens to point out, "People do not commit crime because they are black or poor or sick or ignorant or unemployed or live in ugly homes," but, "such conditions are demonstrably responsible for most crime—for nearly all crime that is foreseeable and can be prevented." Many less critical observers have leaped to the conclusion that such conditions cause crime.

Clark has put his finger on the elements of the third level (theory), where explanation takes place. Although certain factors, that are highly associated with crime, such as poverty, do not cause it, they are in some ways responsible for it; they are contributing factors in the overall process by which one explains crime. What is needed is a theory that explains why these correlation's exist and how one factor (poverty), called the *independent variable,* causes the other factor (crime), called the *dependent variable.* In physics, for instance, scientists moved from the descriptive level (things fall down), to the correlational level (things universally fall down at the same rate), to a theory (gravity is a force operating on all unsupported objects, drawing them toward the center of the earth). Finally, when a theory is tested repeatedly and survives the tests, it is said to be a law (the law of gravity).

Criminology f,llows the scientific lead in moving from facts of crimes to patterns of crime-facts to a theory. In the case of rape, the absence of theft can lead one to exclude robbery or any gain of property from the complex of causal factors. This would mean that rape is not a means to such an end (robbery), but must instead be a means to some other end. This is where the theory-construction process gets complicated: Just what is it, or what combination of factors, that explains the rapist's behavior?

The approach to an explanation depends in part on the starting point. In our time social study has been divided into several disciplines. Psychology, sociology, geography, economics, and others have claimed some portion or aspect of the study of social behavior. Each discipline is tempted—sometimes beyond resistance—to insist that its approach and its explanations are superior to all others. For example, as between biology (with its emphasis on genetics and neurology) and sociology (with its emphasis on the social environment), there is endless debate on the balance of nature and nurture in the explanation of behavior, each claiming it has more of the "why" than the other. But most of social sciences have come, a bit reluctantly, to the view that there are many causes of behavior, that no one approach, let alone any single theory, has a monopoly on inquiry or truth. Indeed, there is an abundance of "truth" in the study of crime. Thus, the following pages begin with a survey of several theories of crime, then move to a discussion of conditions correlated with crime, and finally to the raw numbers and facts of crime and its consequences, where law enforcement has its greatest concern.[3]

Character and Constitution. Another way to look at the causes of behavior involves a distinction between a person's constitution and his character. The concept of *character* is a rather old-fashioned approach to explaining behavior. It suggests factors such as conscience, honesty, virtue, and so forth. There is surely something to it because people speak of it as if it influenced choices and actions. However, good and evil, virtue and vice, folly and wisdom, courage and cowardliness, prudence, honesty, and other ideas associated with character do not lend themselves very well, if at all, to scientific inquiry. Hence they have not interested the scientists who have investigated the causation of criminal activity. But there is something to be said for examining what the poet Coleridge called the "abandoned and malignant heart."

Equally internal explanations of criminal activity are chemistry and biology which focus on the *constitution* or body. Body type, endocrine system, disfigurement, and intelligence level have been suggested in the past as influences of behavior. In the mid-nineteenth century the pioneering criminologist Cesare Lombroso observed, among other things, that tatoos were closely correlated with criminality. In more recent years there has been considerable interest in chromosomal explanations, such as the XYY theory, which holds that the presence of an extra chromosome results in a disportionately high incidence of criminal behavior. More ambitious explanations of behavior are now developing from the study of brain chemistry. This is leading rapidly to a range of drugs that promise to control violent behavior. The field of sociobiology, with ideas like territorial imperative, has emerged in the last decade to influence the thinking of criminologists, too.

Psychology and Psychiatry.   The chemistry of the brain is a study within the realm of psychiatry, which is concerned with genetic aspects, early experiences, and other influences, principally those of close relationships that shape a personality. The physiological and especially the neurological aspects require that practitioners of psychiatry be medical doctors. Psychology is the study of human behavior in general, with emphasis on the normal personality.

The psychological and psychiatric fields are complex, yet fairly familiar in general. The name *Freud* summons up the familiar ideas of id, ego, and superego. Since Freud, psychology has fragmented into numerous "schools"—and they war among themselves as to which has superior explanations and therapies. Now, however, just as it is overcoming the public resistance that has made mental health a subject to be kept in closets, as patients have been kept in institutions, out of sight and undiscussed, there is a growing disenchantment with psychiatry. But there is value in it for law enforcement nonetheless. For instance, during the spate of skyjackings in the 1960s, law-enforcement agencies called on the field of psychology to develop "psychological profiles" of persons considered likely to be skyjackers, to help airline personnel recognize and cope with them. Another case of the value of psychology is the approach of the New York City police team that goes into action in hostage cases, with a perfect record of never losing a hostage, an offender, or a police officer while successfully carrying out its rescue and apprehension operations. They have learned psychological techniques of "talking" such persons into giving up, without the last—but sometimes needed—resort of the police rushing in with guns blazing, which too often ends with loss of life. The "crisis intervention" techniques of the police now being used successfully in family fights are informed techniques based on a psychological understanding of situations of conflict.

Society. Sociologists shift their attention from the internal focus of psychology to an external focus on the environment. There is, however, no sharp distinction: psychologists are concerned about the effects of parents, brothers, sisters, and others; sociologists are concerned about the choices made by the person. Indeed, much of criminology draws from the hybrid discipline of social psychology.

The social explanations of crime rely on three basic social phenomena: social structure, social process, and labeling. The *social-structural* theories emphasize the place of the person, or "where he or she comes from," so to speak. The *social process* theories emphasize what happens to the person along the way after he or she begins the social journey from the social-structural origin. *Labeling* theories emphasize a special event in the process, the "tag" applied to a person when he or she becomes a "delinquent" or "criminal."

The principal social-structural theories are *anomie* theory and *subcultural* theory. Anomie theory originated with the French sociologist Emile Durkheim and was applied by Robert Merton to crime in this country. The anomie theory emphasizes a condition of normlessness or a weakness of society's norms to induce the person to accept the goals of society or the means of attaining them. Ordinarily one accepts society's goals and means. If not, the person must retreat from or rebel against both the goals and the means, or follow the means ritualistically without regard for the goals, or choose unacceptable means (that is, deviant or criminal) if he or she cannot follow the accepted means. A related theory is that of Richard Cloward and Lloyd Ohlin, who say that deviance is explained by *differential opportunity,* or the unavailability of some of the accepted means. Persons in such circumstances will turn to other openings, perhaps to crime, if better opportunities are blocked.

The subcultural theorists assert that society is composed of a dominant culture and one or more subcultures, such as lower-class ethnic groups or immigrant national groups. The subculture will have its own distinctive goals and means, just as it has its own values, norms, and other elements of a culture. These values, however, may conflict in some ways with those of the dominant culture and when that occurs the result may be what the dominant culture has defined as deviance or crime. For instance, if carrying a knife is a means of demonstrating "macho" qualities in a subculture, it may conflict with the law that follows the values of the dominant culture, in which one does not carry a knife. This poses problems for the police officer: does he permit "them" to have "their" standards and behaviors unchallenged or does he enforce the law equally?

The *social process* theories begin with an insistence that the person's position in society by no means determines behavior as rigidly as the structuralists suggest. Most people, even in subcultures, do not engage in much criminal behavior. But some do, and the process theories explain it by reference's to imitation or learning. E. H. Sutherland's theory of *differential association* states that people learn from close personal groups through communication of certain prescribed forms of behavior. If the definition of one's behavior is categorized as criminal behavior rather than lawful behavior, the person will be inclined toward crime. Another process theory, which depends less on the person's associates, is the *self-concept* theory: If one's self-concept is good, one will tend toward law-abiding behavior; if not, one tends toward law-breaking behavior.

Labeling is the third major sociological explanation. One aspect of this theory emphasizes society's treatment of its members: it treats as criminals those it has labeled criminals. Criminal law is, in a sense, the cause of crime, for without the label the behavior is not criminal. The second aspect of the labeling theory emphasizes the effect of the label: Persons labeled as criminals will tend to act as criminals, to become what society says they are. This self-fulfilling prophecy tendency has been influential in the development of diversion programs, in which young people are spared the labels of "delinquent" or "criminal" to avoid the behavior or acting out of the prophecy that the theory predicts. Many patrol officers have understood this intuitively and have practiced a kind of informal diversion program of their own, taking many youngsters home to avoid the deeper trouble of juvenile proceedings.

Geography, Economics, and Politics.   Another approach to the phenomena of crime looks still further beyond the person, beyond relations with other persons, even beyond groups and classes, to determinants that are less social and less personalistic—specifically, to geographic, economic, and political factors. "The earth itself has something to do with the societies that appear upon its surface," says sociologist Robert Bierstedt in *The Social Order*.[4] There can be disagreement on the extent of geography and climate on society and human behavior, but little if any disagreement on the fact that there is some. Suicides occur more frequently in certain months than in others. Crime rates are higher in summer than in winter. The incidences of peculiar behavior ("lunacy") are higher under a full moon than at other times.

The geographical configurations of a community influence the problems, techniques, and style of law enforcement, as observed in Chapter

7. Likewise, they influence other activities, including crime. Cattle grow in certain regions on ranges rather than feed lots, which makes rustling much easier there than where the cattle do not roam. It may be that the looting that accompanied the 1977 blackout in New York City, in contrast with the peaceable blackout of 1966, resulted from the fact that the earlier blackout occurred in the fall, the later blackout in July.

Natural resources vary widely, even more so than climate. This influences patterns of transportation and industry, for instance, and, consequently, patterns of criminal activity. The famous bank robber Willie Sutton robbed banks because, he said, "That's where the money is." Similarly, thefts of heavy construction equipment occur where highway construction goes on, which is determined in part by geography. Smuggling occurs along seacoasts.

Geography is microcosmic as well as macrocosmic, meaning it has a smaller as well as a larger focus. The design of the community, the arrangement of buildings on the land, the very shape of buildings themselves have been found to influence behavioral patterns of criminal activity. Jane Jacobs, in *The Life and Death of American Cities,* observed that some slums with the usual criminogenic, or crime-causing conditions (such as poverty), were significantly free of crime. Her important insight was that there was something in the quality of communications and relationships in those neighborhoods that contained, controlled, or displaced the criminal activity which would presumably have otherwise occurred. Architect Oscar Newman elaborated this insight in his book *Defensible Space,* the thesis of which is that environmental design importantly influences the kinds and amounts of crime, and that this design is within the control of the designers, who can shape the buildings and their layout on the land in ways that will minimize criminal activity. The Pruitt-Igoe housing development in St. Louis, once thought to be the perfect "high rise" low-income housing project, concentrated so much crime in a small area that it became unliveable and was torn down.

Law enforcement has an interest in geography at this level that it cannot have in geography at the levels described earlier. The patrol officer cannot influence the design of a community, but the "architect" of criminal-justice policy at its highest levels does have an interest and influence over the design of policies, hence the design of communities. The city leaders can be persuaded by the police commissioner to begin a street-lighting program, for instance. Evidence indicates that such programs have an initial crime-displacement effect, which makes it clear that communities can influence criminal behavior by "geographical" changes.[5]

The *economic* explanation of criminal activity involves several levels. One, the most fundamental, is the materialist explanation associated with Marxism. According to Karl Marx, writing in the nineteenth century, society (and its institutions, relationships, processes, change, and so forth) is rooted in material conditions, principally the economy. The economic system of the feudal society determined the nature of the government and its society. Likewise, the economic qualities of capitalism determined the "bourgeois" qualities of its politics and its social life. Marxists like the criminologist Bonger have argued that economic conditions, systems, and relationships likewise determine distinctive kinds of criminal behavior, which are peculiar to the economic system within which they occur. One criminologist, William Chambliss, has traced the changes in the laws of vagrancy, demonstrating that the changes in the law responded to the "changing needs" of the dominant classes of England at various times, as changing the definition of vagrancy had the effect of "criminalizing" forms of status and behavior that had not been deemed criminal previously.[6]

At another level the economic explanation accounts for the nature of the business system, which in turn produces different kinds and amounts of criminal activity. For instance, as the business system moves increasingly away from the use of cash, theft begins to involve the substitutes for cash, principally the forgery of checks. As the "cashless" society becomes more dependent upon the electronic transfer of funds from one account to another, theft increasingly will involve the use of computers.

At yet another level of economic explanation, the method of analysis employed in economics has been put to use in explaining that some criminal activity is due not to social or psychological factors, but to opportunity and a kind of "cost-benefit" analysis: Persons with a predisposition to crime, when they spot an opportunity, will think about what they stand to gain and lose from crime. This leads law enforcement to emphasize programs that reduce opportunities.

The *political* explanation of crime is derived from—and essentially the same as—the *conflict theory* in sociology, or the growing concern for the lack of harmony in the community. In the last decade or so there has been less confidence that law and its administration reflect widespread agreement on values. Instead of consensus, the conflict theorists argue that there is a sharp division between those with political power to secure their social and economic position and those without such power, who are held off or actively repressed. This is political because it concentrates on the governing of the polity or the goals of the community and the policies directing its governmental agencies, including the police. In short, those who lose with ballots (like those who lose with bullets) will have less access to material goods, security, freedom, and opportunity. Some of the more radical criminologists of this persuasion would insist that the government is really under the thumb of an elite that rules despite the expressions of political sentiment at the polls. They contend that all the trappings of democracy are manipulated for their benefit behind the scenes; what is on stage is calculated to entertain and distract the public, like the "bread and circuses" for the mobs of the Roman Empire. The meaning of this, insofar as it is valid, is that the police can no longer be sure that they serve the public as a whole—if there is no "whole," but rather an elite and a mass. Instead, police officers must see themselves as agents of the privileged few. The naked truth of that, if it is true, must be unsettling; cops cannot assume that they serve the cause of law and order, they must ask whose side they are on.

Conditions and Correlates of Crime.   At the middle of explanation, where correlations are established, criminology has another contribution to make to law enforcement. Law-enforcement policy and operations can gain from data that have been found to have a relationship—a correlation—with crime. Information at this level can be helpful in predicting crime frequencies, even if the causes of crime are not known. Gwynn Nettler has identified several correlates of serious crime: age, sex, social status, race, nationality, unemployment, ghettoes, and urbanism.[7] Each factor promises to aid in the analysis of crime, especially its changes in the future. Age, for instance, correlates highly: Younger persons commit more crimes than older persons, at least of the violent sort. This means, if other things hold equal, that violent crime (which is caused mainly by young people) will decline per person with the aging of the offspring of the baby boom. Sex, too, correlates highly: Far more males commit crimes than females. These correlations can be established with some precision, but they must be used cautiously, because projections cannot be made with all other things assumed to be equal. Women's liberation appears to be having an effect on female criminality: Women have access to situations now, because of their more varied employment, that give them opportunities to commit certain kinds of crime once the prerogative of men, such as those crimes peculiar to the business world. Liberation from a "culture-bound" gender are loosening the constraints that kept females from engaging in juvenile gang activity (except as "camp followers") and in behaviors once thought "unladylike," such as violence.[8]

Social status, as manifested in occupation, income, wealth, class, and education level, indicate crime rates, usually negatively: The higher the status, the lower the criminality (at least for crimes of violence). Urbanism yields a correlation: The sheer size of a community correlates strongly and positively with crime, as does the proportion of people employed in manufacturing.

Nettler argues that culture is the key to controlling crime, and that community is the condition of culture. Thus, whatever erodes the bonds of community contributes to increases in crime. Such increases can be anticipated by increases in factors that undercut community: (1) "physical relocation of large masses of people," (2) crowding, (3) social mobility, (4) "relative deprivation (or what people think they lack)," (5) child neglect and misuse of youth (e.g., "Schools that shame children, or imprison them, . . . that provide no moral models"), (7) mass media's glorification of criminals, (8) the "comforting chemicals," (9) the growth of anarchy and decline of authority, which put distance between parents and children, and finally (10) laws and their enforcement ("laws without force are criminogenic"). To the extent that these conditions can be quantified, predictions can be made of changes in crime rates. This is of great importance to law enforcement and should be encouraged and supported as yet another bridge of criminology theory and criminal-justice practice.[9]

The Quantity of Crime

The quantities of crime—the frequencies, rates, trends upward and downward—all supply data that is indispensable to the scholar who inquires into causes, to the politician who shapes policies and measures that influence the conditions of crime, and especially to the police and criminal-justice administrators who apply organizational, strategic, and tactical responses to crime. Moreover, the rates of crime are the aspect to which the public responds in the first instance, just as a specific criminal act is what a victim responds to. The aggregates of crime reported in the rates veil the qualities of those specific crimes, however. This important dimension of crime will be taken up after some discussion of the quantitative aspect.

The principal source of crime data in the United States is the *Uniform Crime Reports* (UCRs). Compiled by the FBI from reports submitted by some 8000 police agencies, the UCRs are relied on heavily by many researchers into crime. The UCRs report figures on the following crimes, the first seven of which are commonly called the index crimes:

PART I OFFENSES:

1. criminal homicide
2. forcible rape
3. robbery
4. aggravated assault
5. burglary—breaking or entering
6. larceny—theft (except motor-vehicle theft)
7. motor-vehicle theft

PART II OFFENSES:

 8. other assaults (simple)
 9. arson
10. forgery and counterfeiting
11. fraud
12. embezzlement
13. stolen property; buying, receiving, possessing
14. vandalism
15. weapons; carrying, possessing, etc.
16. prostitution and commercialized vice
17. sex offenses (except forcible rape, prostitution, and commercialized vice)
18. narcotic drug laws
19. gambling
20. offenses against the family and children
21. driving under the influence
22. liquor law violations
23. drunkenness
24. disorderly conduct
25. vagrancy
26. all other offenses
27. suspicion
28. curfew and loitering laws (juveniles)
29. runaways (juveniles)

One of the highlights of the UCRs is the "crime clock" (Figure 9.1) which indicates the frequency of certain crimes in terms of time.

The trends in rates are represented in Table 9.1. The 50 percent increase is of course much greater than the increase in population. On the other hand, 1977 is estimated to show a decrease from 1976, the leveling off predicted from the demographic effects of time on the baby boom of the postwar years.

The UCR charts graphing robberies and thefts are especially interesting, and are illustrated in Figures 9.2, 9.3, and 9.4.

The crime rates in the United States take on meaning in terms of their relativity to earlier years and to other countries. The former has been indicated in Table 9.1, the latter is suggested in the observations of David H. Bayley comparing Japanese and American crime rates:

> The number of crimes committed annually in Japan in recent years is actually lower than 25 years ago. . . . The crime rate . . . is declining; in 1974 there were 112 crimes committed for every 10,000 persons. (This

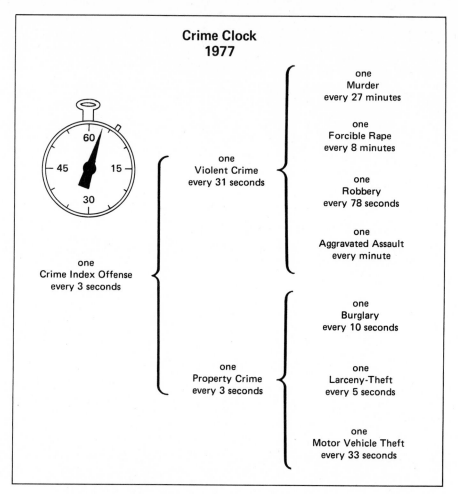

**Crime Clock
1977**

one
Crime Index Offense
every 3 seconds

one
Violent Crime
every 31 seconds

one
Property Crime
every 3 seconds

one
Murder
every 27 minutes

one
Forcible Rape
every 8 minutes

one
Robbery
every 78 seconds

one
Aggravated Assault
every minute

one
Burglary
every 10 seconds

one
Larceny-Theft
every 5 seconds

one
Motor Vehicle Theft
every 33 seconds

Figure 9.1 (*Source:* Federal Bureau of Investigation, *Uniform Crime Reports 1977* [Washington, D.C.: GPO, 1978], p. 6.)

includes all penal code offenses, no matter how trivial, except for traffic violations.) . . . In 1974 (in the United States), there were 480 [index] crimes for every 10,000 persons. In other words, there are over four times as many serious crimes per person in the United States as crimes of any sort per person in Japan.[10]

The reliability of the UCRs has been challenged by scholars for several reasons, among them the practices of the police, which can distort the reports in ways indicated in Chapter 5. Also, the definitions of crimes

TABLE 9.1
National Crime, Rate, and Percent Change

Crime Index offenses	Estimated crime 1977		Percent change over 1976		Percent change over 1973		Percent change over 1968	
	Number	Rate per 100,000 inhabitants	Number	Rate per 100,000 inhabitants	Number	Rate per 100,000 inhabitants	Number	Rate per 100,000 inhabitants
Total	10,935,800	5,055.1	−3.3	−4.0	+25.4	+21.7	+62.7	+50.0
Violent	1,009,500	466.6	+2.3	+1.5	+15.3	+11.8	+69.7	+56.4
Property	9,926,300	4,588.4	−3.8	−4.5	+26.6	+22.8	+62.1	+49.4
Murder	19,120	8.8	+1.8		−2.6	−6.4	+38.6	+27.5
Forcible rape	63,020	29.1	+11.1	+10.2	+22.6	+18.8	+99.0	+83.0
Robbery	404,850	187.1	−3.7	−4.4	+5.4	+2.2	+54.0	+42.0
Aggravated assault	522,510	241.5	+6.4	+5.6	+24.2	+20.4	+82.2	+67.9
Burglary	3,052,200	1,410.9	−1.2	−2.0	+19.0	+15.4	+64.2	+51.3
Larceny-theft	5,905,700	2,729.9	−5.8	−6.6	+35.8	+31.8	+69.6	+56.3
Motor vehicle theft	968,400	447.6	+1.1	+.3	+4.3	+1.1	+23.6	+13.9

Source: Federal Bureau of Investigation, *Uniform Crime Reports 1977* (Washington, D.C.: 1978), p. 35.

vary from state to state, introducing some inconsistencies in the reports of crimes. The 8000 agencies reporting their jurisdiction's crimes are only part, although the bulk, of the 40,000 police agencies in the nation. More important is the volume of unreported crime, some of which is known to local police but not reported by them to the FBI, but most of which, however, is not reported to the police at all. Long suspected, this so-called dark figure of crime was measured initially in a study done for the President's Crime Commission in 1967 and, more definitively in a continuing study by the Census Bureau for the Law Enforcement Assistance Administration. It confirmed the suspicion that there is a significant "dark figure" of unreported crime, as Table 9.2 indicates.

Although the police could respond that unreported crimes have no operational significance for them (because they can only respond to what they are told about), the police could not pass off the survey's findings of reasons for nonreporting of crimes: Varying with the kinds of crime, between 10 percent and 20 percent said it was because the police would not want to be bothered; one-third to two-thirds said nothing could be done; and another one-quarter said their victimization was not important enough (Table 9.3). These findings have troubled the law-enforcement community because the reasons reflect negatively on the police. They have led to reforms, principally in programs to assist victims and witnesses in the trial process. Other responses (did not want to take time, a private matter, did not want to get involved, fear of reprisal, and victimization reported to someone else) are also of concern to the police because they indicate something of the public's attitudes and knowledge

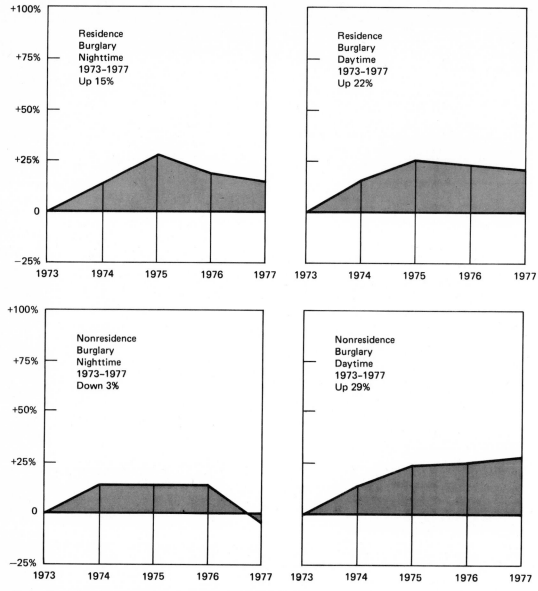

Note: Burglaries of unknown time of occurrence are not included.

Figure 9.2. (*Source:* Federal Bureau of Investigation, *Uniform Crime Reports 1977* [Washington, D.C.: GPO, 1978], p. 25.)

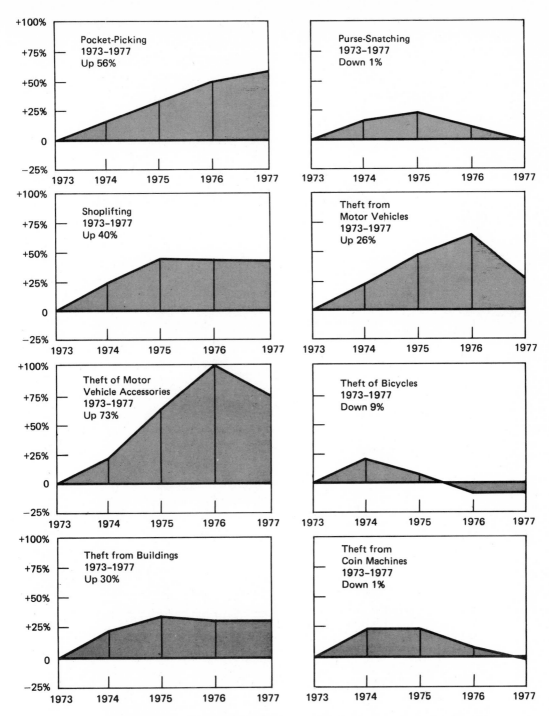

Figure 9.3. (*Source:* Federal Bureau of Investigation, *Uniform Crime Reports 1977* [Washington, D.C.: GPO, 1978], p. 29.)

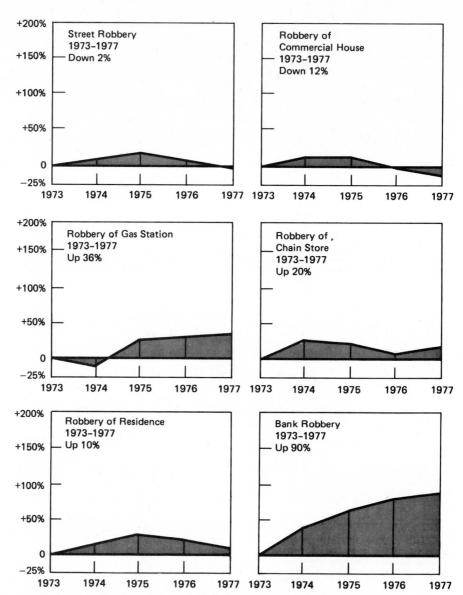

Figure 9.4. (*Source:* Federal Bureau of Investigation, *Uniform Crime Reports 1977* [Washington, D.C.: GPO, 1978], p. 18.)

TABLE 9.2
Estimated Number of Personal, Household, and Business Victimizations, By Reporting to Police and Type of Victimization, United States, 1975[a]

Type of victimization	Total		Reported to Police		Not Reported to Police		Don't Know Whether Reported to Police	
	Number	Percent	Number	Percent	Number	Percent	Number	Percent
Personal victimization:								
Rape and attempted rape	151,055	100	84,999	56	66,056	44	0	0
Robbery	1,121,374	100	597,249	53	519,267	46	4,858	0
Robbery and attempted robbery with injury	353,493	100	229,768	65	121,387	34	2,339	1
Serious assault	207,114	100	138,221	67	67,632	33	1,261	1
Minor assault	146,380	100	91,548	63	53,755	37	1,077	1
Robbery without injury	467,595	100	276,462	59	189,827	41	1,306	0
Attempted robbery without injury	300,285	100	91,019	30	208,053	69	1,213	0
Assault	4,176,056	100	1,888,249	45	2,243,469	54	44,338	1
Aggravated assault	1,590,080	100	878,320	55	698,065	44	13,696	1
With injury	543,175	100	353,612	65	183,342	34	6,222	1
Attempted assault with weapon	1,046,905	100	524,708	50	514,723	49	7,474	1
Simple assault	2,585,976	100	1,009,930	39	1,545,404	60	30,643	1
With injury	687,352	100	329,173	48	352,656	51	5,523	1
Attempted assault without weapon	1,898,624	100	680,757	36	1,192,748	63	25,119	1
Personal larceny with contact	513,952	100	177,606	35	333,935	65	2,410	0
Purse snatching	119,096	100	76,532	64	42,564	36	0	0
Attempted purse snatching	60,912	100	11,160	18	49,752	82	0	0
Pocket picking	333,943	100	89,913	27	241,619	72	2,410	1
Personal larceny without contact	15,455,660	100	4,014,300	26	11,275,190	73	166,170	1
Household victimization:								
Burglary	6,688,964	100	3,252,549	49	3,410,292	51	26,123	0
Forcible entry	2,251,869	100	1,641,474	73	598,498	27	11,897	1
Unlawful entry without force	2,959,734	100	1,125,573	38	1,827,196	62	6,965	0
Attempted forcible entry	1,477,361	100	485,502	33	984,598	67	7,261	0
Larceny	9,156,711	100	2,479,407	27	6,633,769	72	43,534	0
Under $50	5,615,914	100	865,244	15	4,729,099	84	21,571	0
$50 or more	2,707,605	100	1,439,354	53	1,255,026	46	13,225	0
Amount not ascertained	277,922	100	46,504	17	226,250	81	5,168	2
Attempted	555,270	100	128,305	23	423,394	76	3,571	1
Vehicle theft	1,418,725	100	1,008,870	71	393,256	28	16,599	1
Completed	910,253	100	829,163	91	70,918	8	10,172	1
Attempted	508,472	100	179,707	35	322,338	63	6,428	1
Business victimizations:								
Robbery	261,725	100	236,010	90	23,693	9	2,022	1
Burglary	1,518,339	100	1,210,725	80	273,904	18	33,710	2

[a]Subcategories may not sum to total because of rounding.
Source: Michael R. Gottfredson, et al., eds., *Sourcebook, Criminal Justice Statistics 1977* (Washington, D.C.: Law Enforcement Assistance Administration, 1978), p. 302.

concerning aspects of law enforcement on which the police have some influence. The police can help to make it worth taking time to get involved and to do so free of fear of reprisal.

The apparent plateauing of crime rates, whether reported in the UCRs or the LEAA reports, is encouraging—unlike the 1973 decline, which was followed by increases in the next years. But the straight-line projection of a downward trend may be deflected from its trajectory by intervening factors such as changing values, weakening norms, decreasing opportunities, increasing political conflict, and other causes indicated by crime theorists. Just as the factor of women's liberation seems to have

TABLE 9.3
Reasons Given for Not Reporting Personal and Household Victimizations to Police By Type of Victimization, United States, 1975[a]

Type of victimization	Total victimizations not Reported	Nothing could be done		Victimization not important enough		Police wouldn't want to be bothered		Did not want to take time	
		Number	Percent	Number	Percent	Number	Percent	Number	Percent
Personal victimizations:									
Rape and attempted rape	66,056	14,820	22	7,596	11	6,094	9	1,707	3
Robbery	519,267	197,925	38	120,239	23	73,164	14	24,458	5
Robbery and attempted robbery with injury	121,387	51,918	43	22,595	19	22,001	18	1,243	1
Serious assault	67,632	29,412	43	12,383	18	12,821	19	1,243	2
Minor assault	53,755	22,506	42	10,212	19	9,180	17	0	0
Robbery without injury	189,827	68,953	36	33,832	18	33,017	17	7,830	4
Attempted robbery without injury	208,503	77,054	37	63,812	31	18,147	9	15,385	7
Assault	2,243,469	503,326	22	624,810	28	151,590	7	71,172	3
Aggravated assault	698,065	178,122	26	146,172	21	53,898	8	41,266	6
With injury	183,342	40,210	22	31,737	17	13,223	7	4,626	3
Attempted assault with weapon	514,723	137,912	27	114,435	22	40,674	8	36,640	7
Simple assault	1,545,404	325,204	21	478,637	31	97,693	6	29,906	2
With injury	352,656	48,717	14	78,368	22	21,947	6	6,226	2
Attempted assault without weapon	1,192,748	276,487	23	400,270	34	75,746	6	23,680	2
Personal larceny with contact	333,935	185,552	56	71,218	21	34,051	10	12,162	4
Purse snatching	42,564	26,793	63	9,632	23	1,175	3	1,175	3
Attempted purse snatching	49,752	30,307	61	10,805	22	4,868	10	3,917	8
Pocket picking	241,619	128,452	53	50,782	21	28,008	12	7,069	3
Personal larceny without contact	11,275,190	4,816,170	43	4,036,270	36	896,800	8	427,060	4
Household victimizations:									
Burglary	3,410,292	1,736,646	51	1,035,374	30	409,502	12	95,702	3
Forcible entry	598,498	291,520	49	135,641	23	88,023	15	17,055	3
Unlawful entry without force	1,827,196	972,938	53	523,111	29	191,099	10	50,692	3
Attempted forcible entry	984,598	472,188	48	376,622	38	130,379	13	27,955	3
Larceny	6,633,769	3,207,843	48	2,977,590	45	803,905	12	231,652	3
Under $50	4,729,099	2,153,535	46	2,494,021	53	563,290	12	141,071	3
$50 or more	1,255,026	748,316	60	204,641	16	157,879	13	66,486	5
Amount not ascertained	226,250	107,101	47	111,952	49	30,848	14	9,849	4
Attempted	423,394	198,892	47	167,156	39	51,888	12	14,245	3
Vehicle theft	393,256	187,100	48	107,905	27	59,234	15	18,187	5
Completed	70,918	18,695	26	10,685	15	6,169	9	2,292	3
Attempted	322,338	168,405	52	97,220	30	53,065	16	15,895	5

[a]Subcategories may not sum to total because of rounding.

Respondents may have given more than one reason for not reporting the victimization to the police, the row sum of the "reason for not reporting to the police" may exceed "total victimizations not reported."

intervened in the projections based on sex alone, so the rates of violent crime may be altered by other intervening factors. The juvenile population is decreasing relative to the population as a whole, but not the rates of juvenile crime—rates that are responding to unidentified factors: Violence is practiced at younger ages and gang activity is turning from the defense of "turf" to commercial shakedowns, residential robberies, and forays—like guerilla raids—into the outer world for attacks at sports and entertainment events.[11]

Moreover, the dimension of recent violence is less alarming in its amount than its kind: terrorism, randomness (the "senseless killings"), multiplicity—murders by the dozen (by the 20's, no less, in California,

TABLE 9.3 *(Continued)*

It was a private matter		Did not want to get involved		Fear of reprisal		Victimization was reported to someone else		Other		Not ascertained	
Number	Percent	Number	Percent	Number	Percent	Number	Percent	Number	Percent	Number	Percent
20,276	31	6,417	10	10,840	16	7,141	11	23,822	36	0	0
60,321	12	20,326	4	39,423	8	67,221	13	110,624	21	2,440	0
15,262	13	8,766	7	10,291	8	8,278	7	33,128	27	1,302	1
10,224	15	3,713	5	6,443	10	3,469	5	15,313	23	1,302	2
5,038	9	5,053	9	3,848	7	4,808	9	17,814	33	0	0
18,881	10	11,560	6	15,813	8	35,380	19	34,044	18	1,137	1
26,179	13	0	0	13,319	6	23,563	11	43,452	21	0	0
561,631	25	73,174	3	112,626	5	377,810	17	438,945	20	24,709	1
178,161	26	37,033	5	46,677	7	92,193	13	148,122	21	3,845	1
60,489	33	9,462	5	12,870	7	36,352	20	33,426	18	0	0
117,672	23	27,571	5	33,807	7	55,841	11	114,696	22	3,845	1
383,471	25	36,141	2	65,949	4	285,617	18	290,823	19	20,863	1
118,773	34	12,486	4	15,484	4	88,941	25	67,000	19	2,448	1
264,698	22	23,655	2	50,465	4	196,675	16	223,823	19	18,415	2
20,522	6	3,596	1	4,445	1	54,885	16	63,147	19	2,469	1
2,518	6	1,250	3	1,198	3	8,591	20	4,771	11	0	0
1,411	3	0	0	0	0	3,720	7	12,235	25	1,229	2
16,592	7	2,346	1	3,247	1	42,574	18	46,141	19	1,240	1
379,720	3	60,970	1	46,330	0	2,812,100	25	1,372,870	12	101,850	1
257,214	8	40,339	1	27,511	1	303,605	9	705,620	21	21,366	1
65,658	11	13,540	2	7,279	1	56,948	10	150,529	25	3,419	1
170,639	9	20,589	1	16,823	1	154,120	8	337,573	18	7,366	0
20,917	2	6,202	1	3,409	0	92,537	9	217,519	22	10,581	1
455,978	7	42,522	1	32,577	0	264,406	4	927,239	14	59,139	1
290,705	6	26,138	1	19,115	0	165,431	3	508,204	11	39,606	1
142,405	11	14,004	1	6,960	1	70,028	6	288,238	23	15,476	1
13,378	6	0	0	1,434	1	6,467	3	29,069	13	1,643	1
9,490	2	2,381	1	5,069	1	22,481	5	101,729	24	2,415	1
25,971	7	1,082	0	5,666	1	26,478	7	89,784	23	1,172	0
21,421	30	0	0	3,466	5	4,898	7	21,458	30	0	0
4,551	1	1,082	0	2,199	1	21,580	7	68,326	21	1,172	0

Source: Michael R. Gottfredson, et al., eds., *Sourcebook of Criminal Justice Statistics 1977* (Washington, D.C.: Law Enforcement Assistance Administration, 1978), pp. 302–313.

Houston, and Chicago), and so much of it involving cruelty, especially torture, and bizarre sexual and even ritualistic overtones. The public responds more to occasional incidents of this kind—the half dozen shovings into the path of onrushing New York City subway trains—than to the hundreds of routine homicides. So we turn now to the character, rather than the quantity of crime.

The Character of Crimes and Criminals

The definitions, causes, correlates, conditions, and rates of crime begin to take on meaning when abstractions are fleshed out with the human element. It is this element that the experience and imagination of the police and the community translate into weights of harmlessness or of horror. Bringing the generalities down to specifics requires attention to the range of offenses that fit a particular category of crime. Theft, for instance, ranges from "stealing the pennies off a dead man's eyes" to the ghoulish stealing of a corpse itself. Auto theft ranges from joy-riding, which is sometimes treated distinctly in the law because there is no intention of permanently depriving the owner of property, to stealing fleets of cars. Prostitution ranges from high-class call girls at thousands of dollars a night to two-bit streetwalking whores, with variations involving sadomasochistic homosexual prostitution and hustling "chickens," or young boys, preyed upon by "chicken hawks," or middle-aged men.

The synonyms for crimes and criminals indicate the range and subtlety of differences. Stealing, pilfering, filching, snitching, swiping—all connote different degrees of theft. Novelist John Barth, in *The Sot-Weed Factor,* presents six pages of words for *whore*—from *hooker, quail,* and *frisker* to *harpy* and *didler.*[12] White-collar crime, which is a matter of getting something for nothing, or for less than what a full and fair deal calls for, takes numerous forms: bankruptcy fraud, bribes, kickbacks, payoffs, computer crimes, consumer fraud, illegal competition, deceptive practices, credit-card fraud, checking schemes (such as check-kiting), embezzlement, insurance fraud, pilferage, receiving stolen property, securities theft and fraud—to name only a few.

Confidence games occur in forms ranging from the so-called big con of the sort made famous in the movie *The Sting* to less ambitious schemes such as "high dice," "pigeon drop," "spanish prisoner," "shell game," "badger game," and "Murphy game." "High dice," for example, preys upon the greed of the victim. One con artist (A) engages the "mark" (M) in conversation; the second con artist (B) appears, looking stupid or bewildered; A goes to see what is going on and returns to report to M that B has a lot of money but is afraid to put it in a bank and will do so only with help and some sign of good faith—but that A and M can make off with B's money by tricking him. B then explains that if M will add a lot of his money to B's money, B will trust him to deposit it and then meet him later to make arrangements for withdrawal later on; M withdraws his own money and returns to A and B; A puts it into an envelope with B's money; then, while B distracts M, A switches it for a similar envelope containing paper; M gives B a phony address, then gives A another phony address, and goes off thinking B is thinking M is heading for the bank and thinking A is thinking there will be a rendezvous of A and M; M thinks he will never see A or B again—and he is right! Variations on this game bilk hundreds of people, many of them elderly, of their savings.

The badger and Murphy games victimize, too, but not so sympathetic a victim. In the Murphy game the mark goes with a prostitute to her room, whereupon her partner bursts in as her husband, angrily threatening the mark, who "buys off" the "husband" and leaves very much relieved—of his money, as well. The Murphy game is very common: the mark pays what he thinks is a pimp to get him a prostitute, but when he goes where the "pimp" says he should go, of course there is no one there.[13]

The criminal class is not an undifferentiated aggregation of actors. There are categories of criminals, distinguished by the kind, degree, and frequency of their criminal activity. Shoplifters, for example, can be divided into "heels," or professionals, who earn a living from it; "boosters," or occasional shoplifters who supplement their living with it; and "snitches," or amateurs, who do it now and then, not out of need but for fun.[14]

More elaborate typologies have been constructed, which are helpful in understanding the variety of criminals. Gibbons and Garrity, for example, developed the following typology of property offenders: Professional thieves define themselves as criminals who employ technical skills in their activities and who regard the police as occupational risks. Professional "heavies" are similar except they employ violence or its threat in their crimes, tending toward armed robbery and burglary rather than con games. Nonprofessional property offenders likewise conceive of themselves as criminals, but not skilled criminals, and engage in violent crimes without technical skills. Auto thieves and joy-riders are swaggering, repetitive offenders who conceive of themselves as criminals but not violent and have low-level skills and hostility to law enforcement. The "naive check forger" regularly commits checking offenses without the skills of a professional and because of personal problems rather than outright gain. The white-collar offenders, embezzlers, and professional "fringe" violators are professionals with a sideline of illegal activity, such as doctors performing illegal abortions.[15]

The variations finally become a series of specific crimes and criminals as one gets closer to them; the forest becomes one tree after another. For the police officer the crimes come one by one, each one differing from another in its details. For the student's understanding of crime there is no substitute for some attention to the details of particular crimes. Only one can be sampled at this point, but it is a classic, immortalized in the reporting of novelist Truman Capote in his best seller *In Cold Blood*. The book is a richly detailed account of the killing of a Kansas farm family, the Clutters—Herb and Bonnie and their children, 16-year-old Nancy and 15-year-old Kenyon. Perry Smith and Richard Hickock had made their way to the Clutter farm, where they believed a great amount of money was kept in a safe. They tied up the Clutters, each one in a separate room, then they taped their mouths, and finally—to get rid of any witnesses—they killed them, one by one. In the confession of Smith and the reconstruction by Capote, the episode went like this:

> ". . . I knelt down beside Mr. Clutter. . . . But I didn't realize what I'd done till I heard the sound. Like somebody drowning. Screaming under water. I handed the knife to Dick. I said, 'Finish him. You'll feel better.' Dick tried—or pretended to. But the man had the strength of ten men—he was half out of his ropes, his hands were free. Dick panicked. Dick wanted to get the hell out of there. But I wouldn't let him go. The man would have died anyway, I know that, but I couldn't leave him like he was. I told Dick to hold the flashlight, focus it. Then I aimed the gun. The room just exploded. Went blue. Just blazed up. Jesus, I'll never understand why they didn't hear the noise twenty miles around."
>
> . . . The voice plunges on, ejecting a fusillade of sounds and images: Hickock hunting the discharged shell; hurrying, hurrying, and Kenyon's head in a circle of light, the murmur of muffled pleadings, then Hickock again scrambling after a used cartridge; Nancy's room, Nancy listening to boots on hardwood stairs, the creak of the steps as they climb toward her, Nancy's eyes, Nancy watching the flashlight's shine seek the target (She said, Oh, no! Oh, please. No! No! No! No! Don't! Oh, please don't! Please! I gave the gun to Dick. I told him I'd done all I could do. He took aim, and she turned her face to the wall); the dark hall, the assassins hastening toward the final door. Perhaps, having heard all she had, Bonnie welcomed their swift approach.[16]

The Impact of Crime

The initial impact of crime is experienced by the immediate victim—the one whose throat is cut or life savings gone. The police officer is present for much of the initial victimization; he or she sees the suffering up close. Beyond that, the impact of crime extends like ripples from a pebble thrown in a pool. Police officers are aware of these, too. They see the sons and daughters home from college to support the family, they see the store windows boarded up, they see the neighborhood deserted at night, its businesses moving out, its elderly retreating into their rooms. Victimization reinforces the officer's sense of urgency. The impact also translates itself through community sentiment into policy decisions of increased spending on police protection, more aggressive preventive patrol, and other measures that influence law enforcement.

The impact of crime can be divided into four kinds, according to its direct/indirect or tangible/intangible qualities. The *direct, tangible* impact includes the costs of physical injury (ambulance, hospitalization, medical expenses), employment costs (wage losses, replacement workers), property damage (repainting school walls, refurbishing burnt-out apartments), family costs (baby-sitters, transportation of relatives). The *direct, intangible* consequences of crime include emotional effects (feelings of fear, loss of companionship, insecurity) and changed behavior (avoidance of certain areas).

The *indirect, tangible* effects of crime include the individual's loss of productivity, full or partially; rehabilitation; foregone purchases; increased insurance premiums. Business productivity declines as the quality of the community declines, as better workers leave the neighborhood, as patronage diminishes. Costs go up as premiums increase, as protective measures are employed—at a lowering of profit, of funds for reinvestment, of dividends to be spent by shareholders, of the economic activity generated by investment and spending. Less is produced but at higher prices; the wealth of the community declines with the deterioration of the quality of life. Finally there are *indirect, intangible* effects: emotional changes in the individual, altered style of living, changed patterns of family activity, deterioration of family quality, loss of opportunity, reduced social contacts, loss of confidence in government. The community weakens in its bonds, disintegrating into pockets of frightened individuals; the affluent flee to the suburbs or into high-rise bastions; more is invested in social controls than constructive enterprises such as business, education, art, science. Tax revenue goes down, and with it the quality of the public sector's services. Cultural activities and opportunities decline or shift elsewhere. Facilities and entire areas are abandoned. Finally, the very conditions and prerequisites of civilization itself erode.

The economic impact of crime is represented in Figure 9.5, a graph from the President's Crime Commission report. Increasing cost is suggested by the change over time in local government spending on criminal justice, as indicated in Table 9.4.

Little has been done to quantify and to measure the effects of crimes. So, fear is assumed to be the feeling of most citizens. But it is worth noting that one attempt to analyze the victim surveys gives rise to some optimistic inferences:

1. Perceptions of crime trends: Although most respondents in the surveys thought that their own chances of being victimized had gone up in recent years, more people perceived rising crime as a national, rather than neighborhood, problem.
2. Fear of crime: Respondents in various age, sex, race, and income groups differ considerably in fear of crime, but whether or not one has been the victim of crime during the past year does not appear to have a major effect on fear. In addition, people tend to feel less threatened close to home than in other neighborhoods.

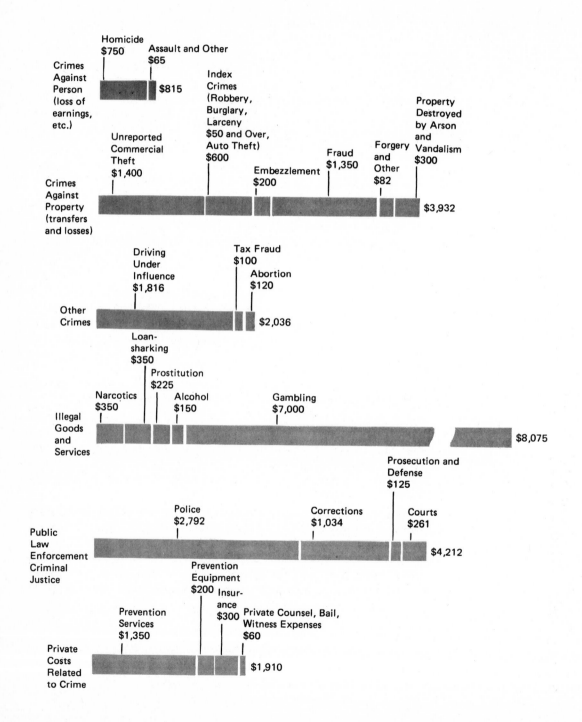

TABLE 9.4

Criminal Justice Expenditure, By Level of Government and Type of Activity and Expenditure, United States, Fiscal Years 1971–1975

	Local Governments									
	Amount					Percent Increase or Decrease (−)				
Activity						1971 to 1972	1972 to 1973	1973 to 1974	1974 to 1975	1971 to 1975
	1971	1972	1973	1974	1975					
Total criminal justice system	6,662,697	7,372,509	8,094,225	9,129,864	10,501,604	10.7	9.8	12.8	15.0	57.6
Direct expenditure	6,620,807	7,281,248	8,052,232	9,092,370	10,448,612	10.0	10.6	12.9	14.9	57.8
Intergovernmental expenditure	75,545	91,261	90,249	115,395	144,501	20.8	−1.1	27.9	25.2	91.3
Police protection	4,489,045	4,978,854	5,405,423	5,984,077	6,817,005	10.9	8.6	10.7	13.9	51.9
Direct expenditure	4,487,825	4,948,354	5,403,036	5,981,711	6,813,407	10.3	9.2	10.7	13.9	51.8
Intergovernmental expenditure	21,327	30,500	32,697	52,985	64,620	43.0	7.2	62.0	22.0	203.0
Judicial	912,310	973,918	1,082,257	1,227,391	1,412,763	6.8	11.1	13.4	15.1	54.9
Direct expenditure	910,545	965,260	1,075,479	1,222,562	1,404,672	6.0	11.4	13.7	14.9	54.3
Intergovernmental expenditure	5,561	8,658	13,824	11,729	17,226	55.7	59.7	−15.1	46.9	209.8
Legal services and prosectuion	295,415	350,150	398,783	476,793	542,440	18.5	13.9	19.6	13.8	83.6
Direct expenditure	294,779	348,351	396,899	474,609	539,854	18.2	13.9	19.6	13.7	83.1
Intergovernmental expenditure	787	1,799	2,553	2,627	2,967	128.6	41.9	2.9	12.9	277.0
Public defense	50,969	63,573	79,283	101,445	127,938	24.7	24.7	28.0	26.1	151.0
Direct expenditure	50,961	63,430	79,240	101,281	127,772	24.5	24.9	27.8	26.2	150.7
Intergovernmental expenditure	123	143	257	522	545	16.3	79.7	103.1	4.4	343.1
Corrections	895,420	961,338	1,066,000	1,240,815	1,471,470	7.4	10.9	16.4	18.6	64.3
Direct expenditure	857,168	911,282	1,035,434	1,213,338	1,433,535	6.3	13.6	17.2	18.1	67.2
Intergovernmental expenditure	47,425	50,056	40,275	46,456	58,170	5.5	−19.5	15.3	25.2	22.7
Other criminal justice	19,538	44,676	62,478	99,343	129,988	128.7	39.8	59.0	30.8	505.3
Direct expenditure	19,529	44,571	62,144	98,869	129,372	128.2	39.4	59.1	30.9	562.5
Intergovernmental expenditure	321	105	643	1,076	1,007	−67.3	512.4	67.3	−6.4	213.7

Source: U.S. Department of Justice, Law Enforcement Assistance Administration and U.S. Bureau of the Census, *Trends in Expenditure and Employment Data for the Criminal Justice System 1971–1975* (Washington, D.C.: U.S. Government Printing Office, 1977), p. 18, Table 2, p. 19, Table 4, p. 21, Table 8, p. 22, Table 10.

3. Attitudes about crime and respondent behavior: There is a strong tendency for people to believe that the fear of crime affects *other* people more than it affects them. The fear of crime does not appear to be a major motivating factor involved in some of the specific behaviors that respondents were asked about.

4. Evaluations of local police: Most respondents rated their local police rather highly, even while believing that police performance needed to be improved. Evaluations of the police were not strongly affected by actual experience with victimization, by the belief that crime is increasing, or by fear of crime, but there were major differences across race and age groups in the evaluations expressed.[17]

Most of the responses of the individual and the community are of a simple but sometimes expensive sort. For instance, the individual may

Figure 9.5. Economic Impact of Crimes and Related Expenditures (estimated in millions of dollars). (*Source:* President's Commission on Law Enforcement, *The Challenge of Crime in a Free Society* [Washington, D.C.: GPO, 1967], p. 33.)

alter behavior, in the simple form of more cautious glances at dangerous times and places, to more aggressive learning of martial arts for self-protection. The individual may carry a whistle, on the simple side of warning, or mace, on the more ambitious side; or offensive weapons, from a cane to a firearm on the more ambitious side. Residences may be equipped with dead-bolt locks and other devices for making entry more difficult, lighting and alarm systems (including dogs, human guards, and electronic systems) to the most advanced electronic devices. Guards may range from a dog (and dogs range from barking warners to silent killers), to humans (ranging from subscription patroling services to full-time armed guards stationed about the premises).

The response of the public to crime would seem likely to reduce crime. But the effects are in part "counterintuitive," not quite what one would "logically" suppose they would be. In a searching study, *The Impact of Crime,* John E. Conklin has found that public responses to crime may lead to more crime, not less.

> Crime generates suspicion and distrust, thereby weakening the social fabric of a community. Viewing ex-convicts as outsiders makes it difficult for them to become reintegrated into society, forcing them back to a life of crime and enhancing the crime problem. Crime leads people to avoid others and to take self-protective security measures, both of which actions erect barriers between the residents of a community. By diminishing social interaction and reducing natural surveillance of public areas, informal social control over potential criminals may be weakened and crime rates may increase.[18]

Communal responses extend from street-lighting projects to redesign of the environment. Neighborhoods have begun civilian patrolling, augmenting the police with radio-equipped patrols on foot or in cars. There comes a point in this stepped-up civilian activity when its nature changes, when it threatens to cross the line from auxiliary law-enforcement activity to vigilantism or civilian displacement of the official agencies of criminal justice. That may be "socially constructive vigilantism," in Richard Maxwell Brown's terms, or "socially destructive vigilantism."[19] The former is legitimate civilian justice where government has either not yet arrived (as on the frontier) or has been taken over by criminal elements. On the other hand, when civilian justice takes over merely out of displeasure with the official system, usurpation has occurred—the legitimate has been replaced by the illegitimate, and the outcome is "lynch law." For the first time in decades, there is concern for the nature of the citizen's participation in law enforcement: Might it go too far? But how far has it gone and how far might it go yet before it goes too far? "Support Your Local Police" would seem to have elicited far too little citizen activity so far, but a few ominous signs have appeared, such as vigilante executions. The vigilante issue is complicated, however, by the failure so far of any analysis that sheds much light on how and how far it might be desirable to shift some criminal-justice functions to the private sector.

Crime Analysis

The feeling of urgency that the police officer gains from the experience of participating with victims in the consequences of crime, that something must be done, does not translate easily into productive approaches to solving problems. This can come from the introduction of systematic study of crime, from the perspective of the police needs. The precursors of this approach are found in the early efforts of August Vollmer, the pioneer of modern policing, to study crime for the purpose of allocating his personnel as effectively as possible on the beat.

> On the assumption of regularity of crime and similar occurrences, it is possible to tabulate these occurrences by areas within a city and thus determine the points which have the greatest danger of such crimes and what points have the least danger.[20]

The idea of crime analysis was carried further with the proposal by O. W. Wilson, another leader in modern police management, that departments have a unit for crime analysis, to analyze "daily reports of serious crimes in order to determine the location, time, special characteristics, similarities to other criminal events, and various significant facts that may help to identify either a criminal or the existence of a pattern of criminal activity."[21]

This development in law enforcement dovetails with the criminological study of "situational factors" called for 20 years ago by Marshall B. Clinard: "Analyses of the situations out of which crimes or delinquent acts arise might shed light on the problem of why knowledge of a given person's traits and attitudes does not always enable us to predict whether he will or will not perform a delinquent or criminal act in a given situation."[22] More situational analysis needs to be done, but now the initiative may be with the police. One outcome could be the partnership of police and criminology suggested earlier.

One direction crime analysis can take is indicated in the recent study in the "Integrated Criminal Apprehension Program" of the Justice Department's Law Enforcement Assistance Administration. This study develops a process of providing information on crime patterns and trends to assist in law-enforcement-agency planning and prevention operations. The unit would gather detailed reports, such as offense reports, which would show information on crime type, victim type, offense location, offense time, property loss or victim injury, suspect description, modus operandi, witnesses, physical evidence; and arrest reports, which would have information about physical description, alias or nickname, crime charges, accomplices, arrest location, residence, vehicle description, weapons. Other information would be added; the information would be validated and updated. The analysis would contribute to decisions on patrol deployment, investigation leads to link specific suspects to crimes by common elements (as when a "modus operandi" is recognized), and development of crime-prevention programs.[23]

This is the sort of "crime analysis capability" the National Advisory Commission on Criminal Justice Standards and Goals has urged the police to adopt. It would make such information retrievable by cross-referencing, to achieve in large departments the "omniscience" of a one-man department in which all information is gathered and filed by one person. For purposes of the emerging partnership between criminology and law enforcement, the Commission's observation on the twofold vaue of "pattern recognition" is important: "The first attempts to recognize a specific pattern of criminal activity such as burglary. The second is much broader and recognizes a general crime picture developing in areas of the city."[24]

Such "crime-specific" studies based on information gathered systematically and completely, can make possible more studies of crime like Harry Scarr's analysis of burglary patterns. It revealed a burglary "cycle," with elements as follows: needs met by burglarizing (motivation), knowledge of burglary technology, perceived opportunities to burglarize, burglary as the path to meet needs, choice of burglary over other paths to meet needs (comparative advantages), the burglary attempt, conversion of burglarized goods, satisfaction for the act, reinforcement (high income for short work-week). The strategy for reducing burglaries that emerged from the study was "interdiction of the burglary cycle, taking those actions based—to the greatest degree possible—on whatever we discover to be the empirical situation." Such "interdiction" would be accomplished by reducing the perceived opportunity (making the residence always appear occupied), reducing the effect of burglary technology (with more resistant locks and windows and better lighting), and interfering with conversion of burglarized goods (by marking them, by keeping little cash on hand). For the police, the recommendation was encouragement of citizen action to reduce the simpler types of burglaries so the police could concentrate on the more skillfully executed burglaries.[25]

Crime analysis can reveal "the anatomy of a scam" (for example, a planned bankruptcy) by organized crime, which reveals information that can be useful in preventing or detecting such crimes. The "three-step scam" illustrates what has been learned about the process:

1. A new corporation is formed, managed by a front man or "pencil" who has no prior criminal or bankruptcy record.
2. An initial large bank deposit, as the "nut," is made to establish credit. This money, plus all other money subsequently deposited, is later withdrawn.
3. A large store is rented and orders for merchandise are placed with as many companies as possible. The size of these orders appears to indicate a successful operation.
4. Smaller orders are placed during the first month, and such orders are almost always completely paid in full.
5. During the second month, larger orders are placed and about a quarter of the balance due on such orders is paid.
6. During the third month, using the credit established as a result of payments made from the previous orders, very large orders are placed. Items easily converted into cash, such as jewelry and appliances, usually constitute a large proportion of these orders.
7. Thereafter, merchandise is converted into cash through a fence or a surplus-property operator, normally one with a sufficiently large legitimate inventory to easily intermix the scam merchandise into the normal inventory. The company is then forced into bankruptcy by its creditors, since, according to plan, all cash has been appropriated by the scam operator.

This plan indicates certain systems that business people can watch for:

1. A large deposit in a bank in one area, which is then used as a credit reference with a bank in another area. Bank officials should be alert to this situation.
2. Unusual amounts of credit inquiries on a new, large depositor, or a great many additional inquiries on old accounts.
3. A great many rush or immediate-delivery requests out of line with normal pattern.
4. A customer firm under new management, with information on the principal vague.[26]

Crime analysis for arson, for instance, would make possible more dependable recognition of its eight varieties—fraud fires, to collect insurance; coverup fires, to obscure some other crime; "pyro" fires, to provide sexual gratification to the pyromaniac; "psycho" fires, without pyromania but some other cause, such as paranoia; vandalism fires, for excitment, with neither pyro nor psycho motivations; vanity fires, to show heroism in putting it out; spite fires, for revenge, jealousy, anger; political fires, to demonstrate some political purpose.[27]

This kind of understanding can be the foundation for the design of policing experiments, such as the development of robbery-control programs, which grow out of the analysis of information about the nature, circumstances, frequency, and other dimensions of the crime.[28] This is an important "payoff" of the bridge between criminology's theories and methods, on the one hand, and the policies and practices of criminal justice.

SUMMARY

This chapter began with a look at criminology and its levels: description, correlation, and explanation. This led into a survey of some of the explanations or theories of crime—*internal* accounts, such as character, chemistry, psychology, and psychiatry; and *external* accounts, such as the social, geographic, economic, and political.

Certain conditions and correlates of crime were identified, such as age, sex, and social status. Then some quantities and qualities of crime were presented from the FBI's *Uniform Crime Reports* and the victim surveys, and from some typologies of criminals.

Victimology was presented, with a look at some of the consequences of crime, including the development of "crime analysis."

NOTES

1. Arthur Train, *From the District Attorney's Office* (New York: Scribner's, 1939), p. 6.
2. Ramsey Clark, *Crime in America* (New York: Simon and Schuster, 1970), p. 66.
3. These aspects of crime are discussed in numerous introductory criminology textbooks, but the most complete is Sue Titus Reid, *Crime and Criminology,* 2nd ed. (New York: Holt, Rinehart and Winston, 1979).
4. Robert Bierstedt, *The Social Order,* 3rd ed. (New York: McGraw-Hill, 1970), p. 34.
5. C. Ray Jeffery, *Crime Prevention Through Environmental Design* (Beverly Hills, Calif.: Sage, 1977).
6. William J. Chambliss, "A Sociological Analysis of the Law of Vagrancy," Ronald L. Akers and Richard Hawkins, eds., *Law and Control in Society* (Englewood Cliffs, N.J., Prentice-Hall, 1975), pp. 62–72.
7. Gwynn Nettler, *Explaining Crime,* 2nd ed. (New York: McGraw-Hill, 1978), chapters 7 and 17.
8. Freda Adler, *Sisters in Crime* (New York: McGraw-Hill, 1975).
9. For a text designed to bridge criminology and criminal justice, see James A. Inciardi, *Reflections on Crime* (New York: Holt, Rinehart and Winston, 1978).
10. David H. Bayley, "Learning About Crime—The Japanese Experience," *Public Interest* (Summer, 1976), pp. 55–68.
11. Walter Miller, "The Rumble This Time," in Jerome H. Skolnick, et al., eds., *Crime and Justice in America* (Del Mar, Calif.: Publisher's Inc., 1977), pp. 94–99.

12. John Barth, *The Sot-Weed Factor* (New York: Grosset & Dunlap, 1960), pp. 466–472.

13. Harold J. Vetter and Ira J. Silverman, *The Nature of Crime* (Philadelphia: Saunders, 1978).

14. M. O. Cameron, *The Booster and the Snitch* (New York:Free Press, 1964).

15. Don C. Gibbons and Donald L. Garrity, "Definitions and Analysis of Certain Criminal Types," *Journal of Criminal Law, Criminology, and Police Science* 53 (1962), pp. 28–35.

16. Truman Capote, *In Cold Blood* (New York: Random House, 1965), pp. 244–245.

17. James Garofalo, *Public Opinion About Crime* (Washington, D.C.: Law Enforcement Assistance Administration, 1977), p. 11.

18. John E. Conklin, *The Impact of Crime* (New York: Macmillan, 1975), p. 248.

19. Richard Maxwell Brown, "Historical Patterns of Violence in America," in Hugh D. Graham and Ted R. Gurr, eds., *Violence in America* (New York: Signet, 1969), pp. 43–80.

20. Quoted in Richard P. Grassie, et al., *Crime Analysis Executive Manual* (Preliminary Draft), vol. 1 (Washington, D.C.: Law Enforcement Assistance Administration, 1977), p. 9.

21. *Ibid.*, p. 10.

22. Marshall B. Clinard, "Criminological Research," in Robert K. Merton, et al., eds., *Sociology Today*, vol. 2 (New York: Harper Torchbooks, 1959), pp. 519–520.

23. *Ibid*, vol. 4, pp. 6–30.

24. National Advisory Commission on Criminal Justice Standards and Goals, *Criminal Justice System* (Washington, D.C.: U. S. Government Printing Office, 1973), p. 56.

25. Harry A. Scarr, *Patterns of Burglary,* 2nd ed. (Washington, D.C.: Law Enforcement Assistance Administration, 1973).

26. Edward J. De Franco, *Anatomy of a Scam* (Washington, D.C.: Law Enforcement Assistance Administration, 1973), pp. 5–7.

27. Kendall D. Moll, *Arson, Vandalism and Violence* (Washington, D.C.: Law Enforcement Assistance Administration, 1974), pp. 10–13.

28. Richard H. Ward, et al., *Police Robbery Control Manual* (Washington, D.C.: Law Enforcement Assistance Administration, 1975).

SELECTED READINGS

Frank G. Carrington, *The Victims* (New Rochelle, N.Y.: Arlington, 1975).

John E. Conklin, *The Impact of Crime* (New York: Macmillan, 1975).

Domestic Council Drug Abuse Task Force, *White Paper on Drug Abuse* (Washington, D.C.: U.S. Department of Health, Education and Welfare, 1975).

Gwynn Nettler, *Explaining Crime,* 2nd ed. (New York: McGraw-Hill, 1978).

John Pekkanen, *Victims: An Account of a Rape* (New York: Dial, 1976).

Simon Rottenberg, ed., *The Economics of Crime and Punishment* (Washington, D.C.: American Enterprise Institute, 1973).

Jerome Skolnick, *House of Cards* (Boston: Little, Brown, 1978).

E. Fuller Torrey, *Why Did You Do That?* (Radnor, Pa.: Chilton, 1975).

Harold J. Vetter, and Ira J. Silverman, *The Nature of Crime* (Philadelphia: Saunders, 1978).

10
CONSTITUTIONAL CONSTRAINTS ON THE POLICE

This chapter takes up the limitations on the police that have been developed in the Constitution to balance police authority and individual liberty. It begins with a review of the purposes of criminal justice, demonstrating the conflicts that must be resolved among them. Then it reviews four fundamental values—order, liberty, democracy, and law—that are at the foundation of the American system of constitutional democracy and that must be similarly accommodated to each other. The rules for arrest, search, and seizure are set forth, followed by an introduction to some Supreme Court cases that illustrate the process by which liberty and authority are balanced by the Supreme Court. Finally, the exclusionary rule is analyzed as the means of judicial implementation of the constitutional rules that limit the police.

The Purposes of Criminal Justice

There are certain purposes associated with criminal justice: retribution, deterrence, incapacitation, rehabilitation, and denunciation.[1] These purposes, or the "why" or philosophy of criminal justice, are what it aims (or is aimed) to achieve. The purposes overlap the functions, because social control is a function, a "functional prerequisite of society," as discussed earlier, and also a purpose. Unlike social control, which is to a large extent unconscious, the other purposes of criminal justice are the subject of thoughtful deliberation and some debate, as we shall see, for the various purposes have different implications for punishment and various practices of law enforcement.

SOCIAL CONTROL AS A PURPOSE

Social control is necessary to a society's survival. The community comes to appreciate this most in times of trouble and turmoil. Then criminal justice is seen as a major means of maintaining control that is generally accepted by all but a handful of anarchists, who are convinced that controls are unnecessary, and revolutionaries, whose interests collide with "the system" and its mechanisms of self-preservation. Others, on the other hand, who generally assume the necessity of social control and its employment of the machinery of criminal justice, differ sharply, on the somewhat inconsistent purposes of criminal justice.

RETRIBUTION

It seems to be natural for people to feel, when they are injured or even when another is injured, that the one who hurts should be hurt back. Perpetrators of crime should "pay" for their offenses. Police officers, who see the wounds up close, experience this feeling acutely, even as they get used to seeing the pain of victims. Justice is done, we say, when the evildoer has received his "just deserts," or what he deserves.

Vengeance, or the desire for revenge, is the aim to exact from the offender a payment of pain to satisfy *us,* often in direct proportion to what he or she took or caused, according to the *lex talionis,* or the rule of "an eye for an eye, a tooth for a tooth"—and a life for a life. Many police officers share the feeling of a special satisfaction when "justice is done." Vengeance is a powerful emotion, which many would deny or repress, some by reference to the divine injunction that "Vengeance is mine, saith the Lord." But it is thought by some to be the wiser course to acknowledge the emotion and control it by channeling it through the regularities of the legal process and thereby satisfy it, lest it come to be expressed impatiently through unofficial means, such as a *vendetta* or feud. But when the law does not provide such satisfaction, especially for police officers, there is a strong impulse in some of them to exact the price of justice from offenders in an informal, extralegal way—sometimes through brutality, sometimes through harassment, sometimes, even worse, through unofficial execution by the "Death Squads" of the Brazilian police.

Expiation, by contrast, exacts from the offender some payment of suffering which satisfies *him,* rather than us, by which he "atones" for his sins. There is surely something to the idea of expiation, as anyone knows who has ever felt penitent. Some who feel guilt go beyond penitence to atonement, to some action, some good deed, that makes things better even if not the same as they were. The very idea of repentance comes from penitence, which is also the source of the word *penitentiary,* for repentance was the aim of the Quakers, who developed the first American prisons in the eighteenth century. They thought that solitary confinement with a Bible for prolonged periods of time would lead to repentance. It makes little difference, however, in Herbert L. Packer's view, which version of retribution we prefer, vengeance or expiation: "In the absence of assurance that his sense of guilt is equal to the demands made upon it, we help to reinforce it by providing and external expression of guilt." [2] That is to say, we inflict punishment in the name of retribution to assure that the price is paid.

Vengeance and expiation are the more easily understood aspects of retribution. But it should be noted that there is another aspect, rational rather than emotional, in which philosophical analysis yields the conclusion that the offender brings the punishment on herself or himself. As the philosopher Kant argued, the offender earns the punishment so deservedly that he or she has a right to it. In any case, retribution has more to do with the offense than the offender and leads to the principle that the punishment should be made to fit the crime rather than the criminal, and should be measured objectively and without regard for the characteristics of the offender. The police officer, a very practical person, is likely to feel uneasy about looking backward to the bygone offense rather than forward to the future behavior of the offender and others—and what they might learn from the offender's experience. Yet the officer feels the need for retribution, too, and is in a dilemma because of the retrospective aspect of retribution and the forward-looking aspect of deterrence, the purpose we take up next.

DETERRENCE

This purpose of punishment is concerned not so much with the offense in the past as with offenses in the future. Deterrence, or the purpose of influencing the offender and others, "uses" the offender's experience of paying the penalty to induce him and others not to commit such offenses. Punishment's effect on the offender is called *special deterrence;* the effect on others, *general deterrence.* A fair amount of the action of police officers on the street is a low-level application of deterrence: The officer can (or thinks he or she can) teach a lesson to an offender without recourse to the official machinery of the courts and the institutions of correction.

Deterrence is a *utilitarian* approach in which the penalty is levied not because it is just, in the sense that the offender morally deserves it, but because it has usefulness. It is expected to work to control the future behavior of the offender and of others. The strict utilitarian will not care whether a penalty is just or not, as long as it will work to decrease crime. The British playwright George Bernard Shaw once suggested that it does not really matter if the punished party is guilty, so long as it will have a deterrent effect on others; by contrast, the strict retributionist will not care whether a penalty has a deterrent effect at all, so long as it is just. Both, however, will agree that the punishment must cause pain, for only pain will satisfy vengeance or produce expiation, in realizing the retributive purpose, and "teach" the offender and others not to do such things, in realizing the deterrent purpose.

INCAPACITATION

A potential offender can be kept from committing an offense simply by making it impossible. Death makes future murders by the executed offender quite impossible. Castration is believed to make rape impossible. Amputation of the hand of a thief, as in Arabia, is a handicap to thieves. Incarceration prevents crime at least outside of prison, unless the prisoner can direct criminal operations from behind bars. Modern techniques, such as psychosurgery (brain surgery) and chemotherapy (drug treatment), can alter behavior and minimize propensities to commit violence. As time goes on, such things as brain-implanted electrodes to influence behavior will doubtless be developed. But at the moment there is uncertainty about the effects of incapacitative measures (except death) and growing concern over the ethics of altering the individual, especially against his will. Many police officers are incapacitators, with a commonsense confidence in the effect of jail and turn to the "lockup" for emergency incapacitation.

REHABILITATION

Expiation and atonement may result in reform, but the retributionist will be satisfied if offenders pay for their crime, whether the payment changes them or not. Likewise, special deterrence may reform offenders or at least intimidate them from committing further offenses, but the proponent of deterrence, as a utilitarian, will be satisfied if punishment of the offender has a deterrent effect in general. Rehabilitation, on the other hand, aims to change offenders so that they will "go straight" of their own choice, not out of fear. Rehabilitated convicts will not commit crimes because they are changed behaviorally, they have learned new ways, new rules, new habits, new conduct; they can cope in the future because they have been socialized, educated, trained, perhaps "habilitated" for the first time.

The rehabilitation ideal gained dominance in correctional circles several decades ago as the old retributivist maxim, Make the punishment fit the crime, gave way to the more humane, Make the punishment fit the criminal. The fit was not to be in terms of a likelihood of change, as ascertained or predicted by the judge at the time of sentencing; instead, it was to depend on how long the rehabilitation process might take. This led to the movement to replace fixed sentences (e.g., five years for robbery) with partially *indeterminate* sentences (e.g., three to seven years). The length was left open, within the range set by the judge, to provide the prison, as an institution for rehabilitation, as long a time as it needed (within that range) to bring about the desired changes in the convict. When the rehabilitation succeeded, the convict would be released; if it did not, the convict remained until the end of the maximum term of the sentence. Not many years ago there was talk of making sentences completely indeterminate (e.g., zero to death), so the rehabilitationists would not be limited by either a minimum or a maximum; they could work on a convict for as short or as long a time as necessary to bring about rehabilitation.

The problem with rehabilitation is that so little is known even today about "habilitation" or socialization or education, or what makes people tick, that little can be done with confidence to rehabilitate those whose behavior is criminal. Rehabilitation programs, even those operated under the most promising of circumstances, have been disappointing.[3] A growing number of observers have concluded that the rehabilitation aim should be abandoned or at least lowered to reduce the ability of the rehabilitationists to detain a convict. A corollary of that view is a shift back from indeterminant sentences to shorter periods for rehabilitationists to work in, hence more certainty of the time of release. Police officers have taken a rather dim view of rehabilitation. Jails, which house offenders after their conviction for misdemeanors, have been scandalously weak in their rehabilitation efforts—a testament to the police community's disdain for this approach.

Reconsideration of rehabilitation is underscored by reservations of another sort: By what right does the community, even if it could change behavior, intrude into the privacy, the individuality, the liberty, the autonomy, the dignity of the person, to alter patterns of conduct or style of life—even as the price of crime? The retributionist argues that punishment should have nothing to do with the offender, that offenders should merely serve their time. Detention, which "cramps the style" of a convict, is a sufficient price to pay, they say; a person's integrity should be kept intact, with no intrusion beyond the limitation of liberty. Rehabilitationists have grown sensitive to this aspect of their aim, and many have shifted their approach from a compulsory to a voluntary basis.

DENUNCIATION

A final purpose of punishment is denunciation of the criminal act, the reaffirmation of the morality of the community that holds such acts to be immoral. Police officers, whose morality is usually quite conventional and in harmony with that of their community as a whole, find it easy to accept this purpose.

The relationship of law and morals involves an educational aspect: Crime is condemned by the community's official declaration, through its state agencies (legislature, courts, and police), that certain behaviors are forbidden under penalty of law. Denunciation of certain behavior may not discourage it; it may even encourage it by setting one part of the community against another and reinforcing the values of the "out group" against the "in group." But to denunciationists that is not as important as proclaiming that wrong is wrong and should be punished, as a matter of principle, not pragmatics.

CONFLICTS AND ACCOMMODATIONS AMONG THESE PURPOSES

Social control and *retribution* are inconsistent, as control may be achieved with lower levels of punishment, which the community might employ if its purpose were merely to redress the balance, to reestablish the moral order. Morris R. Cohen, the philosopher, put it this way:

> When Cain kills Abel, the very earth cries for vengeance. The moral order can be restored, or the violation atoned for only by inflicting evil (generally pain) upon the one guilty.[4]

But that might well be attained not only by going well beyond what society requires for control. Indeed, many critics of retribution insist that it simply goes too far.

This possibility is underscored by the *deterrence* approach to criminal justice. What if murder could be deterred almost completely by the threat of a fine of a dollar? It is quite likely that most members of the community would find that outrageous: Homicide, they would argue, must be paid back by something more than a dollar. The life of the victim is worth more than a dollar.

The retributionists would insist that deterrence does not matter: Whether a punishment causes the offender and others to refrain from the prohibited conduct or not, indeed whether it even causes *more* of the same or not, is irrelevant to what is important—the payment of the just deserts. This requires the policy-maker on punishment to strike some balance between the two which will somewhat satisfy the proponents of both positions: enough to satisfy the retributivists; not too much to offend the utilitarians.

Incapacitation offends the retributionist and utilitarian alike: Locking up someone for longer than he or she deserves is immoral; morality justifies detention only for long enough to exact the appropriate punishment—nothing less, nothing more. To the utilitarian, detention is useful for the narrow purpose of preventing crimes by the detainee, but not necessarily useful—and probably harmful—if the period exceeds what is needed to teach a lesson to others. Both the utilitarian and the retributionist would agree that the consequences of freeing a dangerous offender may be unpleasant and unavoidable, given the limits on what their philosophy of punishment would justify. Thus, a balance must be struck to accommodate the conflicting aims of these three approaches.

The problem deepens with the *rehabilitationist* approach, because it conceives of the period of detention not as punishment for retributive or deterrent purposes or even for incapacitation. It would hold people only to make them better, to make them well enough to function in open society without resort to criminal conduct. If an offender is rehabilitated quickly, say in a few weeks, for a heinous murder, the rehabilitationist is content that the purpose of incarceration is achieved and the only legitimate aim of the system has been attained, so the offender must be let go. This, like the deterrent aim, may conflict sharply with the retributivist views and require yet another "balancing act" on the part of the policy-maker who designs the statutory sentencing system and the judge who applies it.

Conflict Among Values

An institution or system of any maturity is likely to be the result of a good deal of accident and blind evolution. But it is also quite likely to have a history of some conscious (if not altogether wise) decisions reflecting the interplay of an assortment of values. The principle, official values of the United States may be found in the Preamble of its Constitution. Law enforcement partakes of those fundamental values more than is ordinarily supposed. "A more perfect union," "justice," "domestic tranquility," "the common defense," "the general welfare," and "liberty" are now, as they were in the 1780s, the principle values in the foundation of public policy. Hence, it is to them that we look for the fundamentals of the ongoing design of a constitutional system of liberties of the people and powers of their government.

Values, whether of an individual or a community or a nation, are seldom in complete harmony. Discord may be minimized but seldom eliminated; the "bad notes" sounded when values collide can be ignored only for a while. This poses a problem for those who have sworn to uphold and defend the Constitution, for in doing so they must accommodate, if not reconcile, competing values. It is a problem for the judges of the highest courts and for the patrol officer as well. This can be seen when four basic values are paired: order and freedom, freedom and law, law and democracy, democracy and order, order and law, and freedom and democracy.

Order and freedom may conflict when a free person acts irregularly or disorderly; and order, conversely, when it is like that of a machine or a colony of ants, is in conflict with the freedom to act other than in the ways prescribed by nature, by priests, or by kings.

Freedom and law may conflict: Law is a system of rules which the exercise of freedom might violate (unless *freedom* is defined as that which can be done within the confines of law). An American judge, Benjamin Nathan Cardozo, put the conflict this way: "Liberty in the most literal sense is the negation of law, for law is restraint . . ." [5] Law and democracy may conflict because the will of the people, like the will of the individual, may override the regularities of a system of rules (unless *law* is defined as identical to the will of the people); conversely, the rules of law may stand in defiance of the will of the people.

Democracy and order may conflict insofar as the will of the people may create disorder; conversely, orderliness may "cramp the style" of the people. Order and law may be in conflict, as Jerome Skolnik has observed:

> Law is not merely an instrument of order, but may frequently be its adversary. There are communities that appear disorderly to some (such as bohemian communities valuing diversity), but which nevertheless maintain a substantial degree of legality. The contrary may also be found: a situation where order is well maintained, but where the policy and practice of legality is not evident. The totalitarian social system, whether in a nation or an institution, is a situation of order without the rule of law.[6]

Freedom and democracy may conflict when the will of the people limits the freedom of the individual, as in what Toequeville called "the tyranny of the majority."

The conflicts between pairs of these values are complicated when three or four of the values are considered together. And it gets even more complicated when the values vary in their meaning. For instance, freedom has both a negative and a positive meaning: The traditional negative meaning is nonintervention by others, but in recent decades freedom has gained a positive meaning—that the individual is *permitted* to do as he or she pleases, but must also be *enabled* to do what he or she pleases. For example, it is argued that it is not enough that women be liberated from restrictions on abortion; their freedom means they must be given the wherewithall to do so. Similarly, a concept like *order* can change with changes in the needs and perceptions of the community. Skolnick makes this clear:

> Depending on the institution or community, there may be quite different conceptions of order, some more permissive, others less. A traditional

martial conception of order, for example, abhors individual differences. The soldier whose bearing or uniform sets him off from his comrades in arms is an abomination to his commanding officer. Even the slightest deviation, such as wearing gloves on a cold day, is forbidden as an expression of differences in individual feelings. . . .

Other institutions or portions of society are traditionally more yielding. The area surrounding the University of Paris is noted for its emphasis upon individuality. Students, artists, writers may be dressed elegantly or poorly, raffishly or provocatively, the mode being considered an extension of the ego, an expression of personality, or perhaps merely an attempt to experiment with novelty. The idea of order in this setting is surely a more permissive conception than the standard military notion. Our conclusion is that conceptions of order seem to be variable and tend to correspond to the requirements of different communities or institutions.[7]

In addition, values are not separable, like cans in a cupboard, so the "consumer" cannot say, "I want so much of this and so much of that." Instead, values are interdependent: The amount of one may depend upon how much there is of another. Edmund Burke, a British critic of the French Revolution, expressed this view:

> The liberty, the only liberty, I mean is liberty connected with order that not only exists along with order and virtue, but which cannot exist at all without them.

Thus, freedom and order are usually deemed correlates, not mutually exclusive opposites, contradicting each other. Instead, neither can exist meaningfully without the other; indeed, each implies the other.

Yet another complication is the ranking of values. The poet Pope said, "Order is Heav'n's first law." Many would rank order highest. Others would rank freedom higher, much as some would put justice higher: "Let justice be done though the heaven's fall." Beyond this is the problem of other values that might be added to the mix, such as economy, efficiency, mercy, and even beauty. This is not merely an academic exercise in the manipulation of abstractions, because the most urgent constitutional issue emerging right now involves the values of order, freedom, democracy, and law. They are entangled in the question of how much police power (order) should be balanced against which other values and in particular against how much of the rights of the accused (freedom), by the extension of due process (law) into juvenile proceedings, prisons, and other institutions, such as the military, schools, and mental institutions, at the initiative of the courts and in defiance of the apparent disinclination on the part of the representative bodies, mainly the legislature (democracy) to take action.

Liberty and Authority in American Criminal Justice

Before examining some of the specific constitutional constraints on police authority, it is a good idea to look at the reconciliation of liberty and authority àt a more general level.[8] First of all, liberty is usually recognized as dependent on authority, or, as Chief Justice Charles Evans Hughes said, "Civil liberties, as guaranteed by the Constitution, imply the existence of an organized society maintaining public order without which liberty itself would be lost in the excesses of unrestrained abuses." The history of freedom of speech, for instance, is a series of clashes between speakers or printers or petitioners and the police or censors. Those liberties, however, have been protected, too, by the self-restraint of police officers, prosecutors, and judges or by their sometimes courageous protection of demonstrations from the passions of the mob.

Second, liberty is relative. It is rarely held to be so pure as to drive its opponents to an anarchistic, or lawless, solution. This follows not so much from any enthusiasm for order as from an appreciation that conflicts between rights, such as freedom of the press and the right to a fair trial, lead to the conclusion that neither one is an absolute liberty. Third, the concept of liberty changes from time to time and place to place. The grand jury is no longer viewed as an essential protector against prosecutorial oppression; instead, it is often viewed as a tool of the prosecutor.

Fourth, liberty of the individual is not seen as necessarily opposed to the interests of society; rather, liberty is viewed as something society itself values because it produces benefits to society through the creative activities of free individuals. The notion of the *marketplace of ideas,* as the free competition of uncensored ideas to see which one prevails by virtue of its truth, is one which permits false or obnoxious ideas to be exposed for what they are. Likewise, the rights of the accused are "tilted," as it were, in their favor in a generally liberal society, because liberty is seen as "all of a piece" and jeopardized generally wherever it is cut back in one part. The benefit of the doubt is on the side of liberty: The case for restriction of liberty must be a strong one for it is to be overriden by the arguments for authority.

The Rights of the Accused

Before continuing the discussion of basic values, it is important to have the constitutional rights of the accused set forth as simply and as concisely as possible.

QUESTIONING

Police officers may question anyone, whether or not they have "probable cause" to believe the person committed or was about to commit a crime. Nor need officers have reasonable suspicion to believe those things. All they need to believe is that the person may have some information about a crime, and they need not even have that, given the police officer's right, like any other citizen's, to merely ask a question.

However, no one is obliged to answer the police officer's question, any more than one is obliged to answer anyone else's questions. The citizen is not even obliged to give a police officer the proverbial time of day or the courtesy of any other response. He may simply ignore the question. The police have no means to compel a person to reply to such questions. The Supreme Court has recently decided that refusal to reply does not, in and of itself, provide a basis for arrest.[9]

If an officer asks someone whom he believes may have information but no involvement in a crime, he need not meet the constitutional requirements pertaining to self-incrimination and right to counsel (the *Miranda warnings,* which are discussed below).

Stop-and-Frisk. A police officer may stop and frisk (or "pat down") someone she or he *reasonably suspects* of having committed or being about to commit a crime. Before the frisk, however, the officer must identify herself or himself. Only if the answers to questions about the suspicions do not come forth or do not satisfy him or her that the person is beyond suspicion can the frisk proceed, and then only if there is *reasonable fear* for safety. The purpose of the frisk is then limited to detecting a weapon, not finding evidence.

Field Interrogation. Questions asked of a person in the field (as opposed to the station house) are very important because they elicit information more spontaneously. The *Miranda warnings* may be required in field interrogations, however, because "custodial interrogation" requires it. This means the warnings must be given when the suspect has been arrested or, if not arrested, when the interrogation will take place in a police setting, such as the squad car. The Miranda warnings should also be given if the situation would seem to be "custodial" *to the subject* of the investigation, or if the situation involves youth or inexperience of the suspect, inhospitable surroundings of the interrogation, the number of the suspect's own people present, and even the time of day—all of which may constitute pressure to talk. The warnings are also required in some states if the officer intends not to let the suspect go or if the suspect feels he or she must answer the questions.

Witnesses, however, need not be given the warnings, nor anyone who simply knows something but is not suspected of involvement, so long as the interrogation does not occur in custodial circumstances or with intent to deprive the subject of freedom or after the subject has the impression that she or he must answer. Thus, although the police officer may question anyone, if the questioning is in circumstances and in a manner giving rise to a compulsion to answer, the warning should be given. The consequences of not giving the warnings are simple: The information obtained may not be used to obtain a conviction (as discussed below).

ARREST

Arrest does not mean mere "arrest" of movement, mere stopping of a pedestrian or a motorist, even if the latter's car is stopped for a traffic violation. Arrest occurs only when there is an indication that the person is to be taken to the police station or before a judge or otherwise into custody. An arrest cannot be made, however, other than with a warrant, unless the officer has *probable cause,* which means enough knowledge of facts and circumstances that a reasonable police officer would conclude that the subject probably committed a felony.

Thus, probable cause is a higher standard for arrest than the suspicion which justifies a stop-and-frisk. But it need not be based on enough evidence to prove guilt ("beyond a reasonable doubt"), nor need it be based on personal observation by the officer. (Personal observation is usually required, however, before an officer may make an arrest for a misdemeanor.) J. Shane Creamer, former Attorney General of Pennsylvania, has listed what he calls "guilt laden facts" that courts throughout the country have recognized as solid building blocks of probable cause:

> flight, furtive movements, hiding, attempt to destroy evidence, resistance to officers, admissions or confessions, evasive answers, unreasonable explanations, fingerprint identification, hair follicle identifications, handwriting comparisons, fabric comparisons, identification of suspects by witnesses, the emergency setting—crime zone or automobile, ballistics, contraband or weapons in plain view, criminal record, hearsay information—informant, fellow officer, or general, expert police opinion, police corroboration, unusual or suspicious conduct, fact of crime or felony.[10]

A *citizen's arrest* is valid if the felony is committed in the citizen's presence or, if outside his presence, if he has *certainty,* not merely reasonable grounds, to believe a felony has been committed.

An arrest warrant authorizes the officer to make an arrest which is valid by virtue of the warrant rather than the circumstances and the judgment of the officer, so long as it is "executed," or carried out, without unreasonable delay.

Force may be used in making an arrest with or without a warrant, but it may only be such a degree of force as is *reasonably necessary* to make the arrest and to protect the officer and others from bodily harm while doing so. Deadly force may therefore be necessary, but only if it is reasonable to assume so. Breaking into private premises, however, is ordinarily permitted only if, after an officer's identification of himself and his purpose, admittance is refused or there is no response (in which case the officer must not only wait a reasonable time but must also reasonably believe that the subject is on the premises). A "no-knock" entry (entry without knocking or stating identity and purpose) ordinarily may not be made without statutory authorization by the jurisdiction, and then only if the officer reasonably believes that the usual procedure will result in the escape of the subject, the destruction of evidence, or danger to herself or others.

Station-House or Custodial Interrogation.   The Miranda warnings, at their fullest, are as follows:

> Before we ask you any questions, you must understand what your rights are.
>   You have the right to remain silent. You are not required to say anything to us at any time or to answer any questions. Anything you say can and will be used against you in court.
>   You have the right to talk to a lawyer for advice before we question you and to have him with you during questioning.
>   If you cannot afford a lawyer and want one, a lawyer will be provided for you free of charge.
>   If you want to answer now without a lawyer present, you will still have the right to stop answering at any time. You also have the right to stop answering at any time until you talk to a lawyer.[11]

It is crucial that the subject *understand* the warnings and *freely waive,* that is, give up, the right to silence or counsel before proceeding; otherwise the information cannot be used. Hence, even if the subject claims to be innocent or volunteers a statement, if there is doubt about his understanding, the warnings should be repeated or restated in other ways or read by the suspect, repeated after an interruption in questioning or when another officer questions the subject. If and when the subject falls silent and refuses to continue answering questions, he cannot be forced to resume.

If a subject signs a statement to the effect that she was given the warnings, understood them, and willingly answered questions without counsel, voluntarily doing so of her own will, her statement will ordinarily be acceptable. Even so, a court may consider the circumstances and reject such a statement, if the suspect was intoxicated, injured, exhausted, physically abused, or in any way weakened.

SEARCH AND SEIZURE

Like arrest, searches are subject to two sets of rules, depending on whether or not there is a warrant involved. If a warrant is not involved, then the search may be made only if it is *incident to a valid arrest* and at the time and place of the arrest. The scope of the search incident to an arrest is extremely limited, being confined to the room where the arrest occurred (and there only to the extent of things visible, except for places the suspect might reach for a weapon). The person of the subject may be searched fully only if there is an arrest, other than for weapons in the stop-and-frisk situation discussed before. There are exceptions in some circumstances (e.g., a vehicle that might have been searched on the spot of the arrest may be searched later if it is inconvenient to get a warrant and it is reasonable to bring the car into the station and then search it). A warrantless search may be made of a building into which a suspect flees, but the search (which is for the suspect) must end as soon as the suspect is apprehended.

Physical evidence and other information may be obtained from the body of the arrested subject, as by photographing, fingerprinting, cutting hair, testing breath, and removing an object from the body (including blood and urine) so long as "shocking" procedures or force are not used, as in pumping the stomach. Also, the arrested person may be "strip searched," "lined up" with others for identification, and required to demonstrate his or her handwriting, voice, and "fit" of clothing.

Searches with a warrant must be based upon *probable cause,* carried out promptly, and limited in the area and specifics of the search. The complaint, on which the warrant is based, must describe in detail the place or persons to be searched and the things to be seized. Items found in the course of the prescribed search may be validly seized, but not items found outside the scope of the search. In other words, if the warrant authorizes search of a mobile home for heroin, a body found in it is validly seized but not burglary tools found in the car parked outside. The search must stop when its purpose, as spelled out in the warrant, is achieved, that is, the search it authorizes. The success of a search in revealing evidence cannot boot-strap a bad search into a good one. In other words, if the warrant authorizes the search of a saloon for bootleg whiskey, the finding of gambling apparatus in the upstairs apartment does not make its seizure valid.

Generally, *probable cause* for a search means enough current information about the facts and circumstances to satisfy a reasonable officer that a crime has been or is being committed and that the thing to be seized is reasonably connected to the crime, and can be found at a particular place.

Reasonable force may be used in executing a search warrant and "no-knock" entry may be made for a search, as for an arrest, if evidence would be destroyed as the result of the announcement. The classic illustration of this is the narcotics flushed down the toilet while the officers wait outside the door.

There are some exceptions to the general requirement of a search warrant: Automobiles may be searched in some circumstances without a warrant, emergencies may justify warrantless searches, and consent eliminates the requirement of a warrant.

Surveillance. Surveillance is a kind of search conducted with the eyes and ears. It may be aided electronically or not. What the officer can see with his own eyes or hear with his own ears, from a public place or from a private place with the consent of the owner or manager, is generally permissible unless the subject is where he can reasonably expect privacy, such as in a public restroom or a hotel room rented for a time.

Electronic surveillance by means of interception of telephone conversations (by wiretapping) is generally permitted only in compliance with federal law. Telephone conversations can be overheard, on the other hand, with the consent of one of the parties to the conversation. Likewise, an informer may be "wired" with his consent and the conversation which is recorded or overheard may be admitted as evidence.

The Constitutional History of Liberty and Authority

Pitted against each other in the definition of constitutional rights are the *liberty* of the accused or the citizen, or "doing what you want to do," as Chief Justice Marshall defined it, on the one hand, and power or *authority* of the police or the state, on the other hand, which Justice Davis said "has all the powers granted to it which are necessary to preserve its existence."

The progress of Anglo-American constitutionalism toward what Chief Justice Stone called "freedom from arbitrary restraint" begins with the document known as the Magna Carta, the Greater Charter of rights exacted by English nobles from King John in 1215. The document concerned the rights of those nobles themselves, rather than common people. But it came to symbolize the rights of all English people and as time went on, the rights it declared were extended to everyone. Among those rights was one in article 39: "No freeman shall be taken, or imprisoned, outlawed, or exiled, or in any way harmed, nor will we go upon or send upon him, save by the lawful judgment of his peers or by the law of the land." This was the origin of "due process of law," which demanded a degree of regularity in the administration of English law, to minimize the arbitrariness of the king's caprice.

Other landmarks in constitutional history are the Petition of Rights (1628), which limited military law and imprisonment without specific charges; the English Bill of Rights (1689), which prevented excessive bail; the American Declaration of Independence (1776), inspired in large part by the "long train of abuses and usurpations" by King George against the colonists; and the American Constitution (1789) and its Bill of Rights (1791).

The Constitution and its Bill of Rights (the first nine amendments) made available to the individual, in federal proceedings, certain rights pertaining to criminal proceedings. There were freedom *from* bills of attainder (loss of civil rights, especially to bequeath property), ex post facto laws (criminalization of conduct already committed), unreasonable searches and seizures, double jeopardy (reprosecution after acquittal), self-incrimination (proof of guilt by the accused's own words), and cruel and unusual punishment; and rights *to* writ of habeas corpus, trial by jury, indictment by grand jury, specification of charges, speedy and public trial, confrontation of witnesses, compulsory process (subpoena) for defense witnesses, counsel, and bail. The Fourteenth Amendment (1866) provided, in state proceedings, that "no person shall be deprived of life, liberty or property without due process of law." Most of the foregoing *federal* rights have been "incorporated" into the Fourteenth Amendment's Due Process Clause by a process of interpreting due process to mean "fundamental to a scheme of ordered liberty," which includes most of those rights. Thus, they have been made applicable to state as well as federal criminal proceedings.

Two Models of the Criminal Process

The development of liberty and authority culminates in two distinct sets of views of what the criminal process ought to be like. Herbert L. Packer called these two positions models, one based on the set of values associated with liberty, the *Due Process Model,* the other based on authority, the *Crime Control Model.* Both models (or abstractions or caricatures) agree that there should be no retroactive (ex post facto) legislation, which makes something criminal after it has been committed; that there should be some degree of distrust of governmental authority, in favor of privacy and autonomy of the individual (which reflects the generally liberal bias of Americans on governmental power, as observed above); and that there should be some adversariness in the procedure, by which the accused and the state play an active role of opposition in the process. Beyond this common ground, however, the models diverge sharply, each reflecting its basis in a different, somewhat conflicting set of values. Packer stated the Crime Control Model in this way:

> The value system that underlies the Crime Control Model is based on the proposition that the repression of criminal conduct is by far the most important function to be performed by the criminal process. . . . In order to achieve this high purpose, the Crime Control Model requires that primary attention be paid to the efficiency with which the criminal process operates to screen suspects, determine guilt, and secure appropriate dispositions of persons convicted of crime.[12]

The Crime Control Model operates on the basis that most detected offenders are in fact guilty. So the Crime Control Model emphasizes the investigative phase of the criminal process for detecting offenders; it deemphasizes the formal trial process. By contrast, the Due Process Model recognizes the unrealiability of witnesses; it emphasizes careful, formal adjudication (in place of informal fact-finding), so the testimony of witnesses can be carefully examined.

This leads Packer to a pair of metaphors, which suggest these differences:

> If the Crime Control Model resembles an assembly line, the Due Process Model looks very much like an obstacle course. Each of its successive stages is designed to present formidable impediments to carrying the accused any further along the process. . . . The Due Process Model resembles a factory that has to devote a substantial part of its input to quality control. This necessarily cuts down on quantitative output.[13]

Accordingly, in the Due Process Model the foundation is the *legal* presumption of innocence, rather than the Crime Control Model's *factual* presumption of guilt.

Packer's two models of the criminal process help one understand some of the issues that are presented when settled rules are reconsidered. The models reveal the competing values that press for supremacy in the resolution of such issues. For instance, the Crime Control Model urges a power to arrest that goes beyond the well-established basis of probable cause to believe the subject has committed, is committing, or is about to commit a crime:

> In short, the power of the police to arrest people for the purpose of investigation and prevention is one that must exist if the police are to do their job properly; the only question is whether arrests for investigation and prevention should be made hypocritically and deviously, or openly and avowedly. It only causes disrespect for law when there are great deviations between what the law on the books authorizes the police to do and what everyone knows they have to do.[14]

Among the measures congenial to this view is the Uniform Arrest Act, proposed a generation ago, which would empower a police officer to "stop any person abroad who he has reasonable ground to suspect"—rather than probable cause to believe—"is committing, has committed, or is about to commit a crime, and may demand of him his name, address, business abroad, and whither he is going." An unsatisfactory answer, under this proposal, could mean detention for up to two hours for further questioning and investigation.

The Due Process Model casts such measures in quite a different light. Placing liberty higher among the values than order and police efficiency, this model holds that nothing less than probable cause should be the exclusive basis for police intervention:

> Any less stringent standard opens the door to the probability of grave abuse, as repeated investigations of police practices have shown. A society that covertly tolerates indiscriminate arrest is hypocritical; but one that approves it legally is well on the way to becoming totalitarian in nature.[15]

The Due Process Model would sacrifice efficiency in the interest of individual autonomy, at least to the point where

> efficient law enforcement will be so heavily impaired by failure to adopt the proposed measure that the minimal conditions of public order necessary to provide the environment in which individuals can be allowed to enjoy the fruits of personal freedom will in themselves cease to exist or be gravely impaired.[16]

Packer thought we were far enough from that point that we could and should concentrate instead on minimizing such illegal practices that the police might already be convertly employing. Furthermore, to permit such practices would encourage police discrimination against "those elements in the population—the poor, the ignorant, the illiterate, the unpopular—who are least able to draw attention to their plight and to whose sufferings the vast majority of the population are the least responsive." Packer provides similarly illuminating treatment of the other major steps in the criminal process and the constraints the Constitution imposes on law enforcement.

The Cases of Constitutional Liberties

The balance between liberty and authority is struck tens of thousands of times a day, as police officers exercise their powers of law enforcement and order maintenance. In doing so they limit the liberty of a citizen to some extent—sometimes more, sometimes less, depending on whether the officer fires a gun, makes an arrest, or merely waves a bicyclist from the sidewalk to the street or holds back a jaywalker from crossing the street in mid-block. In a few of these cases, the officer goes too far, so the defendant resists—sometimes on the street, sometimes in the courts. In the courts the litigation of such issues of power usually begins with a hearing on the suppression of evidence, so that the availability of evidence will be settled before trial. It may be carried by appeals up the hierarchy of courts to the Supreme Court of the United States. There the balance of liberty and authority is stuck definitively and conclusively.

A good illustration of the balancing process is a famous case of stop-and-frisk, *Terry* v. *Ohio,* which reflects the competition between the needs of the police for authority to intervene in the interest of enforcing the law and the needs of the individual for preservation of autonomy and dignity. It is a real, concrete, street-level case of the conflict between order and freedom, which was treated earlier as a theoretical clash of abstractions.

Detective McFadden had observed Terry and another man engaged in what his 35 years as a detective in that neighborhood indicated to him was the "casing" of a store for robbery. Chief Justice Warren of the United States Supreme Court summarized the facts in his written opinion for the majority:

> He saw one of the men leave the other one and walk southwest on Huron Road, past some stores. The man paused for a moment and looked in a store window, then walked on a short distance, turned around and walked back toward the corner, pausing once again to look in the same store window. He rejoined his companion at the corner, and the two conferred briefly. Then the second man went through the same series of motions, strolling down Huron Road, looking in the same window, walking on a short distance, turning back, peering in the store window again, and returning to confer with the first man at the corner. The two men repeated

this ritual alternately between five and six times apiece—in all, roughly a
dozen trips. At one point, while the two men were standing together on
the corner, a third man approached them and engaged them briefly in
conversation. This man then left the two others and walked west on
Euclid Avenue.[17]

After a while McFadden, suspicious by now, came up to the three, identified himself, and asked for their names. When they "mumbled something," he "patted down the outside of [Terry's] clothing," felt a pistol but
was unable to remove it from the coat. He then ordered the men into the
store, removed Terry's coat, took the gun, then patted down the other two
and found yet another gun. The two with guns were charged with carrying
concealed weapons.

The defendants made a motion in the trial court to suppress the guns
as evidence, arguing that they had been illegally seized, since there had
not been an arrest. The prosecution answered with the argument that
there had been a lawful arrest, that the search was incident to a lawful
arrest, hence the seizure of the guns was legal. The trial judge disagreed
with both, saying McFadden had not had probable cause, hence could not
have made a lawful arrest, but that he had a right to pat down the
suspects for his own protection, given his "reasonable cause to believe
they might be armed."

The defendants were convicted of carrying concealed weapons on the
basis of the evidence of the weapons McFadden had obtained in the frisk.
Chief Justice Warren characterized the position of the trial court as
distinguishing "between an investigatory 'stop' and an arrest, and between a 'frisk' of the outer clothing for weapons and a full-blown search
for evidence of a crime." Then the case began to make its way up to the
U.S. Supreme Court.

The Supreme Court majority supported McFadden's action. Chief
Justice Warren's opinion for the majority said, "We think on the facts
and circumstances Officer McFadden detailed before the trial judge a
reasonably prudent man would have been warranted in believing [Terry]
was armed and thus presented a threat to the officer's safety while he
was investigating his suspicious behavior." The issue was, as the Court
posed it, "whether it is always unreasonable for a policeman to seize a
person and subject him to a limited search for weapons unless there is
probable cause for an arrest." The Court, in *Terry* v. *Ohio,* viewed the
issue in terms of the tension between the competing needs of liberty and
authority:

On the one hand, it is frequently argued that in dealing with the rapidly
unfolding and often dangerous situations on city streets the police are

in need of an escalating set of flexible responses, graduated in relation to the amount of information they possess. For this purpose it is urged that distinctions should be made between a "stop" and an "arrest" (or a "seizure" of a person), and between a "frisk" and a "search." Thus, it is argued, the police should be allowed to "stop" a person and detain him briefly for questioning upon suspicion that he may be connected with criminal activity. Upon suspicion that the person may be armed, the police should have the power to "frisk" him for weapons. If the "stop" and the "frisk" give rise to probable cause to believe that the suspect has committed a crime, then the police should be empowered to make a formal "arrest," and a full incident "search" of the person. This scheme is justified in part upon the notion that a "stop" and a "frisk" amount to a mere "minor inconvenience and petty indignity," which can properly be imposed upon the citizen in the interest of effective law enforcement on the basis of a police officer's suspicion.

On the other side the argument is made that the authority of the police must be strictly circumscribed by the law of arrest and search as it has developed to date in the traditional jurisprudence of the Fourth Amendment. It is contended with some force that there is not—and cannot be—a variety of police activity which does not depend solely upon the voluntary cooperation of the citizen and yet which stops short of an arrest. The heart of the Fourth Amendment, the argument runs, is a severe requirement of specific jurisdiction for any intrusion upon protected personal security, coupled with a highly developed system of judicial controls to enforce upon the agents of the State the commands of the Constitution. Acquiescence by the courts in the compulsion inherent in the field interrogation practices at issue here, it is urged, would constitute an abdication of judicial control over, and indeed an ecouragement of, substantial interference with liberty and personal security by police officers whose judgment is necessarily colored by their primary involvement in "the often competitive enterprise of ferreting out crime." ... This, it is argued, can only serve to exacerbate police-community tensions in the crowded centers of our nation's cities.

The Court resolved the tension in favor of a narrowly circumscribed power of the police to frisk a suspect for their own protection.

Having established that such a search is constitutionally permissible, the Court then turned to the question of the scope of the search and found that McFadden's search had not been excessive:

Officer McFadden patted down the outer clothing of [Terry] and his two companions. He did not place his hands in their pockets or under the outer surface of their garments until he had felt weapons, and then he merely reached for and removed the guns. He never did invade [the third one's] person beyond the outer surfaces of his clothes, since he discovered nothing in his pat down which might have been a weapon. Officer

McFadden confined his search strictly to what was minimally necessary to learn whether the men were armed and to disarm them once he discovered the weapons. He did not conduct a general exploratory search for whatever evidence of criminal activity he might find.

In conclusion, the Court stated its "holding" that the police in such circumstances have a power limited in both its kind and extent:

> We merely hold today that where a police officer observes unusual conduct which leads him reasonably to conclude in light of his experience that criminal activity may be afoot and that the persons with whom he is dealing may be armed and presently dangerous, where in the course of investigating this behavior he identifies himself as a policeman and makes reasonable inquiries, and where nothing in the initial stages of the encounter serves to dispel his reasonable fear for his own or other's safety, he is entitled for the protection of himself and others in the area to conduct a carefully limited search of the outer clothing of such persons in an attempt to discover weapons which might be used to assault him. Such a search is a reasonable search under the Fourth Amendment, and any weapons seized may properly be introduced in evidence against the person from whom they were taken.

It is unusual for important constitutional issues to be decided unanimously; instead, there is usually some sharp disagreement which is expressed in dissenting opinions. Justice Douglas, in his dissenting opinion, said:

> I agree that [Terry] was "seized" within the meaning of the Fourth Amendment. I also agree that frisking [Terry] and his companions for guns was a "search." But it is a mystery how that "search" and that "seizure" can be constitutional by Fourth Amendment standards, unless there was "probable cause" to believe that (1) a crime had been committed or (2) a crime was in the process of being committed or (3) a crime was about to be committed.
>
> The opinion of the Court disclaims the existence of "probable cause." If loitering were an issue and that was the offense charged, there would be "probable cause" shown. But the crime here is carrying concealed weapons; and there is no basis for concluding that the officer had "probable cause" for believing that crime was being committed. Had a warrant been sought, a magistrate would, therefore, have been unauthorized to issue one, for he can act only if there is showing of "probable cause." We hold today that the police have greater authority to make a "seizure" and conduct a "search" than a judge has to authorize such action. We have said precisely the opposite over and over again.
>
> . . . The infringement on personal liberty of any "seizure" of a person can only be "reasonable" under the Fourth Amendment if we require

the police to possess "probable cause" before they seize him. Only that line draws a meaningful distinction between the officer's mere inkling and the presence of facts within the officers's personal knowledge which could convince a reasonable man that the person seized has committed, is committing, or is about to commit a particular crime.

. . . To give the police greater power than a magistrate is to take a long step down the totalitarian path. Perhaps such a step is desirable to cope with modern forms of lawlessness. But if it is taken, it should be the deliberate choice of the people through a constitutional amendment.

. . . if the individual is no longer to be sovereign, if the police can pick him up whenever they do not like the cut of his gib, if they can "seize" and "search" him in their discretion, we enter a new regime. The decision to enter it should be made only after a full debate by the people of this country.

After the *Terry* case had established the constitutional permissibility of stop-and-frisk power, the courts shifted their concern from the principle to its limitations—that is, to limitations on police authority to stop and frisk in varying circumstances. For example, what if a police officer observes a person engaged in continuing conversation with several known narcotics addicts, even though nothing was heard nor was anything seen being passed from one person to another. May the officer frisk that person on the basis of his suspicion that the person is buying or selling narcotics, or is at least in possession of them? In *Sibron* v. *New York,* the Supreme Court said that the power of the police to stop and frisk extended only to the sort of situation involved in *Terry,* where there was reasonable suspicion "that criminal activity may be afoot and that the persons with whom he is dealing may be armed and presently dangerous." [18] That situation was not present in *Sibron:* "The suspect's mere act of talking with a number of known narcotics addicts over an eight-hour period no more gives rise to reasonable fear of life or limb on the part of the police officer than it justifies an arrest for committing a crime." Nor did Sibron indicate that he was going for a weapon when he "mumbled something and reached into his pocket," when the officer had just said to him, "You know what I am after." Moreover, the scope of the search was not within the limits established in *Terry,* even if there was danger. McFadden had patted down the suspect, then reached into a pocket and feeling something distinctly like a gun. In *Sibron,* the officer simply plunged his hand into the pocket where he thought he would find narcotics. Even though he was right—and came up with envelopes of heroin—his success was to no avail, given the unreasonableness of the search in light of the rule established in *Terry;* so the evidence should have been suppressed by the trial judge.

What if the frisk reveals what the officer thinks is a weapon, but it turns out to be burglary tools, which it is illegal to possess. The Supreme Court faced that variation on the stop-and-frisk theme in *Peters* v. *New York,* and said the search and seizure were constitutional. The officer had seen Peters and another man moving about suspiciously in a hallway, gave chase and caught one of them, patting him down for a weapon, feeling what he thought was a knife in the man's pocket, but finding instead a burglary tool. The Court said the evidence was admissible in a trial on the charge of possession of burglary tools.[19]

This is the sort of elaboration of a doctrine that takes place when a basic position is established in constitutional law. Once the position is established in principle, it is worked through in the various permutations and combinations of facts that present themselves in the situations the police face in their day-to-day efforts to enforce the law.

The Combination of Constitutional Provisions

The interpretation of the Constitution is complicated when the rights of the individual may rest on one or another or some combination of two provisions. Under the Fifth Amendment, "No person shall . . . be compelled in any criminal case to be a witness against himself. . . ." Under the Sixth Amendment a person is entitled to counsel. Confessions and other statements came to be excluded from consideration in state courts during the 1930s if they were procured from a suspect by means of physical mistreatment. This was accomplished through the Fourteenth Amendment's Due Process Clause: involuntariness of a confession, in the light of the circumstances surrounding it, made its use a denial of "life, liberty, or property without due process of law." The courts developed this conception by adding to the totality of circumstances under consideration, going beyond physical brutality, threats, and promises to less blatant influences, such as extended questioning and secret questioning.

Meanwhile, another constitutional development was occurring along the line of the right to counsel. First, the accused was granted the right to counsel at the trial itself; then (at least in capital cases) during "critical stages" *before* trial; finally, in *Gideon* v. *Wainwright,* the right to counsel before trial was granted in all serious rather than just capital cases. This line culminated in *Escobedo* v. *Illinois,* where there was no suggestion that the circumstances made the statements involuntary. Instead, there had been a denial of counsel when it was requested. Justice Goldberg spoke for the Court:

> . . . no system of criminal justice can, or should survive if it comes to depend for its continued effectiveness on the citizen's abdication through

unawareness of their constitutional rights. No system worth preserving should have to *fear* that if an accused is permitted to consult with a lawyer, he will become aware of, and exercise, these rights. If the exercise of constitutional rights will thwart the effectiveness of a system of law enforcement, then there is something very wrong with that system.

We hold, therefore, that where, as here, the investigation is no longer a general inquiry into an unsolved crime but has begun to focus on a particular suspect, the suspect has been taken into police custody, the police carry out a process of interrogations that lends itself to eliciting incriminating statements, the suspect has requested and been denied an opportunity to consult with his lawyer, and the police have not effectively warned him of his absolute constitutional right to remain silent, the accused has been denied "the Assistance of Counsel" in violation of the Sixth Amendment of the Constitution . . . and that no statement elicited by the police during the interrogation may be used against him at a criminal trial.[20]

The usual uncertainties about the scope of the *Escobedo* principle (Did it apply before police custody began? Did it require a warning of the right?) were soon settled in *Miranda* v. *Arizona* two years later. The Court relied then on the Fifth Amendment's privilege against self-incrimination rather than on the Sixth Amendment's right to counsel. The right to counsel was combined with the protection against self-incrimination, to make the latter meaningful. The Court said:

> . . . there can be no doubt that the Fifth Amendment privilege is available outside of criminal court proceedings and serves to protect persons in all settings in which their freedom from action is curtailed in any significant way from being compelled to incriminate themselves. We have concluded that without proper safeguards the process of in-custody interrogation of persons suspected or accused of crime contains inherently compelling pressures which work to undermine the individual's will to resist and to compel him to speak where he would not otherwise do so freely. In order to combat these pressures and to permit a full opportunity to exercise the privilege against self-incrimination, the accused must be adequately and effectively apprised of his rights and the exercise of those rights must be fully honored.[21]

The *Miranda* principle left open many aspects for later resolution in the usual course of constitutional elaboration, such as the kinds of offenses it applied to, the meaning of *custody,* the meaning of *interrogation,* the phrasing of the warnings, waiver of the right, the use of statements given without the warning for purposes other than proof of the offense (e.g., to "impeach" the witness's credibility, to contradict his statement at trial, to demonstrate perjury). A recent case illustrates the balancing of interests that the Court continues to engage in as it works out the *Miranda* principle, extending it this far in one case's set of circumstances, that far in another. In *Michigan* v. *Tucker* the Court took up one of the "loose ends" left over from *Miranda*—the question of what use might be made of evidence gained from statements made without the benefit of the complete *Miranda* warnings but with merely the advice that the suspect would be provided counsel if he could not afford it himself. The suspect had been asked some questions, and replied that he had been with a friend and later was asleep at the time of the incident. The police checked out his story with the friend and found that Tucker had left the friend prior to the incident and that he had told the friend the next day that he had been with the victim. Tucker argued that not only his statement about being with the friend and being asleep should be excluded from trial, because he had not been given the full *Miranda* warnings, but also the friend's testimony of what Tucker had told him, because the identity of the friend had been disclosed by Tucker in his statement to the police. Justice Rhenquist stated the reasoning of the Court:

> ... when balancing the interests involved, we must weigh the strong interest under any system of justice of making available to the trier of fact all concededly relevant and trustworthy evidence which either party seeks to adduce. In this particular case we also "must consider society's interest in the effective prosecution of criminals in light of the protection our pre-*Miranda* standards afford criminal defendants." ... Here [Tucker's] own statement, which might have helped the prosecution show [Tucker's] guilty conscience at trial, had already been excised from the prosecution's case. ... To extend the excision further under the circumstances of this case and exclude relevant testimony of a third-party witness would require far more persuasive argument than those advanced.[22]

The Exclusionary Rule

The principle way of making the limitations on search and seizure more than mere "paper" protections has been the exclusionary rule, by which illegally seized evidence is excluded from the judicial process. It is invoked usually in a "suppression hearing," in which the judge considers the facts of the seizure and decides whether the police action was within the scope of the authority permitted under the law. Did the officer have probable cause in the case of a search incident to an arrest, or reasonable suspicion, in the case of a frisk? If the judge finds that there was something less than probable cause (or reasonable suspicion in stop-and-frisk), he or she rules that the evidence was illegally seized and declares that it is inadmissible in the trial of the case.

The purposes of this device were stated by Justice Clark in *Mapp* v. *Ohio* in 1961, the case in which the Supreme Court extended the application of the exclusionary rule to all of the states: "Nothing can destroy a government more quickly than its failure to observe its own laws, or worse, its disregard of the charter of its own existence." [23] One reason for the rule was the deterrent effect it was thought to have: police, knowing the consequences of illegal actions (that the evidence will be thrown out), will refrain from illegal conduct. Another reason was that illegally seized evidence ought not to be used by the judiciary: The courts should not profit from the fruits of the unlawful activities of the other branches.

The exclusionary rule drew criticism from its very beginning, long before the Mapp case. When Justice Cardozo, was a judge on the highest state court in New York, he said of the rule: "The criminal is to go free because the constable has blundered." [24] Other jurisdictions, which respect the rights of the accused no less than American courts, get along without the exclusionary rule. Norval Morris and Gordon Hawkins, writing from the perspective of the Commonwealth nations, stated that view:

> The English and Australian position in relation to the fruits of illegal searches and seizures is plainly more reasonable than the American position. We should at once admit the illegally seized evidence on the question of the accused's guilt and later and quite separately pursue diligent disciplinary processes against the policeman who conducted the search.[25]

A good many difficulties with the rule have emerged clearly in recent years. The rule is limited in that most police activity is oriented toward order maintenance rather than production of evidence for law-enforcement purposes. The rule's sanction (exclusion of evidence from trial) is not felt directly by the police, because officers are interested mainly in "clearing" cases or solving them, not seeing them through the trial process to convictions. The sanction is felt instead by the prosecutor, rather than the wrongdoing police officers. Others are influenced more by what they and the police community believe are good (that is, efficient) police practices, not necessarily the highest constitutional standards. So the appeal to conscience will be shaped mainly by what an officer's colleagues prefer, rather than what the judges call for. There is ineffective communication to the police of what the rule calls for, even with training programs and legal advisers. The force of constitutional rules is weakened by their obscurity: The justices on the Supreme Court itself have sometimes complained that they did not understand what the Court was ruling.

The exclusionary rule protects the guilty parties, both the offender "victimized" by an illegal search and the rule-breaking police officer who "victimized" the offender. Conversely, the rule does nothing for the truly innocent, noncriminal victim of a search, who has no criminal proceeding in which to invoke the rule; the criminal defendant at least gains the avoidance of prosecution beyond that point. Innocent victims can only sue the officer or the police department, at their own expense and with little chance of compensation, because actual damages ordinarily are slight. Thus the rule gives rise to disrespect for the law itself and for the courts that administer it. The illegally seized evidence itself is not less probative (heroin is no less heroin) because of the illegality of the seizure, in contrast to coerced confessions, which are intrinsically unreliable. Vital evidence, typically in gambling, narcotics, and weapons cases, is excluded; without it the prosecution fails. To the public and the police, the reasons for the rule (deterrence and integrity of the process) are less impressive than its effects (a guilty criminal goes free). The rule induces the police to lie, to make up facts to justify their conduct, even to carry packets of drugs or a weapon to plant on a subject (whose word usually will not be taken over that of the police officer). The police thereby corrupt themselves and the system.

The rule operates demoralizingly by means of a hearing at which the police officer becomes, in effect, the accused and the criminal becomes the accuser. The exclusionary rule also introduces into the already drawn-out process of prosecuting offenders a delaying factor (the motions to suppress, the suppression hearing, the arguments on the motion). The rule creates pressure on judges sympathetic to the police to weaken the law of arrest and search, and seizure by interpreting probable cause and other elements of the rules to accommodate the realities of police work. It creates yet another inducement to plea bargaining by introducing into the lawyer's calculations of the likely outcome of the case an additional factor of the likelihood of suppression, which complicates their analysis and prolongs the process. It puts into the hands of the police a power to immunize criminals, if they should cynically or corruptly care to do so, by providing them with a basis for beating the case. The police, frustrated by so much of this, are tempted to use methods such as harassment and confiscation of contraband (especially narcotics and weapons) to control the criminal element, rather than the usual criminal process. The very existence of the rule has distracted officials from developing alternative methods of accomplishing the intended effects of the Amendment.[26]

Donald L. Horowitz, in *The Courts and Social Policy,* an important study of judicial ability to bring about social change, reports that empirical studies of the improvement of police behavior indicate that the rule's deterrent effect is "a sometime, some-crime, someplace thing."

Mapp's effect is not so good as the rule's proponents hoped, nor so bad as its opponents feared. The police are more concerned about convictions than their supposed preoccupation with "clearance" would indicate. They are more influenced by prosecutors and by judicial decisions than they were assumed to be. Moreover, it is not clear than many defendants have been freed as a result of the rule.[27]

Two recent studies have confirmed that the rule has not had a great effect on cases. One study, done by the Comptroller General of the United States at the request of Senator Edward M. Kennedy, Chairman of the Senate Judiciary Committee, analyzed 2804 federal cases in 1978 and found that some 15 percent of the cases that come to the U.S. attorneys involved search and seizure problems but that only 0.4 percent of these cases are declined for prosecution because of search and seizure problems. Of the cases accepted for prosecution, 80 percent of the motions to suppress evidence for search and seizure reasons were denied in cases handled by very large U.S. Attorney's offices, and 90 percent were denied in cases handled by large offices.[28]

The other study of state court-case flows in 13 jurisdictions, using a modern computerized record-keeping system, attempted to find out why there are so few convictions compared to arrests or charges filed. For example, the convictions compared to the arrests ranged in rates from 21 percent in Los Angeles and 33 percent in New Orleans to 46 percent in the District of Columbia and 62 percent in Cobb County, Georgia.[29] Attrition of cases at the point of prosecutorial screening involved little difficulty with due process (search and seizure) compared to other reasons for rejection of cases by the prosecutor. For example, in Los Angeles 37 percent of the rejected cases were referred to other prosecutors for prosecution, 29 percent involved evidentiary problems other than due process questions (e.g., insufficient testimony about a crucial element of the case), 14 percent involved lack of prosecutive merit (e.g., offense was inadvertently committed), 6 percent involved witness problems (e.g., witness failed to show up), and 4 percent involved due process (search and seizure).[30] Likewise, attrition of cases *after* acceptance by the prosecutor had much more to do with factors other than due process. In Los Angeles, lack of prosecutive merit accounted for 26 percent, evidence problems 25 percent, witness problems 21 percent, other and unknown problems 16 percent, and due process 12 percent.[31] The report's summary made the point this way: "Contrary to conventional wisdom, due process violations accounted for very little of the case attrition. The few cases that were dropped for due process reasons (mainly search and seizure problems) were largely drug cases, as might be expected, since many drug cases involve professional crimes." [32]

Alternatives to the Exclusionary Rule

If concern for the effects of the exclusionary rule should decline, there would probably be a decline of interest in the alternatives. Some interest will remain because, as the 13-city report observes "those issues may be substantial in terms of legal theory." [33] The rule may be less appropriate than the alternatives. One alternative is the tort remedy, by which the victim of an unlawful search sues the police officer for trespass or invasion of privacy in a civil suit. The possibility is supposed to keep police officers in line. This, however, puts the victim in the hands of a lawyer and at the mercy of the legal system, about which there is so much concern and criticism. Even if the plaintiff should win his suit, probably after a long delay, he is then dependent on the resources of the defendant, and the typical police officer is "judgment proof," or not so well-to-do that a civil judgment against him would yield much for the compensation of the plaintiff. These limitations dilute the deterrent effect the tort approach is supposed to have. In any case, it has not been used much.

Such limitations on the conventional tort approach suggest improvements of the sort Chief Justice Burger called for in his dissent in the *Bivens* case: "Congress should develop an administrative or quasi-judicial remedy against the government itself to afford compensation and restitution for persons whose Fourth Amendment rights have been violated." [34] Bills were introduced in Congress in the early 1970s to create an administrative mechanism to enable victims of such searches to file a complaint with an administrative agency, newly created for the purpose, which would decide the illegal-seizure issue and make an award of compensation, if appropriate. Discipline of offending police officers would be left to their police agency. So the court, in the trial of the case against the criminal defendant, would be unburdened by the illegal-seizure issue and justice would not be defeated by the actions of an errant officer, which are extraneous to the question of the accused's guilt.

Another approach is the creation of an *ombudsman,* an official the Scandinavian countries have developed to represent the interests of complainants against government agencies. The police agency would have such an official to investigate complaints of illegal seizure of evidence, to recommend compensation, to recommend disciplinary measures, and so forth. There has been a great deal of interest in the idea of the ombudsman in recent years. But it is still not well accepted, let alone found in very many places in the American system of government.

The approach that has attracted the most interest has been the so-called rule-making approach, by which police departments develop detailed rules aimed at providing better guidance to police officers, hence more assurance that illegal seizures will not occur. The rules would be a basis for departmental discipline of its own members. This approach will be developed further after the topics of discretion and dissonance are developed in the next chapter, because the rule-making approach deals with both of those problems as well as the problem of the exclusionary rule.

SUMMARY

This chapter began with a discussion of the purposes of criminal justice: social control, retribution, deterrence, incapacitation, rehabilitation, and denunciation. This discussion highlighted the inconsistencies among these purposes and the need for resolving the differences by some accommodation of one to another. This process of adjustment is involved also in the resolution of differences among fundamental values such as order, freedom, democracy, and law.

The historical process of balancing liberty and authority was described, leading up to today's rules on the rights of the accused that pertain to questioning, stop-and-frisk, field interrogation, arrest, stationhouse interrogation, search and seizure, and surveillance. The balancing process was then put into the context of Packer's two models of the criminal process, the *due process model* and the *crime control model*. Then some cases were examined, mainly *Terry* v. *Ohio*, as illustrations of the work of the Supreme Court in balancing the values of order and freedom, the aims of crime control and due process, and the interests of the police and of the individual. The chapter concluded with an analysis of the exclusionary rule, by which the courts attempt to maintain the balance of liberty and authority in criminal cases.

NOTES

1. Herbert L. Packer discussed them in his *Limits to the Criminal Sanction* (Stanford, Calif.: Stanford, 1968), pp. 34–70.
2. Ibid., p. 38.
3. Robert Martinson, "What Works?—Questions and Answers About Prison Reform," *Public Interest* 35 (Spring 1974), pp. 22–54.
4. Quoted in Abraham S. Goldstein and Joseph Goldstein, eds., *Crime, Law and Society* (New York: Free Press, 1971), p. 47.
5. Benjamin Nathan Cardozo, *The Paradoxes of Legal Science* (New York: Columbia, 1928), p. 94.
6. Jerome H. Skolnick, *Justice Without Trial*, 2nd ed. (New York: Wiley, 1975), pp. 7–8.
7. Ibid., p. 10.
8. Robert E. Carr, et al., *American Democracy in Theory and Practice*, 4th ed. (New York: Holt, Rinehart and Winston, 1960), pp. 510–513.
9. *Brown* v. *Texas* (No. 77-6673).
10. J. Shane Creamer, *The Law of Arrest, Search and Seizure*, 2nd ed. (Philadelphia: Saunders, 1975), p. 19.

11. John G. Miles, Jr., et al., *The Law Officer's Pocket Manual,* 1974 ed. (Washington, D.C.: Bureau of National Affairs, 1973), p. 87. This is a more complete statement of the warnings than most departments require.
12. Packer, *Limits of the Criminal Sanction,* p. 158.
13. Ibid., pp. 163, 165.
14. Ibid., p. 177.
15. Ibid., p. 179.
16. Ibid., pp. 179–180.
17. This and the following passages from *Terry* v. *Ohio* are from Vol. 392 of the *United States Reports,* beginning with p. 1, cited 392 U.S. 1 (1968).
18. This and the following passages from *Sibron* v. *New York,* 932 U.S. 40 (1968).
19. *Peters* v. *New York,* decided together with *Sibron.*
20. *Escobedo* v. *Illinois,* 378 U.S. 478 (1964).
21. *Miranda* v. *Arizona,* 384 U.S. 436 (1966).
22. *Michigan* v. *Tucker,* 417 U.S. 433 (1974).
23. *Mapp* v. *Ohio,* 367 U.S. 643 (1961).
24. *People* v. *Defore,* 242 N.Y. 13 (1926).
25. Norval Morris and Gordon Hawkins, *The Honest Politician's Guide to Crime Control* (Chicago: University of Chicago, 1969), p. 101.
26. Several of the foregoing reasons are developed in Dallin Oaks, "Studying the Exclusionary Rule in Search and Seizure," *University of Chicago Law Review* 37 (1970), pp. 665–753.
27. Donald L. Horowitz, *The Courts and Social Policy* (Washington, D.C.: Brookings, 1977).
28. Comptroller General of the United States, *Impact of the Exclusionary Rule on Federal Criminal Prosecutions* (Washington, D.C.: General Accounting Office, 1979).
29. Kathleen B. Brosi, *A Cross-City Comparison of Felony Case Processing* (Washington, D.C.: Institute for Law and Social Research, 1979), p. 10.
30. Ibid., p. 16.
31. Ibid., p. 20.
32. Ibid., p. 69.
33. Ibid., p. 18.
34. *Bivens* v. *Six Unknown Agents,* 403 U.S. 388 (1971).

SELECTED READINGS

David Fellman, *The Defendant's Rights Today* (Madison, Wis.: University of Wisconsin Press, 1975).

Macklin Fleming, *The Price of Perfect Justice* (New York: Basic Books, 1974).

Donald L. Horowitz, *The Courts and Social Policy* (Washington, D.C.: Brookings, 1977).

Jerold H. Israel, and Wayne R. LaFave, *Criminal Procedure: Constitutional Limitations* (St. Paul, Minn.: West, 1975).

Leo Pfeffer, *The Liberties of an American* (Boston: Beacon, 1956).

Claude R. Sowle, ed., *Police Power and Individual Freedom: The Quest for Balance* (Chicago: Aldine, 1962).

Lloyd L. Weinreb, ed., *Leading Constitutional Cases on Criminal Justice* (Mineola, N.Y.: Foundation, 1974).

11

LAW ENFORCEMENT UNLIMITED: DISCRETION AND DISSONANCE IN POLICE AUTHORITY

This chapter takes up the problem of discretion—the range of choices available to the patrol officer in the enforcement of the law and the maintenance of order. It examines some of the reasons for a degree of discretion and some of the reasons for limiting it. The chapter then reviews the approaches to governing the exercise of discretion, emphasizing the development of rules by police agencies in consultation with the community. The implication of this—a political role for the police—is explored as the basis of a discussion of what is called the "dissonance in police authority," or the lack of harmony between legality and legitimacy of police power on the one hand, and illegality and illegitimacy on the other. The chapter concludes with some directions for reform by which illegal but legitimate police actions can be made legal, and illegitimate but legal actions illegal.

The Problem of Police Discretion

As Judge Charles Breitel defined it, *discretion* is "the power to consider all circumstances and then determine whether any legal action is to be taken. And if so taken, of what kind and degree, and to what conclusion."[1] A wide range for personal judgment conflicts, however, with John Adams's idea that ours is "a government of laws, and not of men." The problem of discretion arises out of the police officer's position, caught in a dilemma, the source of which is the tension between law and order, according to Skolnick.

> The police in democratic society are required to maintain order and to do so under the rule of law. As functionaries charged with maintaining order, they are part of the bureaucracy. The ideology of democratic

bureaucracy emphasizes initiative rather than disciplined adherence to rules and regulations. By contrast, the rule of law emphasizes the rights of individual citizens and constraints upon the initiative of legal officials. This tension between the operational consequences of ideas of order, efficiency, and initiative, on the one hand, and legality, on the other, constitutes the principal problem of police as a democratic legal organization.[2]

The need for law gives rise to the ideal of the rule of law, or "government of laws," to minimize the effects of the "human factors" in ruling. On the other hand, the need for order maximizes the power of the state, hence of the police officer, and permits to it (and him) a wide-ranging discretion, unlimited or limited very little by rules, so as to increase the free play of judgment. The problem is that the officer's judgment might be wise or foolish, benevolent or malevolent, kind or cruel, good or evil, helpful or harmful.

The discretion of patrol officers, like the discretion of the prosecutor, makes it possible for them to make a choice among potentially chargeable crimes, therefore of whom police will arrest, of whom the district attorney will prosecute. The difference between these two officials is that the discretion of the prosecutor is widely acknowledged and generally considered to be legitimate. The discretion of the police, however, has only recently come to be recognized, but is not widely acknowledged and rarely (again, at least until very recently) considered to be legitimate.

Yet it is clear that the police have a vast amount of discretion—and exercise their power within a wide range, uncontrolled by, and even defiant of, rules specified by legislative bodies, which make laws presumably with the intention that they will be implemented. For example, if a speed limit is set at 40 miles per hour by county ordinance, but the police choose to arrest only those who exceed 50 per hour, one may well ask who gave them authority to change the rule, to permit drivers an extra 10 miles per hour above the statutory maximum? This is to say nothing of the selection of drivers to be issued tickets among the total number of speeders who are ignored or given written or spoken warnings. Who authorized the police to exercise such a selectivity in their law-enforcement practices? The answer is that no one did; they assumed the power because it seems sensible to do so. Full enforcement of the traffic laws would require many times the number of police officers on the force. In any event, the legislature has observed "selective enforcement" of its laws for so long that, as Kenneth Culp Davis observes, we must infer that the legislature approves this administrative amendment of the law, this alteration of policy in the course of its implementation, as a reasonable response to the realities of the situation.[3] But this amounts to something quite different from the understanding most people have of law-enforcement authority, as the President's Commission stated:

> At the very beginning of the process—or, more properly, before the process begins at all—something happens that is scarcely discussed in law books and is seldom recognized by the public: law enforcement policy is made by the policeman. For policemen cannot and do not arrest all offenders they encounter. It is doubtful that they arrest most of them. A criminal code, in practice, is not a set of specific instructions to policemen but a more or less rough map of the territory in which policemen work. How an individual policeman moves round that territory depends largely upon his personal discretion.[4]

Two studies have indicated the range of factors that influence the judgment of police officers in the exercise of their discretion. Nathan Goldman, using a sampling of police in four communities, found the following determinants of selection or arrest:

(a) The policeman's attitudes toward the juvenile court.
(b) The impact of special individual experiences in the court, or with different racial groups, or with parents of offenders, or with specific offenses, on an individual policeman.
(c) Apprehension about criticism by the court.
(d) Publicity given to certain offenses either in the neighborhood or elsewhere may cause the police to feel that these are too "hot" to handle unofficially and must be referred to the court.
(e) The necessity for maintaining respect for police authority in the community.
(f) Various practical problems of policing (e.g., distance to the court).
(g) Pressure by political groups or other special interest groups.
(h) The policeman's attitude toward specific offenses.
(i) The police officer's impression of the family situation, the degree of family interest in and control of the offender, and the reaction of the parents to the problem of the child's offense.
(j) The attitude and personality of the boy.
(k) The Negro child offender is considered less tractable and needing more authoritarian supervision than a white child.
(l) The degree of criminal sophistication shown in the offense.
(m) Juvenile offenders apprehended in a group will generally be treated on an all-or-none basis.[5]

Another set of reasons for the selective invocation of the criminal sanction was found in the research of Wayne R. LaFave, author of one of the studies in the American Bar Foundation's Survey of the Administration of Criminal Justice: (1) Ambiguous statutory language causes the police to resolve their uncertainty on the side of caution, lest the uncertainty be resolved later in civil litigation for false arrest. (2) Conduct, such as loitering, may have been declared criminal as a basis for investigatory arrests, which the police permit unless some additional reason is present. (3) Conduct may be criminalized broadly to avoid loopholes. For example, gambling might be defined to include social gambling to avoid the difficulties of theoretically distinguishing between social and professional gambling, leaving to the police the decision in each instance. (4) Conduct may be criminalized to reflect community ideals, for the uplifting effects of law but, as in the criminalization of adultery and fornication, without a serious intention that it be strictly enforced. (5) Conduct which is no longer regarded as intolerable may not have been decriminalized because the legislature has not updated the criminal code. (6) Minor offenses, for which a warning—at most—is called for, may be covered by the statute but not singled out for arrest, especially if no one is injured or complains. (7) Conduct reflecting subcultural standards, such as the carrying of knives by blacks, may be left alone, resulting in confiscation but not arrest. (8) Unenforcement is common in cases of uncooperative victims, who do not or will not support police intervention because the victim prefers some other remedy, because of the relationship of the victim and offender (battery victim continues to live with her assailant), or because the victim is a member of the offender's family. (9) Similarly, when the victim is involved in the criminal activity, arrest of the other party seems inappropriate. (10) Arrest is avoided when it would be ineffective, as in many cases of public drunkenness. (11) Arrest is also avoided where it would cause loss of public respect and support, where charitable gambling is customarily supported by churches. (12) Arrest is avoided when nonarrest would benefit law enforcement, as when an informer is "licensed" to continue his criminal behavior in exchange for his service as informer. (13) Arrest is avoided where nonarrest would harm the offender or victim less than an arrest, as when the officer knows that a "good boy" who has not been in trouble before can be "straightened out" with a reprimand.[6]

LaFave also points out that discretion also permits the police to make arrests in cases when they ordinarily would not. (1) Arrest may be made in a situation, as in family disputes, when the police anticipate that they will be back again and again, so they make the arrest sooner rather than later. (2) Arrest is made to maintain respect for the police, as when a subject has been abusive. (3) Arrest may be made to create an impression of full enforcement, as when social gambling, which is ordinarily tolerated, becomes notorious and is stopped from time to time for the sake of appearances. (4) Arrest may be made to punish someone who is suspected of other criminal activity, by its harassment effect. (5) Arrest may be made for investigation of another offense or offender, as when a traffic or vagrancy arrest is made to provide an opportunity for interrogation about someone or something else.[7]

Selective enforcement of the foregoing kinds is the focus of much of the study of discretion. But, as Herman Goldstein points out, there are other important forms of discretion which do not get much attention. One is the discretion to select among *objectives*. For example, the police department's style of policing, whether it emphasizes law enforcement, order maintenance, or service, is in part a matter of the department's selection, for which it has substantial discretion.

Second, police have discretion not only as to whether or not they should intervene, but if they do so, by what means:

> . . . the officer must often decide, under great time pressure, whether to conduct an investigation, whether to freeze a situation, whether to stop and question, whether to frisk, whether to make an immediate apprehension, or whether to use force. And once the initial determination is made, several of these alternatives require additional discretion. Thus, if the officer decides to investigate, determination must then be made about the scope and intensity of the investigation to be undertaken.

Third, after that decision, the police must decide how to dispose of the case. As Goldstein puts it:

> They may decide to arrest and prosecute, or to use some alternative to the criminal justice system—to warn, mediate, or make a referral; to use the juvenile justice system or the mental health system. They may decide to charge a person with violating a city ordinance rather than a state statute, or they may decide to do nothing.

Fourth, the police have discretion in choosing what investigative methods they will employ:

> They can decide to frisk; stop and question; search persons and property; use informants; conduct surveillances, eavesdrop or wiretap; take photographs and motion pictures; go undercover; infiltrate an organization; employ decoys; or in other ways place themselves in a situation that invites a person intent on committing a crime to attempt it.[8]

Dealing with Discretionary Decision-Making

The discovery that the police have wide-ranging discretion in the decisions they make, coupled with identification of the many considerations that influence their decisions—some legitimate, others illegitimate—gave rise a decade or so ago to a movement to infuse rules into the decisions of police. This was part of a growing concern about the problem of discretion generally, as it is exercised by regulatory agencies of many kinds, as well as by those in the criminal-justice system. One of the leaders of the movement to deal with discretionary decision-making is Kenneth Culp Davis of the University of Chicago Law School. His book, *Discretionary Justice,* set forth his formulation of *confining, structuring, and checking* discretion. Davis's thesis is a simple one: discretion cannot and should not be eliminated because it enables administrators to take circumstances into account; but it can and must be controlled for excessive or unnecessary discretion, so that the right "mix" of rules and discretion will limit the officer's judgment yet free it in a framework of guidance and flexibility that will yield appropriately individualized decisions.

The means of accomplishing this objective is a process that is simple enough in principle but administratively quite complex. *Confining* discretion, or eliminating some of it and limiting much of the rest of it, means "fixing the boundaries and keeping discretion within them." This can be done to some extent by sharpening the statutory definitions of offenses.[9] For example, in place of a statutory provision that criminalizes disorderly conduct in very broad language, so that a police officer would have the power to arrest someone for almost any irregular or peculiar behavior that might have upset someone (even the officer), the offense might be defined much more specifically with standards limiting what the officer can do. An illustration of the confining process at the legislative level is the definition of disorderly conduct that had been included in S.1, the earlier bill for the revision of the federal criminal code:

> A person is guilty of an offense [of disorderly conduct] if, with intent to alarm, harass, or annoy another person or in reckless disregard of the fact that another person is thereby alarmed, harassed, or annoyed, he:
>
> (1) engages in violent, tumultuous, or threatening conduct;
> (2) makes or causes unreasonable noise;
> (3) uses abusive or obscene language, or engages in obscene conduct, in a public place;
> (4) obstructs vehicular or pedestrian traffic, or the use of a public facility;
> (5) persistently follows a person in or about a public place or places;
> (6) solicits a sexual act [as it is defined in Chapter 8] in a public place; or
> (7) engages for no legitimate purpose in any other conduct that creates a hazardous or physically offensive conditions (§1861).

But such a legislative effort needs to be supplemented by an administrative process in which the police agency itself would continue the "sharpening" process (e.g., making the elements of disorderly conduct even more specific, tailored to the nature of the community), in what Davis calls a "movement from vague standards to definite standards to broad principles to rules."[10] An illustration of such rules is the following section from the "Model Rules for Law Enforcement," which follows a section on frisk and search incident to an arrest involving a motor vehicle:

Wider Search When Probable Cause Exists to Believe Seizable Items Are in Vehicle

When Permitted. . . . Whenever a full-custody arrest is made of a person in a motor vehicle or of a person in close proximity to a motor vehicle from which he has just departed or into which he is about to enter, and the arresting officer has probable cause to believe that the vehicle contains seizable items [contraband, a weapon, anything used in committing a crime, loot, or other evidence of crime], the vehicle may be searched without a warrant for those items as soon as practicable.

Scope of the Search. An officer making a motor vehicle search under [this rule] may search only those areas of the vehicle which could physically contain the evidence sought.

Manner of the Search. Whenever possible, an officer shall open a locked trunk or glove compartment by means of a key rather than by force. If keys are not available, instructions shall be obtained from a superior as to the method to be used in opening the locked trunk or glove compartment.

Time and Place of the Search. It is not necessary to keep the prisoner near the vehicle during this type of search. Searches under [this rule] should be conducted at the scene of the arrest as soon as the prisoner is placed in secure custody. In those cases when it is not feasible to conduct the search at the scene of the arrest (e.g., hostile crowd, bad weather, heavy traffic, absence of needed equipment, delay so search warrant can be obtained, or unavailability of keys), the vehicle shall be secured in police custody at all times until it is searched, and the search shall be conducted as soon as practicable.

Search of Vehicle Passengers. If, following a search of a motor vehicle under [this rule], the officer has not found the seizable item sought, he may search the occupants of the vehicle if (1) the item he is seeking could be concealed on the person and (2) he has reason to suspect that a passenger has the item. This search may be made even though the officer does not have probable cause to arrest the passenger.

"Frisk" of Vehicle Passengers. If the officer reasonably suspects that a passenger in the motor vehicle is armed, he may "frisk" him for weapons.[11]

Rules such as these would provide officers with much better guidance than they receive from their own reading of cases, the interpretations provided by commentators, or even the manuals that are available, which distill the holdings of the cases into general statements.

Davis's concept of *structuring* discretion takes over within such narrowed confines of discretion "to control the manner of the exercise of discretionary power within the boundaries," to "regularize it, organize it, produce order in it, so that [administrators'] decisions affecting individual parties will achieve a higher quality of justice." He suggests seven methods of structuring: plans, policy statements, rules, findings, reasons, precedents, and fair informal procedure.[12]

Davis's third process, *checking* discretion, derives from the American experience with judicial review of executive and legislative action, but it is a broader process than the usual review of a subordinate by a superior. Instead, checking would be "by a colleague on the same level, or by one or more subordinates, by legislative committees or their staffs, by an official critic known as an ombudsman, by private organizations, by the press, by an administrative appellate tribunal, or by a reviewing court."[13] This, too, would make for a complicated process of policing.

Above all, Davis emphasizes that each method was to be *open* because "Openness is the natural enemy of arbitrariness and a natural ally in the fight against injustice." This would bring another new dimension, "government in the sunshine," to law enforcement.

Davis's views were reflected in the American Bar Association (ABA) and National Advisory Commission recommendations. Like Davis, the ABA's Advisory Committee on the Police Function appreciated the need for discretion: "The nature of the responsibilities currently placed upon the police requires that the police exercise a great deal of discretion—a situation that has long existed but is not always recognized."[14] Again, like Davis, the committee recognized that police discretion should be limited: "Since individual police officers may make important decisions affecting police operations without direction, with limited accountability, and without any uniformity within a department, police discretion should be structured and controlled."[15] The commission expressed doubt that the legislatures would accomplish much "confining" of discretion through statutory redefinitions, so it took the approach Davis had urged, of administrative responsiblity:

> Police discretion can best be structured and controlled through the process of administrative rule-making by police agencies. Police administrators should, therefore, give the highest priority to the formulation of administrative rules governing the exercise of discretion, particularly in the areas of selective enforcement, investigative techniques, and enforcement methods.[16]

With Davis on yet another point, the commission urged open rule-making: "In its development of procedures to openly formulate, implement, and reevaluate police policy as necessary, each jurisdiction should be conscious of the need to effectively involve a representative cross-section of citizens in this process."[17]

The ABA Commission then presented a range of "checking" approaches "for ensuring that the police are made fully accountable to their police administrator and to the public for their actions." Among the methods they urged were education and training; rewards or status, compensation and promotion; supervision by prosecutors and judges; development of policies; community involvement; sanctions such as exclusion of evidence, criminal and tort liability of officer and agency; injunctions; local complaint-handling procedures; internal, departmental administrative review; and external review by civilian review boards and ad hoc groups.[18]

Not long afterward, the National Advisory Commission on Criminal Justice Standards and Goals, a commission appointed by the Administrator of the Law Enforcement Assistance Administration, reporting in 1973, likewise reflected Davis's views:

> Every police agency should acknowledge the existence of the broad range of administrative and operational discretion that is exercised by all police agencies and individual officers. The acknowledgement should take the form of comprehensive police statements that publicly establish the limits of discretion, that provide guidelines for its exercise within those limits, and that eliminate discriminatory enforcement of the law.[19]

The commission urged interplay between police agency and legislature, as Davis had, aimed at confining discretion by eliminating the wide-ranging authority that enhances discretion of the sort likely to produce undesirable results:

> Every police chief executive should have the authority to establish his agency's fundamental objectives and priorities and to implement them through discretionary allocation and control of agency resources. In the exercise of his authority, every chief executive:
> - (a) Should seek legislation that grants him the authority to exercise his discretion in allocating police resourcee and in establishing his agency's fundamental objectives and priorities;
> - (b) Should review all existing criminal statutes, determine the ability of the agency to enforce these statutes effectively, and advise the legislature of the statutes' practicality from an enforcement standpoint; and
> - (c) Should advise the legislature of the practicality of each proposed criminal statute from an enforcement standpoint, and the impact of such proposed statutes on the ability of the agency to maintain the existing level of police services.[20]

Rule-making, incidentally, bears upon the exclusionary rule, as the ABA Advisory Committee's commentary once indicated:

> . . . the conclusion reached with increasing frequency is that the exclusionary rule either must be made more effective, by means such as [stimulation by legislatures and courts of rule-making efforts by police agencies] or must be supplemented, and perhaps eventually replaced, by much more effective and less costly methods, particularly effective administrative control over police behavior.[21]

Rule-Making and the Community

The approach to the problem of police discretion is (according to these recommendations) to be implemented by the police in consultation with the community. This means that the different organizations and the multitude of individuals comprising the police, on the one hand, and the community, on the other hand, must somehow be connected. Varying interests must be brought together in structured ways for channeling information, sustaining deliberation, focusing decisions, and carrying them out. The police and the community must, in a complex process, focus their efforts on the selection and balance of functions, the design of specific limits on police authority, particular techniques of intervention and disposition, and specification of rights and remedies—down to the dotting of *i*'s and the crossing of *t*'s in each phrase of the rules.

The open quality of the rule-making approach was suggested by Davis and recommended by the ABA Advisory Committee with reference to certain major institutions of the community (the legal profession, the colleges and universities, and the news media) and beyond, to a more generalized relationship: "Each jurisdiction should be conscious of the need to effectively involve a representative cross-section of citizens in this process." The President's Crime Commission's Police Task Force had suggested advisory committees made up of citizens in the policy-making process: "The citizens' advisory group or policymaking board has the advantage of involving the community in the decision-making process, thus giving a broader base than would otherwise exist for the acceptance and support of enforcement policies."

The National Advisory Commission on Criminal Justice Standards and Goals was even more explicit:

> Every police chief executive should provide for maximum participation in the policy formulation process. This participation should include at least:

   (a) Input from all levels within the agency

   (b) Input from outside the agency as appropriate—from other government agencies, community organizations, and the specific community affected.[22]

The Commission's commentary elaborated on that last point:

> Formal and informal contacts with governmental agencies, business and professional groups, labor organizations, other private groups or individuals known to have interest or expertise, police-community meetings, and community surveys are among the means that might be used.[23]

The openness of the rule-making process relates to the general effort of the police to relate to the community, as the National Advisory Commission recommended:

> Every police agency should recognize the importance of bilateral communication with the public and should constantly seek to improve its ability to determine the needs and expectations of the public, to act upon those needs and expectations, and to inform the public of the resulting policies developed to improve delivery of police services.[24]

The Commission urged special attention to racial and ethnic minorities and to non-English-speaking persons. It also called for a specialized unit "built-in" to the larger agencies. Such units would attend to police-community relations on a full-time basis, building and maintaining lines of communication and gathering information about community sentiment.

The Police, the Community, and Politics

The rule-making approach, if it were coupled with such openness to the community, would involve the police deeply in the community, drawing on it for its input on goals and objectives, limitations on authority, and limitations on discretion. The other side of the coin, when the police don't measure up, requires the development of mechanisms of accountability and calls for yet another conjunction of police and community: in the means by which complaints are registered, examined, and disposed of. If the police are to be held responsbile for their actions, there must be some control by the community. The community must relate closely to the process by which sanctions are leveled against the party at fault. The accountability process, like the rule-making process, with emphasis on responsibility, plunges the police deeply into the thicket of values, beliefs, principles, opinions, interests, prejudices—in short, into the politics of the community at its deepest levels, in the sense of politics discussed in Chapter 7.

This involvement of the police in politics collides with long-held beliefs and institutional constraints that are opposed to the mixing of politics and police. This tradition of nonpolitical law enforcement began in America soon after corruption itself began to grow—which was immediately after the formation of the first municipal police departments, before the Civil War. Corruption was rightly recognized as related to politics. Some of the early characteristics of police agencies, deriving from the populistic democracy of those Jacksonian times—such as elected police chiefs, appointment of police for short terms, direct political control of political boards, and partisan influence throughout—were eliminated in favor of reforms such as state control of local police and "civil service" aimed at protecting the police and their department from the patronage or "spoils" system of politics (to the victors go the spoils, including police jobs and promotions). Many restrictions were placed on the police to keep them from involvement in politics. They were kept from holding office, running for office, campaigning for candidates, contributing financially to candidates, and engaging in political activity, such as membership in political parties or clubs. Such restrictions are still common, although they are being moderated in many places, mainly under the force of the First Amendment (free speech permits even public employees to engage in political speech and other activity deemed to be "assembly and petition").

The effort to purge policing of politics has not been completely successful, even though the worst excesses of party influence on the police have been virtually eliminated. James Q. Wilson calls attention to the presence (in only two of the eight cities he studied) of police involvement in politics "in the narrow sense," mainly influence by the political machine. The other cities, however, were not exempt from a kind of politics that is all but unavoidable—the influence of political culture, the influence of "community interests and expectations." As Wilson puts it:

> . . . The community is a source of cues and signals—some tacit, some explicit—about how various police situations should be handled, what level of public order is deemed appropriate, and what distinctions among persons ought to be made. Finally, the police are keenly aware of the extent to which the city government does or does not intervene in the department on behalf of particular interests.
>
> Thus, police work is carried out under the influence of a *political culture* though not necessarily under day-to-day political direction. By political culture is meant those widely shared expectations as to how issues will be

raised, governmental objectives determined, and power for their attainment assembled; it is an understanding of what makes a government legitimate.[25]

Not only is politics of the partisan kind persistent and politics of the cultural kind unavoidable, but the police are driven into politics by yet another factor in addition to the thrust of the rule-making approach. This additional factor is corruption. Despite the removal of the police from the most excessive forms of political influence, corruption has continued and it plagues the police and the public to this day. The most complete study of corruption was done by the Knapp Commission appointed by Mayor John V. Lindsay of New York City. From its 1973 report the public has learned the lingo of corruption: *pad* means regular payoffs at monthly or biweekly intervals; *score* means a one-time payoff; *gratuities* are small, occasional, but sometimes regular payoffs like a cup of coffee or a meal or a Christmas payment. We have learned the amounts involved: Scores of $5,000 to $50,000 are not uncommon—even a $250,000 narcotics payoff (reliably rumored but unverified); pads high enough that the "nut" or share to each participating officer could come to $300 or $400 per month in midtown Manhattan and $1500 in Harlem. We have learned that the factors influencing corruption are, in order of their influence, the officer's character, department branch (plainclothes detectives have more opportunity than uniformed officers), area (Harlem, as noted, and certain other parts of the city are more lucrative), assignment (mobile duty makes for more opportunity than guard duty), and rank (the higher the more money).

The Commission's recommendations included many of an internal, managerial sort, such as the creation of an Inspectional Service Bureau; complete and centralized personnel records so investigators can obtain information on suspected officers more easily; adequate expense money, especially "buy money" for undercover narcotics purchases and payments to informers, so officers will not obtain their expense money corruptly; assignment of rookies to carefully screened senior officers (who would comprise a new classification of "Master Patrolmen") as partners to minimize socialization into corruption; creation of incentives to meritorious behavior.

Other recommendations involved collaboration of police and public. To reduce exposure of officers to corruption, the Commission recommended the repeal of criminal laws against gambling and prostitution, and recommended the control of them, if at all, by civil measures; development of noncriminal measures of narcotics control; and regulation of business by nonpolice agencies. To reduce temptations, the Commission recommended using special investigators to detect bribe offers and penalize bribers. To exert attitude changes, the Commission recommended lateral entry into supervisory ranks and a National Police Academy, like the military academies, to prepare highly qualified candidates for lateral entry into police careers. Finally, to cultivate public support, the Commission recommended providing progress reports to citizens complaining of instances of corrupt conduct, and by providing the public, especially the media, with periodic reports of action taken in corruption cases.[26]

Lawrence W. Sherman reviewed the experience with police corruption in four cities, including New York City, which had experienced recent scandals, and found that corruption had reached high levels in police organization for some of the reasons the Knapp Commission identified, such as opportunities presented by policing victimless crimes and demands of motorists and merchants for favoritism. Outside of New York City he found that politicians were part of the problem of police corruption.[27] Thus, it appears that there is a close relationship between the police and the public, directly or through politicians, for dishonest purposes. The need is for a relationship with honest purposes.But it will still be a political relationship because it will require deliberation and decisions on the laws the community wants and how it wants them enforced.

An inventory of the political aspects of law enforcement cannot ignore recent developments that have "politicized" the police. One is the emergence in the 1960s of "law and order" as a political issue emphasizing the police. This has made their purposes a political issue, raising questions in the political arena of what the police do and do not do, and what they should and should not do. The supporters of the police emphasize what the police should do, usually overestimating what they can do. The politicization has also been in a negative vein with the attack on the police "pigs" in the 1960s as a symbol of the authority against which countless demonstrations were mounted. These called attention to what the police should not do. The police themselves have aggressively "politicked" on certain issues, such as the Civilian Review Board in New York City in the mid-1960s. In addition, policemen have emerged as political leaders and two major cities, St. Paul and Philadelphia, have elected former policemen as mayors.

The police are in politics for yet another but less familiar reason. The very origin of the word *police* is the ancient Greek word *politeia,* which is the root of the words *polity, policy,* and *politics.* This links the police by definition to the political community (polity), to its governing purposes and principles (policy), and to the activities, science, art, and conduct of public affairs (politics). Indeed, an early meaning of police is not institutional (police department), but functional: "The regulation and control of a community, especially for the maintenance of public order, safety, health, morals, etc."[28] Thus, the definitions suggest that the police are central to the politics of the community. It may well be that the problem of politics and the police has not been one of too much to do with each other but of too much to do of the wrong kind.

The idea of involving the police in politics need not be alarming. Politics is of course highly charged, sometimes even explosive: when ballots won't do, bullets will. But the police officer deals daily with highly emotional issues, many of them explosive in the most literal sense. The patrol officer becomes an expert in "the art of the possible." He knows rough-and-tumble, give-and-take. If politics is the "authoritative allocation of values," as political scientist David Easton put it in a very influential definition, the police officer does it all the time. He or she strikes the street-level balance among the values of order, liberty, freedom, and law. He designs adjustments and accommodations, on the spot and instantaneously, even if only by intuition. They live that cardinal virtue of democracy, tolerance, and they bring harmony where there is discord. If not successful all of the time in the practice of politics in these senses, the police officer is successful often enough that the community might have some confidence in the ability of the police to play a higher role in the politics of allocating values, harmonizing discord, striking balances, and making adjustments at the level of policy and rules. An understanding of the political character of the police and their promise for effective leadership in the higher politics of community life is the basis for the working through—and perhaps working out—of the final area of difficulty in this chapter. It is to the vexing problem of dissonance in police authority that we now turn.

Dissonance of Legality and Legitimacy

Dissonance is an issue that is emerging now in law enforcement that is best taken up at this point—after the problem of discretion and some of the proposed solutions have been surveyed, including involvement of the police in the politics of the community. The issue, put simply, is that in law enforcement the legal is sometimes illegitimate, and the legitimate is sometimes illegal. In other words, what police officers are empowered to do (that is, to arrest) may be—and often is—inappropriate. Conversely, what may be—and usually is—appropriate in the circumstances is not within their power. Specifically, in the recurring situation of domestic dispute between spouses, what police have the legal authority to do, that is, make an arrest of one party or another for some offense (and ordinarily there is an offense present in a strictly legalistic interpretation: the husband has hit the wife or she has threatened him), is often counterproductive. Instead, a more sensible course, even if it is not a permanent solution, is to compel the husband to leave (to cool off in a movie or a motel), or to remove the wife and children to a shelter of some sort. But the police have no authority to do that—except by coercing the action under the threat of more severe consequences if they arrest one or the other.

James Q. Wilson noted the dissonance between the imperatives of maintaining order (and not always by means of legal instruments such as arrest) and enforcing the law (which is generally thought to be done only with legal instruments):

> Some or all of these examples of disorderly behavior (a fight, a tavern brawl, and an assault on an unfaithful lover) involve infractions of the law; any intervention by the police is at least under the color of the law and in fact might be viewed as an "enforcement" of the law. A judge, examining the matter after the fact, is likely to see the issue wholly in these terms. But the patrolman does not. Though he may use the law to make an arrest, just as often he will do something else, such as tell people to "knock if off," "break it up," "go home and sober up." In his eyes even an arrest does not always end his involvement in the matter. In some sense he was involved in settling a dispute; if and how he settled it is important both to the parties involved and to the officer himself.[29]

The ABA Advisory Committee elaborated on the ways in which the officer intervenes in these and other disorderly matters to settle them, short of arrests for the specific conduct involved:

1. Resolving conflicts, for example, disputes between individuals such as husbands and wives, landlords and tenants, neighbors, business people and their customers; and disputes between groups, such as protesters and an agency of government, one religious sect and another, one racial group and another, labor and management, etc.
2. Ordering people to move away from a particular site, for example, spectators or bystanders at the scene of an accident, crime, fire, or conflict; the persons involved in a conflict that erupts or threatens to erupt in one of the situations described in [1] above; or at the scene of a parade, speech, or an informal gathering.
3. Stopping and questioning people, for example, on suspicion of criminal activity, with regard to the criminal activity of others, or merely to acquire information with which to carry out any of the wide variety of activities for which the police are responsible.
4. Taking or sending people to locations where they can get immediate help or shelter, for example, to their own residences, a hotel or residence of friends or relatives; or a hospital, mental institution, detoxification center, or temporary shelter for the young or the aged.
5. Finding caretakers for people unable to take care of themselves, for example, a spouse, parent, or other relative, a friend or neighbor.

6. Referring matters to court for private prosecution, for example, informing parties to a dispute that they may seek to initiate a prosecution on their own by filing a complaint with a court, which, if approved, will result in the issuance of a warrant or a summons.

7. Referring matters to an agency or individual in a position to provide assistance, for example, another governmental agency, a private social agency, a minister, a health service, or a lawyer.

8. Issuing warnings (with or without threat of subsequent surveillance), for example, putting a person on notice not to do a certain act, not to omit doing a certain act, not to repeat an action or to continue to fail to act, to stay away from an area or to get out of a certain area.

9. Threatening to report, for example, issuance of instructions to correct a condition or to cease from engaging in a specific form of activity with the threat that a continuance will result in a report being made to, for example, a governmental agency, parents, school officials, an employer, a spouse, etc.

10. Engaging in surveillance, for example, keeping a situation under observation—overtly or covertly—with the objective of acquiring additional information or evidence, with the objective of providing a sense of security, or with the objective of discouraging certain forms of activity.

11. Frisking and searching of persons and searching of vehicles and premises, for example, in connection with an arrest or, independent of an arrest, as a means of protecting an officer, acquiring evidence of a crime, acquiring information generally, or simply making the presence of the police known.

12. Confiscating illegal objects, for example, drugs, guns, gambling devices, paraphernalia, or money—either in connection with an arrest or simply as a means of removing such items from use and circulation.

13. Trading immunity from enforcement for information or cooperation, for example, allowing a narcotics user, a petty gambler, or a prostitute to continue to operate despite evidence of a violation of the law in exchange for their providing information leading to the identity and prosecution of those engaged in more serious forms of behavior.

14. Detaining persons temporarily, for example, the use of arrest and subsequent detention for purposes other than prosecution, such as further investigation, safekeeping, or simply harassment.[30]

The ABA Advisory Committee observed:

> Some of the methods currently being employed by the police are contrary to law. Others are without lawful authority, neither permitted nor prohibited by law. Some are within the scope of lawful authority, but of a questionable effectiveness or propriety. Many of the methods used are sensible, fair, and practical responses to problems that confront the police.[31]

For instance, the method of detention for investigation, safe keeping, or harassment is contrary to law (except perhaps in extreme cases of persons suspected of having critical information pertaining to a kidnapping in progress or a bombing or skyjacking incident announced but not yet taking place). Resolving conflicts (at least by persuasion, "human relations" techniques, or recently developed "conflict management" methods) and stopping and questioning people are in a limbo between actions clearly permitted and prohibited to the police. The police officer's authority to detain a suspect after asking a question and getting no answer has not yet been resolved by the United States Supreme Court. Surveillance is of questionable effectiveness for providing security and of questionable propriety for discouraging certain forms of activity. However, many of the other methods and some varieties even of the interventions given above are quite "sensible, fair and practical."

The police power to arrest or to use or threaten to use force has been grudgingly granted, in jealous protection of constitutional liberties. Less attention has been given to techniques *less* heavy-handed than arrest. Although there is no or doubtful authority to do most of the other things the police do, Goldstein points out that most of those actions "may seem less disruptive and intrusive than an arrest made with the intention of prosecution." Such actions do give rise to complaints because they interfere with the individual; some, moreover, because they are illegal now. Nevertheless, Goldstein's central point is very important:

> . . . one of the values in identifying these alternative forms of action is to
> subject them to more careful scrutiny, with the full expectation that
> this will result in some current police practices being eliminated, some
> being modified, and some, although currently illegal but apparently
> desirable, being legally authorized. Limited forms of authority, if
> provided, will obviate the need for a more disruptive form of
> intervention.[32]

Goldstein says the alternative modes of disposition of cases, like the alternative modes of intervention, should be recognized and, where legitimate, legalized:

> Rather than perpetuate the notion that these police actions outside of the
> criminal justice system are reluctantly and infrequently employed, it
> is far preferable—especially given their frequency—to recognize them as
> clear and, if properly used, appropriate alternatives.[33]

Thus the juvenile-justice system, hospitalization, lesser criminal laws (such as city ordinances, carrying lower penalties), mediation, referral to other agencies, providing information, recommendation of prosecution by the individual apart from the officer's intervention, arranging temporary custody, and doing nothing at all—are in many instances fully legitimate alternatives to the criminal-justice system. The engagement of police and community in rule-making must focus on them.

The ABA Task Force's understanding of this issue led it to this recommendation:

> The process of investigation, arrest, and prosecution, commonly viewed as an end in itself, should be recognized as but one of the methods used by police in performing their overall function, even though it is the most important method of dealing with serious criminal activity. Among other methods police use are, for example, the process of informal resolution of conflict, referral, and warning. The alternative methods used by police should be recognized as important and warranting improvement in number and effectiveness: and the police should be given the necessary authority to use them under circumstances in which it is desirable to do so.[34]

The National Advisory Commission later made a similar recommendation on alternatives to arrest, subject to appropriate limitations:

> Every police chief executive should establish policy that guides the exercise of discretion by police personnel in using arrest alternatives. This policy:
>
> (a) Should establish the limits of discretion by specifically identifying, insofar as possible, situations calling for the use of alternatives to continued physical custody;
>
> (b) Should establish criteria for the selection of appropriate enforcement alternatives;
>
> (c) Should require enforcement action to be taken in all situations where all elements of a crime are present and all policy criteria are satisfied.[35]

On the value of this Goldstein concluded:

> Acknowledging the various dispositions used by the police in this manner achieves several desired objectives. It identifies the criminal justice system as but one of the several forms of disposition available to the police and, therefore, places the system in more appropriate perspective vis-à-vis the totality of police functioning. It reflects the abandonment of the concept that the system is the principal means by which the police operate. Identification of the alternative dispositions gives recognition and proper status to methods commonly and properly employed by the police which, in the past, have often been viewed as questionable or less satisfactory than the criminal justice system. And it makes more apparent the need to

provide police with adequate forms of disposition for the matters they are called upon to handle.[36]

The systems analysis urged in Chapter 7 combines with the crime analysis called for in Chapter 9 as the foundation for the identification of the auxilliaries of the police department and the other agencies of the criminal-justice system and the approaches that can make police intervention more effective.

It will objected—and in matters as important as these powers of the state it *must* be objected—that the authority to arrest is sufficient, that arrest alone should be used, that arrest implies all of the lesser powers urged in these recommendations, and that the protections against abuse of arrest are well developed. But there are simply too many situations that call for action less severe than arrest, and the protections in the limitations on the arresting power are not fully effective guarantees against abuse of the lesser alternatives. As the ABA Task Force's commentary stated,

> . . . the naive assumption that police need only authority to arrest has resulted in such ambiguity that the potential for abuse is greater than it would be if adequate attention were given to determining what kinds of authority police do need and then carefully defining the specific authority which is needed (to assist a drunk, settle a family disturbance, disperse a crowd).[37]

The arresting power does not include the lesser powers except by the intimidating effect of the threat of arrest. That may create the appearance of acquiescence to a patrol officer order, but it is in truth merely a consent to "an offer you cannot refuse." Instead, as the committee argues,

> The use of some alternative methods such as taking the drunk to a detoxification center, an order to "move on," or a "stop and frisk" raises important police questions which ought to be squarely faced, as was done in *Terry* v. *Ohio,* rather than assuming the existence or nonexistence of the authority based upon an analysis of the authority to arrest in the particular situation.

Moreover, the committee continued, "There are instances in which the police ought not to be able to make an arrest when other more effective, less intrusive methods are available."[38]

And that is a final challenge on this frontier of constitutional development: To mark out the limits of police authority, where it should be *less* than the power to arrest, perhaps *even* when an offense has been committed but committed within a context of other considerations which justify something less than the heaviest, although legal, power of arrest. And that is a task that calls for discriminating analysis, sensitive to the heritage of liberty yet responsive to the situational imperatives of modern policing.

SUMMARY

This chapter examined police discretion, the idea of government under law, and the need for some flexibility in law enforcement. It looked at several reasons for *selective enforcement,* some of which are legitimate, others illegitimate. It examined Davis's approach to discretion: confining, structuring, and checking it. Then it put this "rule-making" approach into the context of the community and the politics in which the police would find themselves involved as they consulted with the elements of the community in the development of rules on police functions and procedures.

The chapter then took up the dissonance of legality and legitimacy, or the conflict between legal means to illegitimate ends and nonlegal means to legitimate ends. The rule-making approach, with its consultation in the community, was suggested as an approach to bringing about a consonance of ends and means.

NOTES

1. Wayne R. LaFave, *Arrest: The Decision to Take a Suspect into Custody* (Boston: Little, Brown, 1965), p. 63.
2. Jerome H. Skolnick, *Justice Without Trial,* 3rd ed. (New York: Wiley, 1975), p. 6.
3. Kenneth Culp Davis, *Police Discretion* (St. Paul, Minn.: West, 1975), pp. 80–82.
4. The President's Commission on Law Enforcement and Administration of Justice, *The Challenge of Crime in a Free Society* (Washington, D.C.: U.S. Government Printing Office, 1967), p. 10.
5. Nathan Goldman, *The Differential Selection of Juvenile Offenders for Court Appearance* (Hackensack, N.J.: National Council on Crime and Delinquency, 1963), pp. 129–132.
6. LaFave, *Arrest,* pp. 83–143.
7. Ibid., pp. 144–152.
8. Herman Goldstein, *Policing a Free Society* (Cambridge, Mass.: Ballinger, 1977), pp. 94–99.
9. Kenneth Culp Davis, *Discretionary Justice* (Urbana, Ill.: Universtiy of Illinois, 1971), pp. 52–96.
10. Ibid., p. 57.
11. Project on Law Enforcement Policy and Rulemaking, *Searches, Seizures and Inventories of Motor Vehicles* (Tempe, Ariz.: Arizona State University College of Law, *no date*), pp. 6–9.
12. Ibid., pp. 97–141.
13. Ibid., p. 142.
14. Task Force on Urban Police Function, *Urban Police Function,* 2nd ed., Tentative Draft approved February 12, 1979 (Washington, D.C.: American Bar Association, 1979), p. 43.
15. Ibid., p. 44.

16. Ibid., p. 46.
17. Ibid., p. 49.
18. Ibid., pp. 60–70.
19. National Advisory Commission on Criminal Justice Standards and Goals, *Police* (Washington, D.C.: U.S. Government Printing Office, 1973), p. 21.
20. Ibid., p. 21.
21. Advisory Committee on the Police Function, Task Force on Urban Police Function, *Urban Police Function,* Tentative Draft (Chicago: American Bar Association, 1972), p. 158. The Committee did not, however, make the same statement in the second edition.
22. National Advisory Commission, *Police,* p. 53.
23. Ibid., p. 54.
24. Ibid., p. 29.
25. James Q. Wilson, *Varieties of Police Behavior* (New York: Atheneum, 1975), p. 233.
26. *The Knapp Commission Report on Police Corruption* (New York: George Briziller, 1973).
27. Lawrence W. Sherman, *Controlling Police Corruption* (Washington, D.C.: Law Enforcement Assistance Administration, 1978).
28. *The Random House Dictionary of the English Language* (New York: Random House, 1966), p. 1112.
29. Wilson, *Varieties of Police Behavior,* p. 17.
30. Task Force on Urban Police Function, *Urban Police Function,* p. 29.
31. Ibid., p. 28.
32. Goldstein, *Policing a Free Society,* p. 38.
33. Ibid., p. 39.
34. Task Force on Urban Police Function, *Urban Police Function,* p. 27.
35. National Advisory Commission, *Police,* p. 21.
36. Goldstein, *Policing a Free Society,* pp. 40–41.
37. Task Force on Urban Police Function, *Urban Police Function,* pp. 33–34.
38. Ibid., p. 34.

SELECTED READINGS

American Bar Association, *The Urban Police Function* (Chicago: American Bar Association, 1972).

Burton Atkins and Mark Pogrebin, *The Invisible Justice System: Discretion and the Law* (Cincinnati, Ohio: Anderson, 1978).

Kenneth Culp Davis, *Discretionary Justice: A Preliminary Inquiry* (Urbana: University of Illinois Press, 1971).

———*Police Discretion* (St. Paul, Minn.: West, 1975).

Herman Goldstein, *Policing a Free Society* (Cambridge, Mass.: Ballinger, 1977).

Wayne R. LaFave, *Arrest: The Decision to Take Suspect into Custody* (Boston: Little, Brown, 1965).

William Ker Muir, Jr., *Police: Streetcorner Politicians* (Chicago: University of Chicago Press, 1977).

National Advisory Commission on Criminal Justice Standards and Goals, *The Police* (Washington, D.C.: Law Enforcement Assistance Adminstration, 1973).

Charles E. Silberman, "The Wisdom of Solomon, the Patience of Job: What the Police Do—and Don't Do," in *Criminal Violence, Criminal Justice* (New York: Random House, 1978), pp. 199–252.

Jerome Skolnick, *Justice Without Trial,* 2nd ed. (New York: Wiley, 1975).

James Q. Wilson, *Varieties of Police Behavior* (New York: Atheneum, 1975).

Four

THE POLICE OFFICER TODAY AND TOMORROW: THE PERSON, THE PROFESSIONAL

Part Four plunges into the aspects of law enforcement that are growing in importance. One is the study of the police officer's "human dimension." The officer is far from a robot programmed to patrol with emotionless efficiency; instead, he or she is a very human being, with a full set of frailties and feelings, who is called upon time and time again to make extraordinarily difficut decisions under the most trying of conditions in a complex kind of "people work." The police officer's decisions on the street call for much more than a law enforcement agent—the officer must be a practitioner of law, social worker, psychiatrist, psychologist, even a paramedic and much more. Chapter 12 deals with these aspects of the police officer, including the influences on attitudes and behavior, the exercise of discretion beyond—and even in conflict with—the law and departmental rules and regulations. Special attention is paid to the informal but very important impact of an officer's peers on both the perception of the work role and the behavior in it, especially the additional tension between the expectations of peers and the formal organization.

Chapter 13 focuses on a special aspect of what novelist and former policeman Joseph Wambaugh has called "emotionally the most dangerous job in the world," one involving high levels of pressure. The social, emotional, and physical stresses of police work are examined in detail as they arise out of anticipations of danger, exercise of authority, disruptions of normal rhythms of life, marital frictions, and stress-related physical ailments such as coronary disease, diabetes, ulcers, and low back pain, all of which take a heavy toll on those in law enforcement work.

This final part of the book comes to its conclusion with the Chapter 14 examination of a quite different, yet highly personal aspect of policing—its professionalization. The chapter concentrates on the qualities of traditional professions—how law enforcement compares and how it measures up to an alternative conception of professionalism (which emphasizes rational, managerial aspects of law enforcement). It reviews the controversy over the relationship of higher education to law enforcement and attempts to resolve the issue by discriminating among three kinds of knowledge in law enforcement and the three modes of learning that correspond to them: experience, training academy, and university. The chapter concludes with the pros and cons of professionalization and its prospects for the future.

12

THE POLICE OFFICER TODAY: THE HUMAN DIMENSION

People in our society typically display a great deal of misunderstanding about the nature of police officers and their work. Seldom is the police officer thought of as simply another human being—a worker, a spouse, a parent, a taxpayer—someone possessed of basically the same feelings, strengths, and weaknesses as other people. Irrespective of whether the police are revered as heros and champions of law and order or reviled as facists and foes of individual liberty, they and the things they do remain somehow qualitatively different, set apart from the rest of society. In the course of considering police officers as fellow human beings involved in the complex business of "people work," we will examine and seek to dispel widely held myths and stereotypes about who police officers are and what they do.

The Nature of Police Work

The term *police work* immediately brings to the public mind a kaleidoscope of remarkably consistent and predictable images: a police car with siren wailing and lights flashing as it races to the scene of a robbery in progress; a patrol officer crouched in combat position with gun trained on an armed suspect; a detective (replete with trenchcoat and quizzical expression) examining the scene of a crime or interrogating a suspect. Our thinking about the nature of what the police do is dominated by a conception of them as basically crime fighters, "supercops" whose days and nights are made up of an unending stream of exciting and dangerous experiences as they wage war on crime. The very expression *war on crime,* which became popular during the sixties and still lingers on, inescapably leads to a conception of the police officer as a front-line domestic soldier, a kind of urban guerrilla enlisted on the side of law and order.

Our tendency to think of today's police officer as exclusively preoccupied with crime is no accident. Rather, it is the direct result of our particular history and culture. Over a period of many decades, Americans have been socialized to view the police from the standpoint of what has been called a Dick Tracy mentality. Robert Carter explains the origin of this perspective:

> ... the 1920's and early 1930's were difficult times for America and Americans. Prohibition, followed by the Great Depression, and combined with gross deficiencies in law enforcement contributed to mounting frustrations about crime and criminals. Out of these frustrations, skilled cartoonists such as Chester Gould, Jerome Siegel and Joe Schuster, and Bob Kane produced mythical, make-believe crimefighters who could "stamp out crime" on the street. A new breed of American heroes—SUPERcrime-fighters—was inked on drawing boards and a tradition was born. ... These new heroes were created and were continued in the media—the comic strips, the comic ('funny') books, radio, television and the wide screen of the neighborhood theatre.[1]

The line separating the real police officer from his or her media-created counterpart has become ever more blurred over the years. Today's citizen, steeped in an almost daily exposure to the behavior of television and motion picture "supercops," often imputes to the police in the community the same patterns of work activity and skills, and the ability to ferret out crime and criminals successfully. It follows that the citizen is accordingly dismayed—if not outraged—by the seeming inability of real police officers to maintain a level of success in dealing with crime which is comparable to that of the media police. Because the citizen expects resolution of even the most complex crimes and the arrest of a suspect in the space of a 30- or 60-minute television program (with time out for commercials) our citizen is astonished to read in the morning newspaper that the police actually clear by arrest only about 21 percent of all serious crimes reported to them.[2]

Despite the seeming inability of the police to deal effectively with rising crime rates, the public has clung even more tenaciously in recent years to a media-derived faith in their omnipotence when it comes to the subject of crime. It is almost impossible to overemphasize the importance of the mass media—particularly television, which commands an ever greater portion of the daily attention of citizens—in shaping American perceptions of the police and the work they perform. The media, likewise, exert a strong influence on the ways the police view themselves as well as the things they do. The sociologist Charles Horton Cooley long ago pointed out that each of us comes to fashion a self-concept on the basis of the feedback we receive from others as to what kind of person they see us as being—something that Cooley called the *looking-glass conception of self.*[3] If the collective mirror of self made up by the public reflects an image back to the police that identifies them primarily as crime fighters and calls upon them to do certain things based on television and motion picture impressions of their work, they will behave accordingly, to a large extent. As a case in point, few experienced police officers have not at some point in their careers found themselves consciously or unconsciously playing into media stereotypes of their role. Thus, for example, the patrol officer carefully picks up a discarded soft-drink bottle with a pen while he is on a prowler call (and discards it a few blocks away), simply because of a citizen's insistence that it might have some evidential value. Or he heroically (but imprudently) drives at breakneck speed in pursuit of a traffic violator, or rushes a building known to contain an armed mental patient, because television police regularly do such things and the public holds the same set of role expectations for their real-life counterparts. Goldstein has written of the extent to which the working behavior of investigators is heavily influenced by media-derived stereotypes of police detectives:

> The extent to which the police detective has been popularized—in fiction, in motion pictures, and on television—has had a profound effect upon the way police detectives actually operate. Many of the techniques employed by detectives today are more heavily influenced by a desire to imitate stereotypes than by a rational plan for solving crimes. The myths and fantasy that pervade detective operations deter the police and the public from examining the utility of what it is that detectives in fact do.[4]

Most of the stereotypes held about police work by the public center upon the belief that most of a officer's work time is spent dealing with criminals and enforcing laws. These stereotypes depart radically from the actual nature of the occupational role. While estimates of the percentage of time devoted to law-enforcement matters vary somewhat from city to city, studies make it abundantly clear that the average officer spends only a small part of his or her normal work hours dealing with the business of crime and criminals. The vast majority of the officer's day is consumed by activities that are best defined as order maintenance, conflict management, or peace keeping—rather than law enforcement. Wilson, for example, found in a study of the Syracuse, New York, police department that only 10 percent of the calls dispatched to officers were related to the enforcement of laws. About 30 percent were for order maintenance.[5] Similarly, in Chicago, only 22 percent of calls involved crimes against persons or property,[6] while in Kansas City the figure was 32 percent.[7] A national survey conducted for the International Association of Chiefs of Police reached the conclusion that "the percentage of the police effort devoted to the traditional criminal law matters probably does not exceed 10 percent."[8]

The kinds of things that the police spend most of their time doing—things that fall into such amorphous categories as "order maintenance" and "peacekeeping"—are many and varied. They encompass such diverse tasks as handling noise complaints; locating the owners of stray dogs; giving directions to motorists; helping citizens who are locked out of their homes or cars; dealing with the mentally ill, elderly, and infirm; and mediating interpersonal conflicts of every conceivable type.[9]

Some of the non-law-enforcement activities of the police might easily be performed by anyone of reasonably average intelligence. It takes little in the way of specialized skill or knowledge to write a parking ticket and place it on the windshield of a car, or to spot and report a broken street light. Other tasks routinely undertaken by police officers, however, would test the mettle of a well-trained psychiatrist or social worker. Family disturbances, for instance, represent some of the most difficult and sensitive nonenforcement problems regularly dealt with by the police. Indeed, some 22 percent of all police deaths and 40 percent of police injuries occur in the handling of domestic calls.[10] Whatever their particular level of education and training may be, police officers do not enjoy the luxury of confronting the disputants in a family argument after the fact, in the calm and neutral setting of a counselor's office. Rather, they must deal with them and other troubled, angry, frightened people in an atmosphere of charged emotion as the problem is actually unfolding. Patrol officers do not see the severely depressed mental patient in the antiseptic and controlled setting of the hospital psychiatric ward, but perhaps perched precariously on the ledge of a building and threatening to jump, or with a cocked revolver in his mouth. Given the fact that police officers must routinely deal with extremely complex human problems in a time frame of minutes, and sometimes seconds, the wonder is that they are so often successful in resolving—even if only temporarily—the situations that lead to their involvement. As the senior author wrote in the wake of spending some months working as a patrolman:

> I found myself progressively awed by the complexity of tasks faced by men whose work I once thought was fairly simple and straightforward. Indeed, I would like to take the average clinical psychologist or psychiatrist and invite him to function for just a day in the world of the policeman, to confront people whose problems are both serious and in need of immediate solution. . . . I would like the prison counselor and parole officer to see their "client," Jones—not calm and composed in an office setting, but as the street cop sees him: beating his small child with a heavy belt buckle, or kicking his pregnant wife.[11]

Because they are actors who are heavily involved in the business of dealing with other human beings under trying and stressful circumstances on a routine basis, one would expect that police officers would receive extensive training and preparation for the human dimension of their work. This is not the case. It has been pointed out repeatedly that the overwhelming majority of training received by police officers is devoted to preparing them strictly for law-enforcement activity—which will consume perhaps 10 or 15 percent of their occupational lives. So it is that today's officers are typically well-steeped in such subjects as criminal law, self-defense, and firearms use when they leave the police academy, but are sadly deficient in human relations skills.

A growing number of police departments in recent years, recognizing the failure to adequately equip officers to meet the social and psychological responsibilities of their profession, have initiated a variety of programs in the area of human relations and conflict management.[12] The continuing reluctance of most law-enforcement agencies to go beyond efforts aimed at preparing officers for their crime-fighting responsibilities alone must be related to the earlier mentioned matter of community expectations and public stereotypes about the things the police do. To apply the looking-glass concept on an organizational level, if citizens define police work as dealing entirely with criminal law enforcement, police agencies will structure both their training and work activity to correspond as closely as possible to this public definition of the situation.

Citizens' perceptions of police work as primarily law enforcement must be related not only to images conveyed by the mass media, but to impressions fostered by the police themselves. In an effort to allay public anxieties about crime, police departments typically project an exaggerated image of the amount of time and effort they devote to criminal matters, as well as their ability to deal successfully with them. The reluctance of many citizens to take seriously recent "Help Stop Crime" programs aimed at securing massive public involvement in crime prevention must be related at least in part to the fact that police agencies have traditionally assured citizens that they possess sufficient expertise and personnel resources to do the job alone.

For their part, the police have historically overemphasized their role as crime fighters and played down their more common work as keepers of the peace and providers of social services, simply because our society proffers rewards for the former but cares little for the latter. The public accords considerable recognition and esteem to the patrol officer who becomes involved in a shootout with an armed robber or who chases and apprehends a rapist, and therefore so do the officer's peers and superiors. However, little if any acclaim is extended to an officer who is exceptionally successful in dealing with mentally ill people or embattled husbands and wives. Similarly, a police department which can boast solutions and arrests in a number of very newsworthy cases has acquired considerable political leverage in its attempt to obtain such additional resources as raises, personnel, and equipment. A department which has launched a highly successful crisis intervention program or that is providing its line officers with valuable human-relations training receives no comparable gains either in its political strength or its standing in the community.

On a psychological level, the tendency of both the police and the public to define police work as something that basically involves dealing with crime and criminals can be meaningfully related to the physical symbols surrounding officers and their role. Such things as the gun, badge, handcuffs, and nightstick, which collectively comprise the everyday work tools of police officers, exert a powerful psychological impact on both the police and the public with whom they either interact or at least are observed by. However infrequently they may actually use these implements, they are inescapably powerful symbols that strongly proclaim their owners as people who are routinely preoccupied with crime and criminals. As Niederhoffer has observed, "The policeman is a 'Rorschach' in uniform. His occupational accoutrements—shield, nightstick, gun, and summons book—clothe him in a mantle of symbolism that stimulates fantasy and projection." [13]

Nowhere in this mantle of symbolism is there anything that defines police officers as people primarily involved in the business of social service and conflict management. Rather, every aspect of the physical persona they constantly present to themselves and others symbolically emphasizes their involvement with law violation and the use of force. Small wonder, then, that police officers typically experience a sense of role conflict in many of their attempts to interact with others on a helping or therapeutic level. Unlike social workers, psychiatrists, or counselors, each of whom usually interacts with willing clients in a neutral setting, without the presence of symbolic reminders of force and legal authority, police officers must typically confront an uncooperative clientele and do so in an atmosphere charged with coercive authority. Because the human mind naturally strives to maintain a state of internal harmony or consistency, it tends to reject elements of thought that produce conflict, or what Festinger terms *cognitive dissonance*. [14] In the case of police work, the attempt of officers to maintain a helping or service orientation frequently conflicts with the ideology of wielding authority and enforcing laws, and so often tends to be rejected in the interest of internal harmony and because the public, the police organization and the police subculture all place greater value on crime fighting than on peacekeeping activities.

Police Officers as People

"Most cops are on a big power trip—they really need to push people around." "Without that gun and badge they really feel insecure." "My next-door neighbor is a policeman. He seems like a pretty ordinary guy to me." Comments such as these reflect a debate that has long existed not only among the citizenry but among members of the social-science community as well. Just what kinds of people are police officers? In what ways are the roughly 600,000 people who make up American law enforcement different from workers in other occupations? Just what sorts of things seem to set them apart from other human beings in our society? We can attempt at least partial answers to these and other questions about police officers as people in light of modern research on the subject. We would do well to consider those aspects of police work that most readily distinguish it from other forms of work in American society.

DEALING WITH DANGER

Typically, each job generates its own ways of thinking and acting on the basis of activities it involves. As Skolnick observes, "Doctors, janitors, lawyers and industrial workers develop distinctive ways of perceiving and responding to their environment." [15] The same is true of police officers. Just as illness becomes a focal theme in shaping the perceptions and behavior of medical doctors, the presumed existence of various forms and sources of danger around them comes to strongly influence what police officers see and do, even the ways they feel. Of all the elements that exist in the police officer's occupational environment, danger has been emphasized time and again in law-enforcement literature as one of the most important determinants of police attitudes and behavior. It is interesting to speculate as to just why this should be so, especially in light of the previously observed fact that law enforcement is statistically less dangerous than such jobs as agricultural and construction work, mining and firefighting.

Long before he or she ever seriously considers a career in law enforcement, the future police officer is being subtly conditioned by the mass media—television, motion pictures, novels, magazines, and newspaper articles—to think of police work and danger as more or less synonymous. Any single evening's perusal of the police shows on television will reveal countless police officers engaged in a series of confrontations with dangerous criminals. The mass-media-derived equation of danger and police work extends into very early childhood. Ask any little boy or girl on a preschool playground what the police do and the answer, while it may contain such things as helping children and being "our friend," will surely tend to focus on "catching bad guys" and "shooting guns"—elements that we have already seen to be extremely infrequent occurrences in the lives of most real police officers.

The police-officer-to-be carries such perceptions of the police role from the sandlot games of cops-and-robbers and the viewing of television shows dealing with the dangerous exploits of fictional police to the police academy in the form of a set of implicit and unspoken—but very real—role expectations. The mass media have thus infused the aspiring police officer with the belief that she or he is about to embark upon an occupation where confrontations with dangerous individuals and situations are extremely common. Rather than confronting the officer-to-be with the primarily human service nature of the role, various aspects of the police-academy experience itself serve to greatly intensify the perception of police work as something that is basically preoccupied with managing and surviving physical danger. First, a disproportionate amount of training time at the academy is spent in the mastery of subjects that stress the role of the police officer as something akin to a combat soldier fighting an interminable war. Subjects ranging from firearms and self-defense training to patrol procedures and emergency-vehicle operation have the common theme of preparing the neophyte patrol officer to confront dangerous individuals and events on a routine basis. Time after time during the months at the academy, the recruit is challenged by instructors who are themselves veteran street officers to vicariously project himself or herself into the position of a hypothetical patrol officer handling a volatile disturbance such as in-progress robbery or buglary, armed suspect, or other potentially dangerous event.

The impact of such didactic examples on the recruit's emerging perceptual set toward his new occupation is greatly influenced by the recitation of countless "war stories" by instructors—actual street incidents that graphically drive home the message that dangerous individuals and events of the sort being discussed actually *do* exist and await the recruit upon his graduation from the academy. The actual frequency with which dangerous individuals and events are encountered by patrol officers even in high-crime areas becomes distorted and greatly magnified under a barrage of such stories gleaned from perhaps 15 or 20 years of police experience. Rather than being juxtaposed against the vast number of service situations which make up the bulk of an officer's field activity during his career, the infrequent occurrences represented by "war stories" leave the recruit with the erroneous impression that dangerous encounters are everyday events. Looked at from a perceptual standpoint, danger becomes elevated to the status of "figure" while, ironically, the infinitely more common service aspect of the police role is relegated to "ground." Recruits quickly come to overperceive the actual risk of injury or death associated with their new profession, as academy instruction drives home the danger message. The following exhortation from the senior author's range instructor to the recruit class of which he was a part illustrates the dynamics of academy socialization into what might be called the *danger mystique* of police work:

> "There were one hundred thirty-two policemen killed in the line of duty in this country last year," Quinn said. He took a gun from one of the recruits. "Ninety-five of them were killed with one of these things." He paused for a moment to let his words take effect. "Every one of those one hundred thirty-two guys had one basic thing in common," he said. "They all planned on going home at the end of their shift. Don't ever be ashamed of being scared when you get out there. In fact, make it a point to get scared and stayed scared." He wiped his forehead with the handkerchief again. "You show me a street cop today who says he isn't scared every time he puts a uniform on and I'll show you a liar or a fool—either way, he's a dumb bastard that I don't want to have to work with." [16]

The emotional impact of such statements is both dramatic and long-lasting for the recruit. From an abstract, statistical standpoint, 115 casualties in an occupation that includes over 600,000 people may make police work sound relatively safe. For the academy recruits, however, who hear such statements constantly and hear them against a backdrop of vividly told accounts of police injuries and deaths in the line of duty, the business of policing soon appears to be pervaded with dangerous individuals and events. Coupled with being repeatedly warned about the ubiquitous dangers that characterize the officer's occupational world, recruits are frequently called upon to engage in simulation and role-play exercises which require them to act out the assumption of pervasive danger. Under the watchful eyes of instructors and academy classmates, they learn how to approach suspicious individuals, stop "hot" cars, and approach buildings containing possible robbers or burglars, "cool out beefs" and separate disputants with minimal danger to themselves and other officials.

It is fair to say that prior to their entrance into the police academy, recruits share pretty much the perceptions of society at large: The world is a reasonably safe place, at least when it comes to the conduct of one's everyday life and work role. Danger is a relatively remote thing, something associated with the television or the newspaper, or at least rarely encountered on a personal level. This fundamental perception of life and the world as basically positive changes with the socialization process represented by the police-academy experience.

Vast numbers of environmental stimuli previously thought of as neutral to positive gradually take on an aura of danger and threat. The darkened backseat of a car, the absence of a clerk behind the counter of all all-night market, a clean car with a dirty license plate, an evening jogger, a hitchhiker, someone wearing a jacket on a warm night—none of these events was even worthy of notice prior to entrance into the police academy.[17] Now they become parts of a steadily growing repertoire of perceptions which sets the police apart from other members of society, a "perceptual shorthand" that enables the officers to quickly recognize and categorize potential threats to their safety.[18] While most citizens move through everyday life in a relatively trusting frame of mind, recruits soon learn that theirs is an occupation where nothing is to be accepted at face value. Everything is at least potentially something other than what it is represented to be, and even the most commonplace of things has the potential for danger. As Lewis observes,

> From the day a police recruit enters the academy . . . he is bombarded with admonitions to "be careful" and is repeatedly assured that he runs a substantial risk of injury, even while performing the most innocuous tasks.[19]

The recruit, as a direct result of a combination of different socializing influences, thus comes to perceive police work as a dangerous occupation. These include: the definition by the public and the mass media of the police role as something involving almost constant danger; the actual content and methods of training utilized at the police academy, much of which is consciously designed to heighten the recruit's perception of danger in individuals and events regarded as ordinary or inconsequential by other people; the frequent discussion of incidents involving injury or death to police officers by instructors throughout the academy period; finally, the widespread presence of various physical symbols in the academy environment which provide mute testimony that the job about to be embarked on will involve routine confrontations with danger. The gun, nightstick, and handcuffs—occupational accouterments the recruit comes to handle and use on a regular basis during his or her time at the academy—serve to symbolically define danger as an integral part of police work, in much the same way as a medical student's regular handling of scalpel and syringe come to define illness as an inescapable aspect of a doctor's work.

Certainly it should not be concluded from what has been said thus far that police recruits should not be prepared to perceive danger in their work and take steps to protect themselves from it. To be sure, danger does exist in the police officer's world. The number of officers killed and injured in the line of duty must be relatively small in relation to the total volume of police in the country; yet, as Skolnick observes, ". . . <u>the police</u>

are the only peacetime occupational group with a systematic record of death and injury from gunfire and other weaponry." [20] Occupations such as mining and construction work may be statistically more dangerous than policing; yet death and injury within them are rarely the direct result of intentional harm inflicted by a fellow human being—something which certainly cannot be said of police work.

Granted, then, that the police do face some danger in the course of their work; it is eminently reasonable and desirable to caution them about its existence and to adequately prepare them to respond to such threats to their safety as might arise. The problem is not that the police are trained and socialized to confront danger and the admittedly important crime-fighting aspects of their role, but rather that such an inordinate degree of emphasis is placed on these areas that officers are left both ill-prepared and poorly motivated to deal with the complex array of noncriminal situations and individuals that confront them daily and consume the overwhelming majority of their work time.

The recruits begin to anticipate danger with a curious mixture of excitement and anxiety. On one hand, they are aware that confronting dangerous individuals and situations will inevitably pose certain risks to their safety; yet they are equally aware that success in managing such encounters represents the primary means for securing validation of their new identity as police officers, and for obtaining such rewards as are available from both peers and superiors within their new profession. It is because virtually the entire reward system in the police officer's world—everything from public acclaim to pay, promotion, and prestige among one's peers—is so inextricably tied up with handling danger well and often that the officer spends his or her entire career in anticipation of such encounters. From rookie to seasoned veteran, it is the "hot" or "heavy" (dangerous) call that officers throughout the country live for. As Van Maanen observes:

> The heavy call represents everything the policeman feels he is prepared for. In short, it calls for police work. Such calls are anticipated by the patrolman with both pleasure and anxiety, and the recruit's performance on such calls is in a very real sense the measure of the man. A Union City Sergeant described the heavy call to me as follows:
> "It's our main reason for being in business. Like when somebody starts busting up a place, or some asshole's got a gun, or some idiot tries to knock off a cop. Basically, it's the situation where you figure you may have to use the tools of your trade. . . . You know down deep that this is why you're a cop and not pushing pencils somewhere." [21]

Officers, young and old alike, develop a repertoire of "war stories" based on their handling of "hot" or "heavy" calls over the years, the telling (and occasional exaggeration) of which serves to validate their identity as a police officer in the eyes of self and others. The telling of any number of stories based on far more common human-service situations that officers have become involved in during their careers could never accomplish this same end, for most police in American society are viewed by themselves and others as basically and ultimately crime fighters.

On the streets as patrol officers, recruits quickly discover that dangerous situations are nowhere near as common as both their training and informal socialization have led them to expect. Yet the danger mystique is kept alive and strong by several means. Participation in the informal subculture of patrol officers involves new officers in almost constant discussions of danger and the technology and behavioral means available for dealing with it. In locker-room, patrol-car, and coffee-shop conversations with other officers, attention invariably seems to shift at some point to the topic of danger: the relative merits of .357 magnum versus .38 revolvers and different types of ammunition, the optional or increasingly required wearing of bullet-proof vests on duty, where on the body it is best to strike an assailant or whether it is best to use a nightstick or a heavy metal flashlight.

Added to such discussions are germane "war stories" drawn either from the personal experiences of officers or from the experiences of officers known to them. Through shift after shift, call after call, talking and thinking about danger keeps alive the fantasy of incipient danger and thereby the possibility of organizational, peer, and societal rewards. A massive industry has grown up over the years around the collective fantasy of pervasive danger shared by line officers and police administrators alike. One has only to peruse such popular police trade publications as *Law and Order* and *The Police Chief* to gain a quick appreciation of the sheer number of large business firms that have a strong vested interest in sustaining among American police officers a perception of their role as involving primarily the management of dangerous individuals and situations. Such publications are jammed with page upon page of sensational advertisements for everything from quick-draw holsters to sap gloves and high-powered weapons.

Even though their actual day-to-day work experiences amply confirm the fact that policing basically involves the provision of a wide variety of human services having little if anything to do with danger and crime, patrol officers are repeatedly drawn back to an anticipation of the latter by the combined influence of their training and the socialization they receive from peers and administrators alike. Why, after all, are they carrying the weaponry that is always supposed to be kept within reach if danger is not an omnipresent reality on the job? Such incidents involving danger that do occur within the officer's perceptual field—

whether they involve him, other officers within the department, or officers within other agencies—have an impact upon the officer that is disproportionate to their actual frequency and importance. In other words, dangerous individuals and events become so amplified through individual thought and peer discussion that they serve to greatly heighten the individual officer's expectation of and perception of danger in the work environment.

An officer in a distant city is shot during a holdup attempt. An officer within one's own department is beaten by a drunk driver during a car stop. Rather than being kept in perspective against a backdrop of the things police spend most of their time doing and the relative infrequency with which they are killed or injured, such isolated incidents are quickly elevated through peer interaction to the status of imminent possibilities in one's own work.

An officer's perception of danger in the environment is sustained only by his knowledge of injuries and fatalities suffered by other men and women who do the same things he does. Viewing the world as basically a dangerous place is also heavily influenced by an officer's frequent personal exposure to death and injury involving nonpolice members of the population. While most of the members of any given community are effectively insulated from exposure to the trauma and horror of major-injury automobile accidents, shootings, stabbings, and suicides, police officers must regularly witness the aftermath of such events. The frequency with which law-enforcement officers must confront death and injury is suggested by a questionnaire survey conducted within the Charlottesville, Virginia, police department:

> When questioned regarding potentially unpleasant situations encountered, the respondents, who included patrolmen, detectives, and their supervisors, indicated that they observed minor bleeding three times a month, life-threatening bleeding once every three months, an injured adult three times a month, an injured child once every two months, the victim of a severe assault slightly more than once every two months, and a dead person about once every three months.[22]

Not surprisingly, whatever preservice views of the world as a basically safe place the officer held soon begin to give way to a perception of life as infused with danger and potential threat. The senior author has described elsewhere the still-vivid trauma of witnessing death for the first time as a police officer:

> We worked our way through the crowd of people outside and entered the bar just as a flashbulb exploded. When my eyes recovered, I saw a form sprawled on the floor next to an overturned chair across the room. I looked at the dead man for the first time. He was a black man in his

mid-twenties. His mouth was slightly open in a look of surprise and he still smelled of cologne or after-shave lotion. The eyes were glassy. I saw the small dark hole in the center of his broad nose. Coagulated blood covered the paisley shirt he wore, stained the bar's light wooden floor well beyond the white chalk line someone had drawn around the body. A wide-brimmed felt hat lay on the floor directly behind and to the left of his head. So this was what it looked like, I thought. Violent death. So still. So much blood from such a small wound. I stood and handed the cameraman back his flashlight. How many people had I seen shot to death on television and in movies over the years? I wondered. It had never looked anything like this before. I felt a chill and stepped back from the body.[23]

It is an extremely short inferential step from the discovery that such things happen to other people to the realization that they might befall him as well. Indeed, Neiderhoffer suggests that the police officer's frequent exposure to illness and injury in the normal course of his work serves to transform him into something of a latent hypochondriac:

Specific duties connected with the police role sometimes induce a subdued form of hypochondria. Whenever someone calls an ambulance, a policeman goes to the scene to render aid and obtain the necessary information for police records, thereby quickly becoming an intimate of nurses, interns and doctors. The hospital becomes his hangout where he is periodically called to complete the police reports required in a great variety of hospital cases. . . . Policemen watch doctors operate, help dress wounds, discuss symptoms.[24]

Danger thus comes to take on an added dimension in the police officer's life. In addition to the menace posed by thieves, muggers, pimps, the mentally ill, and other individuals from whom they have been conditioned to anticipate danger, daily work experience as patrol officers also reveals that danger is constantly present in everyday events against which they cannot readily take steps to protect themselves. Heart attacks, drownings, automobile crashes, and other manifestations of the cruel hand of fate randomly work in the lives of people all around them—people with whom they deal every day—leave officers all to aware that they, too, may be struck by lightning at any instant.

Experiences involving noncriminal situations, because they occur with such frequency in the careers of officers and involve such close contact on their part, serve to vividly dramatize to them the brevity of life and the ephemeral nature of health and well-being, things which other people usually take for granted:

I investigated two fatal accidents where three young people were killed in less than one week. I actually had to take their bodies out of the cars and also make the family contact, telling the parents their son was dead. At the time it was very routine, but a short time later when the investigation was all over, I got to thinking how these young lives were just starting and just that quick it had ended. These young people really thought they were living, having a car, going to parties at the end of a school year, and then, that fast their lives had ended.[25]

How do the police deal with the inevitable sense of personal vulnerability which comes from having to regularly witness death and suffering, and being involved in work that they and others define as highly dangerous? One study that sought to examine the fear of death among male patrol officers found that their death anxiety, surprisingly, did not differ from groups of mail carriers and male college undergraduates studied. Indeed, rather than exhibiting the kind of reluctance to deal with the subject one might expect, the patrol officers studied were even more cooperative in taking the test than the other two groups studied, something which led the researchers to conclude that the patrol officers were less defensive about death and had likely worked through personal anxieties about it, at least in part. The study reached the conclusion that in terms of conscious death anxiety, police officers closely resemble other adult males.[26]

In order to function successfully in their occupational environment, new patrol officers must develop psychological and interactional mechanisms to effectively neutralize such phenomena as death anxiety and morbid fears of suffering personal harm in the course of their work. Such sentiments are, of course, understandable by-products of the training and socialization they have received since entering the police world. Yet they are equally dysfunctional, given the fact that they must regularly confront injury, death, and situations and individuals which they have been conditioned to perceive as potentially dangerous. The new officer can scarcely summon the courage to walk into a skid-row bar where several men are fighting with pool cues, order an unruly crowd to disperse, or walk into a darkened warehouse where a silent alarm has been activated, if he is chronically and severely frightened. He must find ways to assure himself as well as those with whom he deals that he is really not afraid— even in situations where anyone might reasonably be frightened.

Some such self-assurance may be derived by periodically emphasizing to self and others that police work is really not all that dangerous, despite the training and socialization to the contrary one has received. As Skolnick observes:

> Policemen themselves do not necessarily emphasize the peril associated with their work when questioned directly, and may even have well-

developed strategies of denial. The element of danger is so integral to the policeman's work that explicit recognition might induce emotional barriers to work performance.[27]

However, because they have been trained and conditioned to perceive so many things as potentially dangerous, and therefore are subject to frequent feelings of fear and insecurity, new patrol officers gradually evolve a specific psychological defense mechanism to help allay such dysfunctional anxieties and to enable them to do the things that they must. In the face of potentially dangerous individuals and events, the new officer's mind adopts what psychologists call *reaction formation, that is, the repression or driving into one's unconscious of thoughts that are unacceptable, and the conscious assertion of their very opposite.* Like the proverbial unmarried man or woman who compensates for unacceptable sexual impulses by expressing an outward attitude of intense prudery, patrol officers soon appropriate a defensive facade of confidence and even aggression as a means of dealing with underlying insecurities and anxieties occasioned by the danger mystique they have been socialized to accept.

The hypothesized existence of such a defense mechanism renders intelligible the notorious "badge-heaviness" of rookie officers, expressed in a surface display of bravado, hyperaggressiveness, and sometimes downright recklessness in the presence of menacing circumstances. Extremely insecure in their new role and trying desperately to convince themselves and other officers that they are capable of surmounting the challenges and dangers their work poses, new patrol officers struggle to prove themselves unafraid and confident in every new situation. Los Angeles police psychologist Dr. Martin Reiser has identified the resulting set of attitudes and behaviors as "the John Wayne Syndrome":

> This is a condition in which the individual tends to swagger and talk tough. He is somewhat badge-heavy in manner, feels that emotion is unhealthy and tends to keep his feelings locked inside under tight control. He feels he must always be right and cannot admit his fallibility or making a mistake.[28]

It is new officers, far more than either seasoned veterans or patrol officers with several years of street experience, who need the personal reassurance attendant on provoking a belligerent drunk into a fight, charging into a family-disturbance call without waiting for a second officer, or piloting 5000 pounds of metal at potentially lethal speeds in pursuit of a misdemeanant. In addition to adopting an extremely aggressive attitude toward encounters involving danger, crime, and criminals, new officers also quickly come to adopt a surface attitude of extreme callousness toward the manifestations of death and physical suffering that they soon begin to witness. The horror attendant on seeing a three-year-old child who has been decapitated in an automobile accident or witnessing the physics of a depressed elderly person's self-inflicted shotgun blast must somehow be denied, somehow kept from reaching the level of conscious emotion, if one is to carry on. Elements of the resulting veneer of callousness and ostensible insensitivity in the face of tragedy are also found, of course, among other practitioners who must regularly witness death and suffering. Hospital emergency-room personnel such as doctors, nurses, and the emergency medical technicians who work in ambulances similarly often provide examples of this dimension of reaction formation. The senior author recalls his own adaptation to the trauma of death and human suffering as a rookie patrolman:

> How many times during those months as a policeman, I wonder, did I joke about a particular shooting, stabbing, or killing, or casually discuss over a cigarette or coffee a horrible automobile wreck I had just worked? Like emergency medical personnel, policemen come to treat even death lightly, to deny its significance just as they deny so many of the other harsh realities of their world.[29]

By discussing the dynamics of reaction formation as largely characteristic of new police officers, it should not be concluded that this condition is confined to them. To be sure, the phenomenon of "badge-heaviness" or the "John Wayne syndrome" is also found among some experienced officers who remain chronically insecure and anxious about their role over the years, and who must therefore constantly prove themselves. Yet reaction formation tends to wane among most officers with time on the streets. With experience in dealing with the people and events that make up a police officer's world comes a simultaneous sense of increasing confidence in one's ability, and a recognition that most of the things encountered are actually far less menacing and formidable than they were once believed to be.

In concluding our discussion of danger and the police role, it is important to realize the extent to which danger becomes a powerful determinant of the attitude and behavior of officers, notwithstanding the fact that its existence is largely illusory in the daily work world of most police officers. As a result of their occupational training and socialization, police officers come to anticipate danger from a great many environmental stimuli. It matters little that the darkened car approached beside a warehouse does not actually contain a waiting assailant, or that the young black male who puts one hand in the pocket of a windbreaker jacket upon an officer's approach has no weapon. Whether it is real or imaginary, danger is defined by patrol officers as being an omnipresent potential. Just how intense and imminent that potential is seen as being in any given situation or at any particular time will be influenced by such variables as length of service, past experiences, individual personality, and type and area of assignment. Thus, and despite the general tendency of officers to perceive less danger with greater length of service, a veteran officer patrolling a high-crime inner-city area may well manifest more danger anxiety than a recruit assigned to a middle-class suburb. Similarly, an officer who has had a recent violent encounter or one who is participating in a stakeout or other obviously dangerous activity will likely exhibit a high level of danger anxiety regardless of length of service. Whatever the individual officer's personal makeup, experience, or particular assignment, danger remains a free-floating mental reality throughout his or her career. As Kroes observes, "For the patrolman, every call has the potential of becoming a line of duty crisis."[30]

EXERCISING AUTHORITY

To most people, the police officer is the living embodiment of authority. The powerful symbols of the badge, uniform, and firearm serve to dramatically proclaim the role as belonging to someone who wields legal authority on a routine basis. From their first day at the training academy, all recruits learn that they are about to enter an occupation whose basic business consists of directing and controlling the lives of other people, often against their wills. They soon come to expect that exercising authority will form as integral a part of their daily work role as dealing with dangerous individuals and events.

If, during the academy period, recruits develop a somewhat distorted picture of the importance of danger in their occupational environment, they similarly begin to acquire a number of misconceptions about the exercise of authority as it takes place on the streets. As they go about studying countless laws and departmental regulations, officers-to-be begin perceiving these things as an explicit set of guidelines for the use of authority. They rather naively embrace them as something of a legalistic and administrative cookbook whose collective contents will provide them with quick and readily accessible answers to whatever questions concerning the exercise of authority arise in the field. As academy instructors train and socialize recruits in terms of the police department's *official* version of what patrol officers do, the "letter of the law" becomes preeminent in their minds. They begin to believe that exercising authority as a law-enforcement officer simply consists, as the label suggests, of discovering which, if any, laws have been violated in a given situation, and then applying the arrest sanction against those who have violated them.

A substantial part of the training-academy curriculum which is devoted to making the recruit thoroughly conversant with legal and administrative procedures is usually characterized by a strategic avoidance of the term *discretion*. Officially, the department cannot admit either to the public at large or to its own personnel in any formal way the fact that the various laws and procedures it is charged with following form, at most, only a nebulous set of parameters for exercising authority in the real-life situations the police face each day. The police organization, from its training-academy instructors and field supervisors to the upper levels of its command hierarchy, is committed to articulating such myths as full and equal enforcement of the law in all situations and rigid adherence to formal departmental regulations, despite the fact that these things bear little resemblance to the actual realities of police work.

The transition from academy recruit to rookie officer on the streets is accordingly a harsh, traumatic jolt. After months of learning a highly specific set of legal and administrative guidelines for the exercise of police authority, new officers quickly discover that these do not often mesh neatly with the exigencies of their daily work. On the streets, they find that being a law-enforcement officer actually has relatively little to do with enforcing the law. In situation after situation, they discover that they must constantly improvise and make highly informal, subjective decisions regarding the use of authority. The cookbook perspective formed during the academy months is soon cast aside under the pressures of the everyday work role, for it provides little if any guidance in the kind of quick and complex decisions officers are regularly called upon to make. Even when laws have clearly been violated and an arrest can be made, the new officer discovers that such a course of action is often not desirable. Putting in jail the drunken husband who has beaten his wife is soon recognized as, at best, a short-run solution to a highly involved problem, and, at worst, a step which will only exacerbate the situation. Similarly, "busting" the ten-year-old who has been caught shoplifting a candy bar or the chronic inebriate who is creating a disturbance in a bar may appear to be a far less desirable course of action than handling these and other "law enforcement" situations informally and unofficially.

Fresh from the academy and strongly imbued with the myth of full enforcement of the law, rookie patrol officers soon discover the absurdity and impossibility of carrying this lofty principle into practice. "Writing" *every* driver he observes violating a traffic law, regardless of how minor it may be, can mean, at the worst, never getting from one end of a heavily traveled beat to the other during a tour of duty, or, at the least, neglecting other patrol duties he comes to recognize as more important. In like manner, making an arrest whenever any other kind of law violation is witnessed means becoming bogged down in a hopeless quagmire of paperwork and meaningless court appearances.

Prior to coming on the streets as a patrol officer, the young officer blindly accepts the wisdom of the laws which collectively underpin his authority. All laws are viewed as solemn pronouncements of the legislature and society. As such, they command unthinking fealty. The law is a sacred institution into whose service he is about to enter. Its elements are immutable, graven in stone. As the rookie goes about the actual business of policing society, however, his views of the law begin to change dramatically. The institution of law itself gradually begins to assume a secular, profane quality under the weight of everyday contact with it and with the criminal-justice system of which it is a part. Some laws which he is charged with enforcing begin to stand out in the rookie officer's mind as ill-conceived and unwise. He begins to question, challenge, and even nullify a growing number of them through his everday action and inaction. This process is well illustrated by an example drawn from the experience of one new officer:

> One of the first calls I had when I started working a solo car was to a noise complaint at an apartment building over near the college. I could tell which apartment the racket was coming from as soon as I pulled up in front of the place. The guy's stereo was up so loud that the walls of his apartment were practically shaking. I had to knock several times before the people inside even heard me. The moment the door opened this cloud of grass about knocks me over. You should have seen the look on this kid's face when he saw me standing there—scared shitless! I mean I had him by the short ones. I had probable cause right then and there to charge inside and make a case. But all I did was tell him to cut the damn stereo down and get rid of the grass. I'm not going to make an arrest on a chicken-shit thing like that, a couple of college kids doing a number in their own apartment. Hell, it'll probably be legal in a few years anyway.[31]

With the passage of time, officers find themselves relying more and more on such subjective determinations of what are right and wrong courses of action, and less and less on the official pronouncements of criminal law and departmental regulations. They come to recognize and accept the essentially quasi-judicial nature of much of their work, to realize that they, more than any other actors in the entire criminal-justice system have the most crucial role in deciding the fate of those with whom they interact. Everything that happens to an individual in the courts and the correctional system depends ultimately on the officer's subjectively determined action or inaction, for he is at the very beginning of the complicated funnel that is the criminal-justice system. A police officer is a kind of prime mover, a labeling agent par excellence, without whose work the entire machinery of the system could not function.

As they go about the quasi-judicial business of policing their beats—deciding to make arrests here and ignore infractions there, conferring the indelible stigma of deviance on some individuals and not on others—they find that the everyday demands of their work often require them to ignore both the law and departmental regulations. The law prohibits officers from, for example, pulling a particular individual off the street or out of a bar and locking her or him in the back of the patrol car for the purpose of obtaining information about criminal activity. Without the existence of probable cause for an arrest, such an action is tantamount to false imprisonment. Yet, because a patrol officer perceives an individual as a "dirtbag" who is in possession of certain information the officer needs in order to go about the business of protecting society, he consciously makes the decision to nullify the procedural nicety of probable cause in a particular case.

During their months at the academy, recruits learned with great specificity the limitations imposed on their authority by such Supreme Court cases as *Terry* v. *Ohio*. However, in their metamorphosis to working patrol officers, they may nonetheless stop a junkie on the beat whom they *think* is "holding," and promptly conduct a full-blown search for narcotics that patently violates the "stop and frisk" doctrine set forth in the *Terry* case. Even though the officer realizes that the fruits of such an unlawful search will be inadmissible as evidence in court (unless, as sometimes happens, he perjures himself as to the conditions under which he obtained them), the officer may nonetheless feel that taking the drugs in question out of circulation is sufficient reason to circumvent the law.

Such decisions to calculatedly ignore or even violate laws they are officially sworn to uphold do not arise from either sinister motives or disrespect for the institution of law. Rather, they occur because such practical concerns as apprehending criminals and protecting innocent people often make such decisions appear to be sensible and even moral courses of action. Because officers so often see criminals twisting the technicalities of the law to their own advantage at the expense of society, they soon come to rationalize certain departures from the rule of law in their dealings with such individuals. As a rookie still very much imbued with academy rhetoric, the senior author once challenged his riding partner, a seventeen-year veteran, for making an illegal search and seizure on an individual we had stopped for questioning. The ensuing conversation illustrates the extent to which practical considerations in everyday patrol work soon come to eclipse rigid adherence to the rule of law in the life of an experienced officer:

"Something on your mind, Doc?" D'Angelo said.

"Yes, there is, now that you mention it, Angie."

"Well, go ahead, get it off your chest."

"You know as well as I do that searching that fellow's sock back there was as illegal as hell, don't you?" I blurted.

"So that's it," he said as he unwrapped a cigar.

"You're damn right that's it," I said angrily. He shrugged. "So it was illegal. So what?" he said as he lit the cigar.

"So what? My God, how can you say a thing like that? We're supposed to be police officers. If we don't respect the law, how can we expect anybody else to respect it?"

He took a deep gulp of coffee. "That what you think them two back there was doing, respecting the law?" he said. "If I hadn't noticed 'em acting so squirrely, you can be sure they'd of knocked over one of them all-night markets over on Allison by now with the heater the little guy had in his jeans. Maybe hurt somebody, killed somebody doing it."

"I'm not talking about that," I said. "I'm talking about making a patently illegal search, then turning around and using the illegally obtained evidence to justify arresting a man. Now, that's wrong."

D'Angelo frowned, puffing on the cigar in silence for a moment. "Okay, Professor, let's analyze this situation," he said at last. "Let's say we done it your way—just arrested the guy with the gun and let the one with the dope in his sock go 'cause we didn't have no legal grounds to search him. What then?" He leaned back in the seat and folded his arms across his chest.

"Then—"

"Then he'd be back down in the project pushing the shit in his sock next morning, wouldn't he? You heard the check that comes back on both of 'em. They both done time for pushing drugs."

"Sure, they're hoodlums, Angie. But that's got nothing to do with it. We're police officers. We can't go around like a couple of vigilantes meting out curbside justice. We—"

"Hey, don't talk to me about justice, Doc," he said. "I seen too much of it over the years down here." He crumpled his coffee cup and threw it out the window. "Justice, my ass."[32]

In their attempt to do their job to the best of their ability while remaining within the framework of law at all times, new police officers soon realize that they are caught on the horns of a cruel dilemma. On the one hand, they are part of a society whose democratic ethos stresses maximum initiative and efficiency in the production efforts of its members. On the other hand, in the unique occupational situation of police officers, there are systematic legal brakes and restrictions on the extent to which they can display these culturally desirable qualities in their work. Skolnick has best stated the essence of the police officer's problem:

The police in a democratic society are required to maintain order and to
do so under the rule of law. As functionaries charged with maintaining
order, they are part of the bureaucracy. The ideology of democratic
bureaucracy emphasizes initiative rather than disciplined adherence to
rules and regulations. By contrast, the rule of law emphasizes the rights
of individual citizens and constraints upon the initiative of legal officials.
The tension between the operational consequences of ideas of order,
efficiency, and initiative, on the one hand, and legality, on the other,
constitute the principle problem of police as a democratic legal
organization.[33]

Society expects its police officers to be highly effective in dealing with
crime and criminals in a democracy such as ours; yet in the interests of
protecting the principles of individual liberty upon which democracy
rests, it has evolved a body of complex legal restrictions which render
impossible the police officer's achievement of that goal.

How do officers deal with the resulting double bind in which they
find themselves? Largely by a series of informal working compromises,
the existence of which can scarcely be admitted on any official level. As
Goldstein observes,

> If both legal mandates and public expectations are taken literally, and if
> the reality of the situations that the police confront is recognized, the
> demands on the police appear so contradictory that the police task is
> simply unworkable. . . .
>
> The need for compromise—with the law, with administrative
> directions, with public expectations, and even with one's own personal
> ethics—has become an important, albeit unarticulated, requirement of the
> police job. . . . The present system places a high value on the officer
> who is willing to profess that he meets all the demands made upon him
> while making the accommodations needed to avoid conflicts. Many of
> the required accommodations are made at the street level, based upon the
> judgment of line officers, with little guidance and control from officers
> of superior rank.
>
> This situation makes for some rather unusual working conditions.
> Specifically, police officers are often required to ignore their oath of office,
> to ignore much of what is taught in formal training; to bluff or lie, not
> necessarily out of malevolence, but often out of a desire to be helpful in
> the face of the irreconcilable demands upon them.[34]

Such a pattern of behind-the-scenes compromise and accommodation,
however, is not without its risks and perils. These include such problems
as the need for condemnation and disciplinary measures by the police
administration when it is officially brought to light that officers are engaged in some practice that may long have been covertly recognized and

allowed to exist at an informal level. Thus, for instance, officers may ignore a departmental order that stipulates that they not exceed a certain speed limit when making emergency runs. Supervisors and administrators alike may be fully aware that violation of this particular rule has become a working norm, yet choose to do nothing about it unless an officer has a serious accident. Similarly, an officer may have been able to successfully ignore an official regulation requiring him to have his hat on at all times when he is out of his patrol car, until the occasion when an irascible supervisor or citizen decides to make an issue of the rule. Officers may carry "hot load" or high-velocity ammunition in their revolvers in contravention of departmental policy, but woe betide the hapless officer who shoots anyone with it! It is ironic that while the department provides its officers with little if any guidance as to how they should exercise authority and discretion in dealing with the complex choices they must make every day, it nonetheless spells out the mechanics of operating procedures in minute detail. Official regulations tell an officer trying to calm a volatile domestic disturbance nothing about the desirability of different courses of action. Nor do they detail in writing specific measures which the officer might take to neutralize the anger and potential violence present. Alternatively, what they do stipulate is that they shall make certain in presenting themselves on such occasions that their shoes are shined, their hair is cut to certain dimensions, and stipulated items of brass are correctly positioned on their uniforms. Regulations give no guidance about the practical wisdom of making an arrest when a violation of law has occurred, but merely specify the kind and number of forms that must unfailingly be filled out when an officer takes a person into custody.

Official regulations, like the law itself, frequently conflict with what appear to an officer to be the best and most desirable courses of action in the everyday handling of people and their problems. Officers therefore find themselves placed in an unending series of double binds in which they must quickly weigh doing what they feel is the right thing against the possible sanctions which may befall them for exercising their authority in a manner that violates formal departmental policies. The following example illustrates the dynamics of this kind of conflict:

> One night I spotted this car weaving badly and pulled it over. The driver really had a load on so I told him I was taking him in for a breathalyzer test. Then he and his wife—she was even drunker than he was—start pleading with me not to arrest him. She's crying and all about how he'll lose his job if his boss finds out. He says that they don't usually drink but that they were out celebrating a promotion he just got. I figure what the hell. They seem like decent working people, so I give

him a break. I tell them to lock up their car and I radio to have a cab
sent around. I told the guy to go home and get his car the next day when
he's sobered up. They really seemed thankful, but you know what that
sonofabitch did? They leave in the cab allright but as soon as I pull out
they have the cabbie make the block and take them back to their car.
They get in it and drive a few blocks before this asshole runs a light and
broadsides another car. The next thing I know my ass is in the
lieutenant's office.[35]

However eminently reasonable such departures from either departmental regulations or the law may seem at the time, and regardless of
the extent to which they may appear to contribute to accomplishing such
police goals as efficiency and service, they nonetheless expose officers to
a gamut of sanctions ranging from days off without pay to criminal prosecution and civil suit. The latter has become an especially ominous menace attending the informal use of police authority in recent years. Indeed,
lawsuits against officers for everything from failure to act and excessive
force to false imprisonment have reached near-epidemic proportions. The
incidence of such suits skyrocketed some 446 percent between 1967 and
1971 alone.[36] According to Department of Justice estimates, over 14,000
civil suits will be filed against police officers in the United States next
year, which leads many observers to conclude that the police "malpractice" crisis is fast approaching that which has long existed in the medical
profession. Because every call a patrol officer handles contains the potential for advertent or inadvertent violation of laws and constitutionally
protected individual rights, the specter of being sued is constantly present
even in the most mundane situations. Owing to the readiness with which
many large police-insurance carriers will settle cases out of court for
sizable sums rather than risk the expense of a drawn-out legal battle and
possible adverse judgment, officers today often find themselves being sued
even in situations where they engaged in no apparent violations either
of laws or departmental regulations. The following is a good case in point:

Two officers in City X responded to an "unknown trouble" call at a local
tavern one Sunday afternoon. They were met in front of the establishment
by the janitor who informed them that a man brandishing a gun had
walked in the tavern while he was cleaning up and demanded a drink and
money to play the juke box, even though he explained the bar was
closed. The janitor's wife had happened to call while the armed man was
distracted by the juke box and he whispered to her to call the police
before hanging up. The janitor explained to the arriving officers that the
man had dashed inside the tavern's storeroom as soon as he saw their cars
pull up.
    Both officers drew their weapons and took up a position on either side
of the storeroom door, identifying themselves as police officers and

ordering the suspect to come out. After an initial silence of some moments, the suspect jerked the storeroom door open, leveling what later was found to be a .44 magnum revolver at the chest of Officer B———. Officer B——— immediately opened fire, felling the suspect with a rapid series of shots from his service revolver. The suspect, who was left paralyzed from the waist down by the incident, had a long and well documented history of criminal and suicidal behavior. Ballistic analysis of the suspect's gun revealed the presence of a dent from one of Officer B———'s bullets on its ejector rod—something which clearly established that the gun had to be pointed directly at Officer B— at the time he opened fire. This notwithstanding, a $600,000 lawsuit against both Officer B— and the city on the ground of "excessive force " was filed. To the dismay of Officer B—, his partner and the police department, the city's insurance carrier made several settlement offers to the suspect and his attorneys, the most recent of these in the order of $60,000. Both offers were rejected by the plaintiff's lawyers and the case is now before the courts.[37]

Police officers function in a rule-bound environment. The myriad of laws and departmental regulations they are expected to observe to the letter at all times, coupled with the impossibility of so doing, renders them constantly vulnerable to criticism and attacks by the police administration, the courts, the mass media, and community-interest groups as well as individual citizens. Because of this vulnerability and the resulting sense of personal insecurity shared by officers, they have evolved within their own subculture norms designed to prevent outsiders from becoming aware of potentially damaging information and events. Paramount among such norms is a *code of secrecy,* which decrees that officers must keep to themselves and their peers such infractions of official rules and laws as they either observe or become part of in their everyday work. Westley has described the functionality of secrecy in the police officer's world:

> Secrecy stands as a shield against the attacks of the outside world; against bad newspaper publicity which would lower the reputation of the police; against public criticism from which the police feel that they suffer too much; against the criminal who is eager to know the moves of the police; against the law which the police all too frequently abrogate.[38]

In addition to being menaced by the requirements of regularly dealing with danger, crime, and criminals, the police share a sense of recurrent anxiety over the possibility of being disciplined, sued, or even criminally prosecuted as a result of many of the things that they do or fail to do in the course of their work. Certain actions must be kept from the eyes of both officialdom and the public. The prospect of "being called up to Internal" (the department's Internal Affairs Division) produces chills in veteran and rookie officers alike, for ordinary working conduct inevitably means becoming caught up in a great many rule infractions. Officers quickly become possessed of a large store of guilty knowledge concerning both their own line-of-duty behavior and that of other officers—much of which would be administratively or legally actionable were it to come to the attention of officials or outsiders.

Police officers face many of the same problems of secrecy and security maintenance as other subcultures and groups that must operate in threatening, rule-bound environments. Prison inmates, for instance, also face a myriad of regulations which seek to govern every aspect of their daily life within the institution. Regulations minutely define exactly what articles of clothing can and cannot be worn, how many razor blades and other personal articles can be kept in one's cell at any given time, what parts of the compound one may not enter, whom one is allowed to correspond with, and on and on. As in the case of police offifcers, prison inmates find adherence to all institutional rules both inordinately frustrating and impossible from a practical standpoint. Violations are extremely widespread. So, too, is the threat of institutional officials becoming aware of them and taking disciplinary action. As a result, and to accomplish the group end of maintaining security, prison inmates, like the police, evolve a strong code of secrecy. The prison "rat" or informer becomes a pariah in the institutional world, a despised outcast against whom sanctions ranging from ostracism to beating and death are applied by the peer group. Through the application of such penalties, threats to group and individual security that result from the leakage of damaging information are held to a minimum.

Much the same dynamics of security maintenance may be found in the police subculture—with the qualification that peer-group rejection is the prevalent sanction employed by police officers as a group to assure secrecy. The physical punishment of those who violate group-secrecy norms, while common among prison inmates, is relatively infrequent among police officers.

New officers are taught by their peers from their first day on the job that "pimping" or informing on other officers is absolutely prohibited. Just as they must demonstrate to the members of their new group that they possess the personal and physical qualities necessary to "back up" other officers in dangerous situations, rookie patrol officers must likewise convincingly establish that they can be safely entrusted with potentially damaging information. Until they do so, new officers are treated as outsiders. As Westley has observed:

> The chief threat to the code of secrecy is the initiate, for he is yet largely a member of the outer world, with no emotional involvement with the

group. Therefore, in the beginning care must be taken that he is not given premature access to secrets, and full acceptance occurs only when he is told the secrets. Among the police, the "rookie" is constantly told about the need for secrecy. In fact, there is no area of police work where the code of secrecy is made more evident.[39]

Rather than being "told" a body of secrets at some point when they are deemed trustworthy by their peers, rookie officers inevitably become privy to potentially damaging information about other officers in the course of working with them. A rookie may be helping another officer make an arrest when the other officer loses his temper and backhands the suspect in front of him. A rookie may open the trunk of a patrol car to get a first-aid kit at an accident scene and discover the half-empty vodka bottle his partner has carefully secreted there. Or, while patrolling a remote road or city cemetery late at night, a rookie may come upon another officer engaging in sexual intercourse in the backseat of a marked police car. How rookies manage such instances of exposure to guilty knowledge make up a rite of passage for them. Those who prove themselves trustworthy will be embraced as members of the group and be given free access to virtually its entire store of past and present secrets. Other officers will readily invest proven initiates with all manner of potentially damaging information about themselves and their careers ("Jesus, let me tell you about the time I . . ."). The clearest sign of acceptance by any group is the members' willingness to do and say things in front of an individual that involve breaking various rules of the organization of which they are a part.

While the police subcultural rite of passage surrounding secrecy usually consists of a rookie's chance exposure to a number of situations involving culpable actions on the part of other officers, patrol officers sometimes intentionally stage events to test an individual's trustworthiness and commitment to the group. The following instance, related by a researcher who was not himself a policeman but was seeking information about the "backstage" behavior of officers, illustrates a conscious attempt by officers to discover the loyalty of anyone who comes close enough to secure damaging information about the police:

> I was observing informally one evening with an officer I knew quite well, and after "lunch" (about 10:00 P.M.) he suggested we have a drink. I agreed. While not a frequent event, I had in the past several times shared a drink with on-duty officers. We drove to an almost empty parking lot adjoining a city park, a lot frequented by other cars working this particular district. My friend parked the squad car and opened his ever present attaché case and produced a bottle of brandy from which we took

several sips. Suddenly, there was a loud banging on my side of the car, and there in apparent moral outrage was the squad sergeant, a sergeant I knew only in passing. I sat with a three-quarter full and open bottle of brandy in my hand and had, no doubt, a look of utter chagrin on my face when the sergeant opened the door and ordered me to explain my doings. I looked first to my colleague to no avail; he was tight-lipped and staring straight ahead. I then turned to the sergeant and, with great difficulty, stammered out something like, "Goddamn it, Sarge, I'm sorry, it's my bottle. Jimmy told me not to bring it along." At this point, both my partner for the night and the sergeant broke out in hysterical laughter, and I realized that I had just been made the proverbial sucker of a well-executed practical joke. After a period of mock outrage I joined the laughter, and then all three of us shared another warming nip of brandy. But there was a lesson for all of us in that surface moment of unseriousness. Had I said that the bottle was not mine, the ruse would have still been revealed, although my character might very well have undergone considerable and perhaps irreparable damage.[40]

Despite the humorous overtones of this particular "test" of an outside researcher's loyalty, for new police officers, such tests of loyalty to their would-be peer group often involve agonizingly difficult choices. Time and again during their first weeks of service, rookies find themselves forced to choose between their loyalties to two opposing masters as they are exposed to a growing number of departures from both the law and departmental regulations. Both the police organization and the informal peer group of patrol officers command utter and complete loyalty. While the rookie cannot maintain absolute allegiance to both groups at the same time, each has means for discovering instances of betrayal as well as powerful penalties which it can apply for such perfidy. In the case of the police organization, these usually include prompt termination during the probationary period as well as such lesser sanctions as days off without pay and damaging entries in one's personnel record. For its part, the police subculture can sanction those who deviate from its normative expectations in such areas as secrecy and courage in the face of danger through ostracism and the loss of essential group support.

In the final analysis, the threat of peer rejection looms larger than the threats of officialdom. However much new officers may dread the possibility of such things as loss of pay or even termination, they soon come to realize that they simply cannot function in their everyday work world without the continuous support of other officers. They know that at any moment their very life may depend on others' willingness to come to their aid. The possible loss of informal group support is therefore perceived as extremely threatening and exerts powerful controls over the behavior of officers, as the following incident illustrates. The conversation, at which the senior author was present, took place in the wake of an excessive-force incident in which a handcuffed prisoner had been struck in the head with a metal flashlight. The man had been arrested for an especially brutal rape:

> BILL: (a new officer) "I don't care what you say, Phil. There was no reason for Norton to bust that guy with a light like that! Christ, he could have killed him. . . . [angrily]. It was just plain wrong and if anybody in Internal [Affairs] asks me, I'll say so!"

> PHIL: (a four-year patrolman) "Take it easy [calmly]. The guy was scum. He had it coming. Even if he didn't, are you going to back him over another officer? Don't ever do that, Bill. These guys are your brothers. Remember that. If a guy's wearing blue, he's right in my book and I'll go to the wall with him [very serious]. Be careful. You start acting flaky and you'll be out there some night and put out a '34' [officer needs help call] and nobody'll come."[41]

Beyond such obviously practical considerations as the threatened withdrawal of group support, new officers also come to support their peers rather than the administration out of a deepening sense of genuine emotional commitment to them. In a very real sense, these officers become "family." In the intensely intimate environment that is the front seat of a patrol car, the beat, the locker room, officers learn everything of consequence about one another. Likes, dislikes; strengths, weaknesses; fears and hopes. Off duty as well as on, they spend a large percent of their time together—hunting, fishing, bowling, going on outings with their families. Together they share the dangers and frustrations of patrol work, the practical difficulties inherent in exercising authority, the countless times when both the law and departmental regulations must be violated or ignored in order to get a job done. It is small wonder that the combined effect of such experiences is the production of a highly cohesive subculture whose members are united by extremely strong bonds of solidarity and mutual support.

The rookie officer's movement from the position of an "organization man" who accepts and supports without question all of the laws and departmental regulations he has internalized during his months at the academy, to that of a working patrolman who regularly violates such pronouncements, is a gradual process. It comes about as a combination of daily exposure to the realities of police work, which demand frequent departures from official norms, and increasing personal and emotional integration into a group which has evolved its own ways of dealing with the kinds of problems that make up a police officer's world. In the process of making this transition, the new officer frequently finds himself caught between conflicting loyalties, as the senior author discovered during his first weeks as a patrolman:

> "What did you do then, Professor? What happened? Just tell me in your own words what you remember. Take your time now," the internal affairs man said reassuringly. "Well . . . I jumped out and tried to give Franklin—Officer Griffin—a hand. You know, get the prisoner back under control." I was conscious of an increasing tightness in my stomach as I went on. "We really had our hands full, I mean what with him struggling and being as big as he was." I was lying, I thought. Lying to protect another policeman in what amounted to a felony assault. I had always said, had always believed, that a free society is lost once those charged with enforcing its laws begin to step outside them. Damnit, I still believed it. Yet I was lying just the same. Why. . . . I looked at the IAD man, conscious that I wanted to tell him what had really happened, to tell him about the incredible abuse Franklin Griffin had taken that night before he finally lost control of himself. I wanted to tell him that there are limits to what a policeman, like any other man, can take—that the law and society ask too much sometimes.[42]

Such experiences serve to alienate new officers from the police organization and its formal directives. They also alienate new officers from the law and the criminal-justice system of which the police organization is a part. Rookies discover that the informal uses of authority which the job frequently requires, however well intentioned, make them constantly subject to official challenges, criticisms, and punishment by the legal system. Having come to conceive of themselves as "good guys," champions of society and justice, during their months at the academy, they now find their honor and integrity regularly called into question by abrasive defense attorneys, their truthfulness constantly questioned. They learn that, unlike other people, they are afforded no margin for error by the system of which they are a part. To lie about or embellish the facts of a case to put away an obviously dangerous criminal, to lose one's temper only for an instant in the face of strong provocation, is to place an officer's entire career in jeopardy.

As officers observe firsthand the daily workings of the criminal-justice system, their alienation from it deepens. They see individuals whom they know to be guilty, and in whose apprehension and conviction they have invested great personal time and effort, "walk" on legal technicalities or secure greatly reduced sentences in what to them is the incomprehensible process of plea bargaining. They find themselves risking their personal safety, perhaps even their lives, in a game where the odds seem to be consistently stacked against them. The dismal failures chronicled in official statistics on arrest and conviction take on a personal and deeply depressing dimension. Faced with definitions of their role as that of a crime fighter by the public, the press, and the police organization itself, new officers find that regardless of how much effort they expend, their personal accomplishments in this area are small indeed. A kind of coup de grace in the new officers' deepening alienation from the official system of justice comes when they realize that the system is unwilling or unable to protect even them in those instances that they become victims of crime. The senior author had several bitter personal lessons in the sometimes casual attitude of the justice system toward even serious criminal assaults on the police officers who are its front-line troops during his tenure as a full-time patrolman. One of these involved the reduction of a "resisting arrest with violence" charge against two individuals who tried to wrest the author's service revolver away from him (ostensibly for the purpose of shooting him with it) during the attempt of a street mob to free a prisoner. The author found himself reacting with the same kind of personal outrage and frustration as regular officers, for whom such experiences are commonplace:

> "What did you say?" I frowned as I looked at my partner in disbelief. "Here, read it for yourself." He handed me the memorandum. I coudn't believe what I saw on the paper in front of me. The district attorney's office had let the two people who had tried to grab my gun on West Jackson plead guilty to "breach of peace." "Breach of peace?" I said angrily as we stood outside the assembly room. "That's like saying they didn't do anything more serious than spit on the pavement! You saw what happened out there. Those people were trying to get my gun. They would have killed both of us!" My partner sighed and lit a cigarette as we got inside the cruiser. "What can you say, Doc? That's just the way it goes— most of the time." I started the car. Angie was right, I thought to myself. Nobody really gave a damn about what happened to us: not the courts, not the people we were trying to protect, nobody. I slammed a fist against the steering wheel in frustration.[43]

Events such as the one just described become part of the everyday emotional stress faced by officers. The subject of stress represents an extremely important behind-the-scenes aspect of policing, and one to which we turn our attention in the next chapter.

SUMMARY The widespread public image of the police officer as a robotlike Marlboro Man, who automatically exhibits invariably successful responses to the appearance of crime, constrasts sharply with the reality of modern law-enforcement officers. Indeed, we saw in this chapter that the very expression *law-enforcement officer* is something of an overworked misnomer, which fails to catch the essence of what most of police work is all about. It was indicated that law enforcement is a profession whose ranks are filled, not with omniscient supermen, but rather with remarkably ordinary men and women who—feeling and being vulnerable—often find themselves up against extraordinarily difficult and frustrating situations.

This chapter explored such things as the role of danger and authority in human terms, as powerful determinants of both police attitudes and behavior; and the ways in which such variables as the mass media, the occupational socialization of the police academy, and expectations of the police subculture impinge upon the new officer on a psychological and behavioral level. An attempt was made to trace the social-psychological exodus of new police officers as they move from the antiseptic world of the academy—with its glib and ready answers to each and every problem—to the world of the streets. In the latter patrol officers learn that such things as the law and departmental regulations take on altogether different meanings in light of the tasks and problems they face. On the streets each officer undergoes fundamental changes as a person in his or her thinking about everything from the law and the criminal-justice system to the meaning of life and death and the nature of human beings. The senior author sought to describe many of the human realities of police work on the basis of personal experiences gained during a participant-observation research project during which he worked for some months as a patrolman in a slum district of one large city.

NOTES

1. Robert M. Carter, "The Media Image of Law Enforcement," *Crime Prevention Review* (January, 1974), p. 9.
2. Federal Bureau of Investigation, *Uniform Crime Reports for the United States* (Washington, D.C.: U.S. Government Printing Office, 1975), p. 42.
3. Charles Horton Cooley, *Social Organization* (New York: Free Press, 1956). Originally published in 1909.
4. Herman Goldstein, *Policing a Free Society* (Cambridge, Mass.: Balinger, 1977).
5. See James Q. Wilson, *Varieties of Police Behavior* (Cambridge, Mass.: Harvard University Press, 1968), pp. 18–19.
6. Albert J. Reiss, Jr., *The Police and The Public* (New Haven, Conn.: Yale University Press, 1971), p. 71.
7. Norman L. Weiner, *The Role of the Police in Urban Society: Conflicts and Consequences* (Indianapolis: Bobbs-Merrill, 1976), p. 11.
8. Ibid., p. 11–12.
9. See "What does a Policeman do?" in Alvin W. Cohn and Emilio C. Viano, *Police Community Relations: Images, Roles, Realities* (New York: Lippincott, 1976), pp. 131–162.
10. Arnold P. Goldstein, et al., *Police Crisis Intervention,* (Kalamazoo, Mich.: Behaviordelia, 1977).

11. George L. Kirkham, "A Professor's Street Lessons," *The F.B.I. Bulletin* (March, 1973), p. 8.
12. For a review of programs established in recent years, see Donald A. Leibman and Jeffrey A. Schwartz, "Police Programs in Domestic Crisis Intervention: A Review," in *The Policeman in Transition: A Psychological and Sociological Review,* eds. John R. Snibe and Homa M. Snibe, (Springfield, Ill.: Thomas, 1973), pp. 430–36.
13. Arthur Niederhoffer, *Behind the Shield* (New York: Doubleday, 1969), p. 1.
14. See Leon Festinger, *A Theory of Cognitive Dissonance* (Evanston, Ill.: Row-Peterson, 1957). For an application of this concept to the police role, see Jerome Skolnick, *Justice Without Trial* (New York: Wiley, 1966).
15. Ibid., p. 42.
16. George Kirkham, *Signal Zero* (New York: Lippincott, 1976), p. 35.
17. For a detailed account of the kinds of individuals and situations police are socialized to pay particular attention to, see Thomas F. Adams, "Field Interrogation," *Police* (March-April, 1963), p. 28.
18. This concept is introduced by Jerome H. Skolnick, *Justice Without Trial* (New York: Wiley, 1966), p. 45.
19. Rodney W. Lewis, "Toward an Understanding of Police Anomie," in Harry W. Moore, Jr., *The American Police* (St. Paul, Minn.: West, 1976), p. 166.
20. Skolnick, *Justice Without Trial,* p. 47.
21. Peter K. Manning and John Van Maanen, eds., *Policing: A View From The Streets* (Santa Monica, Calif.: Goodyear, 1978), p. 302.
22. Lewis, *Police Anomie.*
23. Kirkham, *Signal Zero,* pp. 73–74.
24. Neiderhoffer, *Behind the Shield,* pp. 135–136.
25. William H. Kroes, *Society's Victim—The Policeman* (Springfield, Ill.: Thomas, 1976), pp. 63–64.
26. Alexander Ford, "Psychological Reports," State University of New York, 1971.
27. Skolnick, *Justice Without Trial,* p. 47.
28. Martin Reiser, *Practical Psychology for Police Officers* (Springfield, Ill.: Thomas, 1972), cited in Kores, *Society's Victim,* p. 86.
29. Kirkham, *Signal Zero,* p. 76.
30. Kroes, *Society's Victim,* p. 63.
31. Kirkham, author's files (1976).
32. Kirkham, *Signal Zero,* pp. 98–99.
33. Skolnick, *Justice Without Trial,* p. 6.
34. Herman Goldstein, *Policing a Free Society,* p. 10.
35. Kirkham, author's files (1973).
36. See *Police* (March, 1978), "The Liability Crisis: Who Will Insure the Police," by Kevin Krajick, p. 33.
37. From a case in which the senior author served as an expert witness.
38. William A. Westley, "Secrecy and the Police," in Arthur Neiderhoffer and Abraham S. Blumberg, *The Ambivalent Force: Perspectives on the Police* (San Francisco: Rinehart Press, 1973), p. 131.
39. Westley, *Secrecy,* p. 132.
40. Peter K. Manning and John Van Maanen, eds., *Policing: A View From the Street* (Santa Monica, Calif.: Goodyear, 1978).
41. Kirkham, author's files, (1973).
42. Kirkham, *Signal Zero,* pp. 160–163.
43. Ibid., p. 168.

SELECTED   George Kirkham, *Signal Zero: The True Story of a Professor Who Became a Street Cop* (New
READINGS   York: Lippincott, 1976).

Herman Goldstein, *Policing a Free Society* (Cambridge, Mass.: Balinger, 1977).

Albert J. Reiss, *The Police and The Public* (New Haven, Conn.: Yale University Press,
    1971).

Norman L. Weiner, *The Role of The Police in Urban Society: Conflicts and Consequences*
    (Indianapolis, Ind.: Bobbs-Merrill, 1976).

Arthur Niederhoffer, *Behind The Shield* (New York: Doubleday, 1969).

Jerome H. Skolnick, *Justice Without Trial* (New York: Wiley, 1966).

13

PRESSURES ON THE
THIN BLUE LINE:
STRESS IN POLICING

Managing Stress

If we were to ask a random sample of American citizens whether police work is a "stressful occupation," most of them would unquestionably answer that it is. Asked to rank police work against other occupations, most of our respondents would probably accord policing a place near the top of the list when it comes to the daily stresses faced by different classes of workers. Suppose we were to probe further, asking our hypothetical citizens to tell us just exactly what aspects of a police officer's job make it so stressful. What sorts of things would they describe? To be sure, the overwhelming majority would cite such things as having to engage in armed confrontations with dangerous individuals and high-speed automobile chases as being among the most common sources of stress in modern police work, if only because these kinds of obviously high-stress events are portrayed by the mass media as routine occurrences in a police officer's life.

Our sample of citizens would be correct in their belief that police work subjects those within it to high levels of stress on a regular basis; they would similarly be right in their decision to rank policing higher than most other forms of work on a stress continuum. However, they would be wrong in their conclusions as to what sorts of things make police work so stressful. If we asked this imaginery group of citizens to list on a sheet of paper the specific things which pose the greatest risk of physical harm to officers across the country, they would surely place crime and criminals at the top of the list. They would accordingly be surprised to discover that each year far more police officers die by suicide than by weapons in the hands of assailants. Indeed, one major study revealed that there are nearly twice as many police deaths by suicide as by homicide.[1] Niederhoffer has described the unusually high incidence of suicide that has long characterized New York City police officers:

> After the necessary adjustments are calculated, the suicide rate for males in the general New York City population is about 15 per 100,000. The average police rate of 22.7 is almost exactly fifty per cent more than this.[2]

It is not attacks by criminals that exact the largest toll on law-enforcement officers across the nation each year. Rather, it is a series of insidiously subtle and cumulative everyday pressures that produce among police officers as a group an abnormally high incidence of stress-related problems ranging from suicide, alcoholism, and divorce to coronary heart disease, diabetes, and psychosomatic ailments.[3]

Unfortunately, there have been too few formal studies of both the causes and the effects of occupational stress among police officers. The traditional failure to study this subject in depth, as has been done with so many other occupations, probably has a great deal to do with our pervasive cultural stereotype of the police as strong and silent crime fighters who are above succumbing to the kind of emotional pressures and tensions that afflict ordinary human beings. However, such data on stress and policing as have become available in recent years make it convincingly clear that this is far from the case. Fictional media policemen such as Clint Eastwood's *Dirty Harry* may go about performing even the most stressful of police tasks with all the apparent emotion and tension of a well-programmed android. Thus, for instance, in *Dirty Harry* the officer of that name calmly surveys a bank robbery in progress while still munching calmly on the remnants of a hot dog, the slight frown on his forehead suggesting mild annoyance at having his lunch interrupted. In another film Harry passes the time at a grisly autopsy by making flippant remarks to an attractive female partner. Notwithstanding such stereotypes, even a brief period of exposure to real-life police and their work makes it apparent that they are simply ordinary human beings operating under a great deal of daily pressure. As Kroes has written:

> . . . one need only ride around in a squad car with a patrolman to note the patent medications, such as Tums, readily within the officer's reach to realize that something is going on, or look at the medical histories of policemen to see the overabundance of health problems (too many problems to just write off as a consequence of aging). If that is not enough, psychiatrists have blessed the research literature with case histories of mental health problems of policemen, and newspapers have played up incidents of policemen finally breaking under stress and losing control.[4]

In recent years a number of newspaper accounts have described police officers "cracking" under the stress that Kroes alludes to. The following are cases in point:

> In a small town diner in Alabama, a policeman and his wife started quarreling, whereupon the husband took out his gun, killed his wife, then himself.
>
> In a Chicago bar, a cop went into a sudden rage and started shooting.
>
> Police officer Robert Tornsey and his partner were patrolling the streets of Brooklyn in a squad car. It was Thanksgiving night, 1976, and Tornsey was "upset" (as he later admitted) because he had to work on the holiday. Responding to a radio report that an armed man had been seen in a nearby housing project, the two policemen investigated but found nothing. As they left the building, a group of six boys approached. When one of them—15-year-old Randy Evans—walked up and asked if they had come from his apartment, Officer Tornsey pulled out his pistol and killed the boy. A year later in court, Tornsey was found not guilty of second degree murder by reason of insanity.[5]

To be sure, situations involving such dramatic breakdowns on the part of police officers are relatively infrequent occurrences. Far more common in departments across the country are less severe manifestations of on-the-job stress such as alcoholism, divorce, and psychosomatic ailments. We can readily keep track of the number of incidents where police run amuck and injure or kill either themselves or someone else. It is far more difficult to assess the frequency with which, as an occupational group, they experience such low-visibility problems as depression, anxiety, and interpersonal conflict with family and friends. Police officers are socialized and conditioned to keep whatever problems they experience to themselves. As Richard and Fell note, "Too often police officers are expected by society and their fellow officers to behave in stereotyped, tough roles. Stress and emotional upset are handled by being tough, not complaining, and not showing feelings."[6]

The emphasis placed by both society and the police subculture on such personal qualities as strength and the ability to keep oneself from normal displays of emotion result in a kind of *pressure-cooker* syndrome, in which officers present a surface of outward calm to the world around them but remain seething cauldrons on the inside. Despite the maintenance of such a "front" of toughness and perfect self-control, the internal pressures that officers regularly experience as a direct result of their work inevitably surface in a myriad of destructive ways. If the police officer is normatively prohibited by the expectations of others from admitting to himself and those around him that he is experiencing emotional problems, he is *allowed* by society and his peers to become "sick" in the literal sense of the word. He cannot have an anxiety neurosis or a phobia surrounding some aspect of his job, but he *may* develop ulcers, low-back pain, or circulatory trouble. To seek the help of a psychiatrist or psychologist for job-related personal problems is construed by self and others as a sign of weakness, but to visit a medical doctor or enter a hospital for treatment of some physical malady renders one blameless.

The extremely high—and growing—incidence of stress-related physical problems among police officers suggests that such difficulties often represent an "acceptable" symptomatic reaction to tremendous emotional stresses which the officer is experiencing. Gastrointestinal upsets, headaches, ulcers, stiff neck, hypertension, vague "flus" and the like for many officers represent unconscious psychosomatic mechanisms for escaping or coping with job-related anxieties. Jacobi reports that between 33 and 45 percent of all line-of-duty disabilities experienced by Los Angeles police officers fall into the amorphous category of "low back syndrome."[7] In a similar vein, the Bureau of Compensation reports that the leading cause of claims submitted by California police officers is cardiovascular disorders and ulcers.[8] Significantly, police officers as an occupational group show an abnormally high incidence of both arteriosclerotic heart disease and diabetes mellitus—two major physical diseases which have been closely linked to emotional stress by researchers in recent years.[9]

In addition to psychiatrists and clinical psychologists, police officers themselves are beginning to show signs of recognizing the degree to which those in their line of work experience serious problems in personal and social adjustment as a result of occupationally induced pressures. Thus, for instance, the International Conference of Police Associations (ICPA) recently conducted a national survey involving some 20,000 officers in cities of various sizes and locations in order to discover perceptions on the subject of stress. The results clearly reveal the extent to which officers see serious stress-related problems among their peers:

> Each officer was asked whether he noted any serious problems among his five closest associates. The responses: 37% noted serious marital problems [28.8% of those surveyed were divorced, compared to 13.8% for white urban males generally]; 36%, serious health problems; 23.4%, alcohol problems; 21%, problems dealing with their neighbors; 21%, problems dealing with their children; nearly 10%, serious problems with drugs.[10]

No one knows how many of those with such problems are potential Officer Tornseys—human "time bombs" that might explode at any given moment under the cumulative pressure of everyday problems built up by their work. Beyond the obvious importance of selecting for police work only those individuals who are revealed by careful psychological screening to be of sound mental health, it is equally important to monitor even the most emotionally stable officers throughout their careers for stress-related problems that may begin to appear. Adequate counseling and psychotherapeutic services should be continuously available to all officers on a confidential basis, and utilization of them should obviously be required where indicated.

Too often, because the police organization itself becomes caught up in the "Marlboro Man" mystique that surrounds its officers, police officers are simply left to fend for themselves in the face of serious personal problems. As one officer aptly put it, "Hell, even some guy bucking rivets in an aircraft plant can go see a plant psychologist if he gets uptight. We've got nobody."[11] Even when an officer becomes involved in a traumatic line-of-duty situation, such as a shooting or killing, he is typically returned to duty as if nothing unusual had happened.

A growing number of psychiatrists and psychologists have expressed serious concern over the failure of most departments to provide readily accessible counseling and psychiatric services to officers. Psychiatrist Edward Shev, on the basis on his extensive clinical work with officers in several large departments, has a grim prediction: "At least 40% of all police don't receive help with their problems. Half of these will assault their wives and children, and 10% to 20% of that half will either kill or be killed by family members."[12]

Given the effects of police stress—the ulcers and heart attacks, the suicides, alcoholism, and divorce—just what are the kinds of work pressures that bring these things about? It is possible to identify and discuss a number of specific *stressors* which characterize the police officer's role. Certain of these, such as shift work and the inability to freely express such emotions as anger and frustration, are shared in common with a number of other occupations. Others, however, such as danger, trauma, and hostility toward the courts and the criminal-justice system, tend to set police work apart from other occupations.

SHIFT WORK

A great many of the interpersonal and even physical problems experienced by police officers are closely linked to shift work. Humans are basically diurnal animals.[13] They have accordingly built around themselves a society in which most people accomplish the business of living and interacting with others during the daylight hours. Night is a time for low levels of activity, a time for sleep and recharging the human body's complicated machinery. Each of us operates throughout life on the basis of a twenty-four-hour pattern of bodily activity known as *circadian rhythm.* Very simply, the highly involved set of physiological functions that make up our bodies, such as body temperature, heart rate, metabolism, hormone production, and the sleep cycle, become geared to regular hours of activity and inactivity. For most people, circadian rhythms are based on daylight activity and remain remarkably constant year in and year out. The body and its biological elements operate with the stability of a well-regulated clock.

Police work is basically night work, or, more accurately, night work punctuated by periods of day work. As shift workers, police officers find themselves forced to fluctuate constantly between being diurnal and nocturnal creatures. In the three-shift structure which characterizes most departments, line patrol officers will spend one month on a day shift (7 or 8 A.M. to 3 or 4 P.M.), followed by month-long evening shift (3 or 4 P.M. to 11 P.M. or midnight), and finally by a midnight shift (11 P.M. or midnight to 7 or 8 A.M.). In some departments shift rotations occur even more often, taking place on a biweekly or even weekly basis.

Such changes in work schedules involve serious tampering with the rhythms of an officer's body, mind, and social relationships. From a physical standpoint, no sooner has an officer's body become geared to a particular set of hours for working, eating, and sleeping than it is time to jolt the physical machinery and its circadian rhythms with a different set of hours that must be adapted to. All police officers can attest to the regular digestive and sleep difficulties they experience anew each month as their bodies struggle valiantly to reset the "clocks." Kroes describes one study that sought to discover the extent of such problems among officers:

> In this study, ninety-three out of one hundred police officers surveyed mentioned disruption of eating habits as a problem resulting from changing shift routines. Over 30 per cent of the same officers also mentioned disruption of sleep habits as a problem.[14]

Because so much of police work is night work, officers must become accustomed to securing most of their sleep during the day. This fact by itself poses problems. Research has demonstrated that daytime sleep is physiologically less satisfying than nighttime sleep.[15] Beyond this, it is obviously more difficult to secure. All around the police officer tossing fitfully in bed are the noises of a diurnal society in full gear: horns, traffic, television sets and radios going, phones ringing, children bouncing balls against the walls. The police officer is, in a word, out of phase with society's normal activity cycle, a fact which poses serious problems of personal adjustment both for the officer and his or her family. As Kroes observes:

> The [police officer's] wife must maintain two households, the normal daytime schedule for herself and the children and a separate schedule for her husband. This is quite taxing on her as she must prepare separate meal schedules, coordinate separate sleeping schedules, try to keep the children from making too much noise during the day when her husband is asleep, jumping to answer the phone on the first ring so as not to disturb her sleeping husband, and so on. Further she must often be alone at night, a condition which can be very unsettling for many women.[16]

Such conditions of family life certainly make understandable the extremely high incidence of divorce among police officers as an occupational group. The spouse of a police officer cannot experience many of the social and personal events which most couples come to take for granted: She is frequently sound asleep after a hard day of working at a regular job or caring for the home and children when her husband walks through the door wide awake after just coming off duty. As a result, everything from their sexual relationship to the satisfaction that comes from normal end-of-day husband-wife conversations suffers. Evening get-togethers with other couples, weekend picnics, family trips, and the like can be undertaken only infrequently. Even the officer's time with his children is severly curtailed by the fact that he is either asleep or away from home during most of the time they are awake and active.

ECONOMIC PRESSURE

With few exceptions, police officers across the country experience considerable economic pressure. While one might well retort, "Who doesn't?" given the inflationary economy in which we find ourselves, the fact remains that police officers as an occupational group are grossly underpaid in light of the frequently complex, demanding, and sometimes dangerous activities they are called upon to engage in. The new thrust toward professionalism in recent years, and the resultant influx of large numbers of college-educated young people, has only served to intensify the economic dissatisfaction of the police. Not surprisingly, Niederhoffer found that the cynicism of college-educated patrol officers was far higher than that of other officers, simply because they entered police work with far greater expectations.[17] One study that compared law enforcement with 23 other high-stress occupations found that the police showed the greatest amount of unhappiness with their salaries.[18] A survey by Watson and

Sterling asked officers, "What is the most important problem you as an individual face?" Fifty-seven percent of those responding answered, "not enough pay."[19]

Widespread dissatisfaction with their economic lot has led officers in a growing numer of departments throughout the country to affiliate themselves with strong police unions and associations in an attempt to secure better pay and benefits. In their mounting frustration, many officers have turned away from conventional police unions, such as the Fraternal Order of Police (FOP) and the Police Benevolent Association (PBA), in favor of more militant organizations such as the Teamsters Union. Indeed today:

> . . . the Teamsters, without much public notice, have become a power in police unionism. At least 10,000 police officers across the country are members of Teamsters locals. Teamsters officials estimate that they bargain on behalf of 15,000 police in about 225 municipalities.[20]

This development has caused considerable anxiety among police professionals and administrators alike, in light of the Teamsters notorious reputation for strong-arm tactics and corrupt leadership. Illegal "wildcat" strikes by officers and mass "sick-outs" or "blue flus" have left police supervisors and the national guard with the task of protecting some communities for tense days that seem like years.

In addition to turning toward militant unionism as a means of alleviating economic pressures, police officers in growing numbers have taken up the well-known practice of "moonlighting," or working a second (or even a third) job. During their off-duty hours many officers can be found, often bleary-eyed and zombielike from lack of sleep, guarding banks, working shoplifting details in department stores, and providing security at bowling alleys and other places of entertainment. Many have also gone into private enterprise in their free time, working as roofers, store clerks, gas-station attendants, real-estate or car sales people—anything to bring in badly needed extra dollars. One resultant problem is that moonlighting, while it may ease an officer's financial pressures somewhat, often only serves to intensify the physical and interpersonal problems that already exist in connection with shift work. As one police officer's wife commented:

> Our home life is usually pretty smooth running and uncomplicated. The opposite is true when he is working a second job. In just a few days he has turned into a crabby individual, who has no time for anything except work. He doesn't eat right or sleep right, he is very nervous, tired, listless, and constantly on the run. He gets up and goes to work at his first job, works eight hours, comes home, changes clothes and grabs a bite to eat, rests a few minutes, then leaves for his second job.[21]

Besides the ravages that working a 12- to 16-hour day inflicts on a police officer's body, mind, and personal relationships, it also greatly impairs the ability to function effectively in a law-enforcement role. In city upon city across the nation, police cruisers are staffed by people who are simply too exhausted to do the complex and demanding work that their job involves, and whose chronic fatigue poses a very real danger to both themselves and others. The following case, drawn from a recent newspaper article on police moonlighting in one city, is quite typical:

> Police officer Phillip Kiracofe sometimes sleeps only an hour before groggily awaking to begin his armed, on-duty patrol of the city. "I actually surprise myself how clear-headed I am," said Kiracofe, 30, a 2-year veteran of the force. "I drink a lot of coffee and I'm able to function." If Kiracofe hardly sleeps before going on patrol, it's because he stayed up all night at his second job as a security guard. It doesn't happen often, he said. But, like many . . . cops, Kiracofe insisted he had no choice but to continue moonlighting at second and third jobs. He has a wife and three young children to support. He said his policeman's salary wasn't enough to pay the bills. . . . He has not had a raise in two years.[22]

Police officers resent having to moonlight long hours just to make ends meet. As one officer put it during a new interview, "A guy should be able to work part-time jobs to buy something special for his family. He shouldn't have to do it just to pay his bills and that's what I've been doing."[23] Pervasive moonlighting, even sometimes by high-level command officers, poses an obvious morale problem. As one officer told the senior author:

> The first night I came on the job right out of the academy what do you think I saw. I pull into this hamburger joint with my T.O. [training officer] to get dinner and there's the goddamn zone commander—in uniform, bars and all—working security in the parking lot. I mean, Jesus, a captain with over twenty years on the job! I asked my T.O., "Is that what I've got to look forward to?"[24]

Precisely because of such harsh realities, a great many officers drop out of their law-enforcement careers in favor of more economically rewarding, conventional jobs.

WORK LOAD

Policing is a "feast or famine" activity when it comes to the amount of work facing officers at any given time. At one end of a work-load continuum, patrol officers on a short-handed day shift may scramble frantically from one call to another as dispatchers stack additional calls in a "holding pattern" like air-traffic controllers. At the other end, officers may fight to stay awake on a midnight watch as they drift monotonously up and down deserted streets. Perhaps the fact that such opposite realities characterize everyday police work led an unknown officer to come up with the familiar phrase, police work is hours of monotony broken by moments of stark terror.

Monotony. Certainly this is the last thing the average person would ever associate with police work, after countless hours of watching television cops race from one felony call to another. Yet monotony, as any real officer can quickly attest, is an all-too-real stress associated with the police role. Indeed, the chronic "underload" of work that is found during certain shifts and on particular beats forms one of the most stressful aspects of a patrol officer's career. Research shows that human beings have an optimal level of arousal and must receive a certain amount of stimulation from their environment if they are to function effectively.[25] Having either too much *or* too little to do subjects an individual to both physical and emotional strain.

Cruse and Rubin, on the basis of a stress study of officers conducted in Miami, concluded that patrol officers as a group often suffer from severe boredom and sensory deprivation, particularly late at night when they receive little if anything in the way of stimulation from their environment.[26] Every patrol officer has had the experience of starting at the sound of an unexpected 4 A.M. time check coming over a radio which has been stone silent for nearly a full hour. He has similarly found himself trying desperately to structure activity—rechecking buildings he examined only a short while before, stopping one of the few cars he sees on the slightest of pretexts—as stimulus deprivation closes in on him during the late hours of the midnight watch. Cruse and Rubin found that ". . . the greatest and most consistent increments of fatigue at the end of a shift clearly occurred when the policeman had the least number of citizen contacts." [27] People need people, and the police are no exception. Cruse and Rubin discovered that as the fatigue and boredom of patrol officers increased in the wake of sensory deprivation, their aggressiveness and tendency to overreact to individuals and situations increased:

> Officers are less controlling and "cooler" in handling citizens when they are kept busy (on Saturday night, for example). That is, an officer will exhibit more controlling behavior toward any single citizen when he has had few citizen contacts and spends most of his time simply riding around in a patrol car.[28]

An officer who is suffering from boredom and the crushing fatigue that accompanies sensory deprivation is far more likely to "pick up on" and overreact to trivial incidents and affronts as a means of escaping the stress he experiences as a result of long periods of "underload." As Kroes observes:

> Private reports from policemen, as well as documented research, have shown that the need for action to avoid boredom is so great that policemen occasionally engaged in marginal activities such as arresting or baiting drunks and hippies just to have something to do.[29]

In addition to such instances of focused overaggressiveness on the part of line officers, sensory deprivation and boredom also lead patrol officers to engage in a variety of delinquent (and sometimes illegal) conduct simply as a diversion:

> Police have a number of ways of coping with this [boredom and sensory deprivation]. Some of them periodically get out of their assigned zone and race along for a few minutes on a super-highway. Some, I have been told (but for obvious reasons did not observe), look for women and engage in sexual intercourse. Some sleep. If one isn't in a two-man car with a partner to talk to, other more common devices for combatting boredom are stopping to chat with other patrolmen or backing up a neighborhood patrol car sent on a call. Some policemen endeavor to "look for action" by self-initiated police-citizen contacts and investigations.[30]

As a new police officer, the senior author soon found himself in the midst of (and gratefully taking part in!) many of the boredom-alleviating activities devised by his peers to make it through the midnight watch:

> The late hours of the first watch were an endless round of delinquent measures designed to keep members of the squad from succumbing to the nightly pressure of fatigue and boredom: one night it was Jack, racing like an old West cowboy down the middle of Main Street, shouting like a madman and firing a blank .22 caliber starter pistol at the closed storefronts. Another night it was Ken and Billy (a black-white team) driving through the heart of their ghetto beat with a small Confederate flag fluttering from the cruiser's antenna and the strains of "Dixie" blaring over the loudspeaker. On yet another it was all of us huddled around a new supervisor's car with a hidden tape recorder as we probed him for explicit details of the preceding night's erotic activity with a notorious prostitute in the local cemetery . . . in retrospect, such actions—childish and delinquent though they were—seem to have been functional devices for mitigating the stress of sensory deprivation.[31]

The other side of work-load-related stress is, of course, having far too much to do in a given period of time. This, too, becomes part of every police officer's lot. At any given instant, without the slightest warning, an officer may be jolted from the depths of sensory deprivation to a condition in which every fiber of his being has to struggle to handle a flood of incoming stimulation:

> I was about to say something when I heard the emergency tone, followed by our car number. "Two Lima Ninety-five . . . a suicide attempt in progress at Sixteen-fifteen Blainey. Ambulance is en route," the dispatcher said. My partner accelerated and motioned for me to turn on the emergency lights and siren. This was the way things usually happened, I would find. Suddenly. With no warning. Right in the middle of a sentence, a mouthful of food, a cup of coffee, at the most illogical and inconvenient times. A surge of adrenaline punctuating minutes of relative calm. Man down! Robbery in progress! Major injury accident! Domestic disturbance! See the woman! And almost always the calls would come without the precious luxury of time. Time . . . time to think situations through, time to analyze them, dissect them. Time to weigh the desirability of different courses of action.[32]

Significantly, modern medical research has shown that individuals who regularly work under time pressure run a substantially greater risk of coronary heart disease.[33] It is not surprising that police officers as a group have a relatively high incidence of heart attacks. Police officers are perforce people who live by the clock. From the moment he receives an assignment over the air, an imaginary clock is ticking in the back of his mind, urging him to hurry—to get to the location, find the suspect, render whatever assistance is needed, handle the call and write the report. He knows all to well (and knows that his supervisor knows) the average time within which he should complete different kinds of assignments and check back in. With lights and siren going, he threads his way through peak-hour commuter traffic, fighting the omnipresent enemy of time as he tries to reduce the number of streets that separate him from another officer in trouble, an injured person, or a fleeing felon. Time. Always there seems to be either not enough or too much of it in an officer's life. Either way, high levels of physical and emotional stress result.

Under conditions of work overload, the police officer's mind and body are subjected to a highly stressly process known as *polyphasic activity*.[34] Like time pressure, this, too, is highly associated with heart disease and other medical and psychological problems. Polyphasic activity involves trying to do a number of different things at the same time as an individual tries to cope with a large number of different stimuli that are competing for attention. So it is, for instance, that the police officer handling a volatile disturbance call is simultaneously trying to listen to and calm two (and maybe more) angry people who appear to be on the verge of violence. At the same time, he is tensely scanning the room, people's clothing, the position of hands and bodies—trying to assess the possibility of an attack on himself and the best way of protecting himself. He tries to glean individual biographies from eyes and facial expressions; consciously tries to stage a calm and confident front to mask the tension he feels inside; tries to hear the radio on his belt and determine how far away the backup unit is—all these things take place at the same time, and within seconds. Police officers are routinely called upon to operate in polyphasic situations, which place great strain on mind and body alike.

THE ADMINISTRATION

The police organization itself becomes a major source of near-continuous stress for most officers. It was observed earlier that patrol officers are almost constantly in a position of peril with respect to the administration, because the everyday requirements of their work lead them to either ignore or violate many of its official rules. There exist within the police organization a great many ways to apply punishment for violation of regulations and poor performance by officers. On the other hand, however, there are precious few rewards built into the system for those who do well in the police role. As Eisenberg has observed:

> Recognition and compensation for work well done is extremely limited in law enforcement. One can count on being "recognized" for poor performance but good performance somehow stands as the norm or expected behavior. Most of the behavioral monitoring systems are negative in nature and as such generate stress.[35]

The officer who rescues a child from a burning building or who risks his life in a shoot-out with an armed felon is apt to be rewarded by the organization in any number of ways: favorable assignments, promotions, laudatory comments in his personnel file, and the less tangible (but very valuable) favor of ranking superiors. The opportunities to participate in such dramatic and reward-evoking activities, however, are few and far between in the careers of most real police officers—something that is quite in contrast to their fictional television counterparts. The punishment-oriented bureaucracy that characterizes most police departments has simply not evolved many meaningful devices to reward officers for handling well the often complex everyday tasks they are called upon to perform.

Officers accordingly find themselves "on the carpet" for everything from not having a hat on at a car stop or being disrespectful to a citizen to sleeping on duty and accepting gratuities from a merchant at Christmastime. The vast number of daily accomplishments that characterize the careers of most officers—getting lost children home safely, calming disturbances, and obtaining assistance for elderly and mentally ill people as well as average citizens—simply go officially unnoticed and unrewarded for the most part. Surely it is small wonder, therefore, that so many police officers literally live their entire occupational lives in eager anticipation of dangerous and dramatic life-and-death encounters, for these are really the only routes to organizational rewards open to them.

The everyday, street-level experience of most police officers consists of a more or less continuous stream of negative or unpleasant encounters with other human beings. For the most part, an officer deals with a grudging clientele that varies in its manner from the blatant hostility (and sometimes violence) of the criminal to the brusque manner of the average citizen stopped for speeding. The police officer's interventions may be tolerated or resisted by others, but in the final analysis few actually welcome his presence. The fact that his work is so permeated with unpleasantry produces stress, all the more so because the officer is usually prevented by the possibility of administrative punishment from aggressing against the people who represent *stressors,* or causes of stress, for him.

Added to this everyday burden of stress stemming from the negative experiences that make up the police officer's role is yet another burden of unpleasant contacts with the police administration itself. In addition to feeling that the organization stands ready to punish him for even the smallest mistakes while failing to reward his successes, the police officer also often believes that his department will not back him even when he is clearly in the right. In incidents involving such things as the use of force and friction with various sources of power in the community, line officers often accuse their superiors of everything from indifference to selling them out in favor of political considerations. The drawn-out investigations that typically follow such occurrences as shootings and killings by officers are, therefore a major source of stress for people who feel uncertain about the support of their superiors:

> An outsider to the police department cannot imagine the anguish the officer must go through during these interrogations. Knowing this potential problem, the officer needs to know where his superiors stand: will they support and back him, or will they abandon him to the wolves? Many line officers will tell you that in the interest of public relations they are abandoned by their superiors.[36]

Other frustrations with the police organization add to these stresses and uncertainties. Officers fresh from the academy (and perhaps the college or university campus), filled with new ideas and approaches, soon

find themselves hemmed in, straitjacketed by the rigid dictates of a tra-
dition-oriented bureaucracy. Things are to be done, they quickly learn,
the way they have always been done. "The police organization is a paramilitary bureaucracy which rewards conformity and discourages innovation." [37] Everything from outmoded equipment to inane procedures and
tons of mindless paperwork is to be accepted without a question. Officers
may grumble and share frustrations with their peers, but to formally
make their superiors aware of them through the medium of a formal
interview or memorandum is to invite disaster. Officers learn from more
experienced peers, veterans, and seasoned "street cops" that the best way
to "do twenty" and retire is to cultivate the twin virtues of inaction and
quietude in the presence of departmental officials.

As an officer's sense of alienation and frustration toward the formal
organization of which he is a part deepens with the passage of time, he
gradually drops into a kind of "us-them" frame of mind in which the
administration—"them"—takes on the character of an enemy. When this
occurs, the stage is set for vicariously displacing onto the police organization all the tensions and anger an officer builds up as a result of the
nature of the work. The organization becomes a readily accessible target
for the venting of such feelings. Aggressions gradually become personalized and focused on individual representatives of the department, particular "devils" in the command hierarchy who are blamed for everything
and anything that goes wrong. The following instance, drawn from the
senior author's experience is a good illustration of this process:

> I ran two fingers underneath the tight blue collar. Summer was over. The
> temperature was still hovering in the high eighties as we went on duty,
> yet officially summer was over for the police department. Someone in the
> hierarchy of command had said so two days earlier and had ordered
> us to abandon the light, open-collared shirts in favor of long sleeves and
> clip-on ties. Perhaps a deputy chief, I thought, or even the old man
> himself. My partner had ascribed the premature shift to heavier uniforms,
> like almost every other evil visited upon us, to the malevolence of
> Sergeant Bernard. It was "Douche" who had personally drafted the most
> mindless and idiotic of the General Orders, Douche who engineered
> the assignment of involved calls to the members of "A" Squad during the
> last five minutes of the watch, Douche who was responsible for the poor
> maintenance of the black and whites.[38]

Much of the resentment line officers feel toward the administrators
of their departments stems from the fact that, unlike workers in many
forms of business and industry that practice "management by participation," the police are usually allowed no say in decisions that vitally
affect them. Officers are transferred to new assignments, forced abruptly

to change partners or supervisors, and so on, without being given any opportunity to either understand the rationale behind such decisions or to participate in making them. Officers understandably begin to feel like billiard balls, simply knocked about at will by forces around them. Because of such sentiments, more progressive police agencies today are moving away from autocratic management models in favor of actively involving line officers in the decisional processes that affect them.[39]

THE LAW AND THE COURTS

We saw earlier in this chapter how the American legal system, with the many procedural restraints it imposes on the police in the interest of preserving individual liberty and human rights, is a source of considerable frustration to officers. While the United States may well be the best place in the world to be a citizen, it certainly is one of the most difficult countries in which to be a police officer. The latter must toil not only under the burden of legal restrictions that make efficient performance of his or her duties impossible, but also under a rule of law which renders him strictly accountable for every action (or inaction) he engages in—regardless of how constructive or humanitarian the motives might be.

American police officers function daily under high levels of stress generated by the knowledge that the slightest departure from the law on their part renders them instantly vulnerable to attack from a multitude of sources, ranging from the courts to the press and various civic groups. This is quite in contrast to the situation confronting their counterparts in totalitarian countries, where the law may be violated with impunity providing that such violations are viewed by the party in power as being in their best interests. Skolnick describes, for instance, the wide latitude of operation accorded the Soviet Cheka:

> The Soviet regime (and the Chinese Communist as well) adopted a secret police almost immediately on coming into existence. The Soviet secret police, the Cheka, was given broad powers, although it was not until 1924 that even a document was published explaining its existence and purposes. Under this statutory authorization, the main task of the secret police was to act as the investigative and punitive arm of the dictatorship, hunting out and liquidating counterrevolutionary attempts and actions throughout Russia, no matter what their origin. The Cheka was answerable only to the top leadership of the Party and government, although experience was to demonstrate that whatever actions the Cheka considered necessary to defend the dictatorship (of the proletariat), including arrest, imprisonment, and even execution, would be approved by the Party leadership, notwithstanding any formal or legal limitations on its power.[40]

To be an American police officer today is to work each day within a legalistic goldfish bowl, a high-visibility environment where even the smallest legal actions and inactions are apt to be subject to scrutiny. Such police practices as the proverbial back-room third-degree, the beating of suspects with rubber hoses, and hours of withering questioning without benefit of counsel have given way to an era in which the police— in theory, and increasingly, in practice—are held to a minute observation of individual rights, so minute, in fact, that many feel the protection of society has been sacrificed in favor of solicitude for the rights of those accused of crime:

> ... many police officers and citizens believe that recent judicial interpretations of the Constitution and various statutes have unduly and inappropriately inhibited the work of the police and so have made it harder for police to protect the public. Part of this feeling stems, no doubt, from the tense, fast-moving situations in which policemen are called upon to make split-second decisions, and the calm that prevails in the appellate courts while lawyers and judges argue the merits of those decisions, after having searched law books for apposite precedents.[41]

The law itself tends to be a vague source of free-floating anxiety for most police officers. The courts, however, as a very tangible institution charged with the specific responsibility for seeing that the law is carried out, takes on the form of a major stressor in the police officer's mind. A number of different things conspire to make most of the average police officer's contacts with the courts highly stressful experiences.

Police officers are often described as individuals who tend to see people and events in terms of rather rigid categories.[42] Things are either right or wrong, black or white. The individuals the officer arrests and brings before the court are guilty in his mind and deserving of punishment. In the courtroom (and especially "backstage" in the prosecutor's office where most cases are disposed of before they reach the trial stage), the officer discovers that issues are rarely construed in such terms. What to him or her are the fundamental issues of guilt and innocence become secondary to the legalistic strategies inherent in such processes as plea bargaining. The officer watches individuals whom he knows to be guilty either "walk" as a result of technical flaws in a case or secure a major reduction of the original charge due to case-load pressures within the district attorney's office. Even with those individuals who are convicted of crime, the officer discovers on a very personal level the awful truth that as the volume of crime in a society increases, the penalties meted out for it must, ironically, decrease in severity, simply because the system can no longer handle the work required to punish large numbers of offenders. Officers find, therefore, that punishment (which, as believers in individual free will, they feel is the only truly effective deterrent to crime) is often set aside in favor of the sham of "rehabilitation." Seeing such realities of the court system cannot but be a bitter, frustrating experience for most officers. They cannot help personalizing the failures of the courts into a kind of rejection of themselves, after expending so much time and effort to bring a particular individual to justice, only to see everything they have done brought to nothing through plea bargaining, not-guilty verdicts arising from technicalities, and mild sentences.

Those relatively few cases that do get to court usually subject officers to additional stress and frustration. Time after time, they find their veracity and integrity as officers called into question by the very process of which they are a part. Clever defense lawyers, who are far more knowledgable in the law and more articulate in public settings, subject police officers to high levels of stress in the course of trying to damage their credibility:

> [One] tactic is to confront and upset the officer. If [he] can be angered or rattled he will make easier pickings for the defense lawyer and will present a poorer image to the jury. The ordeal an officer goes through can be tremendous. As one officer relates. "Every time I'm on the stand they [defense lawyers] made me feel guilty as hell. The pressures can be overwhelming. Take the case of one officer, who recently suffered a heart attack because of undue job stress. After he recovered, he returned to work, immediately to be faced with a court appearance. . . . A case that he had forgotten and which at the time of the proceedings all lawyers agreed that the officer had acted appropriately. However, this officer, just out of the hospital, was forced to undergo very strenuous cross-examination to justify himself. In the end the court case was thrown out but not before the officer was put through a "wringer." Shortly after this case the officer suffered a second heart attack.[43]

In the courtroom every police officer discovers the depressing reality that the ability to convict most criminals hinges more on the theatrical skills of the attorneys involved than on the individual's guilt or innocence. Very often the assistant district attorney representing the state's case is either fresh out of law school or has little trial experience. More than one officer has come to the shocking realization during a pretrial conference that he understands the relevant law and operation of the courts better than the assistant D.A. he is depending on to present a case well. Confronting the officer on the witness stand, however, is often a seasoned defense lawyer with years of experience.

It is scarcely surprising, in light of these facts and the few successes officers experience at the hands of the courts, that they come to regard them as major sources of stress in their lives.

DANGER AND TRAUMA

No discussion of sources of police stress would be complete without mentioning the important role played by danger, a subject we have already examined at length. It is not the objective reality of danger that becomes an everyday stressor for most police. We saw earlier that confrontations with dangerous individuals and events are relatively infrequent occurrences. Rather, it is the constant anticipation of danger, the minute-to-minute preparedness to deal with it that makes danger a major stressor in an officer's life. Never knowing when or where danger may appear, police officers must keep themselves in a state of heightened alertness, which produces strain on both mind and body over a period of time. Indeed, research suggests that the *anticipation* of dangerous situations may be even more stressful than actually confronting them:

> This state [of heightened alertness] produces effects similar in the body's reaction pattern to actually being in a crisis situation. Thus, though crises may be relatively infrequent, the cop's body is acting as if they are constant: In this way being in a constant state of peak preparedness tends to wear the officer down as much as if he were in actual danger. In fact, research studies have shown that anticipation before confrontation produces more stress than actual confrontation.[44]

In other words, it matters little as far as the physical and emotional strain placed on an officer whether a reported burglary-in-progress call turns out to be valid or whether a suspicious person who abruptly thrusts a hand in his pocket emerges with a driver's license or a gun. The stress leading up to the situation is the same. Hearts pound, adrenaline pumps, and palms become cold and clammy regardless of the outcome of such encounters. It is thus the omnipresent potential of danger in even the most routine encounters that subjects the police to high levels of stress. Even off-duty, officers continue to experience stress as a result of their perception of possibly dangerous individuals and events. As New York police psychologist Harvey Scholossberg observes:

> A police officer tends to remain in a state of stress even in his off-duty hours. . . . They call it a state of "constant readiness." You can go through this job in 20 or 30 years and never get involved in a crisis—but you're always waiting for it to happen. Your mind is always set on that bad guy around the corner." [45]

In addition to the mental anticipation of danger, daily exposure to such traumatic events as suicides, shootings, stabbings, child abuse, and the like also subject the officer to high levels of stress. Death and all the suffering associated with it, for instance, is effectively kept away from most people in our society throughout their lives. On those infrequent occasions when the death of others must be confronted by the average citizen, it is made as palatable as possible by being presented under highly controlled, institutional circumstances where such things as the mortician's art and the clergyman's utterings serve to ease the sting. For police officers, death and human suffering are very different—and infinitely more traumatic. They kneel beside the crushed body of a child at an accident scene and watch life ebb, powerless to do anything. They fight to control the nausea welling in the pit of the stomach as they enter the apartment of a man who has been dead for perhaps a week or more. They confront the teenaged rape victim who has been brutally beaten and murdered. To confront the death of others is to confront the inevitability of one's own eventual death. For police officers, reminders of their own mortality and vulnerability to the same injury and suffering they see around them come all too frequently. Such things may be handled with aplomb by television police officers. For the real officer, however, they are experienced as stressful, because they are, in the final analysis, simply ordinary human beings who are often called upon to function under extraordinary circumstances.

SUMMARY Police work has been rightly described by author Joseph Wambaugh as ". . . emotionally one of the most dangerous jobs on earth." While law enforcement as an occupation is characterized by a far lower incidence of injury and death than such jobs as mining, construction work, and agriculture, it involves a disproportionately high incidence of emotional hazards, which become translated each year into a staggering volume of problems ranging from alcoholism and divorce to coronary heart disease, psychosomatic ailments, and even suicide (one study reports that a police officer who dies during his career is twice as likely to die by his own hand as that of an assailant).

This chapter has explored the chemistry of stress and police work, identifying in the process specific stressors which place severe pressures on the men and women of the thin blue line. We have accordingly examined the impact of variables, including shift work and low pay, the anticipation of danger, and frustration with both the court system and the police administration. We have seen in this chapter that the most serious emotional strains experienced by the average law-enforcement officer are far removed from the high-speed chases and shoot-outs that make up the work world of television and motion-picture police officers. Rather, the actual strains are tied up with such subtle things as seeing the worst of humankind and human problems day after day, personalizing failures of the criminal-justice system, and functioning in a society whose police are expected to be strong and silent types who do not admit to or vent personal frustrations. Stress in the police officer's life infrequently comes from a gun or knife in the hand of a criminal or mentally disordered person; yet it comes silently and repeatedly each day in such forms as time pressure and polyphasic activity, and in countless emotional demands made upon the police officer as a human being.

NOTES

1. L. Guralnick, *Mortality by Occupation and Cause of Death* (Washington, D.C.: U.S. Public Health Service Vital Statistics Special Reports, 53, 1963).
2. Arthur Niederhoffer, *Behind the Shield: The Police in Urban Society* (New York: Doubleday, 1967), p. 101.
3. For an excellent analysis of these and other stress-related problems in law enforcement, see William H. Kroes, *Society's Victim—The Policeman,* (Springfield, Ill.: Thomas, 1976).
4. Ibid., p. 82.
5. From Micki Siegel, "Workaday World of the Cop: Stress, Unending Stress," *Parade* (March 12, 1978), pp. 4–5.
6. Wayne C. Richard and Ronald D. Fell, "Health Factors in Police Job Stress," in William H. Kores, Ph.D. and Joseph J. Hurrell, Jr., M.A., *Job Stress and The Police Officer: Indentifying Stress Reduction Techniques* (Washington, D.C.: H.E.W. Publication No. (NIOSH) 76-187), p. 83.
7. See Jerome H. Jacobi, "Reducing Police Stress: A Psychiatrist's Point of View," in Kroes and Hurrell, *Job Stress,* pp. 85–116.
8. Kroes, *Society's Victim,* p. 82.
9. See W. McQuade, "What Stress Can Do To You," *Fortune,* 85 (1), pp. 102–107.
10. Reported in Siegel, "Workaday World," p. 4.
11. Kirkham, Author's Files, 1974.
12. See Siegel, "Workaday World," p. 4.
13. See Kroes, *Society's Victim,* pp. 29–33.
14. Ibid., p. 32.
15. Ibid., p. 32.
16. Ibid., p. 31.
17. Niederhoffer, *Behind the Shield,* p. 106.
18. Kroes, *Society's Victim,* p. 35.
19. N. Watson and J. Sterling, *Police and Their Opinions* (Gaithersburg, Md.: International Association of Chiefs of Police), 1969.
20. Allen Dodds Frank, "The Wages of Frustration: When All Else Fails, Call The Teamsters," *Police* Magazine (September, 1978), p. 21.
21. Kroes, *Society's Victim,* p. 21.
22. Tallahassee Democrat, "Police Moonlight to Make Ends Meet," (September 7, 1978), p. 10.
23. Ibid.

24. Kirkham, Author's Files, (1977).
25. J. Rubin and D. Cruse, "Police Behavior," *Journal of Psychiatry and Law* 1 (1973), pp. 167–222.
26. Ibid., p. 221.
27. Ibid.
28. Cited in Harry W. Moore, Jr., *The American Police,* (St. Paul, Minn.: West, 1976), p. 174.
29. Kroes, *Society's Victim,* p. 25.
30. Cruse and Rubin, cited in Kroes, *Society's Victim,* p. 23.
31. Kirkham, Author's Files, 1973.
32. George Kirkham, *Signal Zero* (New York: Lippincott, 1976), p. 87.
33. See, e.g., Meyer Freedman and Ray H. Resenman, *Type A Behavior and Your Heart* (Greenwich, Conn.: Fawcett), 1974.
34. Ibid. (The concept is introduced by the authors to describe a highly stressful condition in which an individual is trying to cope with a number of different stimuli at the same time.)
35. Terry Eisenberg, "Job Stress and the Police Officer: Identifying Job Reduction Techniques," in Kroes and Hurrell, *Job Stress,* p. 28.
36. Kroes, *Society's Victim,* p. 14.
37. Moore, *American Police,* p. 122.
38. Kirkham, *Signal Zero,* p. 137.
39. See, e.g., Edward M. Davis, *Staff One: A Perspective on Effective Police Management* (Englewood Cliffs, N.J.: Prentice-Hall, 1978).
40. Jerome H. Skolnick, *Justice Without Trial* (New York: John Wiley, 1966), p. 19.
41. See James Q. Wilson, *Thinking about Crime* (New York: Random House), 1977.
42. Kroes, *Society's Victim,* p. 46.
43. Ibid., p. 63.
44. *Ibid.*
45. Siegel, "Workday World," p. 5.

SELECTED READINGS

George Kirkham, *Signal Zero: The True Story of a Professor Who Became A Street Cop* (New York: Lippincott, 1976).

William H. Kroes, *The Policeman: Society's Victim: An Analysis of Job Stress in Policing* (Springfield, Ill.: Thomas, 1976).

William H. Kroes, Ph.D., and Joseph J. Hurrell, Jr., M.A., eds, *Job Stress and The Police Officer: Identifying Stress Reduction Techniques* (Washington, D.C.: U.S. Department of Health, Education, and Welfare, Public Health Service, Center for Disease Control, National Institute for Occupational Safety and Health, 1975).

Pat James and Martha Nelson, *Police Wife* (Springfield, Ill.: Thomas, 1975).

D. Cruse and J. Rubin, "Police Behavior," (Part I, pp. 167–222), *Journal of Psychiatry and Law,* 1, (2) 1973; also J. Rubin and D. Cruse, "Police Behavior (Part II, pp. 353–375, 1973, *Journal of Psychiatry and Law,* 1, (3).

See also "The Police Personality" (Part IV) in Harry W. Moore, Jr., *The American Police* (St. Paul, Minn.: West), 1976, pp. 92–170.

14
LAW ENFORCEMENT TOMORROW: TOWARD PROFESSIONAL POLICING

This chapter surveys the subject of professionalization in law enforcement: the ideal of professionalization, the reforms that have been proposed and the improvements made in the name of professionalization, and some current problems in professionalization. It begins with definitions of *profession* and how the police measure up to the standards implied in the definitions. The chapter reviews the historical and social context of professionalization and explores some aspects of professional policing—the departmental qualities of professional law enforcement, the relationship of professional police to the community, and the "human dimension" of police professionalism. Special attention is given to a current controversy: the higher education of the police. After consideration of some advantages and disadvantages of professionalization in law enforcement, this chapter anticipates a few of the obstacles and prospects.

Meanings of *Profession*

Policing would seem to be a profession. Not only is it often called a profession, but it is likened in its qualities to other full-fledged professions, as in the FBI Pledge for Law Enforcement Officers:

> I am aware of the serious responsibilities of my office and in the performance of my duties I shall, as a *minister,* seek to supply comfort, advice and aid to those who may be in need of such benefits; as a *soldier,* I shall wage vigorous warfare against the enemies of my country, of its laws, and of its principles; and as a *physician,* I shall seek to eliminate the criminal parasite which preys upon our social order and to strengthen the lawful processes of our body politic.
>
> I shall strive to be both a *teacher* and a pupil in the art and science of law enforcement. As a *lawyer,* I shall acquire due knowledge of the

laws of my domain and seek to preserve and maintain the majesty and dignity of the law; as a *scientist,* it will be my endeavor to learn all pertinent truth about accusations and complaints which come to my lawful knowledge; as an artist, I shall seek to use my skill for the purpose of making each assignment a masterpiece; as a neighbor, I shall bear an attitude of true friendship and courteous respect to all citizens; and as an *officer,* I shall always by loyal to my duty, my organization and my country.[1]

The trouble is that the term *profession* is not fixed in its meaning. Therefore, professionalization of the police means as many things as the words *profession* or *professional* or *professionalism.* Some meanings associated with those words can be put aside for present purposes: One meaning of *professional* contrasts with *amateur* and denotes "money-making" as the principle characteristic, as in the distinction between pro and amateur golfers. But the subject of police professionalism assumes that the field is made up of paid *professionals.* The word also means skilled or dependable, as in "Pete Rose is a real pro." That meaning involves elements of what we deal with here, but it is distinct: all police officers, we will assume, are (or, when they are professionalized, they will be) skilled and dependable.

PROFESSION, TRADE, AND CRAFT

The professions are distinguished from trades and crafts. These terms are seldom used with precision, so there is overlapping and confusion in their usage. Trades, strictly speaking, are lines of work involving manual or mechanical labor of some skill, such as carpentry. Hod-carrying, by contrast, although hod carriers are organized as a trade union, involves manual labor of little skill—hod carriers have only to hoist, carry, and set down bricks in a hod or wooden trough. The bricklayer is the tradesman.

Crafts are likewise lines of work involving manual or mechanical labor of some skill, but they feature a degree of freedom for artistic flair, as in cabinetmaking, which involves carpentry, but also design and artistic embellishment.

Profession is distinguished from both *trade* and *craft* by several criteria, but with some overlapping and confusion, too. The criteria for *profession* in its traditional sense, as exemplified by law and medicine, are, according to Niederhoffer: high admission standards, special body of knowledge, public-service ideal, lengthy period of education, ethical code, licensing of members, autonomous control, professional pride and high prestige.[2]

PROBLEMS OF PROFESSION AS TRADITIONALLY DEFINED

One problem with *profession* at the level of the definition just stated is the availability of alternative definitions. One has to do with certain qualities of efficiency in organization and technique. There have been steady improvements in law enforcement along those dimensions, so some have concluded that professionalization has occurred. But that is not so if one insists instead on the traditional definition, in which efficiency and technology are not necessarily important—and may even be counter-productive, as indicated later in the chapter.

Another problem is that the criteria of a traditional profession can be met superficially, thereby creating the appearance of a profession. But the reality may be mere pretension; the result a "pseudoprofession." Law enforcement must be scrutinized carefully for this possibility.

Historical and Social Context of Professionalization

Some light is shed on professionalization of the police by the history and social context of the profession.

THE HISTORY OF PROFESSIONALIZATION

The established professions—law, medicine, ministry—have a history that reaches back several centuries. Law, for instance, has been considered a profession, with the criteria mentioned above, for at least three hundred years. But the traditional criteria were met with much less difficulty than now. When Abraham Lincoln was admitted to practice law, he had studied only a few law books and was asked only a few questions to test his mastery of the subject. Until a generation ago, many states permitted a man to prepare for law by "reading law" in the office of a lawyer, something like the experience an apprentice in a trade goes through under the tutelage of a master practitioner.

From the time of creation of "professional" police departments, made up of full-time police officers, in the larger American cities before the Civil War, there has been steady improvement of the police in the sense of increased efficiency. This was one of the aims of Sir Robert Peel in England, and it has been the result of the introduction of many improvements. The telephone and the radio greatly improved police communications; the automobile made police mobility much greater—even if only sufficient to keep up with the criminals; and the computer has enhanced the police's "memory."

Along the way, the police moved in the direction of becoming the traditional ideal of a profession. The police function came to be recognized as a distinct line of work with its own special roles and responsibilities. The knowledge involved in the performance of police tasks was put into place in the curriculum of police training academies in major cities. Police officers were sworn by oath to uphold the law, and from that time forward they had the additional powers of arrest. Much of the police officer's work was in the service of the public, in the sense of aiding the citizenry apart from enforcement of the law or the maintenance of order. The police gained an autonomy like that of traditional professions in determining what they do and how they do it, partly as a result of the isolation of the police from the public (which in turn is a result of the public failing to exercise control over the police). Finally, a code of ethics was promulgated for the police by the International Association of Chiefs of Police.

THE SOCIAL CONTEXT OF PROFESSIONALIZATION

The prestige of lawyers, doctors, engineers, architects, ministers, and members of other established professions has attracted the attention and, perhaps, even the envy of those in many other occupations. This has inspired some of those occupations to strive for professionalization as discussed below. At the same time, the public has grown increasingly concerned for its own protection. This has focused on the competency of those in occupations serving, yet threatening the health and safety of the public. The result has been the development of occupational licensing systems which resemble certain aspects of the professions, such as the requirements of a period of education and a demonstration of knowledge prior to admission to practice. This, too, will be discussed. Finally, as modern life grows more complex, especially as the knowledge explosion progresses as a reflection of that complexity, many lines of work have developed their own body of specialized knowledge that resembles in some ways the body of knowledge that distinguishes traditional professions from crafts and trades.

Several occupations have sought the status of profession—in hopes, in part, of attaining also the prestige and other rewards that go with that status. Wilensky, in his classic study "The Professionalization of Everyone?" identifies the traditional professions (except the ministry), along with accounting and dentistry, as "established" professions. He saw librarianship, nursing, optometry, pharmacy, schoolteaching, social work, and veterinary medicine as being in the process of professionalization. New professions, in his survey, were city management, city planning, and hospital administration. Doubtful professions were advertising and funeral direction. Each of these had at least one training school, university school, local professional association, national professional association, state license law, and formal code of ethics.[3]

Occupational licensing systems resemble certain professional characteristics, as in Illinois:

> The license vouches for the competence and integrity of the licensee in a field in which the average citizen is deemed not qualified to make adequate judgments. Thus in Illinois, concern for the public health is responsible for the licensing of the practice of medicine, dentistry, nursing, osteopathy, chiropody, optometry, pharmacy, veterinary medicine, barbering, and beauty culture. In the interest of public safety, architects and structural engineers are required to be licensed. As a protection against fraud, a license is required before a person may act as a real estate broker, insurance agent, or detective.[4]

It is difficult to distinguish the trades from the professions solely in terms of the formal aspects of the licensing systems. In Illinois, minimum educational standards are set, usually include a period of professional or trade-school training; passage of a prescribed examination is required, under the supervision of an examining board, which also may conduct hearings into violations of standards. Members of the boards are endorsed by the occupation's state association and ordinarily belong to it as well. So the funeral directors govern the funeral-directing profession. Good moral character is required of licensees. A license, once granted, may be revoked (or some less stringent discipline imposed) for violation of restrictions on the practice of the occupation. The restrictions take the form of standards of conduct; violations are immoral conduct, unlawful acts, conviction of a crime, improper advertising, failure to display licenses, incompetence, failure to comply with sanitary rules, performance of illegal acts, and exceeding the statutory scope of practice.[5]

There is little difference in these formalities between the licensing of doctors, midwives, lawyers, and barbers. The professionalization of barbers is an interesting case: Barbers have barber colleges, complete with curriculum comprised of survey courses, theory courses, lab courses, seminars of various kinds, and other trappings of universities; examinations for admission to practice; various standards for admission; ethical code; control of the profession through a board—just as if it were a real rather than a spurious profession. The skeptic is entitled to doubt that competence in haircutting calls for much book-learning or other kinds of school work. The skeptic is also entitled to a persuasive demonstration that the professionalization of the police calls for more than experience of patrol work.

A *knowledge explosion* has begun in recent decades, in which the volume of information is growing by leaps and bounds.[6] The proportion of workers in manual labor is declining as the proportion working directly or indirectly with information is increasing. The tasks of modern life appear to grow more complex, demanding greater understanding—which is often in terms of knowledge of operations. The study that social science is lavishing on life reveals complexities that had not been fully appreciated, as in law enforcement, where the simple-seeming job of the patrol officer is now understood to be extremely complex. This knowledge is being developed into manuals and handbooks, reflected in the questions on civil-service qualifying examinations, instructed in the training programs of various occupations, elaborated in the trade journals or magazines, hammered home in seminars at state and national conventions and continuing-education programs of many sorts, including books, cassettes, videotapes, and the like.

The knowledge peculiar to a line of work usually finds expression in jargon or specialized vocabulary. Lawyers have long spoken of *res ipsa loquitur* and other terms and phrases, to the despair of their clients (but to the facilitation of discussion among the "priesthood" who have been admitted to the secrets of the special knowledge of law). *Jargon* means an excessively technical terminology used not only as "shorthand" expressions but to exclude outsiders from understanding, much as if the terms were a code (*signal zero* means "danger; use caution"). Underlying the jargon is often a sizeable body of knowledge that resembles in many ways the sort of knowledge that has been the burden and the joy of traditional professions. It is to this and other traditional criteria that we turn now.

The Police as a Traditional Profession

The status of the police as a profession requires examination of how the police measure up to the criteria of traditional professions (although this, as discussed below, is not the only definition of *profession*). The central elements will be set forth as they have been understood for traditional professions or exemplified by traditional professions. Then the police will be set alongside the criteria to see how they measure up. The criteria are the special body of knowledge, the preparation for entry, the standards for entry, the licensure of members and its consequences, the control of the profession and its practice, the public orientation, and the ethical code.

SPECIAL BODY OF KNOWLEDGE

The traditional professions are characterized by their distinct bodies of knowledge, without which the practitioner is incompetent to practice the profession. The lawyer has a vast library full of books and articles on the many subjects of law: contracts, torts, property, corporations, taxation, and so forth. What a lawyer does—advising clients, securing their rights or powers, negotiating with those who differ with them or with whom they seek to make or break relationships, advocating their clients' interest or position in disputes with others[7]—depends ultimately on knowledge of law. The disposition of a dispute eventually depends on what a court does about it; that, in turn, results from the definition of rights and powers, which is found in statutes, regulations, or court decisions. To be sure, now and then sheer political power or influence overrides the law and its institutions, and in such cases legal knowledge (and even legal rights) count for naught. But for the most part, legal relations and positions are defined by law, and one side prevails or gains the most (or whatever can be gained or protected at all) according to the legal competence of lawyers. Even lawyers who simply know a great many people, whose contacts count for much, are really only shortcutting the communications process. Other things being equal (even in cases of "contacts" or "politics"), the outcome is determined largely by the law—and the person who knows it, or who has it on her or his side (which is largely a matter of the knowledgeability of lawyers), will prevail.

To measure policing against the standard of possession of a special body of knowledge, it is necessary to conclude whether the knowledge of policing is the sort the traditional professions have or whether it is more like the sort of knowledge the trades and crafts have. Does law enforcement have a distinctive body of knowledge that is of the sort possessed by the established professions? Police officers have to learn certain things before they are any good at what they do. They must learn to use firearms, night sticks, mace, handcuffs, and other equipment. Physicians, too, must learn to use certain kinds of equipment: stethoscope, sphygmomanometer, tongue depressor. The techniques of using these do not require lengthy training. What doctors observe with those instruments make sense to them only in light of a vast amount of knowledge learned from medical books. What patrol officers observe makes sense to them only in light of knowledge that is not so much in the head as it is in the "gut," learned not from books but from experience.

Police officers must develop a suspicious frame of mind, for example. In the training academy, instructors tell officers-to-be that they must be suspicious, should look for things that are out of place, and illustrate this with a list of suspicious circumstances (such as a clean license plate on a dirty car, and vice versa). But the cultivation of suspicion requires not classroom instruction but the steady observation of circumstances. By contrast, the development of the physician's diagnostic competence requires more study of recent medical journals than it does personal observation.

Much of the officer's success depends on how well he handles people; that, however, is not something learned in the classroom but with experience. In contrast to the doctor's "bedside manner," which is "gravy," the patrol officer's "streetside manner" is his "meat and potatoes"—not an extra added attraction but the main feature, the essence of his work. Thus James Q. Wilson has concluded that patrol officers are more like craftspeople than professionals.[8]

PREPARATION FOR ENTRY

Knowledge that is mainly reduced to writing and learned best by study of the word rather than by the doing of the practice requires a lengthy period of preparation. The more the knowledge must be learned in the doing of it, the less preparatory study is necessary. Thus, the traditional professions have a long period of preparatory study; the trades, none. The law student has three years of schoolwork before she begins the practice of law; the apprentice carpenter begins doing carpentry immediately.

Police officers, too, used to begin policing immediately. Now most areas have educational requirements: high school, some college, or even a college degree in some departments, followed now by some time in the police academy. The academy experience does not come close, however, to the time in school required for lawyers, engineers, and architects.

HIGH ADMISSION STANDARDS

The professions have had admission standards that constitute a double-check on the educational process. The bar examination for lawyers requires a demonstration of some command of the subject of law in its various subjects, such as contracts, torts, wills, procedure, corporations, property, taxation and so forth. Medicine, too, requires special examination before specialization. Accountants "graduate" from being bookkeepers to being certified public accountants by passing an examination. Similarly with architects and engineers. Future police officers often take a civil-service exam, but that is part of the process of selecting who is able to commence, not who has successfully completed, police training. It resembles the law-school aptitude test rather than the bar examination. Thereafter, police trainees must complete their courses and the exams that come at the end of each one. Standards for admission to the job of policing—to commence in the field training—have been concerned with physical capabilities.[9]

LICENSURE OF MEMBERS

The "ticket" to practice the profession is a license to do whatever is distinctive in what the profession does. For lawyers it is "the practice of law." Their license permits them and only them to practice law; others, not so licensed, may not practice law.

Police officers, when they are sworn, acquire slightly greater powers than the average citizen has to use force, including deadly force, in the protection of persons and property and in making arrests. But the difference is a difference of degree. Professionals, on the other hand, are in exclusive possession of the power to practice their profession. The lawyer is the only one permitted to give legal advice: not just slightly more advice than laypeople can give, but *any* advice at all. The layperson is in trouble if he engages in "unauthorized practice of law." But the citizen who protects others from crime, detects crime, finds criminals, even makes arrests, is not exceeding her powers or entering into the realm monopolized by the police.

AUTONOMOUS CONTROL OF THE PROFESSION AND ITS PRACTICE

The education of the preprofessional, the standards for admission to practice a profession, the definition of what it is that constitutes such practice, and the exclusion of unlicensed persons from that practice are of critical importance in professional life. A profession itself controls those aspects of the profession. The education of lawyers is by lawyers, who decide what should be taught and how it should be taught; lawyers, who comprise the membership of the board of bar examiners, decide what lawyers must demonstrate to meet the standards that lawyers themselves have established; they and other lawyers, among the leaders of the bar association and the judiciary, define the practice of law; lawyers on the courts oversee the process of excluding (and punishing) those who engage in "unauthorized practice of law." This independence of external influence is won by the profession in large part by fulfillment of the next two qualities of a profession.

The police do enjoy a good deal of autonomy in deciding what they will do and how they will do it, but they have won their autonomy largely by default of the public to take charge of law enforcement. The independence of the police from public governance has not been out of deference to their authority, as in the case of traditional professions. Much of the effort to reform the police has been aimed at wresting control away from the police to get it back into the hands of the community and its leaders.

PUBLIC SERVICE IDEAL

A traditional aspect of the profession is *vocational*, not in the usual sense of having to do with a trade, craft, or profession (as in *vocational training* or *vocational counseling*), but in the sense that comes from the literal meaning of the word, a "calling." The lawyer is "called to the bar." The minister is "called" to the ministry. Although professionals, like tradespeople and craftspeople, earn their livelihood from its practice, the orientation of professionals is above or beyond the lucrative, self-interested pursuit of personal gain; instead, it is toward the service of client, patient, or parishioner, on a 24-hour-a-day basis. More important, doctors and lawyers are obligated to provide service without regard to the client's or patient's ability to pay. Lawyers may turn away an indigent client, but if the court appoints a lawyer to represent one, he or she must do so. Doctors experience a much higher ratio of nonpaying patients to paying patients than any department store would tolerate. This "charity" is no doubt the result less of poor business practices than the spirit that obliges doctors to make their services selflessly available.

Along this dimension of public service, there is a paradox in policing that is a problem for the professional quality of the police. Police officers lay down their lives for others; dozens are killed in the line of duty every year. No other profession, other than the military, calls for its members to give that "last full measure of devotion," so it can hardly be deemed an essential characteristic of a profession. Certainly doctors, lawyers, engineers, and members of other established professions do not do so. At the same time, studies of police work indicate that patrol officers spend much of their time in what can only be called public service, as distinguished from law enforcement and order maintenance which some insist are their main responsibilities (some arguing that this should be so to the exclusion of public service altogether). The paradox is that the propensity of the police for self-sacrificial behavior and their preoccupation with public service are diminished in the face of what the police are supposed to do: they are not supposed to give up their lives—it is quite unnatural to do so, however heroic it may be; and they are supposed, by many, to enforce the law and maintain order, not serve the public. In this view, the public service that they provide is incidental to (or the product of) their law enforcement and order maintenance performance—their primary tasks, in other words. If the public is served by these functions, it is in the same sense that the public is served by bus drivers or taxi drivers doing their jobs, but little, if anything, else.

AN ETHICAL CODE

The professions exchange their ordinary ethics for a higher ethical obligation when they gain their independence and their monopoly of the practice of their profession. The code of ethics may be as simple as the Hippocratic Oath, which doctors have traditionally taken; it may be as complex as the lawyer's Canons of Ethics (now their Code of Professional Responsibility). The emphasis is on integrity. The notion of responsibility to the public and to the client is an important aspect of the ethic of the professional. Self-interest is not paramount, as it is conceded to be for the businessperson, who is applauded for the pursuit of profit. Gain for the professional is incidental (ideally) to service to the public.

The emerging professions typically adopt a code of ethics as a first sign of their emergence. The police, too, have a code of ethics:

Law Enforcement Code of Ethics

As a Law Enforcement Officer, my fundamental duty is to serve mankind; to safeguard lives and property; to protect the innocent against deception, the weak against oppression or intimidation, and the peaceful against violence or disorder; and to respect the Constitutional rights of all men to liberty, equality and justice.

I will keep my private life unsullied as an example to all; maintain courageous calm in the face of danger, scorn, or ridicule; develop self-restraint; and be constantly mindful of the welfare of others. Honest in thought and deed in both my personal and official life, I will be exemplary in obeying the laws of the land and the regulations of my department. Whatever I see or hear of a confidential nature or that is confided to me in my official capacity will be kept ever secret unless revelation is necessary in the performance of my duty.

I will never act officiously or permit personal feelings, prejudices, animosities or friendships to influence my decisions. With no compromise for crime and with relentless prosecution of criminals, I will enforce the law courteously and appropriately without fear or favor, malice or ill will, never employing unnecessary force or violence and never accepting gratuities.

I recognize the badge of my office as a symbol of public faith, and I accept it as a public trust to be held so long as I am true to the ethics of the police service. I will constantly strive to achieve these objectives and ideals, dedicating myself before God to my chosen profession . . . law enforcement.[10]

A problem with a code of ethics such as this is its unenforceability: terms like *unsullied* and *malice* are difficult to reduce to operational meanings or standards by which conduct may be evaluated; phrases such as *constantly mindful of the welfare of others* are exhortations which defy application; and injunctions to make *no compromise for crime* and for *relentless prosecution of criminals* beg profound ethical questions of conflicting obligations of the sort explored in Chapter 11. Moreover, a crucial difference between traditional professions and emerging and pseudoprofessions is that the traditional professions have machinery (sometimes rusty) specifically for investigating and deciding charges of ethical impropriety. And they occasionally discipline a member for a breach of ethics. This is absolutely unheard of in the emerging professions, let alone the pretenders: Midwives are not suspended for unethical practices.

Police officers are suspended sometimes, but usually for commission of a crime, not for violation of an obligation found in the ethical code but not the criminal statutes.

Professional Policing as a Rational, Efficient Organization and Operation

The traditional meaning of *professional* is by no means the only one. It has also meant rational, efficient organization and operation, with emphasis on bureaucratic style of administration and technical tools for the implementation of policy. Goldstein describes it this way:

> The professional model stresses operating efficiency, to be achieved by centralized control, clean-cut lines of organization, fuller and more effective use of police personnel, greater mobility, improved training, and increased use of equipment and technology. It also emphasizes the need for integrity and higher education for police personnel.[11]

Along these lines, law enforcement has come closer to approximation of the professional ideal than it has according to the criteria of traditional professionalization.

A model of a professional agency in this sense is the FBI. It has long required its officers to have not only a college degree but a graduate degree. It has emphasized training and continuing education. It has been highly bureaucratized, with detailed controls working through distinct lines of command and communication. It has emphasized information-gathering, technical analysis, and the latest in scientific research and practices. It has enjoyed a high degree of autonomy in its policymaking and decision making. It has been marked by high integrity. Yet the efficiency and independence, the "good soldier" frame of mind, lead to pursuit of goals and practices developed on its own (and some apparently instigated by the Nixon White House), unchecked by other parts of the government or principles of political and ethical priority.[12]

Judged by the professional model as rational, efficient organization and operation, many police departments remain throwbacks to the nineteenth century. But others have approached the ideal. Experiments in the administration of personnel have been conducted and reforms carried out, as described in Chapter 3. If the results are sometimes equivocal, as in the Kansas City patrol experiment (which suggests that crime levels remain the same regardless of whether patrol is intensified, held the same, or eliminated), the important lesson may be the changeability of operations: police agencies are not locked into ancient patterns as if by immutable laws of nature. Certainly mobility has improved dramatically, with patrol vehicles of all sorts carrying police officers quickly to any point in a jurisdiction. Dispatching is much more discriminating and responsive; the 911 telephone number symbolizes (as well as facilitates) the quicker responsiveness of the police. Equipment and technology has improved, especially with the billions of dollars from the Law Enforcement Assistance Administration. Despite all the unnecessary purchases of such equipment as tanks by small-town departments, the bulk of the funds have gone into much more useful equipment, such as improved two-way communication systems, record-keeping systems, and so forth. Finally, training has improved, especially technical training at the level of the police academy.

Higher Education and the Police

American law enforcement did not value higher education very much until the professional model of policing took hold. Then, in the late 1960s, when federal funds became available in the Law Enforcement Education Program (LEEP), police departments, colleges, and universities, and men and women in police work (and aiming for police careers) dramatically stepped up the higher education of the police. In 1967, only 184 institutions of higher learning had programs of law-enforcement instruction; by 1974, some 1030 had police-related programs.

Two measures of the increase in college-educated police officers are the figures from the Dallas Police Department and from Florida. There were only 11 Dallas police officers with college degrees in 1968; by 1975, there were 625—and 21 with master's degrees. In Florida, in 1968, only 6 percent of the local police officers had any college training; by 1975, 23 percent had degrees—and 44 individuals had doctorates.[13]

The value of higher education was borne out by several studies, such as Locke and Smith's, which indicated that higher education reduced the degree of authoritarianism in the personality of police officers.[14] The National Advisory Commission on Criminal Justice Standards and Goals found such research so persuasive that it prescribed for every police agency a requirement for employment of one year of higher education effective immediately (in 1973), then an increase to two years by 1975, three years by 1978, and four years by 1982.[15]

HIGHER EDUCATION RECONSIDERED

With so many police officers now educated and so many others engaged in higher education, it is surprising to find that higher education for the police is being reconsidered. But it is.

Studies that cast doubt on the value of higher education, reinforcing the doubt that skeptics had felt all along, led to the Police Foundation's study by the National Advisory Commission on Higher Education for Police Officers. The main point of the report is this:

> The Commission believes that the best way to educate the police institution for change is to develop the capacity of the police to use knowledge to solve problems. The art of using knowledge includes the habits of working with written and spoken ideas, computational tools, and information gathered from many sources to produce and test new conclusions. Much of the college education that present and future police officers now receive develops those essential habits. But much of it—particularly the courses offered in specialized police education programs—does not. In order to improve the quality of many of these programs, major changes must be made in their curriculums, the level of resource support they receive from their colleges, the qualifications of their faculty, and the nature of their students' educational experiences.[16]

The Commission recommends that the paraprofessional or vocational curriculum be replaced (or at least kept separate if it is lodged within colleges that offer such training because the area lacks a police training academy), because, they argue, it is inappropriate to institutions of higher education (except under such circumstances). Training should instead be confined to the police training academy itself. Colleges and universities, for their part, should respond to the recommendation that "all college programs focusing on issues in policing and criminal justice should provide a broad education that is useful for many careers and for living through an uncertain future, if only because half of all 'preservice' graduates of these programs do not enter police employment." And this, it might be added, is to say nothing of those who enter the field of criminal justice but leave it for another career.[17]

The Commission could not quite make up its mind which of three other models of higher education it preferred for the police. One is the general-education model, in which prepolice students take a wide variety of courses in many fields, learning as they go along the many things—values, disciplines, modes of inquiry—that will be important to them as thoughtful police officers and police executives. The second model, the liberal-arts approach, conceives of criminal justice very broadly, so that the subject is learned by addressing conceptual, theoretical levels of criminal justice, where many basic questions may be found if they are not excluded by a narrow focus. The third model, the professional, concentrates on what it is within the subject of criminal justice that will be of value to police officers as they move up the ranks into executive positions. Police organization and management and other administrative studies are involved in this. This approach emphasizes, by way of an analogy to business, not the programming of computers (which makes students "marketable" as soon as they graduate), but rather the uses and limits of computers in the business world (which will concern a business executive or the boss of the boss of the programmer).

The Commission's report leans toward a *fusionist* approach, which combines the models in the spirit of the philosopher Alfred North Whitehead: "The antithesis between a technical and liberal education is fallacious. There can be no adequate technical education which is not liberal, and no liberal education which is not technical: that is, no education which does not impart both technique and intellectual vision."[18] The fusionist approach would permit the student to take many general courses along with some police-oriented courses. Those, however, would be designed in the liberal-arts fashion of emphasizing not the narrow technical aspects, the "how-to" dimension, but the "why" and "wherefor."

Policing as a Profession and Craft

The question of whether the practice of policing is a profession turns ultimately on the answer to the question of what kind of knowledge is involved in the work. Answering that question also resolves the issue of the role of the colleges and universities in the education of police officers. Some light is shed on this by a distinction the philosopher William James made between knowledge *of* and knowledge *about* something. Sociologist Robert Nisbet describes the distinction in this way:

> Every civilized language except our own, James noted, has two common words for knowledge: *connaitre* and *savoir,* to go no farther than the French. The first is knowledge-by-acquaintance, the knowledge one finds in every occupation, skill, profession or role. Truly "knowledge-of" is indispensable to any culture. The second, "knowledge-about," is the result of sustained, systematic study, of reflection, logic and abstract thinking. It is this kind of knowledge we associate with science and scholarship. This kind of knowledge is hardly indispensable; rather, it is quite recent in human history and still precarious in foundation. Often, tragically, it appears to be in conflict with "knowledge-of," the pride of businessmen, citizens, housewives and the rest of us.[19]

Knowledge *of,* let us say, guns is what a hunter or sharpshooter or police officer needs: how the gun feels, how you move it about, how to squeeze the trigger, how it recoils, how it sounds, how quickly it can be fired again. Knowledge *about* guns is knowledge of a different order altogether: the types of guns, the comparative fire-power and costs of guns, the size and shape, the rules for using guns, for caring for them, storing them, transporting them. There is an area of overlapping, too: knowledge *about* the relationship of police officer to fleeing felon includes the rules on use of deadly force; knowledge *of* the relationship of officer to fleeing felon includes the response of various kinds of people to the officer's drawn gun; application of rules interacts with the response under the circumstances. The former can be taught, perhaps best in a classroom with a book and blackboard; the latter can be learned, perhaps with some tutelage by a veteran, but best of all in an alley with gun drawn in pursuit of the fleeing felon, perhaps best when the fugitive is in the very sights of the officer's gun.

Some of what is discussed in earlier chapters is best studied in the academic setting: for instance, the rules of constitutional limitation on the use of police power. Some of it is *not* studied best in such a setting: for instance, the "rules" of danger in the exercise of police power. Alternatives to the criminal-justice system can be identified for police officers and learned by them from books; likewise, the extent and the limits of their authority to choose between that system and others in the disposition of "order-maintenance" and "public service" cases can be so learned. But not the reactions of a subject to the exercise of that authority: that is knowledge *of* authority, not knowledge about authority. It must be lived to be learned, not read.

This suggests that there are actually *three* kinds of knowledge involved in law enforcement. There is knowledge *about* it, which is best learned in an academic setting. Then there are two kinds of knowledge *of* it: Some of the knowledge of it is best learned in an academic setting, like the knowledge of a professional but removed from the college and university (since others there will have little use for the learning of it) and shifted to a professional school, like a law school. The other kind of knowledge of cannot be learned at all in an academic setting (not even in a training academy). It might be anticipated ("police work is stressful"), but it must be left to the "academy of the street," to patrol work for learning. This three-fold division of the knowledge in law enforcement makes possible a three-fold division of responsibility for teaching it: colleges and universities for "knowledge-about," police academies (like law and medical schools) for the "knowledge-of" which is professional, and police officers themselves on the street, perhaps under the wing of a veteran partner, for the "knowledge-of" which is the craft of policing.

Thus, future patrol officers may learn *about* civil disorder in the university, at the level of its history, what its participants believe and seek by their actions. This gives students a sense of the sweep of history, the change in society, the influence of ideas and values. They may learn *of* civil disorder in the academy, at the level of the rules of constitutional law, statutory law, departmental regulations, of when certain kinds of disorder collide with regulations, of what strategies and tactics are available in such circumstances, of what weapons may be used and in what circumstances and by which units and individuals and for how long, of what kinds of detention may be employed, what kinds of substitutes for the usual booking procedures and detention, of what persons are entitled to see which detainees, and so forth. They may learn *of* disorder in the disorder itself, in their "baptism under fire," when they "see the whites of their eyes," when they sense panic in their ranks (or in the demonstrators' own), when the chemistry and physics of human action in confrontation and riot move leaders and followers in various ways, of what happens when leaders are separated from followers (and they are "on their own"), of what happens when the tear gas goes off, of what a certain look or tone of voice will do with a young student or not do with a battle-hardened riot veteran. It is like the situation of the surgeon: All the anatomy and physiology from medical school, and all the observation of operations, and all the dissection of frogs and human cadavers will tell her where the organs are located and when they are healthy or cancerous, and what surgical techniques are called for, but only an incision will let her know how the flesh "gives" under the scalpel. And even after that, she knows but cannot tell another—and that is the craft of surgery.

This division of the knowledge of policing into three kinds casts some doubt upon the wisdom of the fusionist approach of the National Advisory Commission on Higher Education for Police Officers. If the craft of policing cannot be taught at all, except by a partner or other "master" of an "apprentice," and if the "professional" knowledge of policing is best imparted at the academy, it leaves for the university the teaching of knowledge *about* policing. It leaves a question of whether that knowledge should be conceived of as including the managerial aspects of policing, the sort of thing the police executive would care to know about. This in turn depends on a characteristic of American police that may change but has not changed so far. That is the bottom-level entry of all its personnel, at the level of patrol officer, with a future of many years of what Skolnick called the "constabulary experience" of the American police office at that bottom level, before movement up into the executive ranks, which entails several more years at the level of sergeant.

Students of business management, by contrast, do not enter business at the clerking level; they enter at a lower executive level (although they may have several months of exposure at some of those levels—even the nephew of the boss begins in the mail room). So long as American policing begins with patrolling and keeps the police officer at that level for several years, it makes less sense to expose them to executive-level concerns in their college education along the lines of what the commission called the professional model. Those things can be reserved until later years as education continues, on the job, in the academy, and in the college, as an officer moves up the ranks. But if there is a shift toward lateral entry into policing at executive levels, as there is in the military at second-lieutenant level for college-educated men and women, then it makes more sense for a college education to include such "professional" elements. Otherwise, the liberal arts or general approach would seem to be desirable—for the usual reasons that such an education is valuable.

The Case Against Professionalization of the Police

The discussion so far has suggested that there are limits to the professionalization of the police through higher education: The colleges and universities and what they do best do not lend themselves very well to the development of some of the knowledge that is most important for police work. There are several other considerations, too, that have emerged in recent years, prompted by the experience gained in the professional development of certain police agencies, such as in Los Angeles, and the employment of many men and women who are fully professionalized police officers.

BLUMBERG AND NIEDERHOFFER ON PROFESSIONALISM

Abraham Blumberg and Arthur Niederhoffer, two seasoned observers of law enforcement, both lawyers and one of them (Niederhoffer) a veteran police officer as well, have provided a thorough critique of professionalism in policing.

Professionalism Polarizes the Police. A significant number of professional police officers in an agency would divide the police ranks into professionals ("pros") and conservatives ("cons"). This division would be as deep as the difference between the two kinds of officer, in terms of their experience, their values, their self-esteem, their self-identity, their aims and objectives, their satisfactions, their preferences. The division would also extend far into the department, as the "invasion" of "pros" would initially reach the level of patrol officer but would eventually extend to all levels, up to the highest executive ranks.

A particularly acute division would reflect the differences between educated and uneducated officers. Those possessing knowledge *about* policing would oppose those with knowledge *of* policing, and vice versa; and those with knowledge *of* policing would oppose each other according to whether it was "professional" or "craft" knowledge, learned in the academy or on the street. Invidious comparisons would be made. The life of the college-educated cop could be made very unpleasant. Later, the life of the "uneducated" cop would be made miserable.

The police would be divided into "cosmopolitans" and "locals," or those with a loyalty wider than their organization and those with a loyalty no further than the organization. One of the characteristics of the police so far has been intense loyalty to the police, to fellow police officers, to the agency, to the institution of law enforcement. The professional, on the other hand, in contrast to the "locals," would have a loyalty divided between that set and the ideals of professional policing, the standards of professional policing, especially the constitutional standards, and the esteem of the law enforcement community (professional police officers, police scholars, and leaders of the field). Like the corporation lawyer who divides his loyalty between his company and the law, the bar, and the standards of practice expected in the field (rather than by "management"—either as a science or as his bosses), the professional cop's outlook would be broad rather than narrow.

Professionalization and Minorities.   Recruitment of a "higher" type of person, an educated person or one who, by virtue of education, is better able to cope with the knowledge dimension of police work, collides with the aim of many communities and police departments to recruit minorities, mainly blacks and women, whose educational attainments and aptitudes (as culturally influenced) are less than those of white males.

Professionalization and Radical Change.   Introduction of a handful of professionalized police officers into a department does not make much of a difference, except to them and those they work with closely. But introduction of professionalization into the department means a change in its very nature, from a craft to a profession. A department could "ease" the change into place only by obscuring—or denying—its objectives. The straightforward approach, however slowly it might be implemented, calls for "root and branch" change; the handwriting would be on the wall from the first day.

Professional Policing Is Impersonal.   One quality of traditional policing has been the broad discretion that permitted officers to make allowances for a variety of circumstances and characteristics. But professional policing, at least of the bureaucratic variety, would have policing restricted by many rules and orders prescribed by "right" practices foreordained for each situation. Standardization "by the book" would make the police officer appear to be a coolly efficient, unsympathetic, mechanical person.

Professionalism and the Public and Public Esteem. A bureaucracy tends to close itself off from the public. If professionalization of the police means bureaucratization of the police agency, it will shut off the public. Niederhoffer and Blumberg argue that such a bureaucracy, shrouded in obscurity and operating in secrecy, will result in public hostility.

On the other hand, professions govern themselves: they educate their own members; they set their own standards and administer them; they hear the complaints and discipline their own members. Today, however, the trend is toward community involvement in and external review of those things. This is a dilemma for a profession: Can it be run by the community without losing much of its quality of profession? Or must it insist on its autonomy and resist the wave of the future.

In any event, one aspect of both views of professionalism is a responsiveness to the community's interests and an accommodation of competing claims. This thrusts the police outward from comfortable insularity into a political role. It corresponds to a development in modern business: Instead of being concerned solely with the "bottom line" of profit, the modern corporation is learning that its profit depends in large part on how well it engages the community and the many interests that affect it, such as shareholders, labor, government, media, education. How well law enforcement controls crime may likewise depend as much on how well the police relate to such institutions as it does on their direct engagement of crime.[20]

OTHER RECONSIDERATIONS OF PROFESSIONALIZATION

Another reason for doubting the desirability of professionalization in policing is the importance of discretion to the traditional kind of profession. The modern trend, however, is to limit discretion. This tends to reduce the professional to a robot playing by the book. The bureaucratic concept of profession, however, which aims to reduce discretion, is not so troubled by this.

An important cause for questioning professionalization is the failure of professionalized departments to fare much better against crime than traditional, unprofessionalized departments.[21] This, however, is a problem that calls for precisely the study that social scientists can give—and perhaps such a study will even explain it, with findings that yield recommendations for workable reforms. This is another instance of the bridge between the practice of policing and the scientific inquiry into it.

It accords well with the professional approach that attaches importance to scientific inquiry and reform.

A CONCLUDING OBSERVATION

There are difficulties in this critique of professionalization because some of the "cons" are inconsistent with each other. This owes largely to the interplay of two concepts of the term *professional*. It may be that one of them must fall by the wayside. It may be that both can be reconciled. There is much to be done yet in the analysis of policing in terms of professionalism before that can happen.

The Prospects for Professionalizing the Police

Do these drawbacks of professionalization of the police make it unlikely that it will occur? Not necessarily, but the obstacles are formidable. For example, Franklin G. Ashburn has observed that the police role is less that of professional workers than "semi-skilled para-professional" workers; and without a change in the conception of their work, there can be no real change toward professionalization. Similarly, the public conceives of the police as errand runners, on the one hand, and crime fighters on the other hand, and find the prospect of a professional army of crime fighters in the community somewhat undesirable as a characteristic of a "police state." Yet that conception is belied by the preoccupation of the police with the tasks of order maintenance and public service.[22]

Ashburn sees another obstacle in bureaucratization of the police and the conflict of ordered police work with discretionary police work. He quotes Albert Reiss on this point:

> A command organization threatens professional status because it expects men to follow orders regardless of their judgment. The professional ideal holds that orders are antithetical to the exercise of discretion. . . . All bureaucracies, then, pose problems for the exercise of discretion.[23]

Ashburn concludes that until these problems are solved, "the police officer will continue to work as a 'semi-skilled laborer' and not as a client-centered, service-oriented 'professional.' "[24]

The outlook for professionalization is clouded also by the difficulty of establishing its meaning, as observed above. Some of the qualities of policing that resemble those of the established professions are the very ones that some reformers of the police would change in the name of another brand of profession. Professionals in the traditional sense enjoy a wide-ranging discretion to permit their professional knowledge and judgment to produce decisions in the best interest of the patient or client. While others may ultimately judge those decisions (in malpractice suits, for instance), and disagree with the diagnosis or prescription, hardly anyone would have the professional's judgment constrained by rules other than those the profession itself establishes as the best practice in the circumstances (as in the "drug of choice"). Nor would they take away the freedom to vary the standard practices in a judgment that takes special, sometimes subtle, circumstances into consideration, often at a level of intuition shaped by long experience. The discretion of the police officer, on the other hand, is said by many to be unnecessarily wide, permitting too many inappropriate factors to influence decisions. The police can be expected to resist encroachment on their discretion, hence they will be difficult to professionalize in the rational, bureaucratic sense.

Similarly, the police have enjoyed autonomy, much as doctors and lawyers have enjoyed autonomy. It has been a result, to be sure, of public apathy and police isolation and secrecy, rather than of the authority of the police. But it is autonomy nonetheless and is understandably prized by the police. They will resist its reduction, just as they will resist diminution of their discretion. To be able to do so in the name of a competing notion of profession will strengthen their resistance.

The political aspect of the police is an obstacle to the aim of professionalism. To the extent that the police are a function of the environment, fully responsive to the sentiments, values, and interests of the host community, it would seem to be less than a profession. Professionalism requires more self-definition than mirrorlike response to what the public wants.

The prospects of professionalism in policing depend in large part on what policing will be like in the future. That depends, in turn, on what crime and the community will be like in the future. But the techniques of future study have not been used very much to discern what the problems are likely to be and what can be done about them. It may be that some problems can be dealt with by nonpolice agencies, leaving the police to handle others. What these are will dictate whether the police deal with them as craftspeople, professionals, or bureaucrats.

Perhaps that, coupled with the different kinds of police knowledge, leads one to this formulation, which James Q. Wilson developed: "[T]he police can be bureaucratized for some purposes, professionalized for others, and left alone for still others."[25]

SUMMARY   This chapter reviewed the topic of professionalization of the police, noting the basic problem of the varying definitions of *profession*. It surveyed some of the characteristics of the traditional professions, like law, which have inspired imitation by many occupations. Policing was compared with the criteria by which traditional professions have been judged and also with the criteria of the newer bureaucratic meaning of professional.

The controversy over higher education and the police was discussed and the recommendations of the National Advisory Commission on Higher Education for Police Officers were questioned in the light of the different kinds of knowledge, hence the different kinds of learning necessary in policing: knowledge *about* and knowledge *of,* both in the profession and craft senses.

The case against professionalization was presented: it polarizes a police department into proponents and opponents of professionalization; it retards minority recruitment because it selects more educated, more accomplished, more skilled candidates (hence fewer of the disadvantaged); it draws the police officer as a rational and impersonal practitioner, back from a humane engagement with the people; it increases discretion (hence abuses of discrimination), or it decreases discretion (hence adjustments by discrimination), depending on which concept of profession is preferred; and it has not demonstrably reduced crime in departments where it has been attained.

Finally, the prospects for professionalization were surveyed. The results of that survey only add to the foregoing drawbacks the ambiguity of the role of the police officer as a professional, the ambivalence of the meaning of a professional, and the likelihood of resistance to a reduction in policy autonomy and discretion, as well as the lack of insight into what policing will be like in the future.

NOTES

1. Reproduced in Arthur Niederhoffer, *Behind the Shield* (New York: Doubleday Anchor, 1967), pp. 25–26.
2. Ibid., p. 19.
3. Harold L. Wilensky, "The Professionalization of Everyone?" 70 (September 1964), pp. 137–158.
4. Neil F. Garvey, *The Government and Administration of Illinois* (New York: Crowell, 1958), p. 454.
5. Ibid., pp. 460–464.
6. Daniel Bell, *The Coming of Post-Industrial Society* (New York: Basic Books, 1973).
7. Martin Mayer, *The Lawyers* (New York: Harper & Row, 1967).
8. James Q. Wilson, *Varieties of Police Behavior* (New York: Atheneum, 1975), p. 283.
9. National Advisory Commission, *Police* (Washington, D.C.: U.S. Government Printing Office, 1973), p. 367.
10. Reproduced in Federal Bureau of Investigation, *Uniform Crime Reports* (Washington, D.C.: Government Printing Office, 1972), p. 52.
11. Herman Goldstein, *Policing a Free Society* (Cambridge, Mass.: Ballinger, 1977), p. 2.

12. Compare Don Whitehead, *The FBI Story* (New York: Random House, 1956) with Sanford Ungar, *FBI* (Boston: Atlantic/Little, Brown, 1975).
13. Richard A. Staufenberger, "The Professionalization of Police: Efforts and Obstacles," *Public Administration Review* (November/December 1977), pp. 678–685 at p. 683.
14. Bernard Locke and Alexander B. Smith, "Police Who Go to College," in Arthur Niederhoffer and Abraham S. Blumberg, eds., *The Ambivalent Force,* 2nd ed. (New York: Holt, Rinehart & Winston, 1976), pp. 164–168.
15. National Advisory Commission, *Police,* p. 369.
16. Lawrence W. Sherman, *The Quality of Police Education* (San Francisco: Jossey-Bass, 1978), pp. 1–2.
17. Ibid., p. 3 (italics eliminated).
18. Quoted in Ibid., pp. 77–78.
19. Robert Nisbet, "Knowledge Dethroned," *New York Times Magazine* (Sept. 28, 1978), p. 36.
20. Niederhoffer and Blumberg, *The Ambivalent Force,* pp. 16–17.
21. Goldstein, *Policing a Free Society,* p. 7.
22. Franklin G. Asburn, "Changing the Rhetoric of 'Professionalism,'" *Innovation in Law Enforcement* (Washington, D.C.: Law Enforcement Assistance Administration, 1973), p. 4.
23. Ibid., p. 4.
24. Ibid., p. 8.
25. Wilson, *Varieties of Police Behavior,* p. 283.

SELECTED READINGS

Arthur Niederhoffer, "The Urban Police Department: From Bureaucracy to Profession," in *Behind the Shield* (New York: Doubleday Anchor, 1969), pp. 11–33.

Charles B. Saunders, *Upgrading the American Police* (Washington, D.C.: Brookings, 1970).

Lawrence W. Sherman, et al., *The Quality of Police Education* (San Francisco: Jossey-Bass, 1978).

Richard Stauffenberger, "Professionalization of the Police," *Public Administration Review* (November–December 1977), pp. 678–685.

Norman L., Weiner, *The Role of the Police in Urban Society: Conflicts and Consequences* (Indianapolis, Ind.: Bobbs-Merrill, 1977).

Harold L. Wilensky, "The Professionalization of Everyone?" *American Journal of Sociology* (September 1964), pp. 137–158.

INDEX